WITHDRAWN

DATE DUE			
GAYLORD			PRINTED IN U.S.A.

CENTRAL PLANNING

IN CZECHOSLOVAKIA

CENTRAL PLANNING
IN CZECHOSLOVAKIA

Organization for Growth
in a Mature
Economy

JAN M. MICHAL

Stanford University Press

Stanford, California

1960

Stanford University Press
Stanford, California

Library of Congress Catalog Card Number: 60-11630
Printed in the United States of America

Published with the assistance of
the Ford Foundation

ACKNOWLEDGMENTS

Unless otherwise stated, all data on Czechoslovakia come from the official publications of the Czechoslovak State Statistical Office: *Statistické ročenky* (Statistical Yearbooks), the monthly *Statistické zprávy* (Statistical Reports) and the theoretical monthly *Statistický obzor* (Statistical Review). I express my appreciation for the use of statistical material available in these publications. Data from various Czechoslovak economic reviews and from official statements, as published by the Czechoslovak daily press or broadcast by Radio Prague and Radio Bratislava, also have been used as indicated in the text. In exceptional cases I have used my own computations, estimates, or approximations, which are clearly marked as such.

Statistical data on countries other than Czechoslovakia have been taken, unless otherwise stated, from the *Statistical Yearbooks* and from the *Monthly Bulletin of Statistics* of the United Nations. Among other sources, the publications of the Economic Commission for Europe and the Organization for European Economic Cooperation have been most useful. Occasionally, Soviet, Polish, Hungarian, and East and West German official statistics, as well as statistics from the international part of the Czechoslovak *Statistical Yearbooks*, have been used.

I am greatly indebted to Mr. George F. Ray, Senior Research Officer, British National Institute of Economic and Social Research, who read Chapters 6, 8, and 10 and the Conclusion; and to Mr. Peter G. Elkan (Cantab.), Research Officer of the Institute, who read the Introduction, Chapter 7, and the Conclusion. Both made valuable suggestions which I was happy to incorporate in my book. Mr. Roger Agile (Paris), of the United Nations Secretariat in New York, kindly read and corrected the demographic part of Chapter 1. I profited from the seminar of Dr. A. Nove, London School of Economics and Social Science (University of London), on the economic problems of the Soviet world. Czechoslovak economists also greatly helped me in interpreting the meaning of Czechoslovak statistics; Mr. Keith G. Lumsden, of Edinburgh and Stanford, kindly helped me to solve many theoretical problems. All the shortcomings of this study, however, are my own unshared responsibility.

Miss J. Mary Bosdêt, Her Britannic Majesty's Inspector, Ministry of Education, gave me valuable help in many ways when I was writing the first draft of this book in London. Finally, I wish to thank the staff of the Stanford University Press, particularly Mrs. Elizabeth Spurr and Emlen Littell, for the careful and judicious editorial and technical assistance that has markedly improved the presentation.

JAN M. MICHAL

CONTENTS

ABBREVIATIONS AND SYMBOLS................................. xiii

INTRODUCTION 1

1 POPULATION AND MANPOWER............................... 6

§1. *Basic Demographic Data*, 6.　　§2. *Working Population (Total Labor Force)*, 15.　　§3. *Distribution of the Economically Active Population by Branches of the National Economy*, 23.

2 INDUSTRY 26

§1. *Importance of Industry in the Czechoslovak Economy*, 26.　　§2. *Index of Industrial Production*, 29.　　§3. *Growth of Output by Main Sectors of Industry*, 37.　　§4. *Productivity in Industry*, 40.　　§5. *Some Growth Factors of Czechoslovak Industrial Production*, 45.　　§6. *Output in Physical Quantities of Important Commodities and Manufactures*, 47. §7. *1958 Reorganization of Industry and Prospective Plans to 1965*, 53. §8. *Summary*, 56.

3 CONSTRUCTION 58

§1. *Importance of Construction in the Czechoslovak Economy*, 58.　　§2. *Construction of Housing Units*, 60.

4 AGRICULTURE 64

§1. *Importance of Agriculture in the Czechoslovak Economy*, 64.　　§2. *Index of Agricultural Production*, 66.　　§3. *Factors of Development in Czechoslovak Agriculture*, 71.　　§4. *Impact of Collectivization*, 79. §5. *Prospective Plans Up to 1965*, 87.　　§6. *Summary*, 89.

5 TRANSPORTATION 91

§1. *General Trends*, 91.　　§2. *Rail, Highway, Water, and Air Traffic*, 92.

6 EXTERNAL TRADE 96

§1. *Czechoslovakia's Dependence on External Trade*, 96.　　§2. *Value of Exports and Imports by Main Economic Areas; Balance of Visible Trade*, 98.　　§3. *Commodity Pattern of Trade*, 106.　　§4. *Volume of Trade*,

121.   §5. *Export and Import (Unit) Price Index: Remarks on Exchange Rate and Price Policy*, 124.   §6. *Foreign Trade Net Subsidy*, 130. §7. *Foreign Aid*, 134.   §8. *Summary*, 135.

7 MONEY AND PRICES 139

§1. *The Currency Reform of June 1953*, 139.   §2. *External Value of the Czechoslovak Koruna*, 142.   §3. *System of Prices*, 144.   §4. *Cost-of-Living Index*, 157.

8 STATE BUDGET AND INVESTMENTS 165

§1. *State Budget*, 165.   §2. *Gross Fixed Investments*, 172.   §3. *Basic Funds*, 182.

9 INCOME OF THE POPULATION AND STANDARD OF LIVING 188

§1. *Earnings in the Socialist Sector and Per Capita Income*, 188.   §2. *"Collective Incomes" and Cost of Social Services*, 194.   §3. *Real Per Capita Earnings in Industry, Real Per Capita Personal Income, and Real Social Security Benefits Per Recipient*, 197.   §4. *Some Other Indicators of the Standard of Living*, 202.   §5. *Summary*, 210.

10 NATIONAL INCOME, GROSS PRODUCT, AND EXPENDITURE AGGREGATES 211

§1. *Conceptual Framework of National Income and Social Product in Centrally Planned Economies*, 211.   §2. *Czechoslovak National Income and Expenditure in 1948, Computed by Western and Marxist Methods*, 215. §3. *Czechoslovak National Income by Marxist Definition, 1948–58 Period*, 217.   §4. *Approximations of Czechoslovak National Income, and Gross National Product and Expenditure, Analogous to Western Definition*, 230.

CONCLUSION 238

APPENDIX 245

BIBLIOGRAPHY OF WORKS CITED 265

INDEXES 269

LIST OF TABLES

1.1 Czechoslovak Population by Broad Age Groups [1950, 1955, and projected] 8
1.2 Czechoslovak Population by Five-Year Age Groups in 1957...... 9
1.3 Comparison by Countries of Population in Productive Age Groups 15–59 Years [1950, 1955, and projected]................. 9
1.4 Some Demographic Characteristics [selected years, 1948–58].... 11
1.5 Death Rates by Causes [1955, 1956]........................ 12
1.6 Expectation of Life at Birth [prewar and postwar periods]...... 15
1.7 Economically Active Population [selected years, 1947–57]...... 16
1.8 Distribution of Economically Active Population [selected years, 1947–57] 24

2.1 Per Capita Consumption of Energy [1955, 1958].............. 28
2.2 Per Capita Consumption of Electricity [1956, 1958]........... 28
2.3 Per Capita Consumption of Steel [prewar, 1956, 1957]......... 29
2.4 General Index of Industrial Production [1937, 1948–58]........ 36
2.5 Rate of Growth of Industrial Production [1949–53, 1953–57].... 38
2.6 Industrial Output Between 1948 and 1958 [Czechoslovakia]..... 39
2.7 Index of Employment in Manufacturing [1948, 1953, 1956–58].. 40
2.8 Approximations of Index of Industrial Output per Man-Year [1948, 1953, 1956–58].................................. 41
2.9 Hours Worked in Industry per Week [1948, 1953–58].......... 42
2.10 Approximations of Output per Man-Hour in Industry [1955–58] 43
2.11 Some Factors of Industrial Growth in Czechoslovakia [1949–58] 44
2.12 Czechoslovak Industrial Production [1937, 1948, 1953–58].... 48
2.13 1957 Per Capita Output of Basic Materials, Energy, and Main Manufactures 52

3.1 Housing Units (Dwellings) Completed in Czechoslovakia [1948–58] 60
3.2 Comparison by Countries of Dwellings Completed, 1954–58..... 61
3.3 Comparison by Countries of Housing Available [postwar years].. 62

4.1 Index of Agricultural Production [1948–58].................. 68
4.2 Main Crops [average 1934–38, average 1948–52, and 1956–59].. 69

4.3   Livestock Production [1948/49, 1955/56–1958/59]...........   71
4.4   Yields of Main Crops [average 1934–38, and 1948–58]........   76
4.5   Number of Tractors [average 1949–52, and 1956–58]..........   79
4.6   Use of Commercial Fertilizers [average 1948/49–1952/53, and
       1956/57, 1957/58]   80
4.7   Breakdown of Agricultural Land, Production, and Supplies to the
       Market, by Sectors [Czechoslovakia, 1948, 1951–58]........   82
4.8   Average State Prices Paid for Agricultural Produce [Czechoslo-
       vakia, 1952–58]   84
4.9   Income of Agricultural Population [Czechoslovakia, selected years,
       1951–57]   86

5.1   Railway Transportation, Comparison by Countries [selected years,
       1937–58]   93
5.2   Air Transportation, Comparison by Countries [selected years,
       1937–58]   95

6.1   External Trade [per capita, selected years, 1948–58]............   97
6.2   Czechoslovak External Trade by Main Economic Areas [1948,
       1950–58]   99
6.3   Index Numbers of Value and Volume of Czechoslovak Trade
       [1949–58]   100
6.4   Czechoslovak Imports and Exports by Principal Trading Countries
       [1948, 1953–58]   101
6.5   Foreign Trade, Comparison of Czechoslovakia and Main Trading
       Partners [1957, 1958]   105
6.6   Czechoslovak Imports and Exports by Principal Commodity
       Groups [1953–58]   107
6.7   Main Czechoslovak Imports and Exports of Commodities [1953,
       1955–58]   108
6.8   Pattern of Czechoslovak Trade with European Centrally Planned
       Economies and Its Principal Partners Among European Market
       Economies, by Important Commodity Groups [1958].......   110
6.9   Czechoslovak Commodity Trade by Principal Receiving and Sup-
       plying Countries [1958]...............................   112
6.10   Czechoslovak Trade with 17 European Market Economies and
       Yugoslavia, Exports and Imports by Commodity Groups [1957,
       1958]   120
6.11   Exports of Machinery in 1956...........................   122
6.12   Comparison by Countries of Exports of Metal-working Machines
       and Diesel Engines [1956, 1958].......................   123
6.13   Index of Volume and of Unit Price of Exports, Comparison with
       the West [1937, 1948, 1950–58].......................   123
6.14   Derived Index of Czechoslovak Unit Import and Export Prices
       and of Terms of Trade [1949–58].......................   124
6.15   Long-Term Credits Granted by Czechoslovakia [1956–57, 1958–
       59]   136

7.1   Comparison of Derived Index of Investment Prices with Indices of
      Wages and Salaries [Czechoslovakia, 1949–58]   147
7.2   Estimate of the Cost-of-Living Index of Wage and Salary Earners
      in Czechoslovakia [1948–59]   158
7.3   Consumers' Prices in Czechoslovakia [1937–59]   162

8.1   Czechoslovak State Budget: Planned Expenditures and Receipts
      [1954–58]   166
8.2   Czechoslovak State Budget: Actual Receipts and Expenditures
      [1956, 1957]   167
8.3   State Budgets for 1958 in Some European Centrally Planned Econ-
      omies   171
8.4   Gross Fixed Investments, Excluding General Overhauls, by Cate-
      gories of Investments (at Comparable 1959 Prices) [Czechoslo-
      vakia, 1948–58]   175
8.5   Gross Fixed Investments, Excluding General Overhauls, by Inves-
      tors (at Comparable 1959 Prices) [Czechoslovakia, 1948–58]   175
8.6   Percentage Distribution of Gross Fixed Investments by Economic
      Branches, Share of State Investments in Total Investments
      [selected years, 1949–58].............................   177
8.7   Gross Fixed Investments in Czechoslovakia, Including General
      Overhauls, by Branches of National Economy [1948, 1953–58]   178
8.8   State-Planned Fixed Investments by Economic Branches of Na-
      tional Economy [Czechoslovakia, 1948, 1953–58]...........   180
8.9   Investments Within the State Investment Plan: Comparison of Ex-
      penditures on Gross Fixed Investments and of Completed Basic
      Funds (Capital Assets) [Czechoslovakia, 1948–57].........   182
8.10 Investments Within the State Investment Plan: Comparison of
      Expenditures on Gross Fixed Investments at 1957 and January
      1959 Prices [Czechoslovakia, 1955–58]...................   183
8.11 Basic Funds (Capital Assets) in Czechoslovakia [1953, 1956–58]   184
8.12 Distribution of National Wealth [Czechoslovakia, 1956].......   186

9.1   Monthly Earnings in Czechoslovakia by Economic Branches [1948,
      1953–58]   190
9.2   Stratification of Wages and Earnings in Czechoslovak Industry
      [1957]   192
9.3   Old Age, Disability, and Other Social Welfare Benefits in Czecho-
      slovakia [1949, 1953, 1956–58]........................   195
9.4   Index Numbers of Benefits from National Insurance [Czechoslo-
      vakia, 1953, 1956–58]................................   196
9.5   Cost of Health Insurance in Czechoslovakia [1948, 1953–58]....   197
9.6   Index of Trends in the Cost of Living and in Real Earnings in Man-
      ufacturing, International Comparison [1952–58]...........   198
9.7   Approximation of Average Net Income in Czechoslovakia in 1948
      (Based on Personal Income in National Accounts)   199
9.8   Approximation of Average Net Per Capita Income in Czechoslo-
      vakia in 1956 (Based on "Net Money Income of Households")   200

9.9 Per Capita Consumption of Food in Czechoslovakia [1936, 1948, 1956–58] 202

9.10 Per Capita Consumption of Meat, Fats, and Sugar, Comparison Between Countries [1957–58]............................ 203

9.11 Working Time Necessary to Earn the Price of Basic Foodstuffs, Electricity, and Cigarettes in 1957....................... 204

9.12 Number of Passenger Cars in Use per 1,000 Inhabitants [1948, 1956, 1957–58] 205

9.13 Radio and Television Sets and Attendance at Films, Comparison by Countries [1957–59]................................ 206

9.14 Book Publication and Newspaper Circulation in 1957, Comparison by Countries.. 207

9.15 Foreign Tourist Travel in 1957............................ 208

9.16 Number of Physicians and Surgeons in 1957................ 209

10.1 Czechoslovak National Income by Economic Origin in 1948, Comparison of Marxist and Western Computations.............. 215

10.2 Czechoslovak National Income in 1948, by Western Definition; by Type, Origin, and Expenditure....................... 216

10.3 Distribution of National Income, Compared with Prewar Times [Czechoslovakia, 1937, 1946–48]...................... 216

10.4 Czechoslovakia's National Income by Marxist Definition [1948–58] 218

10.5 Influence of Factors of Growth of National Income (Marxist Definition) [Czechoslovakia, 1949–58]................... 222

10.6 Czechoslovakia's National Income and Gross Social Product by Marxist Definition [1953, 1956, 1957]................... 226

10.7 Czechoslovak National Income by Marxist Definition [1948, 1953, 1956, 1957] 229

10.8 Approximations of Czechoslovak National Income and Gross National Product, Analogous to Western Definition at Market Prices [1948, 1953, 1956, 1957]......................... 231

10.9 Approximation of Czechoslovak Expenditure on Gross National Product in 1956.................................... 235

10.10 Gross National Product and Expenditure, International Comparison [selected years, 1938–57]...................... 236

A.1 Basic National Account Data [selected years, 1948–59; 1960, 1965] 256

A.2 Industry [indices for selected years; 1960, 1965]............ 258

A.3 Construction [indices for selected years; 1960, 1965].......... 259

A.4 Agriculture [indices for selected years; 1960, 1965].......... 260

A.5 Transportation [indices for selected years; 1960, 1965]........ 260

A.6 Foreign Trade [indices for selected years; 1960, 1965]........ 261

A.7 Standard of Living [indices for selected years; 1960, 1965]..... 262

ABBREVIATIONS AND SYMBOLS

...	Data not available
—	None, negligible quantity (less than half of the unit used), or entry not applicable
( )	Official figure which, in the author's opinion, is not an expression of reality; noncomparable index
‖	Interrupted comparability of a statistical series
*	Author's estimate, if the margin of error is unlikely to exceed 5 per cent
†	Author's estimate, with margin of error probably exceeding 5 per cent
‡	Mere guess
CMEA	Council for Mutual Economic Aid (Moscow)
Cz	Czechoslovak, Czechoslovakia
d	Pence (of pound sterling)
din	Yugoslavian dinar
DM	Deutsche Mark (West German mark)
ECE	Economic Commission for Europe of the United Nations (Geneva)
FAO	Food and Agricultural Organization of the United Nations (Rome)
Fr	French franc (old)
Ft	Hungarian forint
ILO	International Labour Office (Geneva)
Kč	Czechoslovak koruna, prewar
Kčs	Czechoslovak koruna, postwar
£	Pound sterling (U.K.)
OEEC	Organization for European Economic Cooperation (Paris)
ROH	Revoluční Odborové Hnutí (Czechoslovak Revolutionary Trade Unions)
rub	Soviet ruble
$	U.S. dollar
Sch	Austrian schilling
SRRC	*Statistická ročenka Republiky Československé*
Zl	Polish zloty

Billion in this book denotes 1,000 million.

INTRODUCTION

The aim of this book is to bring together, from various sources, statistics and general information on Czechoslovakia's economy during the first decade of comprehensive central planning, 1948 to 1958, and to make comparisons with economic developments in highly industrial Western countries as well as in less industrial Eastern European countries. There are two reasons for undertaking such a study:

1. Czechoslovakia provides, for the first time in history, a test case of the efficacy of central planning at a very high stage of industrialization. (In the only other highly industrial Eastern European country, East Germany, the economic system has not been pushed so far toward comprehensive central planning, and the economy has been exposed to extraordinary influences which make an international comparison difficult.) Therefore, Czechoslovak economic development may be of special interest in view of the competition between the two basic economic systems of our times: the "market economy," which, although it may differ from country to country in the extent of state intervention and in the extent of private and public ownership, is based mainly on the interaction of demand, supply, and price on the market; and the "centrally planned economy," under which all means of production (with the exception of rapidly diminishing private land) are owned by the state or by state-sponsored bodies, and most market functions have been replaced by decisions of the central planning authorities.

When comprehensive central planning, based on radical nationalization of industry, transportation, banking, and trade, was introduced in 1948, Czechoslovakia already had a level of output and consumption similar to that prevailing in Western Europe. This similarity in starting levels makes a comparison of both economic *systems* more valid than, for example, a comparison between the United States and the USSR.[1]

The distinction between "centrally planned economies" and "market economies" is, of course, an oversimplification. The difference between Czechoslovakia and Western countries lies not only in this contrast but in the whole social system. Even from a purely economic point of view, it is necessary to qualify the Czechoslovak system as a centrally planned

---

[1] *Soviet Economic Growth. A Comparison with the United States.* Prepared by the Library of Congress for the Subcommittee on Foreign Economic Policy (Washington, D.C., 1957).

economy in a people's democracy on Soviet lines, with emphasis on industrialization and a planned high rate of accumulation (formation of state-owned capital). One can also imagine a centrally planned economy with emphasis on consumption, although so far there has been no example of a practical application of such a system. On the other hand, in the most developed Western European and North American economies, with which Czechoslovakia will be compared in this book, the existing system of parliamentary democracy promotes consumption and often has a restraining effect on (private) capital formation. Yet other types of "market economies" are known, both past and present, which put stress on a very high capital formation: for example, Britain, during the Industrial Revolution, when there was no universal suffrage and the trade unions were suppressed, maintained a high rate of capital formation by keeping wages extremely low and profits extremely high. In more recent times, Japan, under highly centralized political power, also maintained a high rate of capital formation while relying on the market for the allocation of resources. A somewhat special case is Yugoslavia, which combines a planned high rate of accumulation with the use of some market functions.

The existing contrast between Czechoslovakia and the market economies is sometimes described in the West as between a "free" and a "Communist" economy, and in the East as between "capitalism" and "socialism."

Neither the predictions of Marx, Lenin, and Stalin that the capitalist system would collapse nor the assumptions of some Western economists that the Communist centrally planned economy could not develop have proved right so far. The competition between the two systems is likely to go on for a further period of time.[2]

The centrally planned economy, with its tremendous power of marshaling all economic resources toward one single goal, has shown a remarkably fast pace of industrialization. Such a development probably is attractive to underdeveloped countries. However, it may be of interest to compare its over-all economic results with those of a market economy when

---

[2] N. S. Khrushchev forecast future developments in his speech before the Twenty-first Congress of the Soviet Communist Party in February 1959: "One-third of the world's population lives in Socialist countries [i.e., in centrally planned economies], and its share in the world's industrial output is more than one-third . . . When the Seven-Year Plan to develop the Soviet economy has been fulfilled and surpassed [i.e., in 1965], the countries belonging to the Socialist world system, assisted also by the great pace of economic growth in the people's democracies, will produce more than half of the world's industrial output. Thus, the Socialist world system will gain the upper hand over the capitalist world system in the decisive field of human activity, that is, in material production.

a high level of industrialization has been achieved, and to study the comparative economic efficiency of the two systems.

The author does not claim to provide a definitive answer to this problem. His conclusions about the working of central planning in a developed country are only rudimentary. Yet, some striking dissimilarities between the results obtained by the two types of economy emerge from the comparisons. It is hoped that the main differences may be taken up and further analyzed, with due regard to factors of system and factors of policy, by institutions which are better equipped with technical facilities and specialized knowledge.

2. In spite of this broader interest which Czechoslovak economic development may command, only a relatively small part of the recently published wealth of Czechoslovak data has been made available to the Western reader through the valuable publications of the Economic Commission for Europe, the United Nations Statistical Office, the short English edition of the *Czechoslovak Statistical Abstract, 1958,* etc. Some of the Czechoslovak statistics call for special qualifications.

The author has endeavored to correct some shortcomings of Czechoslovak statistics and to close the gaps in order to provide a more coherent picture of Czechoslovakia's economic growth and policies. This may be especially important, since the great role that Czechoslovakia plays in the present competition between East and West seems not to be generally known. In the 1956–58 period, Czechoslovakia exported to other centrally planned economies and underdeveloped market economies in Asia and Africa machinery and equipment worth over half a billion dollars a year, and almost the same value in raw materials, semifinished products, and fuels for industry. Even the USSR is considerably dependent on Czechoslovak supplies. For example, in 1957, one-third of Soviet imports of machine tools, one-third of Soviet imports of power plant equipment, and all Soviet imports of stationary diesel engines came from Czechoslovakia. The scope of economic aid granted by Czechoslovakia is amazing. In the two years 1956–57, long-term credits granted, with only 2 per cent interest and extremely favorable conditions of payment, amounted to some $40 per Czechoslovak inhabitant (the corresponding per capita economic aid granted by the United States—including grants but excluding military aid—was $16, and per capita aid granted by the USSR was $14).[3] Beyond economic aid of this kind, Czechoslovakia is subsidizing other

---

[3] The actual utilization of Czechoslovak and Soviet credits, however, has been much lower than that of U.S. grants and credits.

countries through low export prices. Czechoslovak foreign trade is analyzed in detail in Chapter 6 of this book.

It is hoped that this work may also serve as a general statistical
reference on Czechoslovakia and, to a smaller extent, on other centrally
planned economies in Eastern Europe.

Czechoslovakia's economy will be systematically compared with the
following market economies: Austria (as an example of a small neighboring country with similar consumption habits), France, West Germany, the
United Kingdom, and the United States. It will also be compared with the
following centrally planned economies, wherever data were available to
the author: East Germany, Hungary, Poland, and the USSR. Comparisons
will also be made with Yugoslavia, which Czechoslovak statistics included
in the group of "Socialist countries," although its economy is a combi-
nation of central planning and market system.

The comparison refers in principle to the 1948–58 period. In the
Appendix, however, data on the Czechoslovak economy in 1959 have been
provided, together with the planned figures for 1960 and the targets for
1965 under the third Czechoslovak Five-Year Plan. Important prewar
figures have also been included in several statistical tables.

Absolute figures on Czechoslovak national income and expenditure are
still withheld from official publication. Even if we had accurate figures,
it would not be easy to compare national accounts in Czechoslovakia and
in the market economies; any such comparison, without adjustments,
would be far from perfect. The Marxist and Western definitions of national
income are different, and most relationships, as reflected in national accounts, have quite different meanings in a centrally planned economy and
in a market economy, in view of the differences in pricing.

Therefore, the author had to work over his field of study sector by
sector to build up a mosaic and finally to draw some general conclusions
from it. The economic sectors are examined in an order similar to that
used in the Czechoslovak Statistical Yearbook: population and manpower
(including some purely demographic data), industry, building and construction, agriculture, transportation, and trade. Next comes an explanation of the system of prices in Czechoslovakia and the state budget and
investments. This is followed by comments on real wages and standard
of living, and by an attempt to estimate Czechoslovakia's national income
and national expenditure.

The stress is placed on statistical tables rather than on the text. Most
of the figures speak for themselves.

As to the reliability of the Czechoslovak statistics, the author has discovered no large-scale intentional distortion of the *basic* figures. There seems to be no double-accounting for basic figures in Czechoslovak statistics, i.e., no bogus figures for publication only. However, the way of collecting statistical data may lead to some distortions even of the basic figures. Production data are given an upward bias by the tendency of industrial management to overrate output in order to obtain premiums for overfulfilling the plan; furthermore, rejects and inferior-quality products are also included in output figures, etc. Data on exports probably exclude military aid and possibly a part of the economic aid granted by Czechoslovakia. Data on civilian consumption include some basic foods used in export industries, etc. When allowance is made for these limitations of the quality of data, the basic Czechoslovak figures can be considered as reasonably reliable.

The *index numbers* and other relative figures, however, are subject to more serious qualifications, as described in the individual chapters of this book. The cost-of-living index, for instance, not only seems to be divorced from reality but is not available at all for the period from the beginning of central planning in 1948 until the second postwar currency reform in 1953. Therefore, the author had to complete and modify the official figures by his own estimate. On the other hand, the possible discrepancy between, for instance, the official Czechoslovak production indices and the probable real trend of the volume of output is believed to be smaller than the discrepancy between Soviet official indices and the corresponding Western recomputations of Soviet data.

In some cases, for purely technical reasons, it was necessary to accept a limited international comparability in order to give the Western reader an insight into up-to-date developments in Czechoslovakia. Too great delay would be involved if some Western statistics were to be adjusted to make them compare perfectly with the available Czechoslovak data. For the same reason, approximations have been used that are not methodologically correct but that are of illustrative validity. These are pointed out where they occur.

The author apologizes to the readers who, having plowed through all the computations in this book, may feel that now they know more about Czechoslovakia than they ever wanted to know. Like any other reference book, this one should only be used in small doses for specific purposes. Readers, on the other hand, who seek more detailed data are invited to consult the sources mentioned in the Bibliography.

Chapter 1

POPULATION AND MANPOWER

1. Basic Demographic Data

The present population of Czechoslovakia—in a comparable territory of 127.8 thousand square kilometers, i.e., without Carpatho-Ruthenia, which was incorporated into the USSR at the end of the war—decreased, in terms of midyear averages, from 14.4 million in the last peace year, 1937, to 14.2 million in 1945 and to 12.3 million in 1948. The main factors causing this decrease were the wartime losses suffered by the Czechoslovak armies in the east and west and the deportation and executions of the home population, as well as the postwar expulsion of a great part of the German population and the exchange of Hungarians from Slovakia and Slovaks from Hungary. On the other hand, groups of Czechs and Slovaks who had lived abroad returned to Czechoslovakia after the Second World War. It would not serve any useful purpose in the present economic study to examine these factors in detail. The reader is only requested to bear in mind, when making comparisons with prewar days, that, besides the reduction in territory (for which, unless otherwise stated, a due correction of prewar figures has been made throughout this study), there was a population decline of 14.5 per cent between 1937 and 1948, on comparable territory.

In the decade under study, the changes of population through migration have been negligible. Emigration due to economic considerations, which was rather important at the beginning of this century, has been almost completely stopped. In 1954, 1955, and 1956, respectively, only 2.7, 3.3, and 2.7 thousand people legally emigrated, while 2.0, 2.3, and 1.8 thousand came into Czechoslovakia. Official migration data for the two later years are not available to the author, yet it is safe to assume that they are as low as for 1954–56. Somewhat greater was the flow of refugees to the West in 1948 and subsequent years, which, similarly to the transfer of a part of the German and Hungarian population, is not recognized in the official Cechoslovak migration figures. No reliable statistical data are available, yet most estimates of the total number of refugees since 1948 (up to 1958) are in the range of 60 to 80 thousand; the rate of refugees amounted thus, over a period of ten years, to only 0.4–0.6 per cent of the population. This has been of some political and cultural significance, but from the economic point of view it is of limited importance only; from the demographic point of view it is immaterial.

The increase of the Czechoslovak population between 1948 and 1958 —as given below for the end of each year—is thus almost entirely the net result of natural movement (figures in thousands).

Year	Total	Women Only	Year	Total	Women Only
1948	12,339	6,350	1954	13,023	6,681
1949	12,340	6,349	1955	13,161	6,749
1950	12,464	6,410	1956	13,296	6,816
1951	12,607	6,480	1957	13,414	6,873
1952	12,754	6,551	1958	13,523	6,927
1953	12,892	6,618			

Source: *Statistická ročenka Republiky Československé*, 1959, Table 3.2.

The density of Czechoslovakia's population decreased from 135 persons per square kilometer in 1930 to 105 in 1957. In the latter year it was thus lower than in West Germany (208) and the United Kingdom (211), but higher than in Austria (83), France (80), and the United States (22). It was higher than in most other centrally planned economies in Europe, such as Poland (90), Yugoslavia (71), and the USSR (9), but lower than in East Germany (155) and Hungary (106).

Up to 1958, data on the age distribution of Czechoslovakia's population were published by four broad age groups only, for 1950 and 1955, with projections up to 1970. See Table 1.1. In the *Statistická ročenka Republiky Československé*, 1959, somewhat more detailed data, by five-year age groups, have been published for the first time since the introduction of central planning. These data can be found in Table 1.2. A comparison by countries of the productive age group is shown in Table 1.3.

The changes in marriage, divorce, birth, and death rates between 1948 and 1958 are compared by countries in Table 1.4. These rates are crude;[1] their comparability is thus limited by deviations in age distribution between countries.

In Czechoslovakia in 1958, 17.4 live births per 1,000 inhabitants,

---

[1] The net birth and death rates are not being published in current standard Czechoslovak statistics. Some articles on them have been published in the recent special publication of the Statistical Office, *Demografie*, in 1959. Data on specific natality (birth rate by age of mother) have been published, for the first time since 1948, in *Statistická ročenka Republiky Československé*, 1959, Table 4.14. Data on specific mortality by age groups also have been published in *Statistická ročenka Republiky Československé* (hereinafter referred to as *SRRC*), 1959, Table 4.23.

TABLE 1.1—CZECHOSLOVAK POPULATION BY BROAD AGE GROUPS

(In thousand persons and per cent of total population)

	0-14		15-39		40-59		60 & Over		Total	
	1000's	%	1000's	%	1000's	%	1000's	%	1000's	%
1950:										
Male	1,633	27.1	2,217	36.8	1,551	25.8	619	10.3	6,020	100
Female	1,581	24.8	2,250	35.2	1,695	26.6	854	13.4	6,380	100
Total	3,214	25.9	4,467	36.0	3,246	26.2	1,473	11.9	12,400	100
1955:										
Male	1,876	29.2	2,204	34.3	1,661	25.9	680	10.6	6,421	100
Female	1,794	26.6	2,228	33.0	1,783	26.4	942	14.0	6,747	100
Total	3,670	27.9	4,432	33.6	3,444	26.2	1,622	12.3	13,168	100
1960 Projection:										
Male	1,997	29.6	2,400	35.6	1,567	23.3	772	11.5	6,736	100
Female	1,902	27.0	2,398	34.0	1,653	23.4	1,099	15.6	7,052	100
Total	3,899	28.3	4,798	34.8	3,220	23.3	1,871	13.6	13,788	100
1965 Projection:										
Male	1,991	28.3	2,533	36.0	1,610	22.9	894	12.7	7,028	100
Female	1,890	25.8	2,490	34.0	1,709	23.3	1,232	16.8	7,321	100
Total	3,881	27.0	5,023	35.0	3,319	23.1	2,126	14.8	14,349	100
1970 Projection:										
Male	2,108	28.4	2,684	36.1	1,612	21.7	1,027	13.8	7,431	100
Female	1,993	26.2	2,600	34.2	1,726	22.7	1,278	16.8	7,597	100
Total	4,101	27.3	5,284	35.2	3,338	22.2	2,305	15.3	15,028	100

Data are from the *Economic Survey of Europe, 1957* (Economic Commission for Europe, Geneva, 1958), Chapter VII. Further information can be found in an article by M. Kučera in *Statistický obzor*, No. 9, 1958. Projections for Czechoslovakia have been computed by the Secretariat of the Economic Commission for Europe before the 1955–58 period, when the Czechoslovak birth rate—crude and probably net as well—continued to decrease; therefore, the population in the 0–14 age group is likely to be overestimated.

TABLE 1.2—CZECHOSLOVAK POPULATION BY FIVE-YEAR AGE GROUPS IN 1957

(End of the year, in thousand persons)

Age Group	Male	Female	Age Group	Male	Female
0–4	651.0	616.7	45–49	470.8	493.0
5–9	660.9	629.7	50–54	425.9	458.3
10–14	591.4	575.0	55–59	371.0	417.6
15–19	470.6	461.2	60–64	264.2	340.8
20–24	424.2	417.8	65–69	187.0	253.0
25–29	486.7	489.5	70–74	133.5	192.7
30–34	491.9	514.6	75–79	88.2	123.5
35–39	424.1	443.8	80–84	40.2	59.6
40–44	339.1	357.2	85 & over	20.3	29.3
			Total population	6,541.0	6,873.3

Data from *SRRC*, 1959, Table 3.4.

though still above the level listed in Western European countries, were one-quarter less than in 1948. Over the same period both Germanies and the United States registered an increased birth rate. No far-reaching conclusions should be drawn, of course, without examining the demographic, sociological, and economic factors involved, which would exceed the scope of this economic study. Yet it is fairly safe to assume that, among other factors, the rapid increase in employment of women in Czechoslovakia has had a certain impact on the birth rate. It also contributed in all proba-

TABLE 1.3—COMPARISON BY COUNTRIES OF POPULATION IN PRODUCTIVE AGE GROUPS 15–59 YEARS

(As percentage of total population)

Country	1950	1955	Projection 1970
Czechoslovakia	62.2	59.8	57.4
Austria	61.5	61.2	60†
France	61.5	59.0	59.2†
West Germany	66.8	64.8	...
United Kingdom	58.8	60.9	...
United States	60.7	57.8	58†
East Germany	61.0	60.8	54.3
Hungary	63.2	61.8	57.3
Poland	62.2	60.4	57.1

Data on Czechoslovakia and all other countries with central planning from the *Economic Survey of Europe*, 1957 (ECE, Geneva, 1958), Chapter VII. Data on market economies for 1950 based on U.N. *Demographic Yearbook*, 1951; for 1955 and projection for 1970, from *OEEC Statistical Bulletin—General Statistics*, July 1958, adjusted to the 15–59 age group by data on the 60–64 age group from the United Nations *Demographic Yearbook*, 1957.

bility to a more rapid decrease in the marriage rate and to the higher rate of divorce, as compared with Western Europe, shown in Table 1.4.[2]

Czechoslovakia registered a sharper fall in crude birth rate than other, less industrial Eastern European centrally planned economies. In 1957 the Czechoslovak birth rate was substantially lower than in the rest of the centrally planned area, except East Germany and Hungary, where some special factors were involved.

In view of the rapid decrease in the birth rate in 1958, there was discussion in the Czechoslovak press as to whether one of the causes was the new law permitting "artificial interruption of pregnancy," not only for health but also for economic and social reasons.[3] This brings us to the question of the relationship between the number of live births and the number of abortions, which has a considerable impact upon the birth rate in our time.

In 1957, before the new law on interruption of pregnancy came into force, 30,090 abortions were officially reported; it was officially estimated that the actual number of abortions was three times higher.[4] This means that in Czechoslovakia, in 1957, there was approximately one abortion for every two live births. The ratio of abortions to live births thus seemed to be no lower than the Western European average.

In 1958 the number of reported interruptions of pregnancy (under the new law) jumped. The monthly *Demografie*, No. 2, 1959, reported the following figures (in thousands):

Year	Live Births	Stillbirths	Officially Reported Abortions
1955	265	3	35
1956	262	3	34
1957	253	3	37
1958	235	2	89

The increase in officially reported abortions was accompanied, in all probability, by a decrease in stillbirths and in nonreported abortions. Nevertheless, interruptions of pregnancy seem to have had, in 1958, an

[2] According to Dr. V. Srb, "Naše populační otázky" in *Rudé Právo*, September 2, 1958, there is one divorce for every three marriages in Prague. This suggests another important factor of the high rate of divorce: the high mobility of labor coupled with the housing shortage. For example, many workers—especially white-collar workers—have been transferred from Prague to somewhat remote mining and heavy-industry areas where there is no family housing available. The separation may then lead to divorce.

[3] For example, *Mladá fronta* for January 8, 1959, maintained that the new law was not the only factor in the further fall of the birth rate. It said that, during the first nine months since enforcement of the new law, several hundred girls under 17 years of age had applied successfully for interruption of pregnancy.

[4] *SRRC*, 1958, p. 34. Later, a figure of 37,000 officially reported abortions was published.

TABLE 1.4—SOME DEMOGRAPHIC CHARACTERISTICS

(Crude rates per 1,000 inhabitants, infant mortality per 1,000 live births)

Country	Birth Rates			Death Rates			Natural Increase		
	1948	1957	1958	1948	1957	1958	1948	1957	1958
Czechoslovakia ...	23.4	18.9	17.4	11.5	10.1	9.3	11.9	8.8	8.1
Austria	17.7	17.0	16.9	12.1	12.8	12.2	5.6	4.2	4.7
France	21.2	18.4	18.1	12.4	12.0	11.1	8.8	6.4	7.0
West Germany	16.6	17.0	17.0	10.3	11.3	10.8	6.3	5.7	6.2
United Kingdom ..	18.1	16.5	16.8	10.9	11.5	11.7	7.2	5.0	5.1
United States	24.2	25.0	24.3	9.9	9.6	9.5	14.3	15.4	14.8
East Germany	12.8	15.6	15.6	...	17.3[e]	18.1	15.2	12.8	12.7
Hungary	19.1	17.0	16.0	11.2	10.6	9.9	-2.4	2.8	2.9
Poland	29.2	27.5	26.3	11.2	9.5	8.4	7.9	6.4	6.1
USSR	...	23.7[a]	23.5	...	7.7[b]	7.2	18.0	18.0	17.9
Yugoslavia	28.3	23.5	23.5	13.6	10.6	9.1	19.1	13.0	12.4

Country	Marriage Rates			Divorce Rates[f]			Infant Mortality		
	1948	1957	1958	1948	1956	1957	1948	1957	1958
Czechoslovakia ...	10.6	6.8	7.4	0.97	1.10	1.07	85.5	33.4	29.5
Austria	10.3	8.0	7.9	2.04	1.22	1.17	76.2	44.2	40.7
France	9.1	7.0	7.0	1.15	0.68	0.66	55.9	33.7	31.5
West Germany	10.6	9.0	9.1	1.87	0.81	0.81	68.1	36.4	36.0
United Kingdom ..	9.0	7.8	7.5	0.98[d]	0.57[d]	0.52	36.0	23.9	23.3
United States	12.4	8.9	8.3	2.79[g]	2.29[g]	2.22[g]	32.0	26.4	26.9
East Germany	...	8.6	8.9	2.12	1.25	1.25	89	46	44
Hungary	...	10.0	9.3	1.21	1.27	1.82	94	63	58
Poland	10.8	9.1	...	0.44	0.50	0.55	111	77	73
USSR	...	...	...	...	...	...	...	44	41
Yugoslavia	...	8.6	9.2	1.55	1.05	1.10	116[e]	101	86

Sources: Various issues of the U.N. *Demographic Yearbook* and the U.N. *Monthly Bulletin of Statistics.* For Eastern Europe, in addition, *SRRC*, 1958, the international part; *Maly rocznik statystyczny* (Warsaw, 1958), and the *Statistical Pocket Book of Jugoslavia*, 1958. For the USSR, *Narodnoe Khoziaistvo SSSR v 1958 godu.* For East Germany, *Statistisches Jahrbuch der DDR 1958.*

[a] Figure for 1956. According to the *SRRC*, 1959, international part, this figure was 25.2 in 1956.
[b] 1956.
[c] Figure for 1956. According to official Soviet data, this figure was 17.6 in both 1956 and 1957.
[d] England and Wales.   [e] 1949.
[f] Final divorces per 1000 inhabitants excluding annulments of marriage and legal separations.
[g] Including annulments. Not all States covered.

increased impact on live births, and the corresponding ratio in Czechoslovakia was probably higher than in Western Europe.

The crude death rate decreased faster in Czechoslovakia than in the West. This favorable development was due not only to the slightly dif-

TABLE 1.5—DEATH RATES BY CAUSES

(Deaths per 100,000 inhabitants)

Code No.	Cause of Death	Czechoslovakia 1955	Czechoslovakia 1956	Austria 1956	France 1956	West Germany 1955	England and Wales 1956	U.S. 1955	Poland 1955	Hungary 1956
B 1	Tuberculosis of respiratory system	40.6	36.3	22.2	25.3	16.2	10.9	8.3	48.9	31.4
B 3	Syphilis and its sequelae	3.6	3.6	4.3	2.7	1.7	3.1	2.3	1.0	3.3
B 18	Malignant neoplasm	163.3	166.0	241.3	182.9	191.9	207.6	146.5	65.3	151.3
B 20	Diabetes mellitus	8.7	9.8	9.3	12.4	10.8	7.3	15.5	2.8	6.7
B 22	Vascular lesions affecting central nervous system	87.7	93.7	152.8	144.2	170.0	166.8	106.0	29.0	135.8
B 26	Arteriosclerosis and degenerative heart disease	180.7	176.6	227.1	58.8	178.0	313.3	286.9	18.7	169.4
B 31	Pneumonia	50.6	48.9	46.6	50.6	37.9	50.1	25.4	70.2	65.3
B 47	Motor vehicle accidents	8.5	10.1	20.6	18.6	23.3	11.3	23.4	38.9	7.7
B 48	All other accidents	56.8	57.9	45.6	42.2	34.5	25.2	33.5		29.2
B 49	Suicide and self-inflicted injury			22.8	16.9	19.3	11.8	10.2	5.7	19.6
B 50	Homicide and victims of revolutions and wars			1.5	0.7	1.0	0.6	4.5	1.2	28.4

Data for Czechoslovakia from *SRRC*, 1958; for all other countries from the U.N. *Demographic Yearbook*, 1957. Only the most important causes of death are listed in this table; data on other causes of death, according to the abbreviated international list (sixth revision, 1948), can be found in the sources quoted above; but in Czechoslovak statistics, items B 48, B 49, and B 50 are combined into one figure described as "all other external causes of death."

12

ferent age distribution, extension of medical care, old-age benefits, etc., but also to some interesting trends in death rates by causes. These are given, in comparison by countries, in Table 1.5. Whereas Czechoslovakia succeeded in reducing the death rate due to most infectious diseases (except tuberculosis) almost to Western European levels (but not yet to the American level), it is not at present affected by the very high death rate for illnesses characteristic of industrialized societies with a traditionally high standard of living, such as malignant neoplasm, vascular lesions affecting the central nervous system, arteriosclerosis or other heart diseases.

It may be of some economic and sociological interest to point out the following facts from Table 1.5:

The death rate from tuberculosis is still higher in Czechoslovakia than in the West. The death rate from syphilis is only slightly higher than in Western Europe or the United States, but lower than in Austria. The death rate from motor accidents is lower than in the West, but allowing for the substantially lower level of motorization in Czechoslovakia (see Chapter 9) it is excessively high. The death rates from other accidents, suicide, and homicide are combined, in Czechoslovak statistics, in one single figure. This rate—57.9 deaths per 100,000 inhabitants in 1956— was lower than the corresponding combined figures for Austria (69.9) and France (59.8), but higher than for West Germany (54.8), the United States (48.2), and England and Wales (37.6). The combined death rate for accidents, suicide, and homicide was also higher than in Poland (45.8, including motor vehicle accidents), but lower than in Hungary (77.2, including 28.4 persons officially reported killed for every 100,000 inhabitants in Hungary in the year of the Hungarian uprising).

The conclusion may be drawn that the death rate from at least one of the causes: accidents other than motor vehicle accidents, suicide, or homicide, is higher in Czechoslovakia than in West Germany, the United States, England and Wales, and Poland. Comparability of crude death rates by causes is, of course, limited by varying age and sex structure of the population and by varying diagnosis-consciousness between countries.

Besides death rates by causes, the number of newly reported cases of infectious illnesses may be of some sociological interest. Among the 19 illnesses which are being compulsorily reported in Czechoslovakia, diphtheria and scarlet fever have been declining most rapidly (from 8,611 cases in 1948 to 988 cases in 1957, and from 50,858 to 27,527 cases, respectively). Whooping cough and infectious jaundice have been increasing rapidly (the latter from 983 cases in 1948 to a peak of 50,814 cases in 1954, with subsequent decrease to 24,621 cases in 1957). Dysentery has been spreading regularly from year to year, increasing from 667 cases in 1948 to 11,453 cases in 1957, with only a slight reduction to 10,081 cases in 1958). This has probably been due to the hastily constructed new industrial centers, which lack adequate hygienic facilities. It is interesting to note that the number of cases of tuberculosis also increased, from 20,180 in 1949 to 23,267 in 1957 and to approximately 25,000 in 1958. Of the venereal diseases, syphilis, after reaching a peak of 16,009 newly reported cases in 1951, was reduced to only 1,961 cases in 1957. But the trend of gonorrhea did not change very much until 1957, the number of cases varying between 5,000 and 8,000 a year in the last decade. In 1958 the number of reported cases of gonorrhea fell considerably, to 3,862.[5]

From the demographic and economic point of view, an important fact is that the decrease in the death rate in Czechoslovakia, although larger than in the listed Western countries in the decade under study, was not sufficient to compensate for the still faster decrease in the birth rate; thus, the Czechoslovak lead in natural increase of population, as compared with Western Europe, was very much reduced between 1948 and 1957, and its lag, as compared with the United States, was increased considerably. The Czechoslovak natural increase of population also remains considerably below that in less developed, centrally planned countries, as shown in Table 1.4.

Two demographic phenomena are much emphasized by the Czechoslovak press as a favorable result of the socialist economy: the drop in infant mortality and the prolonged expectation of life at birth (both these phenomena are, of course, closely correlated). The fall in deaths of infants per 1,000 live births in the last decade was, in fact, the greatest in Czechoslovakia among all the listed countries, as shown in Table 1.4. The infant mortality rate of 33.4 per 1,000 live births in 1957 was lower than in West Germany, but still somewhat higher than in France, the United States, and especially the United Kingdom, which has the lowest infant mortality in the world after the Netherlands, Sweden, and Norway.

Expectation of life at birth in Czechoslovakia and in some Western countries is compared, until 1955, in Table 1.6. It appears that the narrowing of the gap between the lower expectation of life in Czechoslovakia and the higher expectation in Western European countries and the United States, which has been going on ever since the thirties, has accelerated in recent years. Yet, in 1955 Czechoslovakia still had a substantially shorter expectation of life than England and Wales, West Germany, or the United

[5] All data on infectious illnesses from *SRRC*, 1958, Table 17.14, and 1959, Table 17.21a.

TABLE 1.6—EXPECTATION OF LIFE AT BIRTH

Country	Prewar			Postwar					
	Period	Years of Age M.	F.	Period	Years of Age M.	F.	Period	Years of Age M.	F.
Czechoslovakia ..	1929–32	51.9	55.2	1949–51	60.9	65.5	1955	66.2	71.2
France	1933–38	55.9	61.6	1950–51	63.6	69.3			
England & Wales.	1930–32	58.7	62.9	1950–52	66.4	71.5	1955	67.5	73.0
United States ...	1929–31	57.7	61.0	1949–51	65.5	71.0	1955		69.5
Hungary	1930–31	48.3	51.3	1948–49	58.8	63.3	1955	64.7	68.8
Poland	1931–32	48.2	51.4	1952–53	58.6	64.2			

Data for Czechoslovaia for 1955 from *Statistický obzor*, No. 3, 1957; other data from various issues of the U.N. *Statistical Yearbook*.

States; but the period for which comparable data are available is too short to make any far-reaching conclusions. It should be stressed, however, that expectation of life further increased in 1956 to 66.6 years for males and to 71.6 for females, followed by a slight reduction to 66.0 and 71.1 years, respectively, in 1957.[6]

2. Working Population (Total Labor Force)

There is a severe labor shortage in several branches of the Czechoslovak economy. Under Czechoslovak law, men under 65 and women under 60, except sick persons and housewives with small children, must work.[7] Besides this legal obligation, there has been considerable economic pressure on the population to enter employment, especially after the loss of the bulk of savings through the second postwar currency reform in 1953. There was a drive to increase the employment of housewives and, until 1958, also a drive to reemploy old people living on small old-age pensions.[8]

Strangely enough, even under these conditions, the percentage of working population in total population, according to computations based on

[6] From *SRRC*, 1959, Table 4.19.
[7] The age limit is 60 or 55 years for special categories of workers and miners.
[8] Since 1958, national committees have decided whether employment of old people is economically desirable. In *SRRC*, 1959, interesting data on the age distribution of "persons working in the Socialist sector of the national economy, excluding agricultural cooperatives"—covering practically all wage and salary earners—have been published (Table 5.14). They indicate that, on September 30, 1958, 12 per cent of the wage and salary earners were over 55, and 5 per cent were over 65 years of age (the corresponding percentages for men being 13 and 6 per cent, for women 10 and 4 per cent, respectively). The average age of wage and salary earners was 38.9 years for men, and 35.4 years for women (*ibid.*, Table 5.13). In agriculture, the average age of the members of cooperatives, and especially of the remaining individual farmers, was much higher (see Chapter 4, Sections 1 and 4).

official Czechoslovak statistics, decreased between 1948 and 1957; e.g., it remains below the corresponding percentage of economically active population in West Germany. This paradox deserves further analysis. The percentage of working or economically active population (including unemployed) depends, of course, on the structure of total population by age groups. This is one of the limitations of comparability of figures in the table "Erwerbspersonen unter der Gesamtbevölkerung" from the international part of the *Statistisches Jahrbuch für die Bundesrepublik Deutschland*, which has been used for comparison by countries, in Table 1.7 in this book. Yet, in Czechoslovakia's case, these factors cannot explain the decrease in the proportion of "working" population in total population, according to official statistics. This proportion depends, of course, also on the definition of "economically active" or "working" population. The new statistics of "persons working in the national economy," as introduced in Czechoslovakia since 1948, include by definition all wage and salary

TABLE 1.7—ECONOMICALLY ACTIVE POPULATION
(In per cent of total population)

Country	Year	Male and Female		Male		Female	
Czechoslovakia	1947	48		64		33	
	1948[a]	46	49	58	64	33	35
	1953[b]	47	49.5	54	61	36	38
	1957[a]	46	49.5	54	60	38	39
Austria	1951	48		64		35	
	1956	51		66		38	
France	1946	52		67		37	
	1957	45[b]		61[b]		29[b]	
West Germany	1950	46		63		31	
	1956	50		68		35	
United Kingdom	1951	46		67		27	
United States	1950	40		58		22	
East Germany	1950	47		64		34	
USSR	1955	43†[,b]		...		...	
Yugoslavia	1953	46		63		31	

Sources: Figures for Czechoslovakia, 1947, and all other countries except the USSR are from *Statistiches Jahrbuch für die Bundesrepublik Deutschland*, 1955 and 1958, tables "Erwerbspersonen unter der Gesamtbevölkerung." Figures for the USSR are estimated by the author, assuming an economically active population of 85 million (from the *Economic Survey of Europe*, 1957) and a total population of 200 million. There is limited comparability for Czechoslovakia between 1947 and later years and limited comparability between countries.

[a] Figures for Czechoslovakia, 1948–57, were calculated by the author, the first figure being based on official statistics on "persons working in the national economy" and the second figure being adjusted, as described in Chapter 1, Section 2.

[b] Excluding the armed forces and all employment with them.

earners, permanent members of cooperatives, self-employed workers (entrepreneurs, including farmers), and members of their families who work permanently with them. Women working in households only are not included. Therefore, in contrast to the usual definition of "economically active population," the new Czechoslovak statistics on persons working in the national economy do not include the unemployed; but this difference in definition does not change the picture, at least in theory, since there are no officially reported unemployed in Czechoslovakia (in practice, there may be some very limited unemployment, as will be shown; yet, the exclusion of unemployed is, under present conditions, only a very minor factor of incomparability between statistics on persons "working in the national economy" and on those "economically active"). A certain portion of women helping in agriculture who usually are included in statistics on the economically active population may also be excluded from the present Czechoslovak statistics on the working population; but this difference also is of limited importance.

In 1947 there were 5,852,000 "economically active persons" in Czechoslovakia, representing 48 per cent of the total population. In 1948, under the new statistics on the "working population," there were only 5,545,000 "persons working in the national economy," although there were no officially reported unemployment and no decrease in the population of productive age. The proportion of working population in total population went down, according to the new statistics, to 46 per cent. On further examination, it appears that only the proportion of working men in the total male population decreased, while the proportion of working women in the total female population remained unchanged. An interruption of comparability between statistics on "economically active" and "working" population, however, makes accurate analysis difficult. Yet, even perfectly comparable data on working population in later years denote a decreasing number of working men up to 1955.

End of Year	"Working Population" (thousands)			Index, 1948 = 100		
	Total	Male	Female	Total	Male	Female
1948	5,545	3,447	2,098	100.0	100.0	100.0
1950	5,577	3,455	2,141	100.6	99.7	102.1
1953	5,762	3,384	2,378	103.9	98.2	113.3
1954	5,909	3,444	2,465	106.6	99.9	117.5
1955	5,998	3,445	2,553	108.2	99.9	121.7
1956	6,059	3,529	2,530	109.3	102.4	120.6
1957	6,066	3,503	2,563	109.4	101.6	122.1

Statistické zprávy, No. 8, 1958; data exclude apprentices; they are slightly different from data in SRRC, 1958 and 1959, Table 5.1, which refer to yearly averages as follows (working population in thousand persons): 1953, 5,683; 1956, 6,047; 1957, 6,100; 1958, 6,105.

The author of the article from which the above figures are taken explains the decreasing number of working men by a decrease in the number of men of productive age (presumably 15–64 years); but the number of men from 15 to 59 years of age *increased,* between 1950 and 1955 (see Table 1.1) by 97,000, and the number of men in the remaining productive age groups 60–64 years also is likely to have *increased,* while the number of working men *decreased* by 10,000 (although the percentage of working men at ages 65 and over probably also increased). Other authors stressed the "longer period of schooling and training of apprentices as one of the factors affecting the rate of employment.[9] But the change in the number of apprentices was too small to explain the discrepancy of at least 107,000 between the change in "working male population" and in "total male population of productive age" in the 1950–55 period.[10]

The most plausible explanation is that certain activities, carried out especially by men, are excluded from Czechoslovak statistics on working population. In fact, *SRRC,* 1958, in an introductory remark to a chapter entitled "Labor" (p. 88), states that "data on persons working in the national economy are not complete. . . . Excluded, e.g., are data on the armed forces from the Ministry of Defense, the Ministry of the Interior, etc."

These, however, were included in the 1947 Czechoslovak statistics on the economically active population; they also are included in Western statistics. To make the 1948–57 statistics on "persons working in the national economy" more comparable with the usual statistics on "the economically active population," the author made adjustments in the tabulation at the top of page 19 (given in thousands of persons).

The reader will see from Table 1.7 that, after this adjustment of data on "working population," the proportion of economically active men in the total male population is roughly the same, and the proportion of economically active women in the total female population is considerably higher, in Czechoslovakia as compared with Western Europe.

Table 1.7 also shows that the percentage of economically active men, even after this adjustment, decreased in Czechoslovakia between 1947 and

[9] Dr. V. Srb and Ing. M. Kučera in *Statistický obzor,* No. 12, 1957, made international comparisons of the working population by age groups and found that the number of working men is lower in Czechoslovakia, as compared with Western Europe, in the youngest and oldest age groups. They seem to have disregarded, however, certain limits of comparability between Czechoslovak statistics on "working population in the national economy" and Western statistics on the economically active population.

[10] Total number of apprentices was as follows, in thousands: 1948–49, 151; 1952–53, 125; 1954–55, 144; 1956–57, 135; 1957–58, 167.

1948:	Working Population (Official Data)	Apprentices	Groups Not Included in Official Data (Armed Forces, Police, Prisoners, etc.)†	Total "Economically Active" Population*
Total	5,545	151	350	6,046
Male	3,447	100	280	3,827
Female	2,098	51	70	2,219
1953:				
Total	5,762	144	450	6,356
Male	3,384	96	360	3,840
Female	2,378	48	90	2,516
1957:				
Total	6,066	135	400	6,601
Male	3,503	90	320	3,913
Female	2,563	45	80	2,688

Assumptions: One-third of the apprentices are girls; one-fifth of other persons excluded from statistics on the working population are women.

1957. One cause is the decreasing proportion of men of productive age in the total male population since 1955. It was stressed in Czechoslovakia that another factor is the better old-age care; this is valid only in the sense that the number of recipients of old-age benefits under national insurance increased, whereas the purchasing power of average old-age benefits was decreasing until 1957 (see Table 9.4). One of the factors of the decreasing proportion of economically active men which should not be overlooked was that a certain number of civil servants, professional people, etc., were compelled to discontinue their activities because of political reasons, and a certain number of former entrepreneurs because of nationalization of their property. If these persons were over 65 years of age, and not obliged to seek employment as wage or salary earners, they ceased to be economically active.

A different distribution of the economically active or working population by legal status (a different "class structure") should also be taken into account when making comparisons between Czechoslovakia and Western market economies.

In 1955, percentages of wage and salary earners in the economically active population were as follows: Austria, 65 per cent; France, 65 per cent; West Germany, 73 per cent; U.S., 82 per cent; the rest were entrepreneurs and unpaid working family members. In Czechoslovakia the corresponding percentage of wage and salary earners in the total "working population" in 1955 was 70 per cent if we consider the members of agricultural cooperatives and their helping family members as self-employed workers, and 76 per cent if we consider them to be wage and salary earners. With advancing collectivization of agriculture, the share of wage and salary earners, including members of cooperatives, in total working population increased to 85 per cent in 1957, and to over 90 per cent in 1958.

The division of the economically active or working population into wage and salary earners, on the one hand, and into entrepreneurs and their helping family members, on the other, depends not only on different statistical definitions, different social systems, and varying concentrations of capital, but also on the varying importance of agriculture in the national economies concerned. If we consider the nonagricultural working population only, the different proportion of wage and salary earners shows more specifically the difference in social system. These percentages in 1955 were as follows: Austria, 85 per cent; France, 80 per cent; U.S., 89 per cent;[11] Czechoslovakia, over 99 per cent.

In fact, practically all the nonagricultural working population in Czechoslovakia today consists of wage and salary earners. The number of nonagricultural private enterprises decreased from 382,000 at the end of 1948 to 47,000 in 1956, and has been further decreasing in later years. Out of 48,000 nonagricultural self-employed workers (entrepreneurs) still remaining in 1956, nine-tenths were over 40 years of age and one-third over 60.[12] At the end of 1957, the "class structure" of the Czechoslovak population was as follows:

	Thousands	Per Cent
Total working population	6,066	100
Wage and salary earners	4,431	73.2
In "private sector"	4	0.0
Members of cooperatives	781	13.0[a]
Agricultural cooperatives	674	11.1
Self-employed farmers	815	13.3[b]
Other self-employed working persons	39	0.5

[a] Rapidly increasing.
[b] Rapidly decreasing.

The extremely small number of self-employed workers in the nonagricultural population implies some important economic and statistical consequences. Among other things, the "average wage in the socialist sector" equals the average personal income of the entire nonagricultural popula-

[11] Figures calculated from the table "Persons in Employment According to Status," *OEEC Statistical Bulletin*, September 1957.
[12] According to Minister of the Interior R. Barák in the monthly *Život strany*, No. 9, 1958.

tion (including wage and salary earners of the state farms). If we add the incomes of the members of agricultural cooperatives and the incomes of the remaining independent farmers, the number of which is shrinking rapidly (see Chapter 4), we obtain the personal income of the Czechoslovak civilian population, a very important figure in view of the lack of published absolute figures on national income at current prices (see Chapter 10). Another important consequence is that, once the independent farmers have disappeared from the economic scene, the distribution of personal incomes, personal expenditures, etc., will be completely determined by state-fixed wages and state-fixed consumers' prices. Then, income tax and other direct taxation will become unnecessary either as a tool to redistribute the incomes, or as a source of state revenue. This is interesting to note in view of Mr. Khrushchev's proposal to abolish the income tax in the USSR.

Now we come to the question of unemployment. It is officially maintained by the Czechoslovak government—contrary to the Polish approach to this problem—that in a centrally planned socialist economy unemployment cannot and does not exist. While in Western market economies unemployment up to approximately 2 per cent of the total wage and salary earners is considered just frictional, the official Czechoslovak definition of full employment should mean that there are no unemployed at all.

In the West, a person is considered to be unemployed if he is unable to secure employment within his customary occupation and within a reasonable distance of his permanent residence. In Czechoslovakia, it is current practice to transfer people from one sector of the economy to another, from one place to another, etc. In 1957, about 32,000 white-collar workers were transferred to manual work in industry. The following computation shows how the increment of manual labor in industry was secured in 1957 and 1958 (in thousands of persons):

	1957	1958
Total gross increase of manual workers	322	311
Voluntary employment	232	202
Organized employment (persons assigned to work by the Labor Protection Office)	25	29
Apprentices leaving school, etc.	13	14
Persons transferred by decisions of higher authorities	5⎱	17
Organizational transfers	15⎰	
Persons transferred from other categories of employment to manual employment in industry	32	49

Source: *SRRC*, 1958, Table 7.17, and 1959, Table 7.20.

From this official computation it follows that in 1957, out of 322,000 new manual workers in industry, 77,000 plus a certain portion of the 13,000 apprentices leaving school have been assigned to this kind of work by decision of authorities. Thus, approximately one-fourth of the increment of manual workers in industry has been "directed" and three-quarters recruited. In 1958 the portion of "directed" manual workers in industry was slightly higher, owing to the transfer of a certain number of civil servants to production.

In spite of the direction of labor, which in fact renders improbable large-scale open unemployment, there has been—as was to be expected—a kind of hidden unemployment, when workers (although on payrolls) could not produce because of shortage of fuel, basic raw materials, or semifinished products, or because of the change in the production program, etc. There is a special term in Czech (and in Russian) for the working time thus spent idly—the so-called *prostoje*.

For instance, in 1953, about 1 per cent of total actual working time in industry (3.1 out of 294.4 working days), and, in 1957, 0.4 per cent (1.2 out of 292.6 working days) were spent idly. To this must be added as hidden unemployment at least a part of the working time spent on "schooling, brigades and other state-imposed duties"—0.6 per cent of the working time in 1953 and 0.9 per cent in 1957—and a part of the "free time granted by the management"—1.3 per cent of total working time in 1953 and 0.6 per cent in 1957. (The above-mentioned brigades are not to be confused with labor-brigade work outside the normal working time, especially on Sundays.) Whereas frictional unemployment due to imperfect mobility of labor in market economies can be avoided under central planning, the "hidden" unemployment of labor due to imperfect mobility of material resources was also near 2 per cent in Czechoslovakia during most years of central planning. It is interesting to note that with the reduction of hidden unemployment in 1957 a certain, though very limited, open unemployment seems to have appeared in Czechoslovakia, as will be discussed below.

In spite of the official theory of total employment in Czechoslovakia, in the sense that everyone can get a job, there have been unofficially reported cases of persons, especially of elderly people and women, having looked in vain for employment for a considerable time. Even in Czechoslovak statistics we can discover evidence of a certain open unemployment at specific dates. For instance, for many years the total employment at the end of the year has always been higher than the average figures for January through December. But in 1957 the official Czechoslovak figure of total employment at the end of the year was lower by 34,000 than the average 1957 employment. The conclusion can be drawn that, at the end of 1957, a certain number of people previously employed were without a job. This is how the yearly average figures and end-of-year figures compare (in thousands of persons):

	1953	1954	1955	1956	1957
Total employment, yearly average...	5,683	5,850	5,956	6,047	6,100
Employment at end of year	5,762	5,909	5,998	6,059	6,066

In 1958, after a drive to reduce the bureaucratic apparatus, the number of white-collar workers at least temporarily unemployed may have been even higher than the unemployment level at the end of 1957, as suggested above. It also is noteworthy that through the new regulation of old-age benefits of March 1958, pensioners are induced—quite in contradiction to previous trends—to give up employment. Women over 60 and men over 65 now need a special permit to be employed. Thus the official theory of nonexistence of unemployment in Czechoslovakia cannot be accepted at its face value, even if "open" unemployment in Czechoslovakia is very low indeed.

3. Distribution of the Economically Active Population by Branches of the National Economy

Distribution of the Czechoslovak economically active population (irrespective of legal status and thus including wage and salary earners, self-employed workers, and unpaid working family members) by branches of the economy is given in Table 1.8. Czechoslovak statistics on "persons working in the national economy" had to be adjusted, as described in the preceding section on working population, to make them more comparable with the Western data on the economically active population.[13]

---

[13] The international part of SRRC, 1958, contains, on page 461, a comparison by countries of the structure of the working population in absolute figures; it involves, however, a serious error. It is entitled "Gainfully Employed Persons," and, in fact, for Czechoslovakia and East Germany the unpaid working family members have been deducted from figures of the total working population. Thus, in 1950, the number of gainfully employed persons in Czechoslovakia has been given as 4,654,000, whereas the economically active population was 5,577,000 (still excluding defense, police, etc.). The number of persons working in agriculture and forestry was 2,160,000, whereas the gainfully employed figure was given as only 1,070,000. In a similar way, the gainfully employed population in East Germany was quoted in 1956 as 7,590,000, whereas, according to official East German statistics, the total of economically active persons amounted to 8,177,000. On the other

TABLE 1.8—DISTRIBUTION OF ECONOMICALLY ACTIVE POPULATION

Country	Year	Number of Economically Active (thousands)	Percentage Share of Economically Active Persons					
			Agriculture, Forestry	Mining, Industry	Building	Transport	Trade	Other
Czechoslovakia	1947	5,852	37.7ᵃ	37.3ᵃ {		4.9	6.5	13.6
"Working population" ...	1948	(5,545)	(42.1)	(29.3)	(4.8)	(5.0)	(6.5)ᵇ	(12.3)
Adjusted*	1948	6,066	39.6	28.6	4.6	4.8	6.1ᵇ	16.3
"Working population" ...	1953	(5,683)	(34.5)	(32.1)	(7.5)	(5.6)	(6.2)ᵇ	(13.7)
Adjusted*	1953	6,356	31.9	31.1	7.0	5.2	6.1ᵇ	18.7
"Working population" ...	1957	(6,100)	(31.6)	(33.6)	(7.7)	(5.9)	(6.7)ᵇ	(14.5)
Adjusted*	1957	6,601	29.6	32.6	7.2	5.6	6.3ᵇ	18.7
Austria	1951	3,360	32.3	28.3	8.0	5.3	8.8	17.3
West Germany	1950	22,074	23.3	33.8	8.2	5.3	9.6	19.8
United Kingdom	1951	22,610	5.1	41.2	6.3	7.7	14.0	25.7
United States	1950	60,037	12.2	28.5	6.2	7.0	18.5	27.6
East Germany	1956	(8,177)	(20.6)	(33.2)ᶜ	(5.9)	(7.1)	(11.4)	(14.8)
Poland	1950	(12,405)	(57.1)	(18.8)	(4.2)	(3.8)	(5.2)	(10.9)
USSR	1955	(85,000)	(43.1)			(59.6)		
Yugoslavia	1953	7,848	66.7	8.0	2.6	2.1	3.1	17.5

Sources: Czechoslovakia: 1947, U.N. *Statistical Yearbook*, 1950; later years, *Statistical Yearbook*, 1958, figures on "persons working in the national economy." Adjustments are described in Chapter 1, Sections 2 and 3. It was assumed that out of the groups not included in statistics on "persons working in the national economy," such as the armed forces, the police, and prisoners, one-fifth are active in mining and industry, and four-fifths come under "Other." The number of apprentices, also excluded from the "working population," is spread proportionally over all categories. Western countries and Yugoslavia: U.N. *Statistical Yearbook*, various issues. Poland: *SRRC*, 1958, international part. East Germany: *Vierteljahreshefte zur Statistik der DDR*, No. 1, 1958. USSR: *Economic Survey of Europe*, 1958 (Economic Commission for Europe, Geneva, 1959); *SRRC*, international part. Percentage shares calculated by the author on the basis of the above sources. For Czechoslovakia, there is limited comparability between 1947 and later years, because of the change in statistical method. Comparability among countries is limited, for all countries, because of different classifications.

ᵃ Probably classifying all persons farming *and* working in industry as active in industry, whereas in later years some seem to have been classified as active in agriculture.

ᵇ Including "public catering" (canteens, etc.)

ᶜ Excluding 7 per cent of the economically active population in private handicraft (*Handwerk*).

Table 1.8 shows that the proportion of the Czechoslovak population active in industry is as high as in the most industrial Western European countries (but remains below that in the United Kingdom). We shall see in the next chapter, on industry, that employment in manufacturing, in fact, increased faster, between 1948 and 1958, in Czechoslovakia than in the Western market economies, with the exception of countries with retarded postwar reconstruction (Austria, Germany). It is interesting to note, in Table 1.8, that the proportion of the population active in trade to the total economically active population is much smaller in Czechoslovakia and other centrally planned economies than in the market economies listed; an exception is East Germany, where a large part of trade, in contrast to other centrally planned countries, has not been nationalized, and where the percentage of persons active in trade has remained relatively high.

More details on the labor force in Czechoslovak industry, agriculture, building, and transport will be given in Chapters 2 to 5.

----

hand, data for Western countries and Poland in the above-mentioned comparison in *SRRC* refer to the total economically active population, including unpaid working family members. For this reason, and in view of some other statistical discrepancies, data for Czechoslovakia and East Germany are not at all comparable with data for other countries included in this computation.

Chapter 2

INDUSTRY

1. Importance of Industry in the Czechoslovak Economy

Industry (which, under Czechoslovak statistical definitions, includes mining, manufacturing, and public utilities such as gas and electricity) has been the main target of economic expansion since the beginning of comprehensive central planning, with a short-lived change of this policy in 1955.

The number of persons working in industry went up from 1,508,000 in 1948 to 2,022,000 in 1958 (including workers and salaried people), or by 34 per cent, as compared with the average increase of the total labor force in the national economy of approximately 11 per cent. In 1948 less than 30 per cent of the working population was employed in industry; in 1953, over 32 per cent; in 1958, well over one-third.

Industry also was the main beneficiary of fixed capital formation. Out of the domestic gross fixed investments of 214.2 billion Kčs (at 1956 prices) over the period 1948–57, 91.9 billion, or 42 per cent, went to industry (excluding the so-called "general overhauls," see Chapter 8, Section 2; under the definition of gross fixed investments as usually applied in the West, industry's share was greater). Industry's share in gross fixed investments financed by the state was even higher, 58 per cent (again excluding the "general overhauls"). "Basic funds" (fixed capital assets) in industry (at 1955 replacement costs; see Chapter 8) increased by 68 per cent between 1948 and 1958, as compared with the over-all increase of basic funds of only 41 per cent in the national economy. Industry's share in existing capital assets (at 1955 constant replacement costs) went up from 24 per cent in 1948 to 29 per cent in 1958.

With these large inputs, industrial production and the share of industry in the national income increased considerably. Under the Marxist definition of national income (see Chapter 10, Section 1), income originating in industry, at 1955 constant prices, rose between 1948 and 1957 by 101 per cent; however, this was less than the rise of the total Marxist national income at 1955 constant prices, and the share of industry in total income at 1955 prices fell from 67 per cent in 1948 to 66 per cent in 1957.[1] Taking these official data at face value, one could surmise that increments of both labor and fixed investments yielded less net output in industry than in the average of the whole national economy. But it is difficult to arrive at a safe conclusion because the above data are distorted by artificial pricing; e.g., prices for heavy industry products were, in 1955, below labor cost whereas prices for consumers' manufactures were much inflated by turnover tax (see Chapter 7, Section 3). In terms of current prices, the share of industry in the Marxist national income went up from 58 per cent in 1948 to 62 per cent in 1957. In view of a very different price structure, and a different definition, the national income data cannot be used for comparisons between countries on the importance of industry. (All the above data are from, or based on, SRRC, 1958 and 1959, Chapters 1, 6, 7.)

Fortunately, there is other evidence available of the existing high degree of industrialization in Czechoslovakia, in comparison between countries.

In recent years Czechoslovakia has had the highest per capita consumption of energy among all the countries listed in Table 2.1 with the exception of the United Kingdom and the United States. This high consumption affords an important proof of industrial expansion, since the civilian consumption of energy in Czechoslovakia is rather limited. For example, the household consumption of hard coal is still subject to rationing, and the number of passenger cars in use is relatively lower than in most Western countries (as shown in Chapter 9). The pattern of energy consumption, however, is different in Czechoslovakia from that in Western market economies. Consumption of electricity per head, shown in Table 2.2, still remains considerably below that in Western Europe, and even below that in East Germany. Yet it should be borne in mind that the share of industry in consumption of electricity is much higher in Czechoslovakia than in other industrialized countries: in 1958 in Czechoslovakia, industry accounted for 83.0 per cent of the total consumption of electricity; in Austria, 61.5 per cent; in West Germany, 71.9 per cent; and in the United Kingdom, 53.0 per cent.[2]

---

[1] In 1958, however, the index of the Marxist national income originating in industry (1948 = 100), at 1955 constant prices, went up to 218, as compared with the index of total Marxist national income of 219 (see Table 10.4), so that the share of industry in the national income again reached 67 per cent.

[2] *Statistický obzor*, No. 1, 1960, pp. 39–40.

TABLE 2.1—PER CAPITA CONSUMPTION OF ENERGY

(In metric tons per head, in hard-coal equivalent)

	1955	1958
Czechoslovakia	3.89	4.68
Austria	1.86	1.93
France	2.17	2.42
West Germany	3.26	3.44
United Kingdom	4.99	4.74
United States	7.77	7.64
East Germany	3.88	4.31
Hungary	1.91	2.07
Poland	2.62	2.84
USSR	2.24	2.89
Yugoslavia	0.50	0.70

Data from U.N. *Statistical Yearbook*, 1959, Table 131.

TABLE 2.2—PER CAPITA CONSUMPTION OF ELECTRICITY

(In kilowatt hours)

	1956	1958
Czechoslovakia	1,092	1,202
Austria	1,356	1,422
France	1,180	1,261
West Germany	1,576	1,640
United Kingdom	1,765	1,882
United States	3,857	3,833
East Germany	1,592	...
Hungary	469	562
Poland	622	687
USSR	897	977
Yugoslavia	279	338

Source: *Statistický obzor*, No. 1, 1960.

TABLE 2.3—PER CAPITA CONSUMPTION OF STEEL

(*In kilograms*)

	Prewar	1956	1957
Czechoslovakia	95	319	361
Austria	69	205	206
France	...	276	302
West Germany	...	417	393
United Kingdom	227	380	372
United States	318	600	568
Hungary	...	...	154
Poland	30	168	174
USSR	103	235	263

Data from U.N. *Statistical Yearbook.*

In the field of steel consumption Czechoslovakia was, by 1956, third in the order of European countries shown in Table 2.3. Both the consumption of steel and the consumption of energy further increased in 1957 and 1958, and they are due to go up rapidly, under the present Five-Year Plan and the third Five-Year Plan, until 1965.

It is noteworthy that per capita consumption of energy is almost twice as high, and that of steel almost one-third higher in Czechoslovakia than in the USSR.

According to *Statistické zprávy* (No. 5, 1958), Czechoslovakia's share in the world's industrial production in 1958 amounted to 2 per cent, which was four times more than its share of the world's population and 20 times more than its share of the world's territory. This comparison is based, however, on the "gross value of output," as described below.

2. Index of Industrial Production

The index of industrial production is computed differently in Czechoslovakia (and other centrally planned economies) than in the West. It is based, not on weighting the physical volume of output in various branches of mining and manufacturing, but on the gross value of industrial output.

Gross value of output should not be confused with gross industrial product. In addition to the wage bill, profits, depreciation, and other components of gross national product, it comprises the aggregate of fuel, energy, raw materials, and semifinished goods consumed at every stage of mining and manufacturing.

Besides the change in the volume of net output, the Czechoslovak official index (gross value) of industrial production also reflects all the changes in the following factors: (1) volume of fuel, energy, materials, and semifinished products consumed per unit of output (including consumption of agricultural and imported materials); (2) volume of services per unit of output (freight transport, communications, etc.); (3) depreciation of basic funds (fixed capital assets) per unit of output; and (4) "roundaboutness" (number of rotations) of industrial materials and semifinished products from one enterprise to another (gross value of output in industry is officially computed as the sum of gross value of output in every industrial enterprise).

The inclusion of the above-mentioned factors involves an upward bias of the index of industrial production. For instance, since the gross value of output is the main yardstick for measuring the fulfillment of the plan and for granting premiums for overfulfillment, there has been a tendency on the part of the managements of nationalized enterprises to increase the gross value (and costs) of output by using the most expensive materials (more costly even in terms of constant prices). The "plan of lowering production costs" seems not to have been a sufficient counteracting measure. Only in very recent years have some additional criteria of performance of industrial enterprises besides "gross value of output" been introduced.

Official criticism has also been directed to the fact that national enterprises often transfer semifinished products to another enterprise to be finished, and every enterprise involved in these transfers includes, of course, the total value of the purchased semifinished products in its gross value of output. This upward bias may have been counteracted by the amalgamation of industrial enterprises in 1958 (see Section 7).

But there are also other sources of upward bias of the index of gross value of output. For instance, the weighting, based on gross value, overemphasizes material-intensive branches of industry, especially heavy industry, which developed much faster than light industry. Consequently, the general index is being inflated by too great weight given to heavy industry. Furthermore, although the "gross value" is based on constant prices, the newly introduced products are sometimes priced at the cost at the beginning of the Five-Year Plan instead of at the current lower cost of output. This kind of upward bias is, however, much less serious in Czechoslovakia than, for example, in the prewar USSR or in other centrally planned economies at a lower stage of industrialization, with a very rapidly increasing variety of products.

Once a high level of industrialization has been achieved, the index of gross value of industrial output shows a stronger correlation with the actual growth of both, net industrial product and the physical volume of output. In fact, the results obtained by the Czechoslovak and East German indices are more comparable with those of the Western indices than with the industrial growth claimed by "gross value" indices in Bulgaria or Rumania. Especially in the years 1953–57, when the expansion of heavy industry was slowed down and marginal costs were taken more into consideration, the upward bias involved in the use of "gross value" of output as a yardstick for industrial growth may have been rather small in Czechoslovakia; on the other hand, during the fast expansion of heavy industry in 1951–53, the Czechoslovak index based on gross value of output probably meant a great exaggeration of the increase in the volume of production.

Far-reaching criticism of the inflating effect of the gross value method of measuring industrial growth has been published in Eastern European countries themselves.[3] In Czechoslovakia, besides the regularly published official index of gross value of industrial production, another index, based on the physical volume of production, is probably being calculated again by the Czechoslovak Statistical Office, but for internal use only. The results of this index have not been published, but its construction has been discussed, in general terms, in *Statistické zprávy*.[4]

Furthermore, the Marxist "net value" of industrial production is being calculated regularly, but no detailed index has been published. Yet the percentage share of net in gross value of industrial production *in 1958* has been published by M. Vojta, of the Czechoslovak Statistical Office.[5] It amounted, averaging the whole industry, to 32.0 per cent. (See also below and Section 3.)

In the West, the Czechoslovak, East German, and Polish method of measuring industrial production by gross value of output was examined and rejected by Dr. Alfred Zauberman,[6] who computed his own index of

---

[3] See, for instance, an article by Zoltán Román in the official Hungarian statistical review, *Statistikai szemle*, June 1957, and a Czech translation of an article by O. Lukácz in *Statistický obzor*, No. 2, 1959.

[4] Ing. J. Zelinka, in *Statistické zprávy*, No. 10, 1958.

[5] M. Vojta, "Čistá vyroba podniku a její praktické využití" (Net Output of Industrial Enterprises and Its Use in Practice), in *Statistický obzor*, No. 2, 1960.

[6] *Industrial Development in Czechoslovakia, East Germany and Poland*, by A. Zauberman (London, February 1958).

industrial production in Czechoslovakia (1937 = 100, calculated for the years 1948 to 1956). His index is based on weighting the series of physical output, but—since it was probably computed at the time of statistical blackout—only one single product was taken as a representative series for a whole industrial branch. For instance, even for the rapidly expanding chemical industry, with a greatly increasing variety of production, one single product—sulfuric acid—was used as a yardstick for the total output of chemicals. Sugar was considered to be representative of the whole food industry, although sugar output, according to official Czechoslovak figures, in 1956 remained below the prewar level, while other food products surpassed it. The only exception, in Dr. Zauberman's construction of the index of Czechoslovak industrial production, is the metal-working industry, for which he used a combined index of several series. Yet, even this combined index seems to give too low results. It shows an increase in output, between 1948 and 1956, of only 87 per cent as compared with 319 per cent increase according to the official index of gross value in engineering. In the corresponding period the number of workmen in the metal-working industry increased by 80 per cent.[7] Zauberman's index would infer that the output per man-year in the metal-working industry went up by less than 1 per cent a year, i.e., by only a very small fraction of the average increase in output per man-year for the whole industry, although the metal-working industry was by far the main beneficiary of industrial investments (41 per cent of all newly built factories between 1948 and 1956 were for engineering alone).

The different expansion of output of the products chosen by Dr. Zauberman and of some other important products in terms of physical units can be gathered from Table 2.11.

The weighting of the industrial branches in the general index of output is another ticklish problem. For instance, Dr. Zauberman's weight for the rapidly expanding metal-using industry is only 24, whereas the field of engineering alone—a somewhat narrower category than "metal-using industry"—according to official Czechoslovak figures, claimed 30 per cent of the total gross value of industrial output in 1948 and 46 per cent in 1957.[8] Even if we allow for the fact that gross value means a greater exaggeration of weight of heavy industry than of light industry, the weight given by Dr. Zauberman to the metal-using industry in the framework of

---

[7] Dr. Zauberman supposed an increase of only 70 per cent in the number of workmen, without giving reasons for not using the 80 per cent figure of the official data.

[8] *Statistické zprávy*, No. 5, 1958, p. 26.

total industrial production seems to be rather low;[9] this is another reason why, in this writer's opinion, Dr. Zauberman's index may somewhat underestimate Czechoslovak industrial growth. More light on this problem will be shed, in the near future, by Dr. Zauberman himself.[10]

Following is a comparison between his index and the official Czecho-slovak index (1937 = 100):

	1948	1950	1953	1955	1956
Official index—gross value of industrial output at 1954 (constant) prices......	108	143	210	243	266
Zauberman's index (1958)	107	123	157	174	184

The *Economic Survey of Europe*, 1958, used the following approach to the question of "how to measure the real growth" in Czechoslovak industrial production. It compared the yearly increases in "gross output" with the yearly increases in what it termed "net output." On further examination, however, it is obvious that the "net output" used in this study is nothing but "national income originating in industry" from *SRRC*, 1958, Table 1.4. Thus, it excludes the output of that part of capital goods which is merely replacing the capital goods consumed in the course of production, but it includes that part of services which enters into the Marxist computation of national income under the heading of "industry" (see Chapter 10), and is subject to distortions by artificial price structure. The "gross output" used by the *Economic Survey of Europe* is nothing but the gross *value* of output, including thus the multiple counting of intermediate products, as described above. Furthermore, the gross and "net" value of industrial production cannot be compared accurately because of a different price base (the gross value of production, as reflected by the official Czechoslovak index of industrial production, is in terms of constant prices of July 1954, whereas the "net value" of output, i.e., national income originating in industry, is in terms of constant prices of April 1955).

The way used by the *Economic Survey of Europe* to measure the "net output" and "gross output" in Czechoslovak industry is, therefore, methodologically not quite correct, and the numerical results obtained may

[9] According to the previously quoted article by Mr. Vojta in *Statistický obzor*, the share of "net value" in "gross value" of output in engineering in Czechoslovakia in 1958 amounted to 42.1 per cent, as compared with an average of only 32.0 per cent for industry as a whole. This would suggest that the share of engineering in total industrial output, based on gross values, is not overestimated, but possibly underrated; but it is difficult to arrive at any definite conclusion in view of the artificial pricing (see Chapter 7, Section 2).

[10] In his new computation of the Czechoslovak index of industrial production, to be published by Chatham House, London, in 1960.

diverge considerably from the actual increase in the physical volume of net and gross output.

Nevertheless, over the entire period of 1948–58, the increase in the "national income originating in industry" (under Marxist definition) may come closer to the real increase in the volume of industrial output than the increase shown by the official index of gross value of production. "National income originating in industry" increased by 101 per cent between 1948 and 1958, while the "gross value of industrial output" went up 170 per cent.

According to the *Economic Survey of Europe*, the yearly increases in "gross" and "net" industrial output compared as follows (in per cent over the preceding year):

	1950	1951	1952	1953	1954	1955	1956	1957	1958[a]
"Gross (value of) output"	16	14	18	9	4	11	9	10	11
"Net output"[b]	5	17[c]	10	6	4	11	9	8	9

[a] Calculated by the author on the bases of Tables 1.5 and 7.9, *SRRC*, 1959.

[b] In fact, increase in national income originating in industry; see Chapter 10.

[c] Probably reflecting also a sharp increase in wages (and subsidies in heavy industry for which no adequate adjustment has been made in official computation of Marxist national income; this is not mentioned in the *Economic Survey of Europe*).

Even if the real volume of industrial production were ascertained, another factor would limit the comparability of Czechoslovak and Western industrial growth. The proportion of damaged goods and rejects in manufacturing seems to be higher in Czechoslovakia than in Western market economies. The rejects, in terms of the percentage of *gross* value of output in industry, have been officially given as follows:[11]

	1953	1954	1955	1956	1957 (Half-Year)
Total for industry	4.0	2.7	1.8	1.4	1.3
Foundries (including extraction of ores)	3.0	2.7	2.6	2.2	1.9
Engineering	1.8	1.7	1.5	1.5	1.4
Construction	1.8	1.7	1.5	1.5	1.4

If compared with the actual physical volume of output, or with the "net value," the percentage of waste would be approximately three times higher than the above percentage figures.

In his comparisons of industrial growth between countries, the author mostly used the official Czechoslovak index of gross value of industrial production, and cautioned the reader, in due course, of the limits of comparability. There were several reasons for doing so:

[11] *Statistické zprávy*, No. 3, 1957.

First, the latest *Statistical Yearbook* of the United Nations has published the official Czechoslovak index (together with the indices for all other countries) and has used it (so far as the author knows) to compute the world index of industrial production.

Second, the present official Czechoslovak index, based on the gross value of output, seems to exaggerate the industrial growth less than did the first Communist index of 1948, although the latter was based on weighting the physical volume of production. Following is a comparison of the prewar index, the index of 1948, and the present index of industrial production (for the postwar years for which the results of the indices were available; rebased, 1948 = 100):

	1937	1948	1949	1950	1951
Physical volume index, prewar weighting, based on 91 series	97	100	108	—	—
Physical volume index, 1948 construction, postwar weighting, based on 298 series	—	100	116	134	153
Index of gross value of output (official present index)	92	100	114	132	150

As can be seen, the present index has given results somewhere between the results obtained by the prewar construction and the first Communist construction of the volume index. This can be partly explained by the fact that the weight given to heavy industry was too low in the prewar index construction and too high in the 1948 index construction.

Third, in spite of the upward bias of the official Czechoslovak index of industrial production, its comparison with the Western indices leads to some interesting conclusions.

Fourth, the author hopes that the new index based on weighting of the statistical series of the quantities produced (which is, or will be, calculated again for internal use of the central planning authorities) may be published sooner or later. If so, the great amount of work involved in computing an index of industrial production on the basis of the published series on quantities of commodities extracted and manufactures produced may be duplicating the work done by the Statistical Office in Prague.[12]

Fifth and last, whenever possible the author has endeavored to use the "income originating in industry" as a certain corrective, however unsatisfactory, of the index of gross value of production.

[12] If such an index were not to be published in Czechoslovakia for a longer period of time, it could be computed (yet hardly with sufficient accuracy) when using the data on the output of more than 300 kinds of commodities and manufactures, from the *SRRC* 1957–59. The most important of these data and some other figures on the quantities extracted in mining and produced in manufacturing can be found in Table 2.12.

TABLE 2.4—GENERAL INDEX OF INDUSTRIAL PRODUCTION
1953 = 100

	1937	1948	1949	1950	1951	1952	1953	1954	1955	1956	1957	1958
Czechoslovakia												
"Net output"[a]	..	68	71	75	87	96	100	104	116	125	135	147
Official index (gross value)	48	52	59	68	78	91	100	104	116	127	140	158
Austria	59	54	72	86	97	98	100	114	133	138	146	150
France	74[b]	79	82	87	98	99	100	110	120	133	145	154
West Germany	77[b]	..	58	72	85	91	100	112	129	139	147	151
United Kingdom[c]	76	83	88	94	97	94	100	107	113	112	114	113
United States[d]	46	78	72	84	90	93	100	93	104	107	107	100[f]
East Germany (gross value)	56	40	49	63	77	89	100	110	119	126	136	150
Hungary[e] (gross value)	..	..	45	58	73	90	100	105	115	104	111	124
Poland (gross value)	26	39	46	59	72	85	100	111	124	135	149	163
USSR (gross value)	27	45	55	69	80	89	100	113	127	141	155	170
Yugoslavia	48	82	92	94	91	90	100	114	132	145	170	188

Sources: Western countries and Yugoslavia: U.N. *Statistical Yearbooks,* 1958 and 1959 and *Monthly Bulletin of Statistics.* Eastern countries: National Statistical Yearbooks, indices rebased to 1953 by the author. All 1958 data are provisional estimates. All indices, unless otherwise stated, include mining, manufacturing, electricity, and gas. Indices for Czechoslovakia of "net output" or Marxist national income originating in industry from *SRRC* 1959, Table 1.5, and of gross value from *SRRC* 1959, Table 7.9; both arithmetically rebased from 1948 to 1953 = 100.

[a] A term used by the *Economic Survey of Europe,* 1958. In fact, the figures refer to "national income originating in industry," under Marxist definition. See Chapter 2, Section 2, and Chapter 10.

[b] Year 1938.

[c] Including construction.

[d] Excluding electricity and gas.

[e] State industry only.

[f] Manufacturing only.

36

The Czechoslovak index of the gross value of industrial production (incorrectly described, in Czechoslovak statistics, as the "index of industrial production") and the index of national income originating in industry under presently applied Marxist definition (incorrectly described, in the *Economic Survey of Europe*, as "net output") are compared, in Table 2.4, with the indices of industrial production in developed market economies, and with indices of gross value of industrial production in other centrally planned economies (basis 1953 = 100). If the official Czechoslovak index is taken at its face value, industrial production rose, over the 10-year period 1948–58, faster in Czechoslovakia than in the listed Western countries (this was due especially to the greater 1958 increase). When measuring the industrial production by Czechoslovak national income originating in industry, under Marxist definition, there was not much difference in Czechoslovak and French industrial growth, and the Czechoslovak increase was smaller than the Austrian or West German increase (which was in fact due to the retarded postwar reconstruction of those two countries; British and American growth lagged behind, partly because of the high level of industrial output already achieved in the first postwar years prior to 1948).

On the other hand, the official Czechoslovak index shows, in Table 2.3, a smaller increase in industrial production than the corresponding gross value indices in other centrally planned economies, except East Germany. This is due, in part, to the flattening out of production increases in a technologically advanced society, in part to the fact that the gross value yardstick exaggerates the industrial growth more at early stages of industrialization, as was mentioned above, than in developed countries like Czechoslovakia. (Lagging output in Hungary is due to the 1956 uprising.)

When making comparisons between countries, two periods should be distinguished: the years preceding the second currency reform in Czechoslovakia in 1953, and later years. Furthermore, an analysis by sectors of industry and at least a rough input-output examination are imperative. Brief reasoning of this kind will be undertaken in Sections 3, 4, and 5.

3. Growth of Output by Main Sectors of Industry

Table 2.5 contains a comparison of the average compound yearly rates of growth of output by main industrial sectors in the periods 1949–53 and 1954–57. In this table the official Czechoslovak index, which—as we now know—may imply a considerable upward bias, has been used. Nevertheless, even on the basis of the official Czechoslovak index, Czechoslovakia was ahead of the Western European countries in increase in total industrial

TABLE 2.5—RATE OF GROWTH OF INDUSTRIAL PRODUCTION

(*Yearly averages, compound rates, percentages*)

	Total Industry		Metal-using		Textiles		Chemicals	
	1949-53	1953-57	1949-53	1953-57	1949-53	1953-57	1949-53	1953-57
Czecho-slovakia	14.1	8.8	28.2[a]	9.5[a]	4.9	7.0[b]	19.2[c]	11.7[c]
Austria	8.5	9.8	7.8	11.4	7.1	7.0	6.0	8.6
West Germany ...	11.6	10.1	15.5	13.2	9.1	7.4	12.4	11.4
France	5.0	9.4	7.1	11.3	2.8	6.1	6.1	12.7
Italy	10.1	8.1	10.1	6.5	2.4	3.3	16.1	11.6
United Kingdom ...	3.5	3.5	4.6	4.3	1.3	0.2	8.8	6.1
Yugoslavia ...	1.9	13.7	8.2	10.6	-7.5	13.7	2.7	26.0

Data for Czechoslovakia based on official *gross value* of output indices, by industrial branches, from *SRRC*, 1958, Table 7.8; data for other countries from *OEEC Statistical Bulletin*.
Comparability of Czechoslovak data with Western data is limited, especially in the 1949–53 period. See Chapter 2, Sections 2 and 3.

[a] Machinery- and equipment-producing industries only; rates of growth for other metal-using branches were probably lower.
[b] Average for only three years, 1953–56.
[c] Excluding production of fats and soap.

production only in the first period. In the second period the market economies in Austria, West Germany, and France achieved a greater (and in Italy almost the same) yearly rate of growth.

Furthermore, Table 2.5 shows that the rapid boom in Czechoslovak industrial production in the first period was brought about by the expansion of engineering, the production of which increased, in terms of "gross value," two to four times more than the physical volume of output in the listed Western European countries, and by the rapid increase in the production of chemicals. The output of the textile industry lagged behind the Western output. In the second period the increase of Czechoslovak output was spread more equally over heavy and light industries.

The more rapid industrial growth in the first period was accompanied by a disequilibrium and inflation. This was the price Czechoslovakia paid for outstripping Western industrial growth in the 1948–53 period (see Chapter 7, Section 1).

In 1958 the growth of Czechoslovak industrial output again outstripped that in Western market economies, with no serious inflation. This was due, among other factors, to the temporary recession in the West, and to stationary earnings in Czechoslovakia (see Chapter 9).

Table 2.6 shows the growth, by branches of Czechoslovak industry, between 1948 and 1958, and the 1958 pattern.

TABLE 2.6—INDUSTRIAL OUTPUT BETWEEN 1948 AND 1958

	Number of Manual Workers (*thousands*)		Gross Value of Output in 1958, in Per Cent of 1948	Percentage Share of Each Branch in 1958 Gross Value of Total Individual Output	Percentage Share of Net in Gross Value of Output, 1958, within Each Branch
	1948 (1)	1958 (2)	(3)	(4)	(5)
Electricity and heat	17	23	278	2.6	40.6
Fuel, coal and oil products	115	147	218	6.5	46.2
Ferrous metallurgy, incl. ore mining	70	109	297	7.7	23.4
Nonferrous metallurgy incl. ore mining	12	13	230	1.4	19.1
Engineering, metalworking	298	511	497	30.4	42.1
Chemical, rubber, and asbestos industry	42	62	405	5.1	27.1
Building materials	61	76	400	3.8	44.6
Woodworking industry ...	85	99	298	4.5	38.7
Wood pulp and paper ...	22	29	211	1.4	30.9
Glass, china, and ceramics	45	50	216	1.5	52.8
Textile industry	203	191	213	7.6	36.0
Ready-to-wear and underwear production ..	72	76	253	2.7	39.6
Leather, shoe, and fur industry	70	67	204	2.7	36.4
Polygraphic industry	17	16	170	0.6	52.2
Food industry, production of fats, soap, and perfumes	126	138	241	20.6	13.4
Other branches	6	11	673	0.6	28.3
Total industry	1,261	1,618	300	100.0	32.0

Sources: *SRRC*, 1959—columns 1 and 2, Table 7.17; column 3, Table 7.9; column 4, Table 7.10. Figures in column 5 are from M. Vojta, "Čistá vyroba podniku a její praktické využití" (Net Output of Industrial Enterprises and Its Use in Practice), in *Statistický obzor*, No. 2, 1960. Unfortunately, no data on the ratio of gross to net output have been published for previous years, so that it is not possible to derive an index of net output by branches of industry. The share of branches in total net industrial output in 1958 can be derived from columns 4 and 5. The above "net" value includes, however, the varying rate of turnover tax by which the share of individual branches in total "net" value of industrial production would be distorted. Furthermore, it is difficult to say whether adequate correction has been made by Mr. Vojta for underpricing of heavy-industry products, as will be discussed in Chapter 7, Section 3.

4. Productivity in Industry

The question now arises: To what extent was the increase in Czecho-slovak industrial production brought about by a higher productivity?

We already know, from Chapter 1 and from Section 1 in this chapter, that the input of the labor force into industry was rather high in Czecho-slovakia. Table 2.7 contains a comparison by countries of employment in industry in Czechoslovakia (wage earners only) and in manufacturing in Western countries (wage earners and salaried workers). In spite of the limited comparability, employment in industry seems to have increased, until 1953, faster in Czechoslovakia than in the Western developed market economies—with the exception of Austria and the United States. Since 1953 employment in manufacturing in France and Austria has been in-creasing faster than in Czechoslovakia's industry. Table 2.3 shows that output also increased faster in those two countries. As compared with less developed centrally planned economies, industrial employment in Czecho-slovakia has been increasing somewhat more slowly.

Table 2.8 gives some very rough approximations of the increase in industrial output per man-year. This is the official Czechoslovak measure of "productivity of labor in industry"; it is based on the index of gross value of output, divided by the index of employment, in industrial pro-duction proper. Output-per-man-year index reflects naturally not only pro-

TABLE 2.7—INDEX OF EMPLOYMENT IN MANUFACTURING
1953 = 100

All Workers including Salaried	1948	1953	1956	1957	1958
Czechoslovakia[a]	89.6	100	106.8	111.0	115.6
Austria[b]	86.7	100	119.5	121.7	121.8
France	96.2	100	102.6	105.8	106.9
West Germany	...	100	120.8	125.8	128.3
Great Britain	92.8	100	106.0	105.9	104.4
United States	88.9	100	98.6	97.3	89.7
Hungary	...	100	110.6	112.9	117.1
Poland[c]	...	100	113.6	117.6	118.2
Yugoslavia[b]	...	100	131.7	142.0	153.0

Index for Czechoslovakia calculated by the author from data on all workers employed in industry, SRRC, 1958, Table 7.14. Data for all other countries from *International Labour Review, Statistical Supplement* (International Labour Office, Geneva, September 1959).

   [a] Including mining, gas, electricity; excluding apprentices. Figures are for wage earners only, not salaried workers.
   [b] Including mining.
   [c] Socialist sector only, including mining, gas, electricity, and sea fishing.

TABLE 2.8—APPROXIMATIONS OF INDEX OF INDUSTRIAL OUTPUT PER MAN-YEAR
1953 = 100

	1948	1953	1956	1957	1958
Czechoslovakia:					
Based on "net output" (see Table 2.4)	77	100	118	126	128
Based on official index of gross value of output	58	100	119	126	135
Official index of productivity in industry	59	100	118	124	134
Austria	62	100	116	120	123
France	80	100	128	136	140
West Germany	...	100	116	118	120
United Kingdom	88	100	109	110	111
United States	85	100	108	110	112
Hungary	...	100	94	99	106
Poland	...	100	119	127	138
Yugoslavia	...	100	110	120	120

Caution! The above indices have been obtained by simply dividing the index numbers of industrial production by the index numbers of employment with no corrections for different coverage. They are based on output indices from the U.N. *Statistical Yearbook*, 1959, and employment indices from Table 2.7 in this book. Data for Czechoslovakia, Hungary, and Poland cover industry including mining and public utilities; for Austria and Yugoslavia data include mining; for other countries, data cover manufacturing only. Because of this and other inaccuracies and limitations of comparability, the above indices should be regarded as approximate trends only. The difference between the above estimate for Czechoslovakia, based on gross value of output, and the official index of productivity of labor in industry (see Chapter 2, Section 4) is due to rounding and to the exclusion of workers not engaged in actual output from the official productivity index.

ductivity of labor proper, but also the fast increase in inputs of investments (see Table 2.11).

Furthermore, like the index of gross value of production, it involves an upward bias. For this and for other reasons, the intercountry comparability of approximations in Table 2.8 is subject to severe limitations. If we allow for the upward bias of the Czechoslovak data, output per man-year seems to have increased no faster than in France over the entire period 1948–58 (since 1953 it has definitely been increasing more slowly than in France, and probably no faster than in Austria and West Germany). On the other hand, it may have increased in the last ten years faster in Czechoslovakia than in the United Kingdom or even in the United States. One of the factors of this development is the different trend in hours worked in industry. Whereas, for example, in American manufacturing the number of working hours per week remained basically the same in the whole 1948–57 period (around 40 hours a week), in Czechoslovakia working hours in industry (including mining) increased, on the average, from approximately 46* hours per week in 1948 to some 50* hours in 1954,

TABLE 2.9—HOURS WORKED IN INDUSTRY PER WEEK[a]

	1948	1953	1954	1955	1956	1957	1958
Czechoslovakia:							
"Normal hours"	46.8[b]	...	50.0[c]	50.4[c]	49.9[c]	48.3[c]	48.3†
"Productively worked"[d] .	...	...	42.7	43.2	42.7	41.2	...
Austria[e]	41.3	43.7	44.6	45.5	45.4	45.0	‖45.0
France[f]	44.6	44.1	44.6	44.7	45.4	45.7	‖45.0
West Germany	42.4	47.9	48.6	48.8	48.0	46.5[g]	‖45.7
United Kingdom	44.9	45.9	46.3	46.4	46.0	45.8	‖45.4
United States	40.1	40.5	39.7	40.7	40.4	39.8	‖39.3

Computation of Czechoslovak data is described in Chapter 2, Section 4. Other data from U.N. *Statistical Yearbook*, for 1958 from *OEEC Statistical Bulletin—General Statistics*. Although an interruption of comparability ‖ has been marked, the OEEC data are fairly comparable with the U.N. data for previous years.

[a] Wage earners' hours in manufacturing unless stated otherwise.
[b] Hours actually worked.
[c] Includes mining and public utilities. Includes salaried workers.
[d] "Normal hours" after deduction of annual leave, illness, accidents, labor brigades, political and other schooling, unauthorized absenteeism, and time spent idly on factory floors because of shortage of material or energy.
[e] Includes mining. Official monthly figures are multiplied by 12 and divided by 52.
[f] Includes salaried workers.
[g] Including services, not comparable with previous years.

and remained well above 48 hours in 1957. A comparison between countries of hours worked in industry per week can be found in Table 2.9. The Czechoslovak figures are based on the author's estimates. No official data on hours worked per week in manufacturing, or in the whole industry, have been published in Czechoslovakia since 1948 (the most recent official figure available on hours worked in manufacturing, in 1948, has been included in Table 2.9). But since 1954, official information on hours worked per day in industry, including mining, is available (e.g., in 1957 the average working day was 8.1 hours). The number of working days per year in industry, including mining, also is known from official information (in 1957, e.g., averaging the whole industry including mining, 292.6 days were worked, including special Sunday and holiday shifts). The author also estimated the number of hours "productively worked," by subtracting the time for annual leave, sickness and accidents, maternity leave, political schooling, and time spent on brigades in other branches of the national economy, as well as for absenteeism and stoppages, from his above-described computations of "normal working hours in industry." This estimate can be found in Table 2.10.

Starting from both the normal hours worked and the productive hours, as described above, an index of output per man-hour in Czechoslovakia's

TABLE 2.10—APPROXIMATION OF OUTPUT PER MAN-HOUR IN INDUSTRY
Index, 1954 = 100

	1955	1956	1957	1958
Czechoslovakia:				
Per "normal" working hour[a]	108	116	124	135†
Per "normal" working hour[b]	108	116	127	140†
Per "productive" hour[b]	108	121	138	...
Austria	106	107	111	115
France	108	117	122	130
West Germany	107	110	120	127
United Kingdom	103	103	105	105

All data refer to industry, including mining, manufacturing, and public utilities. Data for all countries except Czechoslovakia from *Economic Survey of Europe*, 1958.

[a] Based on "national income originating in industry."
[b] Based on official index of gross value of output.

industry was estimated, and compared to a corresponding index in Western European market economies. Czechoslovak figures, based on the index of gross value of production, involve again an upward bias, as described in Section 2 of this chapter. Allowance being made for this, output per man-hour may have developed in Czechoslovakia in a similar way to that in France or West Germany over the 1954–58 period (comparison for previous years is not possible because of lack of data for Czechoslovakia).

A special study would be required to arrive at more conclusive evidence on the development of productivity in Czechoslovak industry. But even if such a study confirmed that, over the 1948–58 period, productivity increased somewhat faster in Czechoslovakia than in Western Europe, this would not necessarily mean that it has reached the Western European level. It must be borne in mind that in the base year of our comparisons, 1948, productivity, as measured by output per man-hour, was extremely low in Czechoslovakia, owing to the economic and political turmoil in that year.

On the other hand, in certain branches of mining and industry, special categories of productivity in Czechoslovakia seem to be on, or even above, the Western European levels. For instance, the output of hard coal per worker underground, per shift, has been reported to compare with France and West Germany as follows (in kilograms):[13]

	Czecho-slovakia	France	German Federal Republic	Saar
1951................	1,640	1,298	1,457	1,617
1956................	1,791	1,645	1,564	1,819
1957................	1,823	1,683	1,586	1,800

[13] *Statistický obzor*, No. 10, 1959.

TABLE 2.11—SOME FACTORS OF INDUSTRIAL GROWTH IN CZECHOSLOVAKIA

(Yearly increase [or decrease] in per cent of preceding year, unless otherwise stated)

	1949	1950	1951	1952	1953	1954	1955	1956	1957	1958
Gross value of output in industry	14.0	15.8	13.6	18.0	9.0	4.7	10.9	9.4	10.2	11.3
Investment goods	14.0*	16.7	18.0	24.2	12.3	3.7	8.8	10.9	9.9	11.8
Consumption goods	14.0*	14.9	9.2	11.1	4.4	5.4	13.1	8.1	10.3	10.6
Gross fixed investment in *billion Kčs*[a]	6.6	7.9	9.2	11.0	9.6	9.6	9.5	11.1	12.2	15.0*,[b]
Increase in gross value of output per billion Kčs investment, excluding "general overhauls"[b]	2.2	2.0	1.5	1.6	0.9	0.5	1.2	0.9	0.8	0.7*,[c]
Number of manual workers	0.6	3.0	4.4	3.2	0.1	1.8	2.2	2.4	3.1	3.4
Investment goods branches	4.1	6.7	8.3	6.7	2.3	1.7	0.9	2.7	3.6	3.4
Consumption goods branches	-2.8	-0.8	0.0	-1.1	-2.8	2.2	3.8	2.1	4.1	3.7
Gross value of output per man-year	13.0	12.4	9.4	14.4	8.8	2.3	7.9[d]	6.8	5.8	7.4
Investment goods branches	10.0*	9.1	9.2	16.0	9.9	1.8	7.6	8.2	6.0	8.1
Consumption goods branches	18.0*	15.2	9.6	12.0	7.1	2.8	8.7	5.0	6.1	6.2
Costs of production ("comparable basis")	...	...	...	...	...	-1.2	-4.7	-0.3	-2.5	...
Real earnings per workman before deduction of tax and compulsory contributions	...	...	-3.0			11.3	6.8	6.1	0.1	0.9

Yearly percentage increase or decrease in gross value of output and gross value of output per man-year calculated on the basis of official index numbers; yearly increase or decrease in number of manual workers on the basis of official absolute figures. Yearly change in real earnings before deduction of tax and contributions on the basis of the pertinent index in Chapter 9 of this book. The ratio of gross fixed investment to gross value of output was computed before publication of data on general overhauls in industry in *SRRC*, 1959; "general overhauls" increased even faster than "investments" under the definitions used in Czechoslovak statistics (see Table 8.4). Therefore, if based on gross fixed investment as usually defined in the West, the ratio of gross fixed investment to gross value of output would decrease even more rapidly than indicated in this table. Slight inconsistencies between increases in gross value of output, in number of workers and in gross value of output per man-year are due to the rounding of official index numbers and to the coverage of workers engaged directly in output only by the official output-per-man-year index, whereas yearly increase in the number of workers as above covers all manual workers.

[a] At 1957 prices, excluding "general overhauls" (see Chapter 8, Section 2).

[b] This figure is 13.0 billion Kčs at current 1958 prices (according to *Results of the Fulfillment of the State Plan of Development of the National Economy of the Czechoslovak Republic*). Prices for capital goods have been reduced by approximately 14 per cent (see Chapter 7, Section 3). Thus, this becomes approximately 15.0 billion Kčs at 1957 prices.

[c] This figure is in terms of the 1957 investment price, as roughly estimated by the author.

[d] According to *Statistické zprávy*, No. 2, 1958, this figure is 8.2 per cent. The quoted percentage increase is calculated on the basis of the "index of production," *SRRC*, 1957, p. 92.

5. Some Growth Factors of Czechoslovak Industrial Production

In Table 2.11 the reader will find the yearly increases of gross value of production as a percentage of the preceding year, percentage increases of gross value of production per billion Kčs of gross fixed investments in industry (an approximation of the marginal gross output–gross investments ratio),[14] percentage increases of gross value of output per man-year (approximation of productivity of labor), and yearly percentage increases in real wages. As far as possible, these figures have been subdivided into capital and consumer goods industries. Such a subdivision, however, has not been possible for fixed investment; yet it can be taken for granted that the greater part of fixed investment has benefited heavy industry. In the years before the currency reform of 1953, and especially after the revision of the first Five-Year Plan in 1951, the bulk of investment may have been reserved for heavy industry and there may even have been some disinvestment in some branches of the consumer goods industry. It is very likely that, over the ten-year period 1948–58, more than four-fifths of gross capital investment was devoted to developing capital goods output and less than one-fifth to consumer goods output.[15]

Nevertheless, the output per man-year was increasing, in most years, faster in the consumer goods industry than in the capital goods industry. Here again, however, we must bear in mind that the output is measured in terms of gross value, with the resulting distortions. Yet it is interesting to note that gross value of output per worker went up—in the decade under study and at constant prices—by 128 per cent in capital goods branches and by 139 per cent in consumer goods branches. One of the factors of this contrast was probably a hasty and irrational drafting of workers into heavy industry.

Official Czechoslovak data on the cost of production, "on a comparable basis," available from 1954 on, have also been included. It is interesting to note that the more the growth of output shifted from capital to consumers' goods, the more the costs of production, at constant prices and with a constant pattern of output, have been reduced (in 1954, 1955, and 1957). This may indicate the relative costliness of the marginal capital goods output at the present stage of industrial development in Czechoslovakia.

[14] According to coverage used in Czechoslovak statistics under the heading "investments," that is, excluding the so-called general overhauls (see Chapter 8, Section 2).

[15] If "general overhauls" are added to official statistics on investments, the portion of gross fixed investments earmarked for heavy industry would be even greater.

The fall in marginal gross value of the output–gross investments ratio during the period of the greatest industrialization drive between 1951 and 1953 is very striking. After the 1953 currency reform, when the yearly increase of output in heavy industry and the flow of new gross investments into industry slowed down, within a year both this ratio (in terms of increase of industrial output per billion crowns invested in industry) and the productivity of labor (in terms of gross value of output per man-year) went up; yet beginning in 1955 (with gross investments being stepped up again), marginal gross value of the output–gross investments ratio started to decline again, though not so sharply as before 1953. If the "general overhauls," as described in Chapter 8, Section 2, were added to the official investment statistics, the decline of the marginal gross output–gross investments ratio would be even more pronounced.

The above description deals with actual results which, in many respects, did not fall into the planned framework. For example, in 1957 capital goods output was planned to increase by 8.1 per cent and consumers' goods output by only 7.3 per cent. The actual increase, however, was greater for consumers' goods (10.9 per cent) than for capital goods (9.7 per cent). At the same time, productivity per man increased by 6.0 per cent as compared with the planned increase of only 5.3 per cent, and the costs of production (on a comparable basis) decreased by 0.6 per cent further than anticipated by the plan. Total output in industry actually rose by 10.2 per cent as compared with the planned increase of only 7.8 per cent, but almost one-sixth of the total number of 1,429 production units did not fulfill their plans of output. Falling short of the plan was output from many branches of heavy industry (extraction of hard coal and iron ore, production of electricity, pig iron, some kinds of rolled steel, metal-cutting lathes, ball bearings, cement and other building materials, etc.), as well as output of some consumers' goods (meat, butter, washing machines, television sets, and possibly other goods not mentioned in the official report on plan fulfillment). In 1958, probably owing to the new organization of industry, with fewer economic units and more efficient control (see Section 7), the results obtained came closer to the plan even in heavy industry.

Real earnings in industry declined, up to 1953, during the industrialization drive. After 1953, when increase of output was more equally divided between capital and consumer goods, real earnings resumed their upward trend, which, however, has been slowed down since 1957.

As will be discussed in Section 7, a new industrialization drive, with more stress on heavy industry again, seems to have started in 1958. This time, central planning authorities are trying to check the inflation involved in such a policy by keeping the increase in real earnings much below the increase in productivity. This attempt is the main reason for the present pricing system (see Chapter 7, Section 3) and for the introduction of a new wage system, as mentioned in Chapter 9, Section 1.

6. Output in Physical Quantities of Important Commodities and Manufactures

After encountering so many uncertainties among the Czechoslovak indices of industrial production and of productivity, we reach safer ground in considering the physical quantities produced by Czechoslovak public utilities, mining, and manufacturing. The relating figures are to be found in Table 2.12 (for the prewar year 1937, the start of central planning in 1948, and the years 1953 to 1958 inclusive). It is interesting to note that during the industrialization drive prior to 1953, output of many consumer goods (like cotton yarn, shoes, motorcars, and motorcycles) decreased considerably; it has recovered to the 1948 level only very recently. On the other hand, it must be borne in mind that from 1957 on, Czechoslovak exports of consumer goods have been increasing too. (See Chapter 6, Section 3.) Table 2.12 also shows, beyond any doubt, that the slowing down of increase (and for steel even a decrease) of output of capital goods during the *détente* of 1953–55 was only a temporary one.

The figures on output of some goods may be of special interest, since they are not available in the *United Nations Statistical Yearbook*, 1958, or in other international statistical publications (for instance, data on output of lead, aluminum, gold, silver, petroleum products, including synthetic gasoline, fertilizers, etc.). The author also included an estimate of the Czechoslovak production of uranium ore, which, however, as opposed to the other official and reasonably reliable figures, may well prove to be wide of the mark. There is the risk of a wide marginal error in this instance, because of the great interest in Czechoslovak uranium mining and because of an absolute lack of relating official data.

Table 2.13 contains a comparison of *per capita* production of some basic commodities and manufactures in 1957. It shows that Czecho-slovakia had achieved a higher per capita production of crude steel than France, but lagged behind the U.K. and West Germany—as well as the United States. On the other hand, Czechoslovak per capita production

TABLE 2.12—CZECHOSLOVAK INDUSTRIAL PRODUCTION
Public utilities, mining, and manufacturing
(In physical units)

	1937	1948	1953	1954	1955	1956	1957	1958
Public Utilities								
Electricity (billion kwh)	4.1	7.5	12.4	13.6	15.0	16.6	17.7	19.6
Manufactured gas (billion m³)	...	0.6	3.0	3.2	3.4	3.5	3.6	3.6
Mining								
Hard coal, net output (million tons)	16.7	17.7	20.3	21.6	22.1	23.4	24.2	25.8
Brown coal, net output (million tons)	17.5	22.6	32.8	36.1	38.7	44.1	48.8	54.3
Lignite (million tons)	0.5*	1.0	1.6	1.8	2.0	2.2	2.2	2.5
Crude oil (thousand tons)	18	...	122	125	107	108	108	106
Natural gas (billion m³)	...	...	0.2	0.2	0.2	0.3	0.8	1.2
Iron ore, crude (million tons)	1.8	1.4	2.3	2.2	2.5	2.5	2.7	2.8
Manganese ore (million tons)	0.1	...	0.3	0.3	0.3	0.2	0.2	0.2
Uranium ore, concentrate (tons)	32ᵃ	35*	50†	...	...	600–900†	...	...
Antimony ore (thousand tons)	16	...	...	...	...	...	...	...
Gold, pure (kg)	309	...	...	...	...	865	1479	...
Silver, pure (tons)	34.3	...	...	...	...	92.9	87.4	...
Metal-making Industry								
Pig iron (million tons)	1.7	1.6	2.8	2.8	3.0	3.3	3.6	3.8
Crude steel (million tons)	2.3	2.6	4.4	4.3	4.5	4.9	5.2	5.5
Rolled steel, excluding pipes (million tons)	1.6	1.8	2.7	2.8	3.0	3.3	3.5	3.8
Steel pipes (thousand tons)	164	...	400	377	389	463	494	521
Lead (thousand tons)	5.1	7.9	13.0	...	...	...	13.3	...
Copper, black (thousand tons)	1.1	...	...	...	...	...	...	...
Aluminum in blocks, primary (thousand tons)	—	—	2.7	15.4	24.4	21.2	16.7	26.4

TABLE 2.12—Continued

	1937	1948	1953	1954	1955	1956	1957	1958
					Metal-using Industry			
Diesel engines (thousand hp)	...	110	462	705	797	705	674	818
Metal-cutting lathes (thousand units)	...	11.3	16.6	14.8	18.5	19.0	22.7	...
Forging machines (thousand units)	...	4.1	3.0	3.1	6.0	5.6	7.8	5.4
Various equipment for metal making (steel rolling, etc.) (thousand tons)	...	9.2	39.0	44.1	37.2	29.5	37.4	...
Locomotives (main line, steam and electric) (units)	74	178	110	93	143	115	156	152
Tractors, all kinds (thousand units)	0.2	9.1	6.5	8.3	12.6	18.0	21.2	24.6
Tractor plows (thousand units)	...	18.0	...	...	9.9	9.8	14.2	...
Passenger cars (thousand units)	12.6	...	7.3	5.4	12.5	25.0	34.6	43.4
Trucks (thousand units)	2.0	7.2	11.4	12.9	10.5	11.0	12.5	14.0
Buses (thousand units)	1.1	1.1	0.6	1.1	1.1	1.2	1.3	1.1
Motorcycles, over 125 cc (thousand units)	14.1	68.0	46.4	55.6	95.8	112.0	138.3	146.6
Light motorcycles and scooters (thousand units)	...	...	...	...	3.6	30.5	51.7	131.7
Bicycles (thousand units)	203	231	259	231	293	346	330	303
Wireless receiving sets (thousand units) ...	149	267	182	109	102	220	255	303
Television sets (thousand units)	—		12	15	17	40	79	134
Domestic refrigerators, all kinds (thousand units)	...	8	8	19	31	58	66	80
Domestic washing machines, electric (thousand units)	...	2	40	133	206	254	292	313
Photographic cameras (thousand units) ...	...	23	65	80	146	164	110	148
Ball and roller bearings (million units)	...	...	8.6	10.2	14.3	18.0	22.7	27.1

TABLE 2.12—Continued

	1937	1948	1953	1954	1955	1956	1957	1958
Chemical Industry								
Sulfuric acid, 100% (thousand tons)	165	215	311	341	383	422	445	463
Nitrogenous fertilizers (thousand tons/N)	25	29	35	39	60	64	74	108
Superphosphates (thousand tons/P_2O_5)	61	54	67	81	98	107	110	117
Staple fiber, excl. glass fiber (thousand tons)	...	...	36.5	37.5	48.9	49.3	47.7	...
Viscose yarn, excl. glass waste (thousand tons)	...	18.0	25.4	25.6	35.8	35.9	32.9	39.7
Chloride of polyvinyl (thousand tons)	—	—	2.3	2.6	2.9	3.4	4.0	4.8
Sulfonamides (tons)	...	18	130	176	222	279	326	369
Fuel Industry								
Hard-coal coke (million tons)	3.5	4.3	6.5	6.8	7.0	7.3	7.5	7.4
Light motor fuels (thousand tons)	...	360[b]	299[c]	329[c]	346[c]	361[c]	375[c]	...
Gasoline for automobiles (thousand tons)	...	...	...	242	...	...	310	335
Diesel and other heavy oils for motor fuel (thousand tons)	30[d]	...	335	369	401	491	654	811
Lubricating oils (thousand tons)	...	70[e]	...	...	...	65	57	72
Kerosene (thousand tons)	73[d]	...	73	76	85	97	110	112
Building Materials, Glass								
Cement (million tons)	1.3	1.7	2.3	2.6	2.9	3.1	3.7	4.1
Lime (million tons)	...	0.9	1.1	1.3	1.5	1.7	1.8	1.9
Bricks, baked (billion units)	0.8	0.9	1.2	1.3	1.5	1.6	1.8[f]	1.9[f]
Sheet glass, all kinds, 4/4 mm (million m²)	...	15.5	17.4	18.1	21.0	22.9	23.8	24.3
Window glass, 1.6–4 mm (million m²)	...	...	8.8	9.1	10.5	12.1	12.0	12.4
Bottles (million units)	...	...	133	158	173	185	201	210
Crude optical glass in blocks (tons)	...	...	29	26	22	26	...	...
Timber, Paper Industry								
Lumber, all kinds (million m³)	...	3.1	4.4	4.1	4.5	4.4	4.4	4.3
Wood pulp (thousand tons)	270	235	293	303	318	323	334	...
Paper, all kinds (thousand tons)	246	260	318	331	345	360	378	404
Newsprint (thousand tons)	49	44†	32	33	34	34	33	35

TABLE 2.12—Concluded

	1937	1948	1953	1954	1955	1956	1957	1958
Textile and Footwear Industry								
Cotton yarn (million tons)	88.7	68.1	63.3	67.4	76.2	81.7	87.5	94.5
Wool yarn (million tons)[g]	27.2	32.0	31.8	29.2	32.2	32.0	33.0	33.1
Cotton fabrics (million m)	377	280	346	344	356	366	386	420
Woolen fabrics (million m)[h]	33	42	40	35	39	37	38	43
Silk fabrics (million m)	31	26	44	42	51	50	52	56
Linen and semilinen fabrics (million m)	39	34	51	50	55	52	56	62
Footwear, leather and rubber (million pairs)	55	53	49	50	52	52	60	68
Leather footwear (million pairs)	36	28	23	23	23	22	28	34
Food and Drink Industry								
Wheat flour (thousand tons)	982[i]	589	922[i]	970[i]	966[i]	993[i]	887[i]	935[i]
Meat, carcass weight, excluding horse meat (thousand tons)	371	163	335	312	345	385	413	415
Meat products (thousand tons)	...	77	139	135	140	145	169	173
Butter (factory production) (thousand tons)	...	22.9	35.3	37.0	43.2	49.1	52.1	58.1
Vegetable oils (thousand tons)	...	72	87	93	91	100	97	102
Cheese, excl. sheep milk cheese (thousand tons)	...	12.9	16.4	23.1	25.0	27.9	...	...
Sugar, refined (thousand tons)	669	517	657	711	659	593	792	856
Beer (million hectoliters)	8.3	8.2[i]	11.0[i]	10.2	10.5	11.1	12.5	12.6
Malt (thousand tons)	120	118	236	241	244	268	285	302
Wine, bottled (million liters)	...	...	26.6	30.2	32.8	...	37.0	48.1
Alcohol, 100% (thousand hectoliters)	992[k]	269	543	557	524	636	710	...

Prewar data: Various official Czechoslovak and U.N. statistics. Postwar data: *SRRC*, 1957, 1958, and 1959; *Statistické zprávy*, and *Statistický obzor*. Grouping of products does not correspond to the organizational pattern of Czechoslovak industry. Most 1937 data refer to prewar territory; yet the share of Carpatho-Ruthenia (incorporated into the USSR at the end of the Second World War) in Czechoslovak industrial production was negligible or none, except for timber, paper, and wheat flour.

[a] Jáchymov area; in recent years, uranium-ore mining has been developed in other areas, especially at Příbram.
[b] Synthetic gasoline from the Stalin Works at Záluží near Most only; author's rough estimate for 1949.
[c] Mostly synthetic gasoline.
[d] 1936.
[e] Author's estimate
[f] 1936.
[g] Probably including mixed yarn, except for 1937 and 1948.
[h] Substantially lower quality.
[i] 1949, author's rough estimate.
[j] Including mixed fabrics, except for 1937.
[k] Economic year 1936–37.

TABLE 2.13—1957 PER CAPITA OUTPUT OF BASIC MATERIALS, ENERGY, AND MAIN MANUFACTURES

	Czecho-slovakia	Austria	France	West Germany	United Kingdom	United States	East Germany	Poland	USSR	Yugo-slavia
Hard coal (tons)	1.8[a]	0.02	1.3	2.6	4.4	2.7	0.2	3.3	2.2[b]	0.1
Brown coal (tons)	3.8	1.0	0.1	1.9	...	...	12.8	...	1.0	0.9
Electricity (thousand kwh)	1.3	0.8	1.2	1.8	1.8	3.7	1.9	0.7		0.4
Crude oil (kg)	8	456	32	76	3	1970	...	64	487	21
Pig iron (kg)	269	281	274	359	282	420	95	131	181	41
Crude steel (kg)	387	360	320	476	429	597	165	188	250	59
Cement (kg)	278	305	289	374	236	291	298	159	141	111
Sulfuric acid (kg)	333	115	364	539	461	829	365	177	226	68
Passenger cars (units per 1,000 inhabitants)	2.6	0.2	16.5	19.0	16.7	35.7	2.0	0.3	0.6	—
Commercial vehicles (units per 1,000 inhabitants)	1.0	0.6	4.6	5.2	5.6	6.4	1.1	0.5	1.9	2.5
Cotton yarn (kg)	7.9	3.7	7.1	8.2	6.4	10.5[c]	3.5	4.3	4.8	0.7
Wool yarn (kg)	2.9	1.7	3.5	2.5	4.7	3.4	1.2	...	0.9	0.7
Leather and rubber shoes (pairs)	4.5	1.6	...	2.6	2.8	3.3	2.2	1.6	1.7[d]	...

[a] Net output.
[b] Including brown coal.
[c] 1954.
[d] Including shoes of textile material; the corresponding per capita figure for Czechoslovakia would be 5.3.

of steel was much higher than corresponding figures for other centrally planned economies, including East Germany and the USSR. Output of passenger cars per 1,000 inhabitants, while being much lower in Czechoslovakia than in Western Europe, is four times higher than in the USSR. The highest per capita production of shoes achieved among all the listed countries is to be explained by Czechoslovakia's prewar tradition in this branch.

7. 1958 Reorganization of Industry and Prospective Plans to 1965

In October 1957 the Central Committee of the Communist Party issued a resolution concerning "principles to increase economic efficiency." Previously, members of the Central Committee and of the government, among them Prime Minister Široký, had indicated that there would be genuine decentralization of planning and genuine autonomy of industrial enterprises. Suggestions were made that no longer should the plan of "gross value of production" be the yardstick for measuring economic efficiency, but sales by individual enterprises. As a necessary precondition, a new, more rational price structure was postulated by some economists, who criticized the lack of real cost analysis, disregard of the profit criterion in investment and output plans, etc.[16] A kind of planned market economy with competing nationalized enterprises seemed to be in the making.

Later development, however, showed that there will scarcely be such a fundamental change in the economic system. In February 1958, a new resolution of the Central Committee of the Communist Party on the organization of the Czechoslovak economy was published.[17] It decreed in

---

[16] Most outspoken on the subject was F. Zeman in *Predvoj*, weekly publication of the Slovak Communist Party, for September 12, 1957: "In individual cases, the price of goods need not be equal to the value, but total prices should, on the whole, correspond to total values . . . [Mr. Zeman apparently understands "value" as prices related to costs; see Chapter 7, Section 3.] In some cases, unavoidably a price is set higher than the corresponding value, because of the discrepancy between active demand and supply of the product in question, or for other reasons. In other cases, commodities may be priced lower than their corresponding values, as actually occurs in our practice, for some capital goods. . . . If, however, prices generally and substantially depart from the values of goods, it is hardly possible to obtain a correct idea of the size and origin of national income, with the result that the planning of the correct proportion of the national economy, in terms of money units, is impaired. . . . A fixed price can easily make one enterprise appear to be highly profitable and another one less profitable, whereas, in fact, the difference is caused merely by prices diverging from values."

[17] *Rudé právo*, February 27, 1958. A related report by Prime Minister Široký was published as a special supplement to *Rudé právo*, February 28, 1958.

detail a new administrative setup of industry, which became effective April 1, 1958, but spoke only in very general terms about a new system of planning and financing the national economy, to be introduced at the beginning of 1959. Meanwhile it was officially stated that the fulfillment of the plan of gross value of production would continue to be one of the dominant economic criteria. The various measures "to advance the material interests of the enterprises and of the working people in increasing output" thus seem to be merely secondary to improving the management, raising the productivity of labor, and reducing technical waste. The new administration of industry of April 1958 was officially called "decentralization of industry," and it did, in fact, reduce the central planning apparatus; the so-called "general managements" for various industrial branches within the central government were abolished and several thousand civil servants were transferred to production. The enterprises have obtained authority to plan part of their supply of raw materials and part of the pattern of investments, etc., but not their production of various commodities. At the same time, the number of enterprises (economic units) in industry and construction was reduced by two-thirds from 1,417 to 382.[18]

Only one enterprise is now "responsible for the supply of a defined group of goods to the whole national economy." Where the 9,584 production units (pits, factories, etc.) could not be squeezed, according to this principle, into the reduced number of economic units (enterprises), the enterprise, entrusted with the production of a certain kind of goods, obtained control over output of the same kind of goods in factories belonging to other enterprises. In this way, a comprehensive system of production monopolies was set up. This, in itself, made any competition of producers on the home market impossible.

Furthermore, the new system of state wholesale prices (see Chapter 7, Section 3) has not been fully based on the principle that wholesale prices should not substantially depart from costs of production. In view of continuing artificial pricing, it is not possible to rely on the market for allocation of resources.

Last but not least, it was officially stressed, in 1958 and 1959, that the central planning authorities will continue to stipulate all the "basic pro-

[18] Of these economic units, 316 are directed by ministries and 67 have the form of a trust. A detailed report on the new setup was published in *Statistické zprávy*, No. 7, 1958, and in *Hospodářské noviny*, Nos. 14–25, 1958. In mining and smelting of metals, for example, the number of enterprises (economic units) has been reduced from 77 to 22; in chemical industry, from 103 to 37, and in heavy machinery production, from 150 to 23.

portions" in the national economy, such as the scope and pattern of output, the scope and pattern of exports and imports, and the rate of accumulation and investments.

In the 1958–59 period the author could detect no tendency to make greater use of the functions of a "socialist market" to allocate resources, although such tendencies certainly existed in 1956. The basic principles of comprehensive, direct, and centralized planning are likely to continue in Czechoslovakia. Only the method of implementing the central comprehensive plan has been revised. In some respects, central planning may even be tightened. This may become necessary in view of the new prospective plans covering 1965, which are linked with Mr. Khrushchev's target to outstrip the industrial production of the capitalist countries.

Announcing the new plans at the Eleventh Congress of the Czechoslovak Communist Party in June 1958, Secretary General Antonín Novotný postulated an increase in the gross value of industrial output by 90–95 per cent by 1965, as compared with 1957.[19] This implies an average yearly growth of 8.5 per cent, a greater annual increase than in the year of economic *détente*, 1954, but a smaller increase than in the average of the last five years, 1955–59. Yet it has to be borne in mind that the yearly percentage increase will start from a higher and higher level. As in every industrially matured economy, it will become more and more difficult to maintain the pace of growth. To see the planned rise in output in proper perspective, it may be useful to translate it into an index on a 1948 = 100 basis: index of gross value of industrial output—1953, 193; 1957, 270; Plan 1965, between 515 and 525.

For an industrialized country like Czechoslovakia, raising the output more than five times within 17 years would be very spectacular. Besides this general analysis, there seem to be specific factors here which might make such a rapid growth very difficult.

In view of the present, almost full employment of labor, the increased industrial output has to rely mainly upon higher productivity per workman, which is planned to go up by 75 per cent until 1965, according to Mr. Novotný. This means a yearly increase of some 7.2 per cent as compared with a 5.8 per cent increase in 1957. The revision of the wage system in the second half of 1958 was already aimed at pushing up productivity per workman; it remains to be seen whether such an accelerating increase in productivity can be achieved.

The planned raise in output is to center again in heavy industry. Mr.

---

[19] Later the plans were changed; see Appendix.

Novotný gave some figures on only the very basic materials, the production of which can be tabulated as follows:

	1955	1956	1957	Plan 1965	Increase 1957–65 in Per Cent
Hard coal (million tons)	22.1	23.4	24.2	35–36	45–49
Brown coal (million tons)	38.7	44.1	49.0	77	57
Crude steel (million tons)	4.5	4.9	5.2	9.2–9.7	77–86
Power (billion kwh)	15.0	16.6	17.7	38.0	175

The above figures seem, however, not to be fully representative for the planned new preponderance of heavy industry. An economist, K. Vašíček, gave per cent figures on the share in total industrial production in terms of gross value to show the shifting pattern of industrial output:[20]

	1955	1960	1965
Power and fuel	3.6	4.6	5.7
Metallurgy and engineering	34.9	39.7	43.8
Chemicals	3.6	4.0	5.0
Consumers' goods and food	40.4	37.4	32.3

The output of basic materials seems to have special priority in these plans for the future; their proportion of total production is to increase, according to Mr. Vašíček, from 27 per cent in 1955 to 32 per cent in 1960 and to 34 per cent in 1965, while the proportion of highly manufactured goods is planned to decrease from 73 per cent in 1955 to 68 per cent in 1960 and to 66 per cent in 1965.

Nevertheless, in September 1959, the Central Committee of the Communist Party approved targets for 1965 under the third Five-Year Plan which are even higher than the goals of output under the prospective plans as described above. The new targets for 1965 will be discussed in the Appendix of this book.

8. Summary

Czechoslovakia has become one of the most industrialized countries in the world, with special stress on heavy industry, as illustrated by its having the third highest per capita consumption of energy in Europe. But even if we take the official Czechoslovak "index of industrial production"—i.e., index of gross value of output—as a yardstick of industrial growth, disregarding its upward bias, industrial output increased faster in Czechoslovakia than in market economies with a comparable starting level of industry (France, Austria) only in the first period, 1948–53.

[20] *Hospodářské noviny*, June 26, 1958.

During that time, industry was draining economic resources from other sectors of the national economy, and inflation and economic disequilibrium arose, which led to the second postwar currency reform in June 1953.

During the 1953–57 period, when economic resources were better divided between industry and other economic sectors, and when industrial output was better balanced between capital and consumers' goods, Czechoslovakia registered slower industrial expansion than France or Austria. Nevertheless, over the entire period under study, 1948–58, industrial production, in spite of the doubtful measuring of growth by the official index of gross value of production, probably increased in Czechoslovakia as fast as it did in market economies with a comparable level of economic development, and possibly even faster. This, however, was not due to better economic efficiency in Czechoslovak industry. Contrary to the situation in developed market economies, industry under central planning in Czechoslovakia claimed a sharply increasing share in national resources. This can be illustrated by the considerably faster rise of indices of the labor force and fixed capital assets in industry, as compared with the average increases for the whole economy:

	1948	1953	1957
Workers in industry	100	112	124
Total working population	100	104	109
Fixed capital assets in industry[a]	100	125	158
Fixed capital assets in the whole economy[a]	100	114	135
Machinery and equipment in industry....	100	138	184
Machinery and equipment in the whole national economy[a]	100	134	181

[a] "Basic funds" at 1955 cost of replacement (see Chapter 8, Section 3).

In 1958–59, a new industrialization drive began, again with stress on heavy industry, and a continuing, fast industrial growth is being planned under the third Czechoslovak Five-Year Plan, up to 1965. The method of implementing the central plan was somewhat revised, but it is safe to assume that the principles of comprehensive direct central planning will be fully maintained. A greater use of "forces of the socialist market," which seemed to be considered by some Czechoslovak economists in 1956–57, is unlikely to take place in the near future.

In contrast to the first industrialization drive in 1951–53, however, much more attention is now being given by the central planning authorities to the danger of inflation, as described in Chapter 7.

Chapter 3

CONSTRUCTION

1. Importance of Construction in the Czechoslovak Economy

Over the period being studied, the importance of construction including assembly work increased considerably. The number of persons employed in construction and assembly work within the whole "building branch" of the national economy increased from 225,000 in 1948 to 361,000 in 1956 and to 365,000 in 1957, according to *SRRC*, 1958, Table 8.6; the official monthly publication of the Statistical Office, *Statistické zprávy*, gives somewhat lower data on persons employed directly in construction and assembly work: 324,000 in 1956 and 328,000 in 1957, decreasing to 327,000 in 1958. Over the ten years 1948–58, the number of persons working in the building branch increased by approximately two-thirds, as compared with the over-all increase of population working in the national economy of only 11 per cent.

The "investments" in the building branch (see Chapter 8, Section 2), at comparable 1957 prices, rose from 195 million Kčs in 1949 (in terms of 1953 currency units; see Chapter 7, Section 1) to 990 million in 1957.[1] Fixed capital assets—the so-called "basic funds," at 1955 costs of replacement (see Chapter 8, Section 3)—increased, over the decade 1948–58, by 189 per cent, as compared with the average increase of basic funds of 41 per cent in the whole national economy (see Table 8.11).

Labor and capital investments in building increased even faster than those in industry. But in contrast to industry, the proportion of construction in the Czechoslovak economy, measured, e.g., by the ratio of national income originating in building to total national income at factor cost,[2] was much lower, in the base year 1948, than the corresponding ratio in developed Western European market economies. This was due, among other factors, to a rapid decrease in population in Czechoslovakia up to 1948 (see Chapter 1, Section 1), while the wartime destruction of buildings was relatively moderate (except in East Slovakia). Furthermore, lack of financial means, after the first postwar currency reform in 1945,

---

[1] From *SRRC*, 1958, Table 6.4.

[2] Under "Western" definitions (see Chapter 10, Sections 1 and 2), only 5.1 per cent in 1948.

put a certain brake on construction in the "private" (non-nationalized) sector of the national economy.

In any case, there was some disinvestment in construction in 1948 (see Chapter 8, Section 2). In spite of the rapidly increasing flow of gross fixed investments from the very low base in 1948–49, the *share* of construction in fixed capital stock (total basic funds) remained rather low: 0.8 per cent in 1948 and 1.0 per cent in 1957, with no change in 1958 (see Table 8.11). The proportion of the economically active population in Czechoslovakia in construction work remained below that in Austria or West Germany, in spite of the rapid increase in the number of persons working in this branch of the national economy in the years 1948–57 (see Table 1.8).

It is difficult to measure the real volume of construction and assembly work in Czechoslovakia, because the relating statistics are complicated by the division of data into building activity within the "building branch" and within other branches of the national economy, by measuring the building activity in terms of "comparable budget prices" instead of comparable actual cost, and by other distorting influences. *SRRC*, 1958, Table 8.1, gives data on construction and assembly work, including building activities in branches other than the "building branch," in terms of comparable budget prices, from which the following index is derived:

1948	1953	1954	1955	1956	1957
100	230	240	249	279	307

In *SRRC*, 1959, data on building and construction have been retrospectively modified. The coverage was changed and all data have been calculated in terms of the new reduced prices and with regard to the new organization of the building enterprises. These revised data suggest an index of volume of construction of 350 in 1957 and 355 in 1958.

It is difficult to say to what extent this increase of three and a half times in terms of budget prices was brought about by an increase in "comparable costs" (at constant prices), and by actual increase in the volume of construction. The relationship between the gross value of construction and the real physical volume seems to be even more unfavorable than a similar relationship in industry. In any case, the greatest part of new construction was earmarked for increasing productive capacity in industry and, from 1953 onward, in agriculture (exclusively for the benefit of the united co-operatives and of the state farms). Only a small part of the volume of construction was devoted to the building of housing units.

The pattern of construction and assembly work by types and branches of the national economy has been as follows (percentage shares on the basis of "comparable" budget prices), including construction carried out by sectors other than "building":[3]

	1948	1953	1956	1957
Total construction	100	100	100	100
New building investments	84.7	79.8	74.9	75.4
In industry	34.5	26.9	23.7	24.0
In agriculture	3.6	10.1	9.9	10.0
In transport and communications	13.6	11.3	5.0	5.2
In housing	20.0	15.1	23.0	22.2
"General overhauls" (see Chap. 8, Sect. 2)..	6.5	8.2	13.7	13.4
Current maintenance	8.8	11.8	13.6	11.2

More detailed information on the actual volume of construction is available only in connection with housing (units completed), which, as shown above, represents only one-fifth of the total construction. This subsector will be discussed in the next section.

2. Construction of Housing Units

Data on the number of housing units completed, their division between state and "individual" construction, and their varying sizes are to be found in Table 3.1. Over the 1949–57 period, 392,000 housing units were avail-

TABLE 3.1—HOUSING UNITS (DWELLINGS) COMPLETED IN CZECHOSLOVAKIA[a]

Year	Dwellings Completed (Thousand units)			Total Floor Space (Thousand m²)			Average Floor Space per Dwelling (m²)		
	T	S	I	T	S	I	T	S	I
1948	21.7	11.9	9.8	1,154	679*	475*	53.2	...	48.5*
1949	29.1	19.6	9.5	1,577	1,116*	461*	54.2	...	48.5*
1950	38.2	27.1	9.1	1,985	1,544*	441*	51.9	...	48.5*
1951	30.9	22.3	8.6	1,489	1,072*	417*	48.2	...	48.5*
1952	39.3	30.4	8.9	1,631	1,199*	432*	41.6	...	48.5*
1953	39.0	29.7	9.3	1,570	1,119*	451*	40.3	...	48.5*
1954	38.2	27.8	10.4	1,503	999*	504*	39.4	...	48.5*
1955	50.6	35.6	15.0	1,986	1,259	727*	39.3	35.4	48.5*
1956	63.7	33.2	30.4	2,525	1,189	1,336	39.6	35.7	44.0
1957	64.3	33.1	31.2	2,588	1,146	1,442	40.3	34.6	46.3
1958	52.6	35.7	16.9	2,002	1,255	747	38.1	35.2	44.2

Data from SRRC, 1958; Statistické zprávy, 1959. In Czechoslovak statistics, independent single rooms, such as in colleges for students and in homes for apprentices, are considered to be "housing units"—described here shortly as "dwellings."

    [a] T—Total construction.
    S—State construction.
    I—Construction by individuals and nonstate organizations.

    [3] From SRRC, 1958, Table 8.1.

able for use—which was not enough by far to meet the minimum requirements of replacing houses that would have been condemned as unfit for
habitation under normal circumstances and of providing houses for the
natural increase of population. In 1958, 380,000 applications of families
for rehousing were on the register. (Those eligible for registration were
families with living space of less than a certain number of square meters
per person. On the other hand, members of the so-called bourgeois classes
were evicted from their flats.) There is a very severe housing shortage in
Czechoslovakia.

Table 3.2 shows that construction of dwellings per 1,000 inhabitants in
Czechoslovakia has been much lower than in any listed Western country.
Furthermore, the newly constructed Czechoslovak housing units are much
smaller than are the average housing units in the West (see Table 3.1).

TABLE 3.2—COMPARISON BY COUNTRIES OF DWELLINGS COMPLETED, 1954–58
(*Per thousand inhabitants*)

Country	1954	1955	1956	1957	1958
Czechoslovakia	2.9	3.9	4.8	4.8	4.0
Austria	5.8	6.0	6.0	4.9	...
France	3.8	4.9	5.4	6.2	6.5
West Germany	11.1	10.9	11.3	10.5	9.4
United Kingdom	7.0	6.4	6.1	6.0	5.5
United States	...	8.0	6.7	6.1	...
East Germany	2.1	2.0	2.0	2.3	2.8
Hungary	2.8	3.2	2.6	5.2	4.3
Poland	3.0	3.4	3.4	4.3	4.5
USSR	7.0	7.7	8.2	10.8	12.9
Yugoslavia	2.0	1.7	2.1	2.5	3.3

Source: *European Housing Trends and Policies*, 1956, 1958 (Economic Commission for Europe,
Geneva, 1957, 1959). U.S. data: United Nations *Monthly Bulletin of Statistics*, No. 5, 1957, and
No. 6, 1958. The comparison between countries does not take into consideration the average size of
dwelling.

The deterioration of the housing situation in Czechoslovakia is obvious
from the following comparison: Inhabitants per room, 1930, 1.40; 1946,
1.36 (after the transfer of the German population); 1950, 1.45; 1955,
1.48.

Comparison by countries of the housing level can be found in Table
3.3. It shows that Czechoslovakia is lagging very far behind Western
European countries listed above.

There are two main factors in this sad state of affairs: (*a*) The funds provided by the state plan for housing construction are insufficient and private persons do not have enough money. Therefore the share of housing construction in total investments is lower than in the West (see Table 8.6). (*b*) The nationalized building industry seems to be very inefficient. It takes, on the average, over 14 months to construct one housing unit of 36 square meters; building takes three to four times longer than in the West. In 1957, the cost of building such a very small housing unit averaged 90,000 Kčs ($12,500 at the official exchange rate), excluding, of course, the cost of the plot and main services.

TABLE 3.3—COMPARISON BY COUNTRIES OF HOUSING AVAILABLE

Country	Year	Persons per Room
Czechoslovakia	1950	1.5[a]
Austria	1953	0.95
France	1954	0.95
West Germany	1953	1.11
United Kingdom	1953	0.77[b]
Hungary	1954	1.5
Poland	1953–55	1.9
USSR	1954	1.7[c]
Yugoslavia	1953	2.4

Source: *European Housing Trends and Policies*, 1956 (Economic Commission for Europe, Geneva, 1957).

[a] Including kitchens if the floor space exceeds 12 m².
[b] Exclusive of vacant dwellings.
[c] Towns and urban-type communities only.

One suspects that such inefficiency could also be discovered in industrial building. In the summer of 1958, the Central Committee of the Communist Party carried a special resolution on "the situation in the building industry," stipulating a great reorganization. In this connection, Mr. Oldřich Černík, Secretary of the Central Committee, stated, in *Rudé Právo* of September 2, 1958: "The building industry is today one of the weakest links in our economy."

In November 1958, a "Letter from the Communist Party to the Population" announced the launching of a vast program to build 1,200,000 new housing units by 1970. More stress was to be put on nonstate construction. If fulfilled, this program would approximately compensate for Czechoslovakia's lag in development of housing construction in Western

Europe up to the present, so that she would merely regain her prewar position in the European setting. Yet it is doubtful whether this ambitious program can be achieved at a time of general stress in all national resources, under the new production drive which started in 1958 and is planned to continue until 1965. The drop in investments in housing[4] and in the number of housing units completed in 1958, as compared with 1957 (see Table 3.1), is not a good start.

In 1959, 67,000 housing units were completed; this was one-quarter more than in 1958, but the nonstate construction fell considerably short of the target.

[4] In the *Economic Survey of Europe*, 1958, it was stated that investment in housing increased in Czechoslovakia. This is a mistake, due to an unclear statement in the Czechoslovak report in the Plan fulfillment 1958; it will be corrected, as far as the author knows, in further ECE publications.

Chapter 4

AGRICULTURE

1. Importance of Agriculture in the Czechoslovak Economy

In contrast to the over-all economic growth, agricultural production in Czechoslovakia remained below the prewar level throughout the period under study. Between 1948 and 1958, output rose, in terms of gross value, as described in Section 2, by approximately one-third. This was a rather moderate increase in view of the fact that 1948 was not a good year for crops, and a very bad year for livestock after the drought of 1947. Throughout the decade under study, output lagged behind increasing demand for farm products. Czechoslovak planning authorities accepted rather reluctantly the need for a certain increase in imports of food, as compared with prewar needs, but they also tried to put a brake on increasing demand by keeping consumers' prices for food high: in 1958, food prices on the average were about 90 per cent higher than in 1948, as compared with the over-all estimated increase of less than 60 per cent in the cost of living (see Table 7.2).[1]

In a market economy, more resources would be attracted to agriculture. This was not so in Czechoslovakia.

The agricultural labor force was reduced sharply, with no over-compensating increase in productivity per worker, as in developed market economies.[2] In 1948, 2.2 million persons, or 39.6 per cent of the economically active population, were working in agriculture and forestry; in 1957, there were only 2.0 million, or 29.6 per cent (adjusted percentages from Table 1.7). Agriculture alone, excluding forestry, suffered an even sharper decrease in manpower. According to the census of December 31, 1948, 2,222,000 people were working permanently in agriculture, but according to the census of February 1, 1958, there were only 1,692,000—a decrease of 24 per cent. Young people, and men especially, were leaving agricul-

---

[1] Nevertheless, in comparison by countries, consumption of food is fairly high in Czechoslovakia (see Chapter 9, Section 6).

[2] In developed market economies, the agricultural labor force also dropped, but productivity per worker increased faster than the growing demand for farm products.

tural work, so that in 1957 the average age of persons permanently working in agriculture was 45 years,[3] and 54.2 per cent of these were women.

The changes in manpower in agriculture will be described in more detail in Section 3b.

Investments in agriculture, though increased between 1948 and 1958, were far from sufficient: until 1953, gross fixed investments in agriculture, including forestry,[4] remained below 2 billion Kčs a year, at constant 1957 prices (approximately 1.3 billion at 1948 prices; for terms of comparable new currency units, see Chapter 7, Section 1). This was not enough to cover current depreciation. Throughout the war, and in all postwar years until 1951–52, there was a net disinvestment in agriculture.[5] From 1953 on, fixed investments in agriculture probably again surpassed the depreciation quota, but the greatest part of them were devoted to accelerating collectivization rather than to rationally expanding agricultural output, as will be described in Section 4.

Over the years 1948–57, 23.7 billion Kčs, at 1956 prices, were invested in agriculture and forestry, or only 11.1 per cent of total gross investments. In state-financed investments, the share of agriculture and forestry amounted to only 5 per cent.

The proportion of agriculture and forestry[6] in the so-called basic funds (capital stock, including domestic animals, at 1955 replacement costs; see Chapter 8, Section 3) amounted to 8.5 per cent in 1948, and to 8.7 per cent in 1957. As will be argued in Chapter 8, Section 3, these percentages cannot be taken at face value. Nevertheless, they show that the very low ratio of capital investment in agriculture to the average capital investment in the national economy did not improve noticeably between 1948 and 1957. (In 1958, the share of agriculture and forestry in total basic funds

[3] *Mladá fronta* reported in August 1958: "The average age of people working in agriculture is increasing. On February 1, 1956, it was 43.6 years; last February it was almost 45 years. Over-age persons, i.e., persons over 60 years of age, on February 1, 1958, constituted 13.5 per cent. . . . A full quarter of all workers in agriculture are between 51 and 60 years old. . . . In some villages, the average age of persons working in agriculture is over 55 years."

[4] Data for agriculture alone are not available to the author. All investment data in this section refer to gross fixed investments excluding "general overhauls" (see Chapter 8, Section 2).

[5] Net disinvestment in agriculture was officially acknowledged in 1948 (see Chapter 8, Section 2).

[6] Data for agriculture alone are not available to the author. Basic funds in forestry were probably increasing faster than in agriculture. In agriculture alone there may have been no increase, and possibly even a slight decrease in the proportion in basic funds in 1957, as compared with 1948 (this was definitely the case in 1953).

increased to 9.0 per cent [see Table 8.11]; this was due to stepped-up investments in the collectivized sector.)

The share of agriculture (excluding forestry) in the Marxist national income went down, in terms of stable (April 1955) prices, from 17 per cent in 1948 to 11 per cent in 1957, according to *SRRC*, 1958, Table 1.6. According to *SRRC*, 1959, Table 1.7, in 1958 the share of agriculture in Marxist national income further decreased to 10 per cent. (See Chapter 10, Sections 1 and 3 and Table 10.2.)

2. Index of Agricultural Production

There is a basic difference in the construction of Western and Czechoslovak indices of agricultural production, similar to the difference in the field of industrial production. Western index numbers are obtained as a weighted average of the physical quantities of crops or livestock products: the Czechoslovak official index is based on gross value of agricultural production, with adjustment made for price movements.

The Western indices are either of gross production, including agricultural products consumed within the production on the farm, such as seed and animal feed, or of net production, excluding the products re-employed for further production.

The Czechoslovak official index of gross value of agricultural production embraces total crops and livestock production, including seed, feed, and other products consumed within agricultural production. But besides this double-counting, there may be other duplications, such as in the transfer of seed, feed, or even livestock between the state and the cooperative or the private sector, or even between two enterprises of the same sector. Every such transfer is brought into the calculation of the "gross value of production." Though such inflating of the index numbers is probably less serious for agricultural than for industrial production, it has to be borne in mind, along with the question (which the author is unable to answer) of whether or not the gross value of crops is calculated in the same way as the physical quantities of crops, described in the general note to Table 4.2, i.e., including harvesting losses. For at least one of the above reasons, Czechoslovak construction of the index of gross value of output in agriculture (at constant prices) involves an upward bias as compared with the Western construction of the index of gross agricultural production.

A semiofficial index of the net value of agricultural production in Czechoslovakia, including wood production in forestry and services rendered by state tractor stations, was calculated by V. Houštka.[7] This index,

[7] *Statistický obzor*, No. 11, 1957.

however, should not be confused with the Western "net production index." Its author was concerned not only with eliminating the production of seed, feed, etc, but with the share of agriculture and forestry in the net national product. Therefore, he adjusted the index of gross output for all the rising material costs of production. There is no doubt about the growing cost of agricultural output in Czechoslovakia during the collectivization drives up to 1955 and again from 1957, as described in Section 4. This index may bring somewhat lower results than the Western construction of "net" agricultural production, even if its author started from faster-rising index numbers than the official numbers, of gross value of output, having included a faster-rising contribution of forestry to the national gross product as well as the services rendered by the state tractor and machinery stations. In view of the quite different construction and different purpose, i.e., to ascertain the development of real costs rather than the physical net agricultural output, this index could not be used for comparison by countries in Table 4.1. In any case, Dr. Houštka's index of net output in agriculture was computed only up to 1955 and was later subject to official criticism. But it may be of great interest to compare the relating index numbers and the "national income originating in agriculture and forestry" under Marxist definition (analogous to "national income originating in industry," see Chapter 2, Section 2):

	1948	1949	1950	1951	1952	1953	1954	1955
Official index of "gross value of agricultural production"	100	111.7	116.7	118.1	113.0	116.9	114.3	127.2
Dr. Houštka's indices: gross value of production in agriculture, forestry, and tractor stations ...	100	111.4	115.9	120.4	118.3	119.5	116.9	134.7
Material costs	100	122.8	123.4	137.0	142.2	159.4	166.4	197.3
Net production	100	104.1	111.1	109.9	103.0	94.0	89.8	94.8
National income originating in agriculture and forestry (Marxist definition)	100	120	132	121	115	127	112	123

As Table 4.1 indicates, even according to the official index of gross value of gross production, Czechoslovak total agricultural production is seriously lagging behind the development of agriculture in Western Europe and in the United States. On the other hand, the remaining centrally planned countries have not achieved a faster rate of growth of agricultural production either (except, perhaps, the USSR—probably owing to the

TABLE 4.1—INDEX OF AGRICULTURAL PRODUCTION

Country	1948	1949	1950	1951	1952	1953	1954	1955	1956	1957	1958
TOTAL PRODUCTION (CROSS)											
Czechoslovakia, index of gross value of production, 1936 = 100	74.8	83.5	87.3	88.3	84.5	87.5	85.5	95.1	97.4	96.8	99.4
OUTPUT OF LIVESTOCK PRODUCTS (CROSS)											
Czechoslovakia, index of gross value in 1955 prices, 1936 = 100......	68	83	94	92	96	81	89	97	104	107	108

Prewar average = 100	1948/49	1949/50	1950/51	1951/52	1952/53	1953/54	1954/55	1955/56	1956/57
TOTAL PRODUCTION (GROSS)									
Austria	71	82	97	92	101	110	105	113	114
France	96	99	111	105	111	117	125	122	117
West Germany	76	92	103	110	113	119	119	117	121
United Kingdom	118	121	122	122	129	129	137	137	145
United States	139	134	128	130	...	142	142	146	150
Yugoslavia		...	80	107	75	109	90	121	101
OUTPUT OF LIVESTOCK PRODUCTS (GROSS)									
Austria	59	73	90	89	100	109	107	112	113
France	96	105	110	106	114	125	129	132	132
West Germany	56	83	94	104	108	114	117	119	121
United Kingdom	94	105	107	113	119	127	137	132	141
United States	125	132	136	143	144	146	150	156	158

Czechoslovak index numbers are from *SRRC*, 1958 and 1959, Table 9.1. They are based on gross value of output at 1955/56 "realization prices" ("weighted average of lower price for compulsory deliveries and higher price for above-quota deliveries). They include all intermediate products and possibly, at least up to 1955/56, also harvesting and other losses. They are not comparable with Western index numbers. Data for all other countries are: Total production, from *FAO Yearbooks of Food and Agricultural Statistics*; output of livestock products, from *OEEC Statistical Bulletin—General Statistics*, No. 5, 1958.

Soviet large-scale plan of using virgin land in Siberia). While in Western Europe total production (of crops and livestock) has surpassed the prewar level by one-fourth, production in Czechoslovak agriculture has remained —even according to the official index—still below the prewar (1936) level. Further evidence of the slow development of agriculture in Czechoslovakia can be found in the international comparison of main crops in Table 4.2 and of livestock production in Table 4.3. Czechoslovak (and probably most other East European) crop data since 1948 are based on "biological crops": they are obtained by multiplying the areas sown by estimated hectare yields, without adequate adjustment for non-harvested areas and for harvesting losses. For some—but not for all—crops in some years, qualifying footnotes have been officially added, as reproduced in Table 4.2. Only recently has this unsatisfactory statistical method been revised.

TABLE 4.2—MAIN CROPS

(Thousand metric tons)

	Average 1934–38	Average 1948–52	1956	1957	1958	1959
WHEAT						
Czechoslovakia	1,513	1,493	1,541	1,525	1,346	1,643[d]
Austria	417	348	570	574	549	...
France	8,143	7,791	5,683	11,082	9,601	10,943
West Germany	2,505	2,656	3,487	3,843	3,693	...
United Kingdom	1,743	2,397	2,891	2,726	2,755	...
United States	19,456	31,066	27,332	25,873	39,796	31,438
East Germany	1,547	1,243	1,086	1,259	1,362	...
Hungary	2,200	1,909	1,845	1,959	1,487	...
Poland	1,963	1,833	2,121	2,319	2,344	...
USSR	...	...	...	...	75,300	...
Yugoslavia	2,467	2,171	1,606	3,103	2,453	...
RYE						
Czechoslovakia[a]	1,577	1,110	1,050	948	937	962[d]
Austria	539	343	434	400	397	...
France	769	573	471	481	430	475
West Germany	3,081	3,042	3,735	3,816	3,728	...
United Kingdom	10	52	25	24	21	...
United States	1,028	524	537	692	825	545
East Germany	2,070	2,516	2,299	2,231	2,353	...
Hungary	710	731	494	487	371	...
Poland	6,851	6,374	6,558	7,437	7,346	...
Yugoslavia	208	248	205	280	241	...

TABLE 4.2—*Continued*

	Average 1934–38	Average 1948–52	1956	1957	1958	1959
BARLEY						
Czechoslovakia	1,109	1,046	1,408	1,362	1,199	1,474[d]
Austria	281	210	385	392	335	...
France	1,074	1,534	6,407	3,626	3,899	4,692
West Germany	1,699	1,397	2,310	2,504	2,414	...
United Kingdom	782	2,060	2,845	3,004	3,221	...
United States	4,495	5,843	8,205	9,518	10,243	9,021
East Germany	1,024	593	834	897	929	...
Hungary	630	654	645	962	735	...
Poland	1,633	1,061	1,123	1,227	1,196	...
Yugoslavia	407	323	344	604	470	...
OATS						
Czechoslovakia[a]	1,212	961	1,034	899	871	944[d]
Austria	438	275	374	340	333	...
France	4,572	3,393	4,604	2,579	2,637	2,770
West Germany	2,843	2,500	2,452	2,228	2,149	...
United Kingdom	2,019	2,852	2,526	2,179	2,172	...
United States	13,973	18,970	16,883	18,884	20,643	14,655
East Germany	1,584	1,188	1,112	999	1,144	...
Hungary	290	213	176	263	192	...
Poland	2,832	2,240	2,259	2,541	2,657	...
Yugoslavia	317	286	324	484	259	...
MAIZE						
Czechoslovakia	225	254	399[b]	445	479	535[d]
Austria	170	120	144	150	155	...
France	541	447	1,738	1,392	1,625	...
West Germany	51	...	20	16	...	...
United Kingdom	—	—	—	—	—	—
United States	53,066	81,971	87,768	86,435	96,520	...
East Germany	22	...	4	4	...	...
Hungary	2,190	2,068	2,043	3,233	2,739	...
USSR	...	5,730	12,500	7,000	16,200	...
Yugoslavia	4,691	3,078	3,370	5,560	3,950	...
SUGAR BEETS						
Czechoslovakia	4,664	4,967	4,585[c]	6,775	6,946	5,000[†]
Austria	1,130	715	1,228	1,333	...	...
France	8,785	8,344	9,700	10,628	...	...
West Germany	4,118	5,820	8,093	9,690	...	...
United Kingdom	3,195	4,525	5,252	4,587	...	...
United States	8,704	9,762	11,802	13,712	...	...
East Germany	5,467	...	...	...	...	...
Hungary	960	1,716	1,948	...	...	...
Poland	5,959	5,966	6,339	7,600	...	...
USSR	...	17,500	32,500	...	...	...
Yugoslavia	509	1,179	1,130	1,551	...	...

TABLE 4.2—*Concluded*

	Average 1934–38	Average 1948–52	1956	1957	1958	1959
			POTATOES			
Czechoslovakia	9,635	7,255	9,635	8,756	6,589	6,100†
Austria	2,845	2,270	3,229	4,034	3,542	...
France	17,158	13,734	18,169	15,114	13,716	...
West Germany	19,603	24,075	26,779	26,302	22,678	...
United Kingdom	5,011	9,444	7,654	5,782	5,645	...
United States	10,024	10,676	11,055	10,865	11,965	...
East Germany	13,649	13,164	13,565	14,529	12,489	...
Hungary	1,990	1,715	2,055	2,707	2,500	...
Poland	38,036	29,727	38,052	35,104	35,836	...
Yugoslavia	1,631	1,486	2,190	3,310	2,620	...

Data are from *SRRC*, 1957, 1958, 1959 (including the international part), various issues of the *FAO Statistical Yearbook*, FAO *Monthly Bulletin of Agricultural Economies and Statistics*, and *Internationale Monatshefte* (Wiesbaden) (for sugar beets only). For certain years and certain countries, there are minor discrepancies in the data from each of the above-mentioned sources, but they are not of a serious nature. Some of the 1958 and 1959 data are preliminary figures only. Postwar data for Czechoslovakia—and probably all other Eastern European countries—refer to *biological crops*, mostly without correction for nonharvested areas or for harvesting losses (see notes *b* and *c*). Besides these two official qualifications (from *SRRC*, 1957, p. 126n.), there may be other serious discrepancies between the data on biological crops and those on actually harvested crops, for which no correction and no qualification have been made. Eastern and Western data on crops should be compared with serious qualifications.

a Including mixed grain.

b Actual harvest lower by 14,000 tons, because maize on 6,500 hectares "did not ripen" (this means that the area harvested was smaller by 6500 ha than area sown on which the official crop data in the above table are based).

c Actual harvest lower by 180,000 tons, because the sugar-beet area harvested was smaller by 8,665 hectares than the area sown.

d From *Zpráva o rozvoji národního hospodářství ČSR* (Report on Plan Fulfillment), 1959.

TABLE 4.3—LIVESTOCK PRODUCTION

(*Thousand head*)

	Prewar			Year: October–September				
	Date of Estimate	Number	Month of Estimate	1948/49	1955/56	1956/57	1957/58	1958/59
			CATTLE					
Czechoslovakia .	Jan. '36	4,376	Jan.	3,663	4,107	4,134	4,091	4,183
Austria	Dec. '39	2,620	Dec.	2,108	2,346	2,325	2,297	2,279
France	Oct. '38	15,622	Jan.–Oct.	15,434	17,572	17,693	17,924	18,466
West Germany .	Dec. '38	12,187	Dec.	10,559	11,552	11,815	11,948	12,065
United Kingdom	June '39	8,872	June	10,244	10,907	10,881	10,956	11,005
United States ...	Jan. '39	66,029	Jan.	78,298	96,804	94,502	93,350	96,851
East Germany ..	Dec. '38	3,645	Dec.	2,879	3,760	3,718	3,744	3,890
Hungary	May '38	1,882	Mar.	2,070*a*	2,170	1,973	1,936	2,004
Poland	June '38	9,924	June	6,345	8,353	8,265	8,207	8,347
USSR	Aug. '38	63,200	Jan.	...	58,800	61,400	66,800	70,800
Yugoslavia	Dec. '39	4,322	Jan.	5,264	5,206	4,947	4,863	5,038

TABLE 4.3—*Concluded*

	Prewar			Year: October–September				
	Date of Estimate	Number	Month of Estimate	1948/49	1955/56	1956/57	1957/58	1958/59
			PIGS					
Czechoslovakia .	Jan. '38	3,358	Jan.	3,242	5,285	5,369	5,435	5,283
Austria	Dec. '39	2,830	Dec.	1,618	2,933	2,727	2,917	2,838
France	Oct. '38	7,127	Oct.	6,424	7,729	7,759	8,131	8,469
West Germany .	Dec. '38	12,280	Dec.	9,381	14,593	14,407	15,418	14,654
United Kingdom[b]	June '39	4,394	June	2,823	5,474	5,974	6,578	5,978
United States ...	Jan. '39	50,012	Jan.	57,128	55,173	51,703	51,559	57,201
East Germany ..	Dec. '38	5,707	Dec.	2,620	9,029	8,326	8,255	7,518[c]
Hungary	Spring '39	3,886	Mar.	5,200[a]	6,056	4,996	5,338	6,225
Poland	June '38	9,684	June	5,818	11,561	12,325	11,999	11,221[f]
USSR	July '38	30,600[c]	Oct.	19,720[d]	52,155	56,482 ‖	44,300[g]	48,500[g]
Yugoslavia	Dec. '39	3,564	Jan.	4,127	4,655	3,725	4,243	5,656
			SHEEP					
Czechoslovakia .	Jan. '38	533	Jan.	459	1,000	956	889	817
Austria	Dec. '39	318	Dec.	454	255	227	207	194
France	Oct. '38	9,875	Oct.	7,510	8,216	8,403	8,573	8,749
West Germany .	Dec. '38	2,097	Dec.	2,491	1,188	1,146	1,127	1,106
United Kingdom	June '39	26,887	June	19,493	23,645	24,796	26,174	27,554[f]
United States ...	Jan. '39	51,595	Jan.	31,654	31,109	30,840	31,337	32,664
East Germany ..	Dec. '38	1,771	Dec.	723	1,807	1,893	2,019	2,247
Hungary	Spring '39	1,868	Mar.	...	1,930	1,873	2,050	2,155
Poland	June '38	1,940	June	1,617	4,223	4,040	3,893	...
USSR	Dec. '37	57,300	Oct.	...	56,482	108,200	120,200	129,600
Yugoslavia	Dec. '39	10,282	Jan.	11,650	11,518	10,622	10,633	11,247

Figures for Czechoslovakia from *SRRC*, 1957 and 1958, and various issues of *Statistické zprávy;* for other countries, from various issues of *FAO Statistical Yearbook*, and FAO *Monthly Bulletin of Agricultural Economics and Statistics.*

    [a] May 1949.   [b] Pigs on agricultural holdings only.   [c] Prewar boundaries.   [d] Average, 1948–52.

    [e] June.   [f] In agricultural enterprises only.

    [g] Data from FAO Bulletin, Jan. 1960; they are obviously not comparable with previous FAO data for the USSR. (The new data are qualified as "in agricultural enterprises only"). It is noteworthy that *SRRC*, 1959, international part, Table 22.13, gave the figures 40,844 for 1956/56 (as compared with the FAO figure 56,482 in the above table), and 44,336 for 1957/58 (in accordance with the FAO figure "in agricultural enterprises").

As in Western market economies, livestock production was developing in Czechoslovakia slightly faster than crop production. But it is still lagging behind the West. (See Table 4.3.)

The slow development of production in agriculture is not in line with the aims of the planners. The "plan of agricultural production" is chronically unfulfilled. In 1956, a 9 per cent increase of over-all production in agriculture was planned, but production rose by only 3.4 per cent. In 1957, a further increase was planned, but production decreased by 1 per cent. The Czechoslovak press is repeatedly publishing complaints about the rapidly increasing need for imports of food.

3. Factors of Development in Czechoslovak Agriculture

There are four main factors in the unsatisfactory development in agriculture, some of which are interconnected: (a) decrease in acreage of available agricultural, and especially arable, land; (b) shortage of manpower; (c) too slow increase in crop yield per hectare and in livestock production, as compared with the West; (d) lagging mechanization of Czechoslovakia's agriculture, and a lower use of chemical fertilizers than in the West. A further factor is the influence of collectivization, which will be discussed in detail in Section 4 below.

a) The total hectarage of agricultural land decreased from the prewar average of 7,756,000 hectares, for 1934–38, to 7,561,000 hectares in 1948;[8] but it decreased still faster in the decade under study, amounting to only 7,377,000 hectares in 1957. Two factors accounted for the decrease in agricultural land: first, forestry land increased from 3,999,000 hectares (prewar average) to 4,066,000 hectares in 1948 and to 4,329,000 hectares in 1957; and second, the land not used for either agriculture or forestry increased from 782,000* to 910,000* hectares, from the prewar average to 1948, remaining relatively constant at 909,000* up to 1957.[9]

---

[8] On a comparable basis, with due regard to the separation of Carpatho-Ruthenia from the Czechoslovak Republic. On the other hand, no adjustment has been made for the very small increase of approximately 5,000 hectares due to a rectification of Slovakia's border.

[9] Before the war, this "unused" land comprised mostly built-up areas, airports, etc., high mountains, inland waterways, and marshes. The postwar figures include a higher portion of actually unused, formerly agricultural, land and fallow land, especially in the "border regions." This may be gathered from the fact that, in Slovakia, the land not used for agriculture or forestry increased only very slightly from the prewar average to 1948 (from 363,000* to 383,000* hectares), but decreased again to 339,000* hectares by 1957. In the Czech regions (Bohemia and Moravia), however, containing the bulk of the "border regions" (to be reinhabited after the transfer of the Sudeten Germans), this "unused land" rose from 389,000* hectares, 1934–38 average, to 527,000* hectares in 1948, and to 570,000* hectares by 1957. The increase of the area not used for either forestry or agriculture, between 1948 and 1957, may be taken as an indication that resettlement in the border regions has not advanced since 1948, but rather has suffered a certain decline. This conclusion is also supported by press reports. Jan Macek wrote in *Hospodářské noviny* of April 18, 1958: "In our border regions, there are still considerable economic resources

Arable land decreased even faster, from the prewar average of 5,602,000 hectares to 5,297,000 hectares in 1948,[10] and to 5,119,000 in 1957. When the lowest point, 5,007,000 hectares, was reached in 1954, the Tenth Congress of the Communist Party set a special target to extend the area of arable land. It should have been extended by 200,000 hectares in 1957, but the actual increase was only 120,000 hectares. In 1957, the area of arable land still remained lower, by 9 per cent, than the prewar average figure for 1934–38, and it was 3 per cent lower than that for 1948. In 1958, the arable land area remained unchanged at 5,119,000 hectares, according to official statistics, but with the qualification that these 1958 arable land statistics also included 15,000 hectares of orchards with crop cultivation, which were not included in data on arable land up to 1958.[11] In 1959, in terms of the new, larger coverage, arable land increased to 5,153,000 hectares,[12] still short of the target set by the Tenth Congress of the Communist Party.

The total sown area decreased from the prewar 1934–38 average of 5,613,000 hectares to the 1949–53 average of 5,121,000, and to 5,105,000 in 1955. Then, following the relaxation of collectivization of agriculture in 1955 (see Section 4 of this chapter), it went up to 5,143,000 hectares in 1956, dropped again to 5,113,000 in 1957, and increased slightly to 5,118,000 hectares in 1958.[13]

Official statistics suggest that, in 1955, the area sown was *greater* by 10,000 hectares than the total arable land (which is certainly due to the exclusion of cultivation of crops in orchards from arable land statistics); in 1957, it was lower by 2,000 hectares (with arable land still excluding orchards under cultivation); in 1958 the area sown was smaller by 35,000 hectares than the arable land (including orchards under crop cultivation).

b) The number of persons working permanently in agriculture decreased by 24 per cent between December 31, 1948, and February 1, 1958 (as mentioned in Section 1 of this chapter). The bulk of this drop in agri-

---

remaining unused. . . . In spite of all efforts, the decline in population of productive age in the agricultural border districts is continuing . . ." The "forbidden zone" near the Czechoslovak border of western Germany and Austria may also account, in part, for the increase of "unused land" in Bohemia and Moravia.

[10] On a fairly comparable basis, with due regard to the separation of Carpatho-Ruthenia from the Czechoslovak Republic. See footnote 8.

[11] From *SRRC*, 1958, Table 9.2.

[12] From *SRRC*, 1959, Table 9.4.

[13] From *SRRC*, 1959, Table 9.11. Data on area sown by main crops can be found in *SRRC*, 1959, Table 9.2, and in various issues of the *FAO Statistical Yearbook*.

cultural manpower occurred during the maximum industrial expansion, ending in 1952, when the number of persons working permanently in agriculture may have been, according to the author's own estimate, as low as 1,600,000†, i.e., 90,000 less than the figure for February 1958. From 1953 on, efforts have been made to stop the rapid decline of manpower in agriculture. According to the official report on plan fulfillment in 1956, the number of persons permanently working in agriculture went up in that year by 95,000. According to the census of December 15, 1956. 1,756,000 persons were permanently working in agriculture. The subsequent new decrease of manpower—to 1,692,000 persons, according to the census of February 1958—occurred in spite of the transfer of some white-collar workers to employment in agriculture; it coincided with a new collectivization drive and a renewed tendency to step up the rate of industrial growth.

The sharp drop in agricultural manpower between 1948 and 1952 was not solely due to directing the labor force into industry; the flight of the younger generation from agriculture was caused also by the increasing discrepancy in earnings in agriculture and other sectors of the national economy, as described in Chapter 9. On the other hand, the reduction of this discrepancy in earnings since 1953 has apparently not been sufficient to make work on collective farms attractive enough.[14] At the beginning of 1958, total manpower in agriculture was less than half of the prewar figure.

There is no doubt that the decrease in manpower has not been compensated by increased productivity per worker, and that a shortage of manpower exists in this sector of the Czechoslovak economy.

c) Changes in yields of various main crops per hectare (Table 4.4) depend, of course, not only on factors that can be influenced by man but also on variations in weather from year to year. Furthermore, Czechoslo-

---

[14] The Czech Trade Unions daily paper *Práce*, on August 2, 1958, wrote: "In the Prague region, there are 3,000 young people out of school who still have not found employment, but the plan of recruiting the labor force for agriculture has been only 56 per cent fulfilled. In the Pardubice region it is necessary to recruit 1,777 young people for agriculture this year, but till now only 800 have reported for work. . . . Many local national committees and many unified agricultural cooperatives have thoughtlessly agreed to the departure of young people from the villages, although they know that the average age of persons remaining in the village and in the cooperatives is often 55 years or even older."

The Slovak Trade Unions daily paper *Práca* wrote on similar lines on July 23, 1958, about the same problem in Slovakia: "In Slovakia 15,381 boys and girls are needed as apprentices in agriculture and cattle breeding . . . but we have acquired only one-third of this number."

TABLE 4.4—YIELDS OF MAIN CROPS

(100 kg per hectare)

	Prewar Average 1934-38	1948	1949	1950	1951	1952	1953	1954	1955	1956	1957	1958
WHEAT												
Czechoslovakia	17.1	16.4	19.5	18.9	19.9	20.5	20.8	15.6	20.4	21.3	20.6	18.3
Austria	16.7	12.8	16.9	17.6	18.2	19.8	23.0	19.0	22.5	22.7	23.3	20.9
France	15.6	18.0	19.1	17.8	16.7	19.6	21.3	23.5	22.8	20.7	23.6	20.8
West Germany	...	21.5	26.8	25.8	28.6	27.6	27.5	26.1	28.9	30.2	31.5	28.3
United Kingdom	23.1	26.8	28.2	26.4	27.3	28.5	30.2	28.5	33.5	31.2	31.8	30.8
United States	8.7	12.1	10.0	11.1	10.8	12.3	11.6	12.2	13.3	13.5	14.4	18.4
Yugoslavia	11.4	13.4	14.1	10.3	12.9	9.2	13.3	7.5	12.8	9.9	15.7	12.3
Hungary	13.2	15.9	14.3	...	...	...	...	11.8	15.7	13.3	15.7	12.5
Poland	14.6	11.7	12.3	12.4	12.8[a]	13.5[a]	12.5[a]	12.8	14.9	14.5	16.0[a]	15.9
USSR	9.3	...	...	...	...	...	...	...	...	...	...	...
BARLEY												
Czechoslovakia	17.0	15.4	17.9	16.8	18.0	18.2	19.2	17.7	20.1	21.1	20.4	17.9
Austria	17.6	11.5	16.8	17.2	17.7	18.1	21.5	20.8	22.2	22.9	22.1	19.4
France	14.5	15.5	16.0	16.3	16.3	16.1	18.6	20.5	20.3	28.1	22.2	21.9
West Germany	21.0	18.6	24.5	24.0	26.2	24.9	26.3	26.2	26.7	27.1	28.7	27.5
United Kingdom	20.9	24.4	25.9	24.2	25.5	25.7	28.4	27.3	32.1	30.3	27.9	28.8
United States	11.6	14.2	12.9	14.6	14.6	14.8	15.2	15.3	14.8	15.7	15.5	17.0
Yugoslavia	9.6	11.1	12.2	8.2	10.9	8.1	12.7	7.6	11.5	9.7	14.7	12.1
Hungary	13.2	15.9	14.3	...	...	...	...	14.1	19.7	15.8	21.2	13.7
Poland	15.7	11.7	12.2	12.7	12.4[a]	14.2[a]	12.9[a]	12.9	15.1	14.6	15.8[a]	16.2

76

TABLE 4.4—Concluded

POTATOES

Czechoslovakia	135	110	102	123	110	118	153	132	127	153	139	109
Austria	137	118	113	139	129	151	184	158	167	178	175	...
France	112	150	98	131	124	118	144	166	147	175	151	139
West Germany	166	205	186	245	216	208	211	225	203	236	234	214
United Kingdom	169	192	173	193	198	199	205	195	180	205	176	170
United States	78	145	145	171	162	168	168	174	180	197	189	202
Yugoslavia	57	75	88	43	72	47	84	73	87	82	116	90
Hungary	73	77	66	...	...	...	...	84	107	93	112	108
Poland	138	108	120	138	102[a]	106[a]	124[a]	135	100	140	127[a]	126

SUGAR BEETS

Czechoslovakia	286	236	220	285	213	206	241	261	285	207	298	299
Austria	262	164	182	281	275	211	289	310	320	283	309[b]	...
France	276	305	264	320	263	213	296	290	281	290	310[b]	...
West Germany	356	300	285	383	...	295	297	355	354	310	374[b]	...
United Kingdom	221	264	239	308	270	262	321	261	271	307	264[b]	...
United States	252	304	333	328	340	343	363	361	370	371	386[b]	...
Yugoslavia	188	190	122	86	193	67	178	159	199	161	203[b]	...
Hungary	207	158	207	...	...	120	238	184	198	169	...	...
Poland	265	190	204	222	168[a]	177[a]	190[a]	183	186	176	225[a]	...
USSR	...	...	...	...	...	...	216[c]	175[c]	...	...	...	...

Data for Czechoslovakia are from *SRRC*, 1957, 1958, and 1959 (for some crops, for 1950 and 1951, they differ slightly from FAO data). Data for other countries are from various issues of the *FAO Statistical Yearbook*, FAO *Monthly Bulletin of Agricultural Economics and Statistics*, SRRC, international part, and from *Statistisches Jahrbuch für die Bundesrepublik Deutschland*, 1958, unless stated otherwise.

[a] Data from *Mały rocznik statysticny* (Warsaw, 1958).
[b] Calculated by the author on the basis of data on area sown and production, from *Internationale Monatszahlen* (Wiesbaden, April 1958).
[c] Data from *Statistički godišnjak FNRJ* (Belgrade, 1957).

vak statistics relating to biological crops, as described in Table 4.2, general remarks, cannot be considered very accurate. Nevertheless, Table 4.4 may be taken as an indication that the yields per hectare between 1948 and 1957 were increasing more slowly in Czechoslovakia than in Western Europe, and yields of some root crops remained below the prewar level.[15]

Under normal circumstances, it would be futile to compare the yields by individual years instead of the averages of several years. But in the specific Czechoslovak case, the varying yields per hectare have a strong negative correlation with the changing industrialization and collectivization drives. This is the reason it is useful to give yearly data on hectare yields.

d) The mechanization of Czechoslovak agriculture and the supplies of inorganic fertilizers were much neglected during the first industrialization period (up to 1953). They increased faster in the years 1953 to 1958. But except for the short-lived relaxation of collectivization in 1954 and 1955, practically all new machinery and most of the fertilizer supply were provided for state farms and unified agricultural cooperatives only. As will be demonstrated in Section 4, this "Socialist sector of agriculture" seems not to have made efficient use of the increased amount of the means of agricultural production.

Table 4.5 contains data on the deliveries of tractors and agricultural machinery, the bulk of which went to the Socialist sector.[16]

Table 4.5 provides an international comparison of tractors; in Czechoslovak agriculture, the number of hectares of arable land per tractor remained much above that in developed Western market economies until 1957.

The use of fertilizers per hectare of agricultural land from 1948/49 to 1957/58 in Czechoslovakia and a comparison by countries of the use of fertilizers per hectare are to be found in Table 4.6.

---

[15] For some other crops which need particular care, the yields per hectare decreased even more as compared with prewar levels. For example, the tobacco yield decreased from 16.3 quintals in 1934–38 to 12.3 in 1955 and to 10.5 quintals in 1956. The hops yield fell from 8.1 quintals in 1937–38 to 7.2 quintals in 1955, to 6.1 quintals in 1956, and to 6.0 quintals in 1957. Contrary to the tobacco area, the hops area decreased, so that the lower yields can by no means be explained by the use of marginal land. Hops, incidentally, are a very important item of Czechoslovak export. The paper *Lidová demokracie* wrote on August 20, 1958: "Our hop gardens are the second greatest in the world . . . Our production is only in fourth place."

[16] The Socialist sector consists of state farms, agricultural cooperatives, and tractor stations. Contrary to Khrushchev's policy in the USSR, the tractor stations in Czechoslovakia were not dissolved until 1959.

TABLE 4.5—NUMBER OF TRACTORS

	Tractors Used in Agriculture (wheeled and crawler) (*Thousands*)				Hectares of Arable Land per Tractor		
	1949–52	1956	1957	1958	1949–52	1956	1958
Czechoslovakia							
Actual tractor units:							
FAO figures	26.1ᵃ	38.8	...	...	211	139	...
Author's estimate	24*,ᵇ	40*	45*	53*	...	129*	97*
In terms of 15 hp units..	...	51†	56.6ᶜ	...	...	101†	...
In Socialist sector	...	46.6	52.7	61.8	...	48	67
Austria	16.8	66.0	78.9	...	107	27	...
France	148.1	396.0	477.5	...	143	50	...
West Germany	169.6	549.9	614.2	...	51	16	...
United Kingdom	325.3ᵃ	435.9	...	...	23	16	...
United States	3,808.7	4,600	4,685	...	50	41	...
Yugoslavia	6.3ᵈ	15.0	20.5	...	1,247	562ᵉ	...
East Germanyᶠ	16.9ᵍ	38.0	39.0	...	...	...	...
Hungaryʰ	13.3	25.5	26.2	...	433	227	...
Poland	29.8	51.8	55.7	...	545ⁱ	317	...
USSR	971.7ʲ	876.8	910.7	...	230ᵏ	140ᵉ	...

Tractors used: Data for Czechoslovakia—author's estimate based on "tractors per 1,000 hectares" and on hectarage data from *SRRC*, 1959, Table 1.1; data in terms of 15 hp units in the Socialist sector from *SRRC*, 1959, Table 9.55. All other data are from the *FAO Statistical Yearbook (Production)*, 1958, Table 95.

Arable land per tractor: Czechoslovakia—based on data on tractors used, and on hectarages from *SRRC*, 1959, Table 9.6 (the figure there is lower than the FAO figures on arable land in Czechoslovakia in 1957). All other data are from FAO *Monthly Bulletin of Agricultural Economics and Statistics*, May 1958.

ᵃ Two-year average.   ᵇ 1948.   ᶜ According to *FAO Statistical Yearbook*, 1958.
ᵈ 1950.   ᵉ Based on arable land, 1954.   ᶠ State farms and tractor stations only.
ᵍ Three-year average.   ʰ Excluding approximately 3,000 "standing tractors."
ⁱ Based on arable land, 1955.   ʲ In terms of 15 hp units.   ᵏ Based on arable land, 1947.

4. Impact of Collectivization

At the beginning of the central planning system in Czechoslovakia, there were four types of agricultural cooperatives. Whereas types one and two are cooperatives as known in the West, types three and four are analogous to the Soviet kolkhozes. Their agricultural land and livestock are collectivized and their members receive shares in profits according to the number of work units performed (but they have small private lots of land on which they can keep their own cattle). At present, only these latter two types are described as "cooperatives" in Czechoslovak statistics, whereas types one and two are included in the so-called "private sector."

TABLE 4.6—USE OF COMMERCIAL FERTILIZERS

	Czecho-slovakia	Austria	France	West Germany	United Kingdom	United States	Yugo-slavia	East Germany	Poland
NITROGENOUS (1,000 TONS N)									
1948/49–1952/53	48.1	22.5	281.7	365.0	209.3	1,171.0	5.9	194.1	93.7
1956/57	93.5	37.8	402.9	527.0	306.9	1,909.4	51.0[a]	225.4	195.5
1957/58	92.1	41.3	483.5	576.4	312.7	2,012.2	95.0[a]	...	...
Kg per hectare arable land, 1956/57	18	21	19	61	43	10	6[a]	43	12
PHOSPHORIC ACID (1,000 TONS P_2O_5)									
1948/49–1952/53	62.9	33.0	454.2	405.5	402.9	1,960.0	9.9[b]	84.2	102.7
1956/57	115.2	59.4	771.2	572.4	375.5	2,170.5	50.0[a]	184.0	156.4
1957/58	112.0	69.3	750.1	586.8	360.0	2,074.6	135.0[a]	...	...
Kg per hectare arable land, 1956/57	23	34	36	66	53	12	6[a]	36	9
POTASH (1,000 TONS K_2O)									
1948/49–1952/53	77.7	27.5	362.1	660.3	215.2	1,243.0	3.2[b]	385.4[b]	174.2
1956/57	186.1	68.8	579.9	878.5	343.0	1,739.0	44.3[a]	459.6	283.8
1957/58	215.7	71.5	679.1	980.1	345.0	1,622.5	70.0[a]	...	...
Kg per hectare arable land, 1956/57	37	38	27	101	48	9	5	88	29

Data for Czechoslovakia are from *SRRC*, 1959, Table 9.59; for other countries from *FAO Statistical Yearbook (Production,)*, 1958, Tables 92, 93, 94. Data on amount per hectare of arable land were calculated by the author on the basis of total consumption data and from data on arable land for 1957, *FAO Statistical Yearbook*, 1958, Table 1, except for Czechoslovakia, where the official figure of 5,119,000 hectares was used (in contrast to the relating FAO figure of 5,392,000 hectares).

[a] Calendar year 1957.

[b] Three year average.

The unified cooperatives (types three and four) developed as follows:[17]

End of Year	Number of Cooperatives	Members (Thousands)	Agric. Land[a] (Thousand hectares)
1951	3,138	109	...
1952	5,848	260	2,300*
1953	6,679	381	2,100*
1954	6,502	304	1,900*
1955	6,795	392	1,834
1956	8,016	395	2,109
1957	11,090	656	3,257
1958	12,140	852	3,996
1959	12,560	...	4,789

[a] Including "private lots" of cooperative members (end of 1955 approx. 110*, 1956 130*, 1957 230*, 1958 310* thousand hectares).

The percentage share in total hectarage of agricultural land under cultivation by sectors (i.e., the land of the state farms and other branches of the state sector, the land of the unified cooperatives, the land of the private sector and the "personal sector"[18]) in the period 1948–58 is to be found in Table 4.7.

Data on the share by agricultural sectors in the total gross value of production are also included in this table. It appears that, in all years, the share of the private sector in total land under cultivation was smaller than its share in production. On the contrary, the state and cooperative sectors had a greater share of land under cultivation[19] as compared with their share in total production. This in itself is proof of the higher productivity of the individual farmers.

Yet, in terms of net production, if one allowed for the high costs of production in the state and cooperative sectors, the better performance of the individual farmers would stand out even more clearly. Practically all new gross investments in agriculture in 1957 went to the state and cooperative sectors. For some inexplicable reason, Czechoslovak data on gross investments exclude machinery and implements in the private sector of agriculture. Yet in 1957 there were practically no private investments

[17] Data through 1958 from *SRRC*, 1959, Table 9.48; for 1959, from the *Results of the Fulfillment of the State Plan of Development of the National Economy of the Czechoslovak Republic*, 1959.

[18] This is the total of private lots of members of the unified cooperatives and small farming units of less than 0.5 hectare, belonging mostly to industrial workers.

[19] The share of state and cooperative sectors in total agricultural land, including fallow land, would be even greater.

TABLE 4.7—BREAKDOWN OF AGRICULTURAL LAND,ᵃ PRODUCTION, AND
SUPPLIES TO THE MARKET, BY SECTORS

(*Yearly averages, in per cent of totals for agriculture*)

	1948	1951	1952	1953	1954	1955	1956	1957	1958
Socialist:									
Agricultural land..	...	24.4	31.1	44.7	41.2	40.5	44.4	51.7	68.2
Production	3.9	21.6	27.6	36.2	33.9	33.8	36.3	39.8	52.7
Supplies to the market	...	28.3	34.8	45.3	45.6	44.5	47.0	49.4	62.1
Private:									
Agricultural land..	...	73.9	66.4	51.8	55.3	56.0	51.8	44.1	26.2
Production	91.9	72.1	64.4	53.8	54.8	55.1	51.8	46.6	28.4
Supplies to the market	...	70.0	63.0	50.5	50.3	50.7	47.7	45.1	32.4
Personal:									
Agricultural land..	...	1.7	2.5	3.5	3.5	3.5	3.8	4.2	5.6
Production	4.2	6.3	8.0	10.0	11.3	11.1	11.9	13.6	18.9
Supplies to the market	...	1.7	2.2	4.2	4.1	4.8	5.3	5.5	7.7

BREAKDOWN OF THE SOCIALIST SECTOR

(*In per cent of totals for all sectors, total agriculture*)

State:									
Land	...	13.1	13.3	13.5	14.4	15.5	16.3	17.0	17.4
Production	3.9	10.9	11.5	12.2	12.8	13.0	12.2	12.7	13.7
Supplies to the market	...	17.7	17.5	18.3	19.8	19.1	18.2	18.6	18.6
Unified cooperatives:									
Land	...	11.3	17.8	31.2	26.8	25.0	28.1	34.7	50.8
Production	...	10.7	16.1	24.0	21.1	20.8	24.1	27.1	39.0

Data are from an article by V. Nachtigal, "Some Data on the Socioeconomic Structure of Czecho-slovak Agriculture" in *Statistické zprávy*, No. 2, 1959. The Socialist sector includes state and co-operative farms, excluding private lots of members of unified cooperatives. The private sector covers individual farmers and, in the first part of the decade, the then existing cooperatives of types one and two. The personal sector covers small farming up to 0.5 hectare (mostly by workers in industry), and private lots of members of unified cooperatives.
ᵃ Land under cultivation only, excluding fallow land.

of that kind, because of the bad financial situation of individual farmers and their fears that they could not escape collectivization sooner or later. The following distribution, in spite of the exclusion of private agricultural machinery from data on investments, provides a picture of investments in agriculture in 1957, by sector (in billion Kčs at 1956 prices):

Total gross investments in agriculture 4.7
State sector 2.2
Cooperative sector 2.5
Private sector 0.04

Obviously, private farms had to face a disinvestment in buildings and machinery. But they had to cope with other kinds of discrimination against them too. They had to pay higher prices for fertilizers and materials and for services provided by the tractor stations than did the state and the cooperative sectors:[20]

	1957 Prices in Kčs per 100 Kg	
	Charged to Unified Cooperatives	Charged to Individual Farmers
Potassium nitrate	43.20	61.80
Ammonium sulfate	56.40	80.60
Nitrogen lime	72.60	103.60
Thomas slag	27.20	38.90
Kalium salt	36.60	52.40
Superphosphate	40.20	57.40
Cement	15.00–17.00	64.00

Not only do the individual farmers have to pay higher prices for the means of production; they also receive lower prices for their produce than do the state and cooperative sectors. Technically, the state prices paid for the same kind of produce are identical for all sectors. But there are lower prices for compulsory quota delivery and higher prices for deliveries above the quota. Their development appears in Table 4.8. Since the individual farmers had much higher delivery quotas to fulfill, their average proceeds were lower. According to the article by J. Nikl (see footnote 20), the so-called "realization prices" (weighted average of quota and above-quota prices) for individual farmers and for cooperatives diverged, in 1956, as follows (index, 1937 = 100):

	Realization Prices Paid	
	To Unified Cooperatives	To Individual Farmers
Total agricultural produce	137.8	130.5
Livestock products	156.5	147.8

It will be noted that the index of prices for agricultural produce, especially those paid to individual farmers, remains below the index of the cost of living (see Table 7.2).

[20] Data from an article by J. Nikl in *Nová mysl*, No. 7, 1958.

TABLE 4.8—AVERAGE STATE PRICES PAID FOR AGRICULTURAL PRODUCE
Index, 1937 = 100

	1952	1953	1954	1955	1956	1957	1958
All products:							
Quota deliveries (compulsory)	78.4	84.3	91.9	97.3	102.3	102.0	100.9
Above-the-quota deliveries	190.8	229.0	222.3	226.1	224.3	221.7	216.7
Weighted average	81.0	89.8	105.6	120.7	128.2	130.6	132.1
Livestock products:							
Quota deliveries (compulsory) .	86.4	89.8	100.2	108.3	112.5	111.5	109.3
Above-the-quota deliveries	236.2	247.8	231.8	236.7	238.3	228.9	229.8
Weighted average	90.8	96.1	117.3	137.0	144.0	145.7	148.1

Data from *SRRC*, 1958, Table 15-12; 1959, Table 15.18. The weighted average indices were obtained by averaging quota and above-quota prices paid to unified agricultural cooperatives and to individual farmers.

In spite of all odds against them, the individual farmers maintained, as late as 1957 and possibly into 1958, higher hectare yields for several crops, potatoes among them. In *SRRC*, 1958, the following comparison of hectare yields by sectors in 1957 is to be found (in 100 kg):

	State Farms	Unified Cooperatives (Types 3 and 4)	Private Farms
Wheat	21.9	22.0	19.4
Rye	17.2	19.2	18.1
Barley	20.6	21.9	19.3
Oats	14.0	18.3	16.7
Legumes for human consumption..	7.4	8.8	10.1
Sugar beets	293.6	318.4	279.6
Potatoes	118.2	140.8	141.3

The above figures refer to biological crops; i.e., they include harvesting losses and unharvested crops. These losses were certainly much higher in the state and cooperative sectors than in the private sector.[21] In terms of actual harvest, the results of the individual farmers would appear more favorable.

The performance of individual farmers in the field of livestock breeding has been clearly better than that of the state sector. Their share in the

[21] According to reports in Czechoslovak newspapers, 500,000 tons of sugar beets and and 1,200,000 tons of potatoes remained unharvested (in the soil) in 1957. Nearly all these losses, and most of the harvesting losses, occurred in the "Socialist" (state and cooperative) sector.

total livestock population (kept by all sectors), as given below,[22] was much higher than their share in agricultural land (see Table 4.7):

Beginning of Year	Per Cent of Total Livestock			
	Socialist Sector	Coopera- tives	Private Lots	Individual Farmers
Cattle 1956............	30.6	16.5	5.8	69.6
1957............	35.1	19.8	6.7	65.0
1958............	48.6	31.0	12.4	47.5
Pigs 1956............	36.9	21.3	8.1	55.0
1957............	38.7	23.6	9.1	52.2
1958............	44.4	29.8	15.6	40.0

Even the report on the plan fulfillment for 1958 stated that the private sector fulfilled livestock product deliveries better than the state and co-operative sectors. Individual farmers provided 34 per cent of cattle for slaughter and 39 per cent of milk supplies and 66 per cent of eggs to the market, although their share in agricultural land, at the end of the year, was only 27 per cent.

The performance of individual farmers is the more remarkable since, besides the material odds against them, the age distribution of persons still working on private farms is very disadvantageous:[23]

	Per Cent of Total Working Persons, by Age Groups				
	Under 21	21–40	41–50	51–60	Over 60
State farms	11.6	41.2	22.9	17.8	6.5
Cooperatives	5.3	29.4	27.0	26.2	12.1
Private farmers	7.2	26.3	24.6	25.3	16.4

In view of the artificially higher costs of production under the system of discriminatory, state-fixed prices, and in view, too, of the lower prices paid to the individual farmers for their produce (see Table 4.8), incomes in the private sector of agriculture were lower than in the Socialist sector. These incomes before taxes, by sectors, including the estimate of incomes in kind, are to be found in Table 4.9. (In the author's opinion, the incomes in kind of the individual farmers—as estimated by a member of the Czechoslovak Statistical Office, Josef Nikl—may be slightly over-estimated.) But these lower incomes of individual farmers were subject to higher direct taxation by agricultural tax. In 1957, 236 million Kčs were levied in agricultural tax from individual farmers, and only 78

[22] Data from an article by J. Bašata, *Statistický obzor*, No. 5, 1958.
[23] Data from *SRRC*, 1958, Table 9.36.

TABLE 4.9—INCOME OF AGRICULTURAL POPULATION AT CURRENT PRICES
FROM SALE OF PRODUCE AND ALL OTHER ECONOMIC ACTIVITIES

(*Kčs per month per person working permanently in agriculture*)

	1951	1953	1955	1956
Total gross money income:				
Unified cooperatives	6,904	9,737	12,824	13,369
Individual farmers	4,990	5,589	6,200	6,616
Net money income:				
Unified cooperatives	3,347	4,856	6,416	6,730
Individual farmers	1,735	2,285	3,960	4,409
Income in kind:				
Unified cooperatives	4,595	6,424	5,293	5,274
Individual farmers	5,548	8,032	6,653	6,895
Total net income:				
Unified cooperatives	7,942	11,280	11,709	12,004
Individual farmers	7,283	10,317	10,613	11,268

Data from an article by Josef Nikl in *Nová mysl*, No. 7, 1958. They are higher (especially for individual farmers) than Bezouška's data on net money income per economically active person in farmers' families (see Table 9.8). One reason is because of the difference in definition of "persons working permanently in agriculture" and of "economically active persons" (Bezouška possibly includes a
larger number of working family members) and to a different classification of occupational groups
(Bezouška has a special category for "wage earners with farming lots"—*kovozemědělci*; part of
higher incomes of this category may possibly be included in Nikl's data on incomes of individual
farmers, etc.).

million from unified cooperatives;[24] thus, the ratios between individual
farmers and unified cooperatives were: agricultural tax, 3:1; agricultural
land (including private lots), 10:9; gross value of output (including
output of private lots of members of cooperatives), 10:8.

The relatively weak results obtained by the state sector have been
admitted by the central planning authorities.[25] On the other hand, the

[24] From an article by Messrs. Mencl and Nikodém on direct taxation, *Statistický
obzor*, No. 11, 1959.

[25] The Central Committee of the Communist Party thought it necessary to take
specific action, in December 1957, to improve the running of "state estates" (which
represent about four-fifths of the state sector, the remaining one-fifth being other
state or publicly owned agricultural enterprises apart from the special organization
of the state estates; they are run directly by various ministries, the army, the Secretariat of the President of the Republic in Lany, etc.). The daily paper of the Communist Party, *Rudé právo*, wrote in this connection on December 9, 1957: "There
are severe shortcomings in the state estates farming. Their production is too expensive. Beginning in 1953, their land increased by 38.3 per cent but their gross production increased by only 26 per cent, and produce brought to the market increased
by only 14.4 per cent. Productivity of labor increased by only 7.5 per cent, which
has no relation to the amount of machinery allotted to them . . ." *Rudé právo*
further complained that the actual losses suffered by the state estates were increasingly exceeding the planned financial losses.

unified cooperatives were praised, up to 1959, for performance superior to individual farmers. In the author's opinion, this cannot be sustained when the input and output in these sectors are compared.

At the beginning of 1959, however, when three-fourths of the agricultural land was already collectivized, a change of policy was announced. A new system of prices paid for agricultural produce by the state was to be introduced, which would offer a lower margin of artificial profits to cooperatives. Lower state procurement prices for quota deliveries, and higher over-quota prices (favoring the cooperatives) have been abolished and a single state wholesale price for agricultural products has been introduced.[26]

In conclusion, let us compare the share of the sectors in the national income originating in agriculture under Marxist definition; the Marxist national income, of course, reflects discriminatory, artificial pricing. In spite of this distortion, it is obvious that the private sector contributed more toward the formation of national income originating in agriculture than was its share in total agricultural land:

1957	State Sector	Cooperative Sector	Personal Sector	Individual Farmers
Percentage share in national income originating in agriculture and forestry[b]	11[a]	20[a]	17	52
Percentage share in agricultural land (average at beginning and end of year)	18*	33*	5*	44*

[a] Including income originating in forestry land. Practically all forestry land is state-owned or collectivized.

[b] Data from *SRRC*, 1958, Table 1.9.

5. Prospective Plans Up to 1965

At the Eleventh Congress of the Communist Party in June 1958, ambitious plans for the development of agricultural output were announced, together with plans for further rapid industrialization. By 1965, total agricultural production is to increase by 40 per cent, as compared with 1957 (in terms of gross value). With the index 1948 = 100, the planned development of gross value of agricultural production is as follows: 1953, 117; 1957, 129; planned for 1965, 181. Thus, agricultural production is planned to surpass prewar (1936) production by one-third in 1965.

Such an increase—for which there has been no precedent in the decade

[26] In a commentary, broadcast by Radio Prague on April 14, 1959, it was stated that, under the old system of double state prices, the state would have had to pay 30 per cent more for agricultural produce by 1965 than it paid for the same amount of produce in 1957. Obviously, this price difference was estimated with regard to the expected full collectivization.

under study—is to be achieved by substantially higher hectare yields and by very intensified livestock production.

The hectare yields are to be increased as follows (in hundred kilograms per hectare):[27]

	Average 1955–57	1957	Planned Average 1961–65
Wheat	21	21	26
Barley	20	20	25
Sugar beets	263	298	312
Hay	35	32	46
Hops	6	6	12

For this purpose, the mechanization of agriculture and the use of inorganic fertilizers are to increase rapidly. According to an article by Karel Vašíček on economic tasks in 1965,[28] the number of tractors in agriculture is to shoot up, from a proportion of one per 165 hectares of agricultural land in 1957 to one per 70 hectares in 1965; production of nitrate fertilizers is to more than double, from 59 kg to 125 kg per hectare between 1957 and 1965.[29]

Nesvadba and Vašíček give identical figures for the target of livestock production in 1965, but their figures (per hectare of agricultural land) for 1957 diverge slightly.

	1957		Plan, 1965
	Nesvadba	Vašíček	
Meat, including poultry (live weight, kg)	135	132	175
Milk (liters)	501	493	730
Eggs (units)	284	...	407

On the whole, the target in agriculture for 1965 seems to be attainable from a purely technical point of view. The Western European countries listed in this book had surpassed prewar total production by one-third already in 1956/57, whereas in Czechoslovakia, such an increase over the prewar level is planned only for 1965. The planned Czechoslovak hectare

[27] According to J. Nesvadba, "Some Data Regarding the Tasks Established by the Eleventh Congress of the Communist Party in the Field of Agriculture."

[28] Hospodářské noviny, June 29, 1958.

[29] No reason is given for quoting the production rather than the use of fertilizers; but even the production figure given by Vašíček does not agree with the data in SRRC, 1957, on production of nitrate fertilizers, according to which production of about 85 kg per hectare, in terms of nitrate, can be calculated. For consumption, see Section 3c. Vašíček's data on tractors do not tally with figures in Table 4.5.

yields in 1965 would still remain below those prevailing in West Germany and at about the same level as those prevailing in France now.

But there are many open questions. It is subject to doubt whether the planned increase in the number of tractors is sufficient to obtain the planned hectare yields, especially in view of the labor shortage in agriculture. Even if the long-term plan is attained, the number of tractors in Czechoslovakia by 1965 would remain below the Western European levels.

The postulated greater intensity of livestock production in 1965 per hectare of agricultural land would surpass the 1955 levels in France and in the United Kingdom (according to Vašíček):

	Czechoslovakia		France	U.K.	Netherlands
	1957	Plan, 1965	1955	1955	1955
Meat, excluding poultry (*carcass weight, kg*) ..	80.8	106	104.1	89.3	267.9
Milk (*liters*)	493	730	563	567	2,514

To attain this goal, according to Vašíček, cattle should increase in the next eight years, by 700,000 to 800,000 head. In the ten years under study here, the number increased from 3,275,000 at the beginning of 1948 (a very low level, in consequence of the drought year 1947) to 4,134,000 in 1957, or by 859,000; but it still remained below the 1946 level of 4,-143,000.

The planned increase in livestock seems to be very overoptimistic, especially in view of the goal to "achieve an overwhelming victory of Socialist production in agriculture" by 1960, which was announced along with the prospective plans for 1965. During the collectivization drives, the number of cattle, so far, has always decreased.

But the main skepticism as to attaining the long-term goals in agriculture arises from the basic economic consideration that, whenever there is a sharp acceleration in industrial growth, other sectors of the economy are affected. The prospective plan for industry, described in the Appendix, will certainly mean a drain on all economic resources. Without large foreign credits, which apparently are not being considered, the expectation of a simultaneous, great expansion in industry, construction, agriculture, and transport, and a simultaneous rise in the standard of living, as promised by the long-term plan, appears overambitious.

6. Summary

During the maximum industrialization drive in Czechoslovakia in 1950–52, the input of both manpower and gross investments into agricultural production was severely curtailed. In later years, some efforts were made to remedy this situation, at least in part. But during a second collectivization wave, from 1955 on, the major part of gross investments was devoted to changes from private to state or collective ownership rather than to over-all expansion of agricultural production. The private sector suffered from disinvestments and extreme shortage of manpower. Collective farming, and especially farming on state estates, was far from rationally handled; productivity was too low, compared with the input of gross investments and other resources in these sectors. Average yields per hectare and amount of livestock have been increasing in Czechoslovakia more slowly than in the Western market economies. Other factors, such as a reduced area of agricultural land, also had an unfavorable influence.

The consequence was that, between 1948 and 1958, whereas agricultural production increased in the developed market economies by more than one-third (in the United States by one-half), surpassing the prewar level, in Czechoslovakia for the same period production increased probably by less than one-third in terms of comparable physical volume (index of gross value of output, with its upward bias, rose by just one-third), and in 1958 still remained below the prewar level.

According to the latest plans, collectivization should be completed in Czechoslovakia by 1960. But even when this transition period is over, and when investments in agriculture are directed more toward the expansion of production than toward the class struggle, as is the case at present, it remains to be seen whether collective farming is superior to individual farming. The recurring experiments in directing Soviet agriculture may be evidence of the difficulties experienced by a centrally planned economy in forcing agriculture—so subject to nature's freakish ways, to which men have to adapt themselves—into a rigid plan. This process probably has a still more valid objection in a small country with intensive farming than in a vast, extensive agricultural area like the Soviet one. Furthermore, it remains to be seen whether an individual farmer's love of the soil and his extreme diligence can, in Czechoslovakia, be compensated by a new collective discipline and responsibility.

Chapter 5

TRANSPORTATION

1. General Trends

As in many other European countries, transportation in Czechoslovakia suffered much during World War II. In the first postwar years, a fairly large share of the national resources was allocated to the transport system, and this trend continued, after the introduction of comprehensive central planning in 1948, until 1953. The number of persons employed in transportation increased from 184,000 in 1948 to 230,000 in 1953. Gross fixed investments went up from 1,857 million Kčs in 1949 to 3,360 million in 1957 (at 1957 constant prices, in 1953 currency units; including investments in the system of communications). Between 1953 and 1957 the increase in manpower was much slower: in the latter year, there were 259,000 persons employed in transportation, only 29,000 more than in 1953.[1] The yearly flow of gross fixed investments to transportation and communications, at 1957 constant prices, was reduced to 3,179 million Kčs in 1957, i.e., 181 million less than in 1953. Over the nine years from 1948 to 1957, the number of persons working in transportation increased by 41 per cent, and capital assets (basic funds at 1955 replacement costs [see Chapter 8, Section 3]) increased by approximately 16 per cent.[2] The traffic increased, however, in the over-all average, by some 160 per cent. The capacity of rolling stock and of other transport installations and the working capacity of transport workers and employees seem to have been very overstrained.

The following tabulation shows the pattern of traffic in 1957, and the corresponding percentage increases over 1948:

[1] Data from *SRRC*, 1958, Table 11.17; excluding apprentices.

[2] This percentage is derived from a weighted average for freight and passenger transportation. It should be pointed out that the depreciation of assets, which is not adequately reflected in statistics on the basic funds, was necessarily higher in transportation than in other branches of the economy. The proportional *share* of transportation in total basic funds in the national economy *decreased* between 1948 and 1957 (see Table 8.11). All data on investments in transportation are from *SRRC*, 1958, Table 6.4.

Transportation	Passenger		Freight	
	Million Net Passenger-km	Percentage Increase over 1948	Million Net Ton-km	Percentage Increase over 1948
Rail	19,048	27	35,291	180
Highway	9,508	304	1,302	260
River	20	0	1,604	155
Ocean	—	—	1,198ᵃ	—
Air	135	145	5	64

ᵃ Million ton-miles.

Railways remain by far the most important means of transportation, and freight traffic is developing much faster than passenger traffic; this seems to be a common characteristic for all centrally planned economies.

2. Rail, Highway, Water, and Air Traffic

a) *Rail.* The total length of railway lines on Czechoslovak territory increased from 13,096 km in 1948 to 13,168 km in 1957. No data on rolling stock have been published. According to unofficial information, the rolling stock is not sufficient for the present traffic load, and the modernization of railways has been very limited. The low percentage of electrified railway lines (0.8 per cent in 1948, 2.1 per cent in 1957) seems to corroborate this information.[3]

In 1948, 74.4 million tons of freight were transported; in 1957, 159.9 million tons; and in 1958, 174.4 million tons. The average transport distance for freight increased from 191.8 net km in 1948 to 247.4 km in 1957. (In terms of tariff-km the increase was from 168.8 km in 1948 to 220.8 km in 1957.)

International railway traffic has no great importance (it may have decreased as compared with 1948; the low in international freight traffic was reached in 1953). In 1957, international traffic accounted for 17 per cent of total freight traffic by rail. The traffic in 1957 was as follows (in millions of tariff ton-km):

Total freight traffic	35.3
Exports by rail	2.1
Imports by rail	1.6
International transit	2.4

Thus the increase in freight traffic was brought about by higher internal traffic. The longer average transport distance and the faster rise of the net ton-km index, as compared with the index of industrial production between 1948 and 1957 (280 as compared with 270 in terms of gross

[3] It is planned to accelerate electrification of railway lines. The plans for this have been examined in the *Economic Survey of Europe*, 1958. According to data in *SRRC*, 1959, Table 11.1, electrified railway lines increased to 4.6 per cent in 1958.

value of production, and less in terms of net value), seem to indicate an increased mobility of goods in Czechoslovakia.

The number of paying passengers carried by rail increased from 415 million in 1948 to 541 million in 1957 and to 537 million in 1958. Contrary to the trend in freight transportation, the average transport distance for passengers decreased from 36.1 net km in 1948 to 35.2 km in 1957. In the author's opinion, this indicates a greater number of short daily journeys to and from work, and a smaller number of long-distance journeys for pleasure.

An international comparison of the index of railway traffic based on passenger-km and ton-km is to be found in Table 5.1. With the exception of passenger traffic in Austria, railway traffic increased in the listed market economies more slowly than it did in Czechoslovakia and other centrally planned countries. One factor affecting transport in the Western countries

TABLE 5.1—RAILWAY TRANSPORTATION, COMPARISON BY COUNTRIES

(Passenger figures in billion passenger-km)

(Freight figures in billion ton-km)

Country	1957 Figures	Index					
		1937	1948	1953	1956	1957	1958
		PASSENGERS					
Czechoslovakia	19.05	45	100	106	111	113	114*
Austria	5.90	57	100	120	137	140	...
France	32.63	88	100	85	101	107	...
United Kingdom ...	36.36	101	100	98	101	108	...
United States	41.7	60	100	77	69	63	...
Hungary	10.22	43	100	184	159	179	...
Poland	38.26	...	100	176	184	188	...
USSR	153.4	93	100	121	145	157	...
Yugoslavia	7.91	46	100	98	118	120	...
		FREIGHT					
Czechoslovakia	39.54	78	100	184	240	277	299*
Austria	7.59	81	100	103	143	148	...
France	53.71	77	100	98	122	130	...
United Kingdom ...	34.14	83	100	105	99	96	...
United States	906.9	57	100	95	102	97	...
Hungary	9.49	69	100	182	181	211	...
Poland	55.25	...	100	157	185	196	...
USSR	1,212.8	106	100	238	322	362	...
Yugoslavia	12.98	53	100	118	160	175	...

Data for Czechoslovakia are from *SRRC*, 1957 and 1958; for other countries from various issues of the U.N. *Statistical Yearbook*. Index numbers were calculated by the author.

with the highest economic development was a considerable shift from rail to highway, air, and inland water transportation. In Czechoslovakia, such a shift has so far been much slower.

b) Highway. Total length of public roads (excluding local roads) increased from 70,037 km in 1946 to 71,530 km in 1957, or only by 2 per cent over a period of 11 years. The Czechoslovak road system seems to have been much less developed and much less improved than the road system in Western market economies.

In 1948, 24.8 million tons of goods[4] were carried by public highway transportation; in 1957, 109 million; and in 1958, 107 million. The number of paying passengers carried by public highway transportation (except municipal) increased from 293 million in 1948[5] to 894 million in 1957, and to 974 million in 1958. In state highway transportation, the average distance of passenger journeys decreased from 11.5 km in 1948 to 10.6 km in 1957. Like the rail situation, this seems to indicate the increasing number of daily trips to and from work.

Private motoring increased in Czechoslovakia much more slowly than in the developed Western market economies; in the general pattern of Czechoslovak transportation it has not yet reached any great importance. (Number of passenger cars will be discussed in Chapter 9, Section 4.)

c) Ocean shipping. Until 1952, Czechoslovakia had no seagoing fleet. In later years, merchant shipping developed as follows:

	1952	1953	1954	1955	1956	1957	1958	June 1959
Number of seagoing ships under the Czechoslovak flag	1	1	3	3	3	3	5	7
Thousand gross registered tons	6.6	6.6	17.3	17.3	17.3	17.3	40.5	61.2
Shipping, in million ton-miles	0.1	—[a]	0.4	1.2	1.3	1.2	...	...

[a] Ship all year under repair.

Although seaborne shipping, in international comparison, is of very limited importance, its increase is remarkable for a landlocked country.

d) Traffic on inland waterways. Total length of navigable inland waterways on Czechoslovak territory increased from 458 km in 1948 to 510 km in 1957. No data on the number and tonnage of river ships have been published recently. In 1948, 0.9 million tons of cargo were carried by river shipping; in 1957, 2.9 million; and in 1958, 3.2 million. The

---

[4] Of this total, 20.9 million tons were by private haulers and 3.8 million by state enterprise. From 1952 on, there were no private haulers.

[5] Of this, 87 million passengers were carried by private haulers and 206 million by state transportation. There was no private highway passenger transportation from 1949 on.

average transport distance for cargo decreased from 680 km in 1948 to 547.8 km in 1957. This may indicate that transportation between Czechoslovakia and the seaports decreased, and that river transportation on Czechoslovak territory was more intensified. In 1948, river shipping carried 2.4 million passengers (mostly pleasure trips); in 1957, only 2 million.

e) Air traffic. The internal air routes in 1948 in Czechoslovakia totaled 3.6 thousand km; in 1957, only 2.1 thousand (the low was 1.3 thousand km in 1954). International air routes, served by Czechoslovak state airlines, totaled 19.7 thousand km in 1948, but only 11.7 thousand in 1957 (the lowest point was reached in 1952, 5.2 thousand km).

In 1948, Czechoslovak airlines carried 101,000 passengers and 3.2 thousand tons of cargo; in 1957, 294,000 passengers and 8.2 thousand tons; in 1958, 408,000 passengers and 9.2 thousand tons of cargo.

In spite of the somewhat accelerated growth in very recent years, Czechoslovak air transportation lags much behind Western developments. This can be established with the help of the international comparison of the index of passenger-km and ton-km flown, in Table 5.2. Between 1953 and 1957, Czechoslovak passenger traffic by air increased also less than the Polish or Yugoslav traffic; but the lower starting base of air traffic in these latter two countries has to be considered.

TABLE 5.2—AIR TRANSPORTATION, COMPARISON BY COUNTRIES

(Passenger figures in million passenger-km)

(Cargo figures in million ton-km)

Country	1957 Figures	Index					
		1937	1948	1953	1956	1957	1958
PASSENGERS							
Czechoslovakia	123.7	17	100	134	212	224	318†
France	3,832.9	7	100	203	443	470	...
United Kingdom	3,857.3	9	100	259	379	432	...
United States	50,308.2	8	100	231	351	397	...
Poland	99.1	46	100	172	368	431	...
Yugoslavia	50.9	14	100	310	499	553	...
CARGO							
Czechoslovakia	2.1	9	100	74	83	91	136†
France	81.5	5	100	213	420	434	...
United Kingdom	81.6	5	100	196	287	321	...
United States	868.8	1	100	230	350	376	...

Data from the U.N. *Statistical Yearbook*, 1958. Index numbers were calculated by the author. Data on Czechoslovakia, in *SRRC*, 1959, Table 11.14, are slightly higher than the UN data in the above table (130.7 million passenger-km in 1957, excluding aerotaxi), but for passenger transport the trend shown in both sources is closely correlated.

Chapter 6

EXTERNAL TRADE

1. Czechoslovakia's Dependence on External Trade

The Czechoslovak economy always has been heavily dependent on exports, especially of manufactured goods, and on imports, especially of raw materials. In 1937 total exports amounted to 20 per cent and total imports to 18 per cent of the current national income. (This ratio does not, of course, reflect the real contribution of foreign trade toward the formation of national income.) The corresponding prewar figures for such a "classical" world-trade country as the United Kingdom were only 11 per cent and 19 per cent for exports and imports, respectively. In 1948, Czechoslovak exports amounted to 18 per cent and imports[1] also to 18 per cent of the current national income, while the corresponding figures for the United Kingdom were 17 per cent and 21 per cent. The ratio of external trade to national income of Czechoslovakia, however, would be misleading from 1948 on because, since the introduction of comprehensive central planning and a state monopoly of external trade, export-import prices have been completely divorced from internal price structure, and the Marxist method of calculating national income is different from the Western method.[2] Per capita exports and imports in current dollars, in

[1] Imports excluded UNRRA supplies.

[2] Assuming that the author's estimate of the Czechoslovak national income, analogous to the Western definition "at market prices" (see Chapter 10) is not far from reality, and under the rather arbitrary but perhaps not unrealistic assumption that the foreign trade net subsidy (as described in Section 6 of this chapter) equals export subsidy (surplus receipts from imports of food and finished products roughly equaling surplus expenditure on imports of raw materials), the following ratios can be obtained: in 1957, exports were 12–14 per cent of national income at market prices and imports were 7–8 per cent. From this angle, the ratio of foreign trade to national income in 1957 appears to be below the increasing ratios in the developed market economies, as well as below the corresponding Czechoslovak ratio in 1948, especially in imports. One serious qualification in the above estimates is that they allow only for the gap between the internal and external price levels (foreign trade subsidy) and not for the dissimilar internal price structure in Czechoslovakia (underpricing of basic raw materials and heavy industry products; see Chapter 7, Section 3). It also should be mentioned that the ratio of exports/imports to national income rather than to gross national product was used, because of uncertainty about the magnitude of GNP in Czechoslovakia in prewar as well as in postwar times.

TABLE 6.1—EXTERNAL TRADE
(*Per capita, in current U.S. dollars*)

		1948	1950	1956	1957	1958[a]
Czechoslovakia	Exports	61	63	105	101	112
	Imports	61	61	90	103	100
Austria	Exports	28		121	138	131
	Imports	42		139	159	153
France	Exports	49		104	115	115
	Imports	84		127	139	127
West Germany	Exports	...		145	167	174
	Imports	...		130	146	145
United Kingdom	Exports	132		173	181	186
	Imports	168		205	222	205
United States	Exports	86		113	121	100
	Imports	49		75	76	72
East Germany	Exports		24	83	103	116
	Imports		27	79	92	103
Hungary	Exports		35	51	50	69
	Imports		34	48	70	64
Poland	Exports		25	35	35	37
	Imports		27	37	44	43
USSR	Exports		10	18	22	21
	Imports		8	18	20	21
Yugoslavia	Exports	10		18	21	24
	Imports	15		26	37	38

Data for 1948 (1950 in the case of the Eastern area countries) and for 1956 are from *Economic Survey of Europe*, 1957, Chap. VI, p. 21. Data for 1957 and 1958 were calculated by the author on the basis of official trade figures for the countries concerned and of official exchange rates. Comparability between countries is limited, especially as between centrally planned and market economy countries, in view of dissimilar foreign trade prices and of varying statistical coverage.

[a] Provisional data.

Table 6.1, reflect somewhat better, though not perfectly, the varying dependence on external trade.

At the end of the decade under study, Czechoslovak per capita foreign trade, in terms of current dollar values, was lower than in the developed Western countries, except for per capita imports into the United States (which is to be expected in a country with such great economic resources). Over the period 1948–57, foreign trade developed substantially more slowly than in continental Western Europe, but faster than in the United Kingdom and in the United States (it has to be borne in mind that British and American trade was already very high by 1948 as compared with the European continent).

For reasons explained below, this way of comparing foreign trade in Czechoslovakia and in the Western market economies makes Czechoslovak trade appear less important than it is in reality. To assess correctly Czechoslovakia's place in world trade, a study of the volume of exports and imports and of export-import prices, as well as a further analysis of the value of trade by regions and by groups of goods, is imperative. It would be well to study Sections 2–5 before drawing any conclusions on the basis of Table 6.1.

It also is stressed that, within the centrally planned area, Czechoslovakia continues to have the greatest per capita external trade, as Table 6.1 shows.

2. Value of Exports and Imports by Main Economic Areas; Balance of Visible Trade

From 1948 to 1957, Czechoslovak total *exports* (f.o.b.) rose from $753 million to $1,356 million, or by 80 per cent. In the same time, exports of all market economies in continental Europe (except Finland and Spain) rose, on the average, by 199 per cent, British exports by 46 per cent, and American exports by 65 per cent in current dollar values.

Total imports (c.i.f.) rose in Czechoslovakia from $754 million in 1948 to an estimated value of $1,500 million[3] in 1957, or by approximately 90 per cent; the corresponding increase in c.i.f. imports, in current dollars, was 109 per cent in continental Europe, 36 per cent in the United Kingdom, and 83 per cent in the United States. (The relatively small increase in American and British trade is explainable by the high level in 1948.)

The current dollar values of imports and exports, and the balance of trade (including the switch from the c.i.f. to the f.o.b. basis for imports, according to Czechoslovak statistics), are shown in Table 6.2, divided into trade with the centrally planned and the market economies, with the latter subdivided into trade with non-Communist, underdeveloped countries. An index of the current values of imports and exports, on a comparable 1948 = 100 basis, is to be found in Table 6.3.

The development of Czechoslovak trade was far from equally balanced between exports and imports and between centrally planned economies and market economies.

Imports from other centrally planned countries were rising steadily, but, until 1957, the rise was slower than the increase of Czechoslovak

---

[3] F.o.b. value was $1,385 million—see general remarks for Table 6.2.

TABLE 6.2—CZECHOSLOVAK EXTERNAL TRADE BY MAIN ECONOMIC AREAS

(*In million U.S. dollars, at current prices*)

	1948	1950	1951	1952	1953	1954	1955	1956	1957	1958
Total imports ..	754	639	897	876	879	933	1,053	1,185	1,385	1,357
Total exports ..	753	779	845	874	994	1,005	1,176	1,387	1,356	1,513
Balance	– 1	140	–52	– 2	115	72	123	202	–29	156
TRADE WITH CENTRALLY PLANNED ECONOMIES										
Imports	297	486	509	630	774	751	803	899	883	1,065
Exports	280	345	538	621	694	698	745	780	970	957
Balance	17	61	–29	9	80	53	58	119	–87	108
TRADE WITH MARKET ECONOMIES										
Imports	474	294	359	255	185	235	308	405	415	400
Exports	456	373	336	244	220	254	373	488	473	448
Balance	–18	79	–23	–11	35	19	65	83	58	48
TRADE WITH UNDERDEVELOPED COUNTRIES OF MARKET ECONOMIES										
Imports	89	...	...	...	55	83	131	131	128	135
Exports	123	...	...	...	71	99	171	235	200	192
Balance	34	...	...	...	16	16	40	104	72	57

All data are converted at the official exchange rate—50 Kčs: $1 in 1948 and 7.20 Kčs: $1 in all other years. Data for 1948 (except for underdeveloped countries) are from *Měsíční přehled zahraničního obchodu*, December 1948; figures refer to special trade, in terms "free at the Czechoslovak border," corresponding roughly to f.o.b. exports and c.i.f. imports.

Data for 1950–57 (except for underdeveloped countries) are from *SRRC*, 1958, and for 1958 from *Statistické zprávy*, No. 2, 1959. They include re-export and switch. All figures are in terms "free at the border of the supplying country," corresponding roughly to f.o.b. exports and f.o.b. imports. Therefore, the import figures for 1950–58 especially are not comparable with the 1948 data. Division of trade between centrally planned economies and market economies was calculated by the author on the basis of trade with individual countries within the central planning area: Albania, Bulgaria, East Germany, Hungary, Poland, Rumania, the USSR, the China mainland, North Korea, North Vietnam, Mongolia, and Yugoslavia.

All data on trade with underdeveloped market economies are from *Statistický obzor*, No. 3, 1959. They cover "formerly dependent (non-Communist) countries" in Africa and Asia; possibly a small amount of trade with underdeveloped countries in South America. These data, including the 1948 import figures, are in terms "free at the border of the supplying country," including re-export and switch. The 1948 imports exclude UNRRA supplies. The 1953–58 export figures exclude military aid and possibly part of the economic aid granted by Czechoslovakia (especially to North Korea and Hungary).

exports to the area. In 1957, these imports jumped suddenly. This was due to a sudden increase in imports from the USSR (by $145 million). This turned the traditional Czechoslovak surplus in trade with the USSR into a deficit of $142 billion, and the previous surplus in trade with the whole Eastern area into a deficit of $87 billion (due in part also to a decrease in export prices, as will be discussed below). In 1958, this trend was reversed again: imports from the USSR were reduced (see Table 6.4), and Czechoslovakia again had a surplus, of $45 million in trade with the USSR, and of $108 million in trade with the whole central planning area.

TABLE 6.3—INDEX NUMBERS OF VALUE AND VOLUME OF CZECHOSLOVAK
IMPORTS AND EXPORTS
1948 = 100

*(Index of value based on yearly totals at current prices; index of volume based on yearly totals
at constant 1955 prices)*

	General		Centrally Planned Economies		Market Economies	
Year	Value	Volume	Value	Volume	Value	Volume
		IMPORTS				
1949	106	115	...	145	...	94
1950	94	112	128	167	72	76
1951	132	131	199	224	87	68
1952	129	133	231	247	62	57
1953	129	144	257	283	45	51
1954	137	159	259	306	57	60
1955	154	176	276	313	75	84
1956	174	197	289	328	99	110
1957	203	233	359	409	101	115
1958	199	248ᵃ	354	425ᵃ	97	131ᵃ
		EXPORTS				
1949	107	117	...	136	...	101
1950	104	139	137	168	82	112
1951	112	140	171	198	74	87
1952	116	152	212	241	54	72
1953	132	180	260	296	48	75
1954	133	189	253	293	56	94
1955	156	227	270	329	82	135
1956	184	269	303	369	107	179
1958	201	295ᵃ	359	449ᵃ	98	174ᵃ

Index numbers of import-export values have been calculated on the basis of dollar values in Table 6.2. The 1948 statistics, however, are not comparable with those for later years, the main difference being the c.i.f. basis for imports in 1948 and the "free border of supplying country" basis for imports in later years. In order to remove this serious source of incomparability, the official c.i.f. import figures for 1948 have been reduced to the "free border of supplying country" basis, as officially used in present-day statistics, as follows (in million U.S. dollars): total imports, 754 to 681; imports from centrally planned countries, 280 to 270; imports from market economies, 474 to 681. The difference is relatively small for imports from centrally planned countries, since the most important countries have a common border with Czechoslovakia. The "centrally planned economies" include Yugoslavia. Index numbers of volume are from *SRRC*, 1958, Table 14.1, p. 315 (their construction has been described by J. Havlíček in *Statistický obzor*, No. 5, 1959).

ᵃ Obtained by linking the official 1953 = 100 index from *SRRC*, 1959, Table 14.1, with the previous official index, 1948 = 100. It should be stressed that the official Czechoslovak data show an increase in the volume of imports in 1958, whereas the ECE index in the *Economic Survey of Europe*, XI, No. 1, Table 4, "Volume of External Trade of Czechoslovakia," shows a decreasing volume of imports in 1958. Having examined the development of Czechoslovak imports and exports of commodities in physical quantities according to Czechoslovak figures as well as according to the foreign trade statistics of Czechoslovakia's trade partners, the author feels that the official Czechoslovak index of the volume of trade in 1958 comes closer to reality than the ECE index.

TABLE 6.4—CZECHOSLOVAK IMPORTS AND EXPORTS BY PRINCIPAL
TRADING COUNTRIES

(In million Kčs)

Country		1948[a]	1953	1954	1955	1956	1957	1958
		CENTRALLY PLANNED ECONOMIES						
Europe:								
Albania	Imp.	0	21	11	14	24	33	30
	Exp.	0.4	48	45	41	36	43	69
Bulgaria	Imp.	85	146	153	175	229	341	298
	Exp.	112	276	282	312	259	243	261
East Germany..	Imp.	77	438	542	705	851	1,039	1,167
	Exp.	71	441	584	574	1,010	952	1,134
Hungary	Imp.	149	529	558	555	467	528	651
	Exp.	160	507	484	461	424	547	557
Poland	Imp.	292	722	581	548	554	432	515
	Exp.	381	733	607	740	714	563	683
Rumania	Imp.	212	259	271	300	205	192	161
	Exp.	171	794	305	270	252	267	272
USSR	Imp.	848	2,476	2,522	2,631	2,808	3,856	3,253
	Exp.	865	2,313	2,510	2,900	3,085	2,866	3,579
Yugoslavia	Imp.	345	—	16	53	48	42	108
	Exp.	376	0	8	44	97	135	180
Asia:								
China mainland	Imp.	0	401	396	437	478	482	655
	Exp.	1	437	464	415	466	585	786
North Korea ...	Imp.	—	—	—	—	6	8	11
	Exp.	—	33	99	34	90	122	85
Mongolia	Imp.	—	—	—	—	0	9	21
	Exp.	—	—	—	0	0	14	33
North Vietnam .	Imp.	—	—	—	1	32	37	22
	Exp.	—	—	—	30	45	29	32
		MARKET ECONOMIES						
Europe:								
Austria	Imp.	129	113	97	120	155	180	150
	Exp.	222	103	93	135	144	148	140
Belgium and Luxembourg..	Imp.	167	44	52	57	91	81	102
	Exp.	116	44	40	61	83	81	72
Finland	Imp.	17	48	34	59	80	96	74
	Exp.	36	118	121	130	157	166	59
France	Imp.	134	27	54	53	91	92	128
	Exp.	147	36	41	51	64	107	127
Italy	Imp.	129	100	63	61	73	69	91
	Exp.	168	78	74	84	89	107	104
West Germany..	Imp.	42	61	121	119	280	431	445
	Exp.	104	106	127	224	364	395	386

TABLE 6.4—*Concluded*

		1948[a]	1953	1954	1955	1956	1957	1958
Netherlands ...	Imp.	293	82	90	88	135	159	114
	Exp.	348	74	76	110	133	125	102
Switzerland ...	Imp.	257	106	121	144	207	171	197
	Exp.	258	90	142	130	153	160	172
United Kingdom	Imp.	550	167	159	202	193	261	233
	Exp.	196	208	192	163	178	248	211
Turkey	Imp.	99	71	100	148	122	116	126
	Exp.	126	89	110	143	147	159	80
Africa:								
Egypt	Imp.	152	80	132	151	241	199	277
	Exp.	61	68	61	83	72	174	328
America:								
Argentina	Imp.	148	16	50	150	86	41	85
	Exp.	77	30	70	165	82	41	69
Brazil	Imp.	80	56	91	155	144	116	114
	Exp.	65	50	91	162	145	98	105
Canada	Imp.	96	2	6	14	209	11	8
	Exp.	35	17	12	23	40	32	41
United States ..	Imp.	262	0	3	4	5	10	7
	Exp.	168	14	20	25	39	44	54
Australia	Imp.	26	72	65	101	110	176	78
	Exp.	81	19	25	30	33	35	33

Import figures for 1948 and later years are comparable only as to countries having a common border with Czechoslovakia ("free at the Czechoslovak border" and "free at the border of the supplying country" being identical). This applies to most of the centrally planned economies in Europe. Imports from other countries are not comparable between 1948 and later years. Comparability of export figures for 1948 and later years is also limited. See remarks to Table 6.2. Source: *Měsíční přehled zahraničního obchodu 1948, SRRC 1958*, Tables 14.3 and 14.4, *Statistické zprávy* 2/1959.

[a] Original data in 1945 currency units converted into new (1953) currency units at the ratio 6.94:1 (see Section 5 of this chapter).

It is difficult to explain the sudden isolated jump in imports from the USSR in 1957. One of the factors may be that the Soviet Union made a lump payment to Czechoslovakia, in goods, for Czechoslovak uranium ore which had been exported exclusively to the USSR in large quantities since the end of the war. (Czechoslovakia's government has been claiming in recent years that the USSR is paying the world market price for uranium, but previous unofficial reports contradict this.) Another possible explanation is that Czechoslovakia received, like Poland, a certain compensation for trade losses suffered under Stalin, although in Prague this has never been publicized. The small Soviet credit granted to Czechoslovakia for the specific purpose "of developing atomic energy" could not account for such a great jump in Czechoslovak imports.

Czechoslovak exports to the centrally planned area were increasing very fast up to 1957. The slight value decrease in that year was probably due to lower export prices charged by Czechoslovakia (see Section 5). In 1958, Czechoslovak exports to the area, even in terms of the new export prices, increased again considerably.

In trade with the market economies, Czechoslovak imports decreased rapidly until 1953. In 1957 they almost regained the 1948 level, but fell again in 1958. Exports to the market economies showed a similar trend, but since 1953 they rose faster than imports from the area. This was mainly due to the spectacular increase in Czechoslovak exports to the economically underdeveloped countries in Asia and Africa between 1953 and 1956. After a certain decline in 1957 and 1958, a new increase in trade with the underdeveloped countries in Africa and Asia was announced for 1959 by Deputy Minister for Foreign Trade Kocour.

Exports to developed Western countries, after a certain recovery from the 1953 low, started decreasing again in 1958.

Table 6.2 contains the difference between the export and import value, which, however, is not really the balance of trade under the usual Western definition, since the import figures exclude transportation costs from the border of the supplying country. (They correspond roughly to f.o.b. values.) If the import figures were based on the c.i.f. value, as is customary in the West, the balance of trade would appear less favorable, especially with the market economies. (For most centrally planned economies in Europe the "c.i.f." and "f.o.b." values are identical, since these countries have common borders with Czechoslovakia.)

The balance of payments, in view of various financial transfers (including compensation for nationalized foreign investment), would be still less favorable than the balance of trade. Unfortunately no relating figures have been made available since 1948. This is how the balance of trade and the balance of payments compared in 1948 (in million dollars):

	With Centrally Planned Economies	With Market Economies	Total
Surplus of f.o.b. exports over f.o.b. imports	+27	+45	+72
Balance of trade (f.o.b. exports over c.i.f. imports)	+17	−18	− 1
Balance of payments (including all invisible trade items and financial and capital transfers)	...	...	−45

It can be assumed that the export figures in Table 6.2 do not include military aid or part of the economic aid granted by Czechoslovakia.[4]

---

[4] E.g., official statistics on trade with Egypt show a Czechoslovak deficit of $23.5 million in 1956 and of $3.5 million in 1957, although Czechoslovakia granted undis-

The current values of Czechoslovak exports and imports in trade with the principal countries, in terms of Kčs, are to be found in Table 6.4. The way in which development of Czechoslovak trade with Poland and Yugoslavia differs from trade with other centrally planned economies is noteworthy. The decrease in trade with Poland and the increase in trade with East Germany are quite remarkable. In 1957, there was a tendency to balance off the old Czechoslovak surplus with Bulgaria, East Germany, and the USSR (the Czechoslovak deficit with the USSR being more than the balancing off of the old, officially reported surplus). This tendency coincides with preparations to establish new price relations within the so-called Socialist world market (see Section 5). But in 1958, a new Czechoslovak surplus in trade with Eastern Europe started to build up again (and this tendency continued in 1959).

Trade with the market economies listed in Table 6.4 increased, over the period under study, in imports most rapidly with the German Federal Republic, and in exports with the United Arab Republic. In terms of turnover (export value plus import value), in 1958, West Germany was Czechoslovakia's most important trading partner outside the central planning area—although Czechoslovak–West German trade decreased as compared with 1957—followed by the United Kingdom and the United Arab Republic.

Table 6.5 provides a rough check of the reliability of Czechoslovak foreign trade statistics by comparing them with those of its trading partners. It is necessary to allow for the different statistical coverage and the different treatment of cost, insurance, and freight, as well as for possible discrepancies in the dollar conversion ratio and for the time lag between "exports" from the point of view of the supplier and "imports" from the point of view of the buyer. Some specific Czechoslovak definitions, such as exports and imports "free at the border of the supplying country" (referred to in Table 6.5 as f.o.b.), should also be borne in mind. In theory there should not be a great difference between Czechoslovak f.o.b. import figures and the counterpart f.o.b. export figures according to the statistics of the trading partners, provided the statistical coverage is about the same. On the other hand, Czechoslovak f.o.b. export data should be

closed but important military aid to Egypt in 1956 and an economic credit of $56 million early in 1957. Another example is Hungary, which received economic aid from Czechoslovakia, after the 1956 uprising, equivalent to $12 million, and in March 1957 a credit for purchase of goods equivalent to $25 million. Yet 1956 official Czechoslovak statistics, converted to a dollar basis, show a Czechoslovak deficit of $3 million, and 1957 figures show an unexpectedly small surplus of only $3 million in trade with Hungary.

TABLE 6.5—FOREIGN TRADE, COMPARISON OF CZECHOSLOVAKIA AND
MAIN TRADING PARTNERS

(*In million U.S. dollars*)

Country	Imports into Czechoslovakia		Exports from Czechoslovakia	
	1957	1958	1957	1958
CENTRALLY PLANNED ECONOMIES				
USSR	551.3	446.8	385.6	512.1
	534.7	489.6	398.1	497.1
East Germany	140.6	...	118.9	...
	144.3	162.1	132.2	157.5
Hungary	75.8	92.9	78.8	78.3
	73.3	90.4	76.0	77.3
Poland	61.1	...	77.8	...
	60.0	71.5	78.2	94.9
Yugoslavia	8.6	19.5	18.9	27.5
	5.8	13.6	18.9	25.0
MARKET ECONOMIES				
Austria	22.6	18.7	18.8	18.2
	25.0	20.7	20.5	19.4
Belgium and Luxembourg	10.1	11.3	11.4	9.4
	11.2	14.2	11.2	10.0
Finland	13.0	9.3	27.1	8.6
	13.3	10.3	23.0	8.2
France	11.8	17.5	13.8	18.5
	12.8	17.6	14.8	17.6
West Germany	55.0	61.3	49.8	49.0
	59.9	61.8	54.9	53.6
Netherlands	9.9	7.9	16.3	13.9
	22.1	15.9	17.3	14.2
Switzerland	17.3	14.8	16.7	15.3
	23.7	27.4	22.2	23.9
Turkey	19.4	15.1	24.0	12.2
	16.1	17.5	22.1	11.1
United Arab Republic	48.7	54.2	21.4	47.4
	24.2	38.5	27.7	23.9
United Kingdom	14.4	13.2	23.3	19.2
	36.2	32.3	34.4	29.3
United States	2.0	1.6	7.9	7.8
	1.4	1.0	6.4	7.5

The upper row of figures for each country is taken from the statistics of the country concerned, in *Direction of International Trade* (U.N. Statistical Papers, Series T, Vol. X); the second row is taken from Czechoslovak statistics in Table 6.4 (data converted into dollars at the official exchange rate of 7.20 Kčs).

Coverage: special trade for all countries, except the United Kingdom and the United States, which is general trade. Valuation—exports: for other countries, f.o.b.; for Czechoslovakia, free at the Czechoslovak border (analogous to f.o.b.). Valuation—imports: for other countries, c.i.f., except for East Germany and the USSR, which are f.o.b.; for Czechoslovakia, free at the border of the supplying country (analogous to f.o.b.). Attribution by countries: as described in the *Direction of International Trade*; for Czechoslovakia, by country of consignment.

lower than the c.i.f. import figures in the statistics of trading partners, the difference increasing with the distance between Czechoslovakia and the trading country.

In fact, there are no great discrepancies between Czechoslovak and opposite foreign statistics to be discovered in Table 6.5 exceeding those that usually occur among Western statistics, except for trade with Switzerland and the United Kingdom. Even if we allow for different statistical coverage, trade with these countries in 1957 and 1958, according to Czechoslovak statistics, appears to be higher than according to Swiss or British statistics. (Such a discrepancy applies also to Czechoslovak imports from Holland in 1957.) It is noteworthy that no great discrepancy appears, in Table 6.5, in trade with Hungary, Egypt, etc., according to Czechoslovak and foreign statistics. Therefore, if Czechoslovak aid granted to those countries is excluded from Czechoslovak export statistics,[5] it is also excluded from import statistics of the receiving countries.

3. Commodity Pattern of Trade

The pattern of Czechoslovak foreign trade by commodity groups changed very considerably in the ten years under study. The most striking feature is the great rise in the export of machinery and equipment for industry. Its share in total exports rose from 7 per cent before the war to 20 per cent in 1948 and to more than 40 per cent in recent years.

Czechoslovak foreign trade by commodity groups, in terms of current dollar values and in percentages of total imports and exports, can be studied in more detail in Table 6.6. The economic thaw in 1953–55, reflected in decreasing exports of machinery and increasing imports of manufactures for consumption, is noteworthy. Nevertheless, imports of consumer goods—except food—remained quite unimportant throughout the period. Imports of fuel and raw materials, and also of machinery, increased from the centrally planned area only.

Data on imports and exports of most important goods, in physical quantities, are to be found in Table 6.7.

Until 1959, very little information was available on trade by commodities *and* by countries. Only in the official monthly *Statistické zprávy*, No. 12 (December), 1959, have data been published on Czechoslovak exports and imports in 1958, in breakdown by more or less detailed commodity groups and by all European countries. They are reproduced in Table 6.8, in a synoptical manner, for all European centrally planned economies including the USSR, for Yugoslavia, and for six of the most

[5] Such a possibility was mentioned in the remarks in Table 6.2.

TABLE 6.6—CZECHOSLOVAK IMPORTS AND EXPORTS
BY PRINCIPAL COMMODITY GROUPS

(Free at the border of the supplying country)

	1953	1954	1955	1956	1957	1958
IN MILLION DOLLARS, CURRENT PRICES						
Imports:						
Machinery, equipment, and tools	123	111	139	203	260	253
Fuel, raw materials	477	493	564	653	748	743
Cattle for breeding, other animals	1	1	0	1	1	0
Foodstuffs, including raw materials for food industry	265	306	305	292	322	313
Consumers' manufactures	13	22	43	37	55	47
Total	879	933	1,053	1,185	1,385	1,357
Exports:						
Machinery, equipment, and tools	421	387	511	559	555	656
Fuel, raw materials	366	390	462	512	463	471
Cattle for breeding, other animals	0	0	0	0	1	1
Foodstuffs, including raw materials for food industry	85	82	72	102	92	107
Consumers' manufactures	121	146	131	213	235	279
Total	994	1,005	1,176	1,387	1,356	1,513
IN PER CENT OF TOTAL CURRENT VALUE						
Imports:						
Machinery, equipment, and tools	14.1	11.9	13.3	17.2	18.7	18.7
Fuel, raw materials	54.2	52.8	53.6	55.0	54.0	54.7
Cattle for breeding, other animals	0.1	0.1	0.0	0.0	0.1	0.0
Foodstuffs, including raw materials for food industry	30.1	32.8	29.0	24.6	23.3	23.1
Consumers' manufactures	1.5	2.4	4.1	3.2	3.9	3.5
Total	100	100	100	100	100	100
Exports:						
Machinery, equipment, and tools	42.4	38.5	43.5	40.3	40.8	43.3
Fuel, raw materials	36.8	38.8	39.3	36.9	34.8	31.1
Cattle for breeding, other animals	0.0	0.0	0.0	0.0	0.1	0.0
Foodstuffs, including raw materials for food industry	8.6	8.2	6.1	7.4	6.9	7.1
Consumers' manufactures	12.2	14.5	11.1	15.4	17.4	18.4
Total	100	100	100	100	100	100

Data are from *SRRC*, 1958 and 1959, Table 14.2. Dollar values are obtained by applying the official exchange rate, 7.20 Kčs = $1.00. Group values do not add up to total value of imports and exports because of rounding.

important trading partners of Czechoslovakia in Western Europe (Austria, Belgium, France, West Germany, Switzerland, and the United Kingdom)—for all important commodity groups.

It is seen from this table that in Czechoslovakia's European trade most of the exports of heavy industry products, such as machinery and equipment for industry, complete factories, instruments, motorcars, tractors, ships, cables, etc., go to Eastern Europe, including the USSR. Czechoslovak exports to Western Europe concentrate more on consumer goods and special kinds of food such as sugar, malt and hops, and eggs, although in 1958 a considerable amount of consumer goods such as textiles, shoes, etc., were exported to the USSR and East Germany. Coal and coke, according to these statistics, are exported to both East and West (although exports to Eastern Europe probably are mainly coke), as are chemicals and nonferrous metals (antimony may be an important item in exports

TABLE 6.7—MAIN CZECHOSLOVAK IMPORTS AND EXPORTS OF COMMODITIES

(In thousand tons, unless otherwise specified)

	1953	1955	1956	1957	1958
	IMPORTS				
Hard coal	4,785	4,066	3,451	2,251	2,576
Oil and oil products	605	1,060	1,176	1,609	1,645
Iron ore	3,038	3,926	3,903	4,923	5,163
Copper	49*,ᵃ	...	27*	...	...
Aluminum	14*,ᵃ	...	18*	...	...
Sulfur	15	28	25	28	38
Sulfuric acid	6	23	16	13	10
Phosphates (as P_2O_5)	51	100	92	96	122
Potash fertilizers (as K_2O)	125	158	186	187	217
Nitrogenous fertilizers (as nitrogen)	16	30	32	17	13
Natural rubber	26	30	38	44	49
Synthetic rubber	13	13	14	9	12
Cotton	61	71	78	83	89
Wool	11	16	18	21	20
Jute	9	11	11	11	14
Hides	14	18	18	22	36
Wheat	569	816	661	974	964
Maize	127	218	301	38	193
Meat, including livestock	35	77	55	54	92
Butter	15	18	6	11	8
Rice	30	40	57	81	74
Coffee	4.3	3.5	3.9	4.5	5.4
Cocoa beans	6.7	8.9	8.4	8.3	9.9
Fruit	108	133	110	106	116
Vegetables	36	46	57	92	63
Tobacco	9	10	13	13	14
Passenger cars (*units*)	7	1,476	5,620	10,549	9,538

TABLE 6.7—*Concluded*

	1953	1955	1956	1957	1958
	EXPORTS				
Hard coal	415	549	556	734	1,506
Brown coal	914	1,177	1,273	1,540	1,266
Coke	1,259	1,198	1,256	1,159	1,045
Steel pipes	203	179	183	145	175
Rolled steel	248	606	534	462	525
Metal-working machines (*units*)	5,427	5,489	7,911	8,481	10,579
Diesel engines (*units*)	4,684	5,173	7,834	10,091	11,482
Dynamos (*thousand units*)	16	10	20	15	...
Wheeled tractors (*units*)	5,947	8,865	9,888	14,445	15,192
Trucks (*units*)	4,554	2,527	2,486	2,602	4,829
Passenger cars (*units*)	6,167	9,441	14,718	15,858	25,037
Motorcycles (*thousand units*)	33	32	51	80	109
Paper	56	59	56	63	66
Cotton tissues (*million meters*)	54	82	124	127	116
Wool tissues (*million meters*)	2.6	2.1	4.6	5.3	3.5
Silk tissues (*million meters*)	3.8	1.8	7.2	8.3	8.8
Leather shoes (*million pairs*)	2.1	2.8	12.0	10.5	14.0
Rubber shoes (*million pairs*)	8.7	10.0	13.9	13.2	13.9
Beer (*thousand hectoliters*)	124	212	226	247	370

Figures from *SRRC*, 1958 and 1959, Table 14.5, and *Statistické zprávy*, No. 2, 1959.
  [a] 1950.

to Western Europe, within metal exports, and possibly silver and gold).

Main Czechoslovak imports from Eastern Europe in 1958 were metal ores, food (grain and butter from the USSR, meat from Hungary and Poland), and fuel (oil from the USSR, coal from Poland and the USSR). The USSR also supplied a considerable amount of textile materials. Main Czechoslovak imports from Western Europe were chemicals, especially pharmaceutical products; a certain amount of machinery was imported from both Western and Eastern Europe (from East Germany and the USSR).

Value data in Table 6.8 may be somewhat distorted by variations in prices charged or paid to various countries for the same commodities (see Section 4 of this chapter).

But recently new information on physical quantities of the main commodities imported and exported have been made available for 1955–58, with corresponding percentage shares of individual countries in Czechoslovak imports and exports of each commodity. In contrast to the above-mentioned data on the value pattern of trade, this information covers not only Europe but the whole world, including such important non-European trading partners of Czechoslovakia as the mainland of China and the United Arab Republic. In Table 6.9, a substantial portion of these statis-

TABLE 6.8—PATTERN OF CZECHOSLOVAK TRADE WITH EUROPEAN CENTRALLY PLANNED ECONOMIES AND ITS PRINCIPAL PARTNERS AMONG EUROPEAN MARKET ECONOMIES, BY IMPORTANT COMMODITY GROUPS, IN 1958

(In million Kčs, free at the Czechoslovak border [exports] and free at the border of the supplying country [imports])

	Albania	Bulgaria	East Germany	Hungary	Poland	Rumania	USSR	Yugoslavia	Austria	Belgium and Luxembourg	France	West Germany	Switzerland	U.K.
CZECHOSLOVAK EXPORTS														
Metal-working machines and equipment	1.3	6.2	42.2	28.3	36.6	9.2	152.6	14.6	2.1	1.0	2.0	8.1	...	3.4
Diesel engines and aggregates	1.7	2.2	...	...	...	...	101.7	...	...	...	...	...	...	...
Machinery and equipment:														
For food industry	...	1.3	2.3	...	...	1.5	19.3	...	...	...	...	...	...	...
For light industry	...	6.8	14.3	4.9	10.1	5.6	50.6	...	...	...	2.6	...	...	...
For building-materials industry	1.1	...	8.6	...	...	...	...	...	...	...	...	...	...	...
Complete factories	5.9	3.1	10.0	7.3	49.7	29.5	425.7	4.3	...	...	...	...	...	...
Instruments, tools, ball bearings, etc.	...	14.7	21.2	12.8	25.2	10.7	45.3	8.7	...	...	...	...	...	...
Railway rolling stock and equipment	...	...	5.9	...	...	...	126.5	...	...	...	...	...	...	...
Tractors and machinery for agriculture	...	6.4	23.3	26.9	36.9	1.5	...	22.6	...	...	11.2	...	1.4	...
Motorcars and spare parts	11.8	19.6	49.2	35.6	85.3	6.0	151.5	16.4	8.1	3.7	1.3	9.7	4.6	...
Motorcycles and spare parts	...	17.4	73.7	...	57.1	3.3	19.5	...	...	0.6	...	...	...	...
Ships	...	...	...	...	...	...	...	...	...	...	...	...	...	...
Cables	...	...	...	...	...	...	109.0	...	...	...	...	...	...	...
Coal and coke	...	13.0[a]	212.2	104.0	...	46.3	...	...	59.0	...	8.7	57.2	...	...
Ferrous metals, including semiproducts	9.9	44.5	114.4	...	52.4	52.4	...	19.2	14.0	6.1	...	81.8	...	...
Nonferrous ores and metals	...	7.6	23.2	12.4	4.9	3.9	18.1	7.1	4.8	2.3	8.2	34.5	15.7	17.7
Chemicals, dyestuffs, varnish, etc.	...	3.8	3.5	...	10.0	...	...	...	...	...	...	...	...	2.0
Rubber goods	9.2	4.1	...	...	14.7	...	...	...	...	1.9	4.6	...	...	...
Building materials	...	...	...	...	...	6.7	...	...	2.8	0.7	...	15.7	3.7	...
Lumber	...	...	...	...	...	...	...	...	...	...	20.4	...	...	...
Timber and wood products for production	...	...	7.8	30.6	...	...	...	...	...	...	...	33.0	6.4	27.3
Paper and wood pulp	3.2	10.5	4.6	13.1	4.4	...	...	3.4[b]	...	3.0[b]	8.3	13.9	3.1	9.7
Raw materials and semifinished products for textile industry	...	9.3	...	...	19.9[c]	...	...	...	...	...	...	...	...	...
Grain (excluding seed)	...	...	...	...	...	...	...	...	10.0	2.0	7.0	1.9	1.9	3.4
Meat and meat products	...	...	...	...	...	...	...	...	...	...	...	...	12.3	5.5
Eggs	...	...	...	...	...	...	...	...	1.1	...	2.9	20.3	9.4	9.3
Hops and malt	...	...	...	6.3[d]	...	...	...	...	...	...	...	...	...	...
Sugar (presumably refined only)	...	...	38.9	4.3	...	6.1	100.7	13.4	5.2	13.2	12.8	19.1	22.4	21.9
Beer	...	...	12.7	...	...	...	12.9	...	...	...	...	1.8	21.9	4.2
Tissues (except technical for production)	1.5	16.1	74.8	11.0	...	7.3	50.7	14.2	...	4.1	...	9.7	4.4	...
Readymade wear and underwear	1.2	5.2	18.7	...	...	...	149.4	3.2	...	1.9	...	2.9	1.1	1.1
Shoes, all kinds	...	1.2	43.1	...	38.0	...	309.0	...	...	4.5	...	3.2	...	...
Consumers' glass, china, ceramics	...	...	6.3	6.3	...	...	44.2	...	...	4.4	5.7	1.3	5.0	5.0
Furniture	...	...	15.1	6.2	...	...	43.2	...	2.0	...	1.1	...	...	...
Pharmaceutical products	1.0	1.0	...	1.4	2.9	2.9	33.5	...	...	...	...	...	4.1	4.2
Household machinery, apparatus, and equipment	4.1	4.1	37.0	3.8	40.3	9.1	24.0	5.8	1.7	1.5	...	...	...	...
Total exports	68.7	261.3	1,134.5	556.7	682.9	272.3	3,579.0	179.6	140.5	72.2	126.8	386.4	172.2	210.8

TABLE 6.8—Concluded

CZECHOSLOVAK IMPORTS

	Albania	Bulgaria	East Germany	Hungary	Poland	Rumania	USSR	Yugoslavia	Austria	Belgium and Luxembourg	France	West Germany	Switzerland	U.K.
Metal-working machinery and equipment	...	...	54.8	...	9.6	...	20.9	...	3.7	1.2	...	17.9	12.5	...
Power production machinery and equipment	...	...	...	...	...	...	56.0	...	11.6	4.1	1.9	8.9	...	...
Light industry machinery and equipment	...	...	39.5	...	...	...	24.3	...	...	...	...	9.5	...	...
Baggers and road-building machinery	...	...	19.3	...	11.3	...	12.5	...	...	...	...	...	...	9.2
Telecommunication apparatus and equipment	...	...	12.1	5.5	...	...	...	...	...	...	...	...	...	...
Typewriters, calculating and other office machines	...	...	39.6	...	...	...	...	...	...	...	...	...	...	...
Complete factories	...	...	39.0	...	14.2	...	36.1	...	...	...	...	...	...	...
Instruments, tools, ball-bearings, etc.	...	...	74.8	...	...	...	26.3	...	...	...	...	...	...	...
Railway rolling stock and equipment	...	25.7	63.0	7.3	...	...	...	...	...	...	...	...	...	...
Tractors and agricultural machinery	...	5.5	7.1	...	...	3.5	...	...	3.4	4.3	2.3	...	12.3	...
Motorcars, including spare parts	...	...	76.8	62.2	...	...	62.9	...	...	...	...	1.6	...	...
Hard coal	...	...	...	25.7	192.8	...	37.2	...	...	...	12.0	...	...	...
Oil and oil products	4.9	...	4.8	4.9	...	26.9	111.7	...	...	...	...	...	...	...
Metal ores and metals, including semiproducts	19.5	48.2	...	220.4	10.6	11.3	253.9	18.7	84.9	23.8	32.5	229.8	37.8	12.6
Chemicals, dyestuffs, varnish, etc.	...	...	108.4	...	...	...	731.4	4.0	10.1	3.3	5.5	38.9	...	...
Fertilizers	...	...	25.5	6.0	...	...	31.6	...	...	...	...	...	...	...
Rubber and rubber goods	...	...	...	...	...	...	34.3	...	...	...	1.9	...	...	...
Timber and wood products for production	...	...	...	...	...	5.7	49.8	1.1	...	...	...	7.8	...	...
Textile raw materials and semiproducts	...	...	30.3	...	...	2.6	69.6	...	1.8	...	...	5.5	...	...
Tobacco	1.3	47.3	...	...	...	...	350.3	5.4	...	34.7	20.8	1.4	12.9	37.1
Grain (excluding seed)	...	...	...	...	...	6.8	636.1	...	...	...	...	...	5.2	...
Oil seeds	...	...	...	...	...	...	18.7	...	...	...	...	...	9.3	...
Slaughter animals	...	...	...	13.8	...	...	...	4.1	...	...	...	...	...	...
Meat and meat products	...	43.8	...	63.7	35.5	5.5	27.5	...	...	...	...	...	...	54.3
Butter	...	...	...	3.8	5.5	...	49.4	...	...	...	...	...	...	...
Fish and fish products	...	...	...	...	3.0	...	22.7	...	...	...	...	...	...	...
Vegetable oils for human consumption	...	...	...	22.7	...	...	15.2	...	...	...	...	...	...	...
Wine	...	9.7	...	3.9	...	...	79.5	...	...	...	...	...	...	...
Household machinery and equipment	...	...	33.6	18.6	...	...	...	...	...	...	...	1.8	5.3	...
Pharmaceutical products	...	...	...	...	...	...	...	...	...	...	1.6	4.2	6.6	6.3
Total imports	30.3	298.3	1,166.4	651.0	514.9	161.0	3,253.3	108.5	149.7	101.6	128.1	444.7	196.9	233.1

All data are from *Statistické zprávy*, No. 12, 1959. Some less important groups of goods have been omitted from this table. The ellipsis (...) indicates that corresponding figures cannot be found in the original source. In most cases this can be interpreted as exports to, or imports from, the countries concerned being of limited importance but not necessarily negligible. The official Czechoslovak foreign trade classification of goods, as used above, lists investment goods first, followed by raw materials, and then food and consumers' goods. Since the above lists of goods are not exhaustive, figures do not sum up to total imports and exports respectively.

a Coke only. b Paper only. c Malt only. d Hops only.

TABLE 6.9—CZECHOSLOVAK COMMODITY TRADE BY PRINCIPAL RECEIVING
AND SUPPLYING COUNTRIES

Commodity	Unit	Receiving Country	Quantity	Per Cent Share
EXPORTS, 1958				
Metal-working machinery	Units	Total	10,579	100
		USSR	1,842	17
		China Mainland	1,607	15
		Poland	860	8
		East Germany	790	7
		Hungary	537	5
Baggers (presumably very large types)	Units	Total	152	100
		USSR	50	33
		China Mainland	29	19
		Hungary	13	9
		Poland	11	7
Diesel engines and aggregates	Units	Total	11,482	100
		China Mainland	5,914	52
		United Arab Republic.	1,161	10
		USSR	848	7
Electric motors (presumably 25-kw and over, including very large types)	Units	Total	31,726	100
		Poland	15,985	50
		USSR	5,030	16
		United Arab Republic.	2,186	7
		Turkey	955	3
		China Mainland	794	3
Complete factories	Million Kčs*	Total	1,172	100
		USSR	559	48
		China Mainland	252	22
		United Arab Republic.	142	12
Wheeled tractors	Units	Total	15,192	100
		Poland	3,131	21
		China Mainland	2,769	18
		Yugoslavia	1,835	12
		France	1,155	8
		East Germany	1,093	7
Trucks	Units	Total	4,829	100
		USSR	2,327	48
		China Mainland	775	16
		Bulgaria	260	5
		United Arab Republic.	201	4
Passenger cars	Units	Total	25,037	100
		East Germany	6,996	28
		USSR	3,519	14
		Austria	1,893	8
		Hungary	1,733	7
		West Germany	1,611	6

TABLE 6.9—*Continued*

Commodity	Unit	Receiving Country	Quantity	Per Cent Share
Motorcycles	1,000 units	Total	109	100
		East Germany	32	29
		Poland	31	28
		USSR	13	12
		Bulgaria	11	10
Bicycles	1,000 units	Total	170	100
		United States	56	33
		Poland	46	27
		Switzerland	13	8
		North Vietnam	10	6
Hard coal	1,000 metric tons	Total	1,506	100
		East Germany	727	48
		Hungary	311	21
		Austria	236	16
		Rumania	149	10
Brown coal	1,000 metric tons	Total	1,266	100
		West Germany	958	76
		Austria	192	15
Coke	1,000 metric tons	Total	1,045	100
		East Germany	529	51
		Hungary	221	21
		Rumania	124	12
Steel pipes	1,000 metric tons	Total	175	100
		USSR	84	48
		China Mainland	30	17
		Rumania	16	9
		Poland	10	6
Rolled steel	1,000 metric tons	Total	525	100
		Hungary	131	25
		West Germany	83	16
		Poland	55	10
		Argentina	35	7
		India	32	6
Sheet glass	1,000 square meters	Total	12,247	100
		Italy	1,667	14
		Canada	1,237	10
		United States	1,131	9
		Netherlands	1,095	9
		Yugoslavia	742	6
Consumers' china and ceramics	Metric tons	Total	9,789	100
		Italy	1,396	14
		USSR	902	9
		United Arab Republic.	801	8
		Rumania	563	6
		Austria	595	5

TABLE 6.9—*Continued*

Commodity	Unit	Receiving Country	Quantity	Per Cent Share
Lumber	1,000 cubic meters	Total	616	100
		United Kingdom	93	15
		Netherlands	87	14
		Italy	86	14
		United Arab Republic.	78	13
		France	77	12
Paper	1,000 metric tons	Total	66	100
		United Arab Republic.	10	15
		United Kingdom	6	9
		Hungary	5	8
		Belgium	3	5
		Italy	2	3
Cotton fabrics	Million meters	Total	114	100
		East Germany	14	12
		Greece	5	4
		Bulgaria	4	4
		Yugoslavia	4	4
		West Germany	4	4
Wool fabrics	1,000 meters	Total	3,484	100
		USSR	715	21
		Belgium	287	8
		East Germany	261	7
		Yugoslavia	243	7
		Iran	199	6
Silk fabrics	1,000 meters	Total	7,455	100
		East Germany	1,127	15
		Burma	1,001	13
		Poland	777	10
		Italy	698	9
		Yugoslavia	325	4
Linen fabrics	1,000 meters	Total	14,333	100
		USSR	3,857	27
		Canada	1,633	11
		United States	1,367	10
		Australia	982	7
		East Germany	562	4
Leather shoes	1,000 pairs	Total	14,030	100
		USSR	10,158	72
		Poland	1,061	8
		East Germany	997	7
		British Africa	634	5
		West Germany	148	1
Rubber shoes	1,000 pairs	Total	13,851	100
		British Africa	2,254	16

TABLE 6.9—*Continued*

Commodity	Unit	Receiving and Supplying Countries	Quantity	Per Cent Share
Rubber shoes	1,000	USSR	1,577	11
(*Continued*)	pairs	Iran	1,572	11
		Rumania	616	4
		Canada	485	4
Hops	1,000	Total	50	100
	custom	East Germany	14	28
	quintals[b]	Belgium	8	16
		France	7	14
		West Germany	5	10
		Hungary	4	8
Malt	1,000	Total	143	100
	metric	Switzerland	25	17
	tons	USSR	19	13
		East Germany	16	11
		Brazil	14	10
		West Germany	13	9
Sugar (presumably refined	1,000	Total	369	100
only)	metric	USSR	121	33
	tons	United Kingdom	51	14
		Norway	34	9
		Switzerland	33	9

IMPORTS, 1958

Commodity	Unit	Receiving and Supplying Countries	Quantity	Per Cent Share
Hard coal	1,000	Total	2,573	100
	metric	Poland	1,567	61
	tons	USSR	1,005	39
Crude oil	1,000	Total	1,377	100
	metric	USSR	1,366	99
	tons	Bulgaria	11	1
Iron ore	1,000	Total	5,164	100
	metric	USSR	3,701	72
	tons	India	494	10
		Brazil	359	7
		China Mainland	156	3
		Sweden	113	2
Pyrites (sulfur content)	1,000	Total	67	100
	metric	Yugoslavia	21	31
	tons	Sweden	13	19
		Greece	11	16
		Bulgaria	11	16
		Norway	10	15
Phosphates (P_2O_5 content)	1,000	Total	122	100
	metric	USSR	74	61
	tons	Lebanon	18	15
		United Arab Republic.	13	11

TABLE 6.9—*Continued*

Commodity	Unit	Supplying Country	Quantity	Per Cent Share
Sulfur	1,000 metric tons	Total	38	100
		USSR	18	47
		China Mainland	13	34
		East Germany	7	19
Potassic fertilizers (K content)	1,000 metric tons	Total	217	100
		East Germany	207	95
		USSR	10	5
Nitrogenous fertilizers (nitrogen content)	1,000 metric tons	Total	13	100
		East Germany	11	85
		USSR	2	15
Sulfuric acid	1,000 metric tons	Total	10	100
		USSR	10	100
Natural rubber	1,000 metric tons	Total	49	100
		Malaya	14	28
		United Kingdom	10	20
		China Mainland	7	14
		USSR	5	10
Synthetic rubber	1,000 metric tons	Total	12	100
		USSR	7	58
		East Germany	5	42
Wood pulp	1,000 metric tons	Total	28	100
		Finland	20	71
		USSR	5	18
		Sweden	2	7
Cotton	1,000 metric tons	Total	89	100
		USSR	47	53
		United Arab Republic.	26	29
		China Mainland	3	3
		Iran	3	3
Wool	1,000 metric tons	Total	20	100
		USSR	5	25
		Australia	4	20
		New Zealand	2	10
Jute	1,000 metric tons	Total	14	100
		Pakistan	11	79
		China Mainland	3	21
Hides	1,000 metric tons	Total	36	100
		Argentina	15	42
		Brazil	11	31
Wheat	1,000 metric tons	Total	964	100
		USSR	938	97
		Hungary	26	3

TABLE 6.9—*Continued*

Commodity	Unit	Supplying Country	Quantity	Per Cent Share
Barley for fodder	1,000 metric tons	Total	88	100
		United Arab Republic.	41	47
		Argentina	26	29
		USSR	21	24
Maize	1,000 metric tons	Total	193	100
		USSR	130	67
		Switzerland	21	11
		Rumania	14	7
		Yugoslavia	10	5
		North Vietnam	8	4
Other fodder	1,000 metric tons	Total	69	100
		USSR	27	39
		Iran	20	29
		Yugoslavia	4	6
		Denmark	4	6
Meat, including animals for slaughter	1,000 metric tons	Total	92	100
		China Mainland	27	29
		East Germany	13	14
		USSR	12	13
		Hungary	11	12
Fish and fish products	1,000 metric tons	Total	43	100
		Norway	14	33
		Iceland	9	21
		USSR	6	14
		Denmark	5	12
		Sweden	3	7
Butter	1,000 metric tons	Total	8	100
		USSR	7	88
		Denmark	1	12
Groundnuts	1,000 metric tons	Total	43	100
		United Kingdom	19	44
		Sudan	11	26
		China Mainland	6	14
		France	4	9
Soya beans	1,000 metric tons	Total	35	100
		China Mainland	30	86
		Turkey	3	8
		United Kingdom	2	6
Sunflower seeds	1,000 metric tons	Total	28	100
		USSR	21	75
		United Kingdom	3	11
		China Mainland	2	7
Eggs	Millions	Total	57	100
		Bulgaria	25	44

TABLE 6.9—*Concluded*

Commodity	Unit	Supplying Country	Quantity	Per Cent Share
Eggs (*Continued*)	Millions	China Mainland	17	30
		Hungary	15	26
Rice	1,000 metric tons	Total	74	100
		China Mainland	37	50
		North Vietnam	16	22
		Burma	10	14
		United Arab Republic.	4	5
Coffee	Metric tons	Total	5,226	100
		Brazil	3,678	70
		Colombia	884	17
		Mexico	286	5
Cacao beans	Metric tons	Total	8,268	100
		Switzerland	2,969	36
		Brazil	2,750	33
		France	935	11
		United Kingdom	842	10
		Netherlands	585	7
Tea	Metric tons	Total	1,376	100
		China Mainland	440	32
		North Vietnam	349	25
		Netherlands	210	15
		USSR	141	10
		India	136	10
Tobacco	1,000 metric tons	Total	14	100
		China Mainland	5	36
		Turkey	4	29
		Bulgaria	3	21
		Yugoslavia	1	7
Fruit	1,000 metric tons	Total	116	100
		Hungary	28	24
		Bulgaria	23	20
		Rumania	17	15
		Turkey	7	6
		Yugoslavia	7	6
Vegetables	1,000 metric tons	Total	63	100
		Hungary	33	52
		Bulgaria	18	29
Passenger cars	Units	Total	9,538	100
		East Germany	4,932	52
		USSR	1,765	19
		France	1,788	19

Data from *SRRC*, 1959, Table 14.5. They include re-export and switch.

[a] In terms of export prices, free at the Czechoslovak border.

[b] 50 kg.

tics is given for 1958. It shows the very considerable Czechoslovak contribution toward the industrialization of the whole Soviet area, and the degree of recent Czechoslovak dependence on imports of raw materials from this area.

Some further figures on Czechoslovakia's trade with her largest trading partner, the USSR, are worth considering.

In 1956, Czechoslovakia imported from the USSR 117,000 metric tons of manganese ore, 129,000 tons of pig iron, 25,000 tons of ferroalloys, 19,000 tons of copper (70 per cent of Czechoslovakia's total copper imports), 13,000 tons of zinc, 12,000 tons of tin, 1,000 tons of lead (which, contrary to increased Soviet supplies of other nonferrous metals, was substantially less than in 1949), and 12,000 tons of aluminum. Manganese ore, pig iron, and nonferrous metals are not included in the newly available statistics on commodity trade in *SRRC*, 1959, and are quoted from other sources.[6] These same sources show the Soviet dependence on Czechoslovak supplies of certain products and commodities: in 1956 Czechoslovakia supplied 100 per cent of Soviet imports of stationary diesel engines, 31.5 per cent of its imports of metal-working machines (40 per cent in 1957), 46.5 per cent of Soviet imports of steel pipe (Czechoslovak exports to the USSR amounted to 85,000 metric tons), 21.5 per cent (6.8 million meters) of Soviet imports of cotton fabrics, 66.3 per cent of Soviet imports of leather shoes, and 100 per cent of Soviet imports of rubber shoes (8.8 and 1.3 million pairs, respectively).

The commodity pattern in trade with the developed market economies can be obtained from Western statistics. In Table 6.10, the commodity pattern of Czechoslovak trade with Western Europe and with Yugoslavia, in terms of dollar values, has been taken from the *Economic Bulletin for Europe*, XI, No. 2. (Data on the commodity pattern of Czechoslovak trade with individual Western European countries or with the Common Market or the Outer Seven can also be found in this *Bulletin*.) The main Czechoslovak exports to Western Europe in 1957–58 were as follows: coal, iron and steel, wood, and food to West Germany; wood and wood products, sugar, and textiles to the United Kingdom; wood, fruit, and vegetables to France. The main import items were as follows: iron and steel, chemicals, machinery, and nonferrous metals, especially copper, from West Germany; machinery, textile fibers, and chemicals from the United Kingdom; textile fibers and motor vehicles from France.

For the commodity pattern of Czechoslovak trade with underdeveloped

---

[6] Article by V. Čáp and O. Dubský in *Hospodářské noviny*, No. 27, 1958; *Rudé právo* of December 12, 1958; *Statistický obzor*, No. 12, 1958.

TABLE 6.10—CZECHOSLOVAK TRADE WITH 17 EUROPEAN MARKET ECONOMIES AND
YUGOSLAVIA, EXPORTS AND IMPORTS BY COMMODITY GROUPS, 1957 AND 1958

*(In millions of current dollars at official exchange rates, exports c.i.f. receiving country, imports f.o.b.
supplying country; data based on non-Czechoslovak statistics)*

Products	With 17 European Market Economies				With Yugoslavia			
	Exports		Imports		Exports		Imports	
	1957	1958	1957	1958	1957	1958	1957	1958
Live animals, meat and products...	2.1	2.2	5.9	0.6	0.2	—	2.2	1.5
Dairy products, margarine	2.8	3.8	1.9	1.0	—	—	—	—
Fish and preparations	—	0.1	6.8	7.1	—	—	0.3	0.6
Wheat	1.1	1.9	0.6	0.1	—	—	—	—
Other cereals, flour, etc.	11.9	10.4	0.1	0.2	—	0.2	0.3	4.6
Fruit and vegetables	8.7	7.5	6.6	6.0	—	—	0.9	1.5
Sugar and products	5.7	11.5	—	—	0.3	2.6	—	—
Other food	0.4	0.4	0.1	0.3	0.2	—	—	—
Fodder	—	—	3.4	0.9	—	—	—	0.2
Beverages	0.3	0.6	2.3	0.8	—	—	1.2	0.8
Tobacco and manufactures	—	—	13.2	9.2	—	—	1.0	3.0
Oil seeds, fats and oils	0.1	0.2	6.0	6.7	—	—	—	—
Animal and vegetable materials...	1.8	1.9	0.9	1.0	—	—	0.2	0.1
Hides and skins, crude and dressed	1.2	0.5	6.7	6.9	—	—	0.4	0.7
Footwear, leather goods, furs.....	3.4	3.1	0.1	—	0.1	0.1	—	—
Wood, round and sawed	23.6	22.5	5.1	3.2	—	—	0.3	0.1
Wood products, incl. furniture, etc.	3.0	3.1	2.5	1.3	—	—	—	0.1
Pulp, waste paper	2.4	2.3	3.6	3.5	—	—	—	—
Paper and manufactures	5.0	4.6	1.8	1.8	0.7	0.4	—	—
Textile fibers	3.9	1.0	13.5	13.8	0.6	—	0.3	0.5
Synthetic fibers	—	—	0.9	1.6	—	—	—	—
Yarn and fabrics	11.4	9.6	5.9	7.3	1.6	1.9	—	0.1
Made-up textiles, clothing	7.7	6.6	0.7	0.8	0.6	1.0	—	—
Lime, cement, bricks, etc.	5.0	5.0	1.1	1.3	0.4	0.3	—	—
Glass, glassware, pottery	11.8	11.2	0.9	1.2	0.5	0.5	—	—
Basic chemicals	10.9	11.0	10.1	9.6	0.7	0.6	0.1	0.1
Pharmaceuticals }	3.7	3.4 {	3.0	3.0	} 0.4	1.0 {	—	0.1
Other chemicals, excl. fertilizers..			12.1	10.1			0.2	0.4
Fertilizers	0.2	—	—	—	—	—	—	—
Coal, coke, briquettes	17.9	16.9	—	—	—	—	—	—
Crude petroleum	—	—	—	—	—	—	—	—
Petroleum products	3.4	2.1	2.2	0.3	0.1	0.2	—	—
Crude minerals, ore, scrap	8.6	6.8	7.0	5.1	0.3	0.4	0.6	0.7
Precious metals, including ore	5.3	3.0	0.9	1.0	—	—	—	—
Iron and steel	17.3	15.6	36.6	41.8	1.1	2.5	0.1	0.6
Nonferrous metals	1.2	1.4	6.5	10.0	0.1	—	0.5	1.2
Copper	—	—	4.7	7.8	—	—	—	—
Aluminum	0.2	0.8	...	...	—	—	—	—
Tin	0.1	—	...	...	—	—	—	—
Metal manufactures, etc.	5.9	5.1	3.9	3.3	0.4	0.4	—	—
Metal-working machinery	8.0	6.2	3.4	5.7	1.1	2.5	—	—
Other machinery, excluding electric	16.2	13.6	17.4	21.7	4.4	5.6	—	—
Electric machinery	5.7	4.2	6.6	8.1	0.9	1.5	—	—
Road motor vehicles	16.8	7.8	3.7	3.0	2.6	2.8	—	—
Ships and boats	—	—	—	0.3	—	—	—	2.4
Other transport equipment	2.3	0.7	0.3	—	0.5	0.6	—	—
Instruments, watches, etc.	3.2	2.5	3.9	3.7	0.6	1.1	—	—
Other commodities	8.4	8.4	4.5	5.9	0.5	1.1	—	0.1
Total	248.3	119.7	210.2	208.3	18.9	27.3	8.6	19.5

Economic Bulletin for Europe, XI, No. 2 (ECE, Geneva, September 1959, Tables D and E). All data
refer to "special trade" and are therefore lower than the "general trade" figures in Czechoslovak statistics. The 17 countries concerned are as follows: Austria, Belgium-Luxembourg, Denmark, Finland,
France, West Germany, Greece, Iceland, Ireland, Italy, the Netherlands, Norway, Portugal, Sweden,
Switzerland, Turkey, and the United Kingdom.

market economies, no comprehensive data are available to the author. Yet it is safe to state that by far the greatest Czechoslovak export items are machinery and equipment, including complete factories, and the main import items are primary products.

Czechoslovak exports of machinery and equipment for production by 1956 were relatively more important than those by Western market economies. Table 6.11 leaves no doubt about this, in spite of severe limitations of comparability. This table shows that, by 1956, 55 per cent of Czechoslovak exports to non-Communist overseas countries (of which the bulk went to underdeveloped countries) consisted of machinery and equipment, whereas in the listed Western European and American exports to nonindustrialized and semi-industrialized countries, machinery and tractors made only 43 and 40 per cent respectively. The 43 per cent share of machinery in Czechoslovak exports to other centrally planned economies also is noteworthy.

Czechoslovakia's position as an exporter of machinery is especially important in some specific fields which seem to have been assigned to it in the framework of the specialization of output, as decided by the Council for Mutual Economic Aid. Table 6.12 shows a comparison by countries of exports of metal-working machines and diesel engines.

Like Czechoslovakia, East Germany is a great exporter of machinery within the centrally planned area. However, the greatest part of East German exports goes to other centrally planned countries rather than to the underdeveloped market economies.

4. Volume of Trade

We have so far been analyzing external trade in current value, which of course reflects all export and import price movements. An index of the volume of external trade (imports and exports at 1953 constant prices) is to be found, together with the index of trade in current values, in Table 6.3 (p. 100). The volume of both imports and exports appears to have been rising faster than their value. This was caused by a fall in export-import prices. A comparison by countries of the volume of exports is contained in Table 6.13, from which the reader may gather that, in Czechoslovakia in 1948, the export volume was nearer the prewar level than in Western Europe, which is a sign of speedy postwar recovery in Czechoslovakia. A study of Table 6.3 indicates that the lag behind Western European volume of exports in later years up to 1953 was solely due to a dip in Czechoslovak exports to the market economies, while volume of exports to the centrally planned area has risen constantly. From 1953 to 1958, the volume of trade in Czechoslovakia rose generally faster than in the West.

TABLE 6.11—EXPORTS OF MACHINERY IN 1956

(In million current dollars and per cent of total exports)

Exporting countries	World		Eastern Trade Area[a]		Overseas Countries[b]		Nonindustrialized Countries		Semi-industrialized Countries	
	Amount	Per Cent	Amount	Per Cent	Amount	Per Cent	Amount	Per Cent	Amount	Per Cent
MACHINERY, EQUIPMENT, APPARATUS, INSTRUMENTS, AND SPARE PARTS FOR PRODUCTION[c]										
Czechoslovakia	$559	40.3	$387	43	$131	55				
Hungary	149	30.3	134	43	10	26				
Poland	154	15.6	...	...	...	...				
USSR	716	19.5	...	...	...	...				
MACHINERY AND TRACTORS[d]										
Nine Western European countries[e]	4,255	16	66	10			$1,218	18	$558	25
United States[f]	2,436	17	—	—			794	18	239	22

Data are from, or based on information in, the *Economic Survey of Europe*, 1957. Calculation of per capita exports of machinery, etc., on the basis of the above figures, may be of interest, even if Western and Eastern data are not comparable: Czechoslovakia, $46.9; nine Western European countries, $19; the United States, $16; the USSR, $4.

In more recent years, Czechoslovak exports of machinery and equipment have been increasing rapidly. In 1958, they reached $650 million; their share in total exports, in current value terms, went up from 40.3 per cent in 1956 to 43.3 per cent. Under the third Five-Year Plan, by 1965 this share is expected to reach 55.3 per cent of total Czechoslovak exports (see Appendix).

[a] All centrally planned economies in Europe and Asia.
[b] Practically equal to exports of machinery and equipment to less developed countries.
[c] Classification by the Council for Mutual Economic Aid in Moscow.
[d] *Economic Survey of Europe*, 1957, items 9-13, Table XI, "Exports by Main Commodity Groups and by Area of Destination."
[e] The six countries of the Common Market, the United Kingdom, Norway, and Sweden.
[f] Limited comparability, as stated in the *Economic Survey of Europe*, 1957.

TABLE 6.12—COMPARISON BY COUNTRIES OF EXPORTS OF METAL-WORKING
MACHINES AND DIESEL ENGINES

(*In million U.S. dollars*)

Country	Metal-cutting Lathes		Forging Machines		Diesel Engines and Aggregates	
	1956	1958	1956	1958	1956	1958
Czechoslovakia	33.6	50.3	10.2	11.4	16.7	24.6
Austria	3.1	3.1	1.0	1.1	...	...
France	13.8	11.5	4.6	4.5	8.0	7.8
West Germany	113.1	46.1	138.0	51.6	47.7	51.8
United Kingdom ...	58.4	8.5	59.1	9.5	60.8	52.3
United States	99.0	126.3	50.3	46.8	77.4	68.8

Data from *Statistický obzor*, No. 2, 1960. The statement was made that Czechoslovakia has become the world's fifth largest exporter of metal-working machines and the sixth largest exporter of diesel engines.

In relation to the centrally planned economies, the volume of both imports and exports rose continuously until 1958, the latest year for which data are available. In relation to the market economies, the volume of Czechoslovak imports also rose until 1958, but the rising trend of export volume was reversed in 1958. (It should be stressed that the figures for 1958 in Table 6.3 are based on *SRRC*, 1959, Table 14.1, and are substantially different from the provisional data on the volume of Czechoslovak foreign trade as published in the *Economic Bulletin for Europe*, XI, No. 1, Table A.19.)

TABLE 6.13—INDEX OF VOLUME (QUANTUM) AND OF UNIT PRICE OF EXPORTS
Comparison with the West

	1937	1948	1950	1951	1952	1953	1954	1955	1956	1957	1958
VOLUME INDEX 1953 = 100											
Czechoslovakia	62	56	77	78	84	100	105	126	149	150	172
Continental Western Europe	69	45	79	94	90	100	114	129	138	149	153
United Kingdom, Iceland, Ireland....	76	82	104	103	97	100	105	111	118	120	116
United States and Canada...........	44	83	75	94	97	100	97	100	116	122	108
UNIT EXPORT PRICE INDEX 1953 = 100 (based on dollar values)											
Czechoslovakia	69	136	101	109	105	100	96	94	94	91	93
Continental Western Europe	...	49	113	86	106	109	100	97	98	101	104
United Kingdom, Iceland, Ireland...	48	107	80	96	102	100	99	100	103	107	106
United States and Canada...........	50	95	87	100	101	100	98	100	103	107	106

Index of volume of Czechoslovak exports is from Table 6.3; index of export unit price for Czechoslovakia is from Table 6.14, rebased to 1953 = 100, except for 1937. These prewar data were obtained by linking index numbers 1937 = 100 from an article by Jaroslav Štefan, "Zahraniční obchod v čs. hospodářství," in *Plánované hospodářství*, No. 2, 1949, with the above index 1953 = 100. Indices of volume of trade and of export unit price for all Western areas are from the United Nations *Monthly Bulletin of Statistics* and from United Nations *Statistical Yearbook*, 1959.

5. Export and Import (Unit) Price Index: Remarks on Exchange Rate and Price Policy

By dividing the current value index by the volume index, a derived import and export unit value, or price index, has been obtained. This will be found in Table 6.14.

TABLE 6.14—DERIVED INDEX OF CZECHOSLOVAK UNIT IMPORT AND EXPORT
PRICES AND OF TERMS OF TRADE
1948 = 100

	1949	1950	1951	1952	1953	1954	1955	1956	1957	1958
Import unit price:										
General	92	84	100	97	90	86	88	88	88	80
From centrally planned economies ...	...	77*	89*	94*	91*	85*	88*	88*	88*	83*
From market economies	...	95*	128*	109*	88*	95*	89*	90*	88*	75*
Export unit price:										
General	91	75	80	76	73	70	69	69	66	68
To centrally planned economies..	...	82	86	88	88	86	82	82	79	80
To market economies	...	73	85	75	64	60	61	60	59	56
Terms of trade:										
General	99	89	80	78	81	81	78	78	75	80
With centrally planned economies ...	...	106*	97*	94*	97*	101*	107*	107*	90*	98*
With market economies	...	77*	66*	69*	73*	63*	69*	67*	67*	75*

Data computed on the basis of value and volume index numbers in Table 6.3.

Over the years 1948–57, the unit price for imports, in the long run, ran parallel, decreasing by 22 per cent, from both the centrally planned and the market economies, with the exception of the Korean war years, when prices on imports from the West rose more sharply than those from the East; on the other hand, import prices charged by the centrally planned economies were still going up in 1952 when prices charged by Western countries had already begun to go down again. In 1958, the unit price index fell more for Czechoslovak imports from the market economies than for those from the centrally planned economies.

In exports, however, price movements were different in respect to the centrally planned and the market economies. After introduction of the state monopoly of foreign trade, export prices in trade with the West started falling more rapidly than in trade with the East. Yet, in 1951, average export prices were about one-sixth lower in relation to both the centrally planned and the market economies. At that time, trade with the West reached its lowest point, and the percentage of exports to the East reached a peak. When a new Czechoslovak drive for exports to the market economies (especially the underdeveloped ones) started in 1954, average export prices to this area began falling rapidly, while unit export prices to the East remained more stable until 1957, though lower than in 1948. In 1957, however, there was a much sharper drop in the Czechoslovak export unit price to the centrally planned economies than to the market economies. Then, in 1958, the unit price index for exports to the centrally planned economies went up again, although it still remained below the 1956 level, while the unit price index for exports to the market economies continued to fall. All the above deductions are, of course, based on a mere assumption that the main factor of the changing unit prices was a change in actual prices other than in the commodity pattern of imports and exports.

An international comparison of the export unit price index, based on dollar values, is contained in Table 6.13. The year 1937 also is included. The table shows that the 1948 Czechoslovak export unit price was more favorable than the Western European export unit price. From 1948 to 1950, the index dropped quite uniformly for Czechoslovakia, Western Europe, and the United Kingdom, although Czechoslovakia—unlike these countries—did not devalue its currency in September 1949. But in order to remain competitive, the foreign trade monopoly reduced export prices, in terms of Czechoslovak koruny, in trade with the devaluating countries by exactly the devaluation ratio of one-third, and by somewhat less in trade with other countries where the increased competition of the sterling and franc area had to be met.[7] A similar procedure was probably used in May 1953 when the exchange rate of the Czechoslovak Kčs was revalued.[8] Export prices in terms of Kčs have most likely been reduced correspondingly to maintain them unchanged in terms of foreign currency. This assessment is supported by the index of Czechoslovak export prices (on a dollar basis), showing no increase between 1953 and 1954; on the contrary, it fell more than the Western export price indices.

The above-mentioned policy is the reason why it is not necessary to

---

[7] Note, for example, the unofficially reported difference in export prices, free at the Czechoslovak border, in terms of Kčs, for the JAWA-250 motorcycle before and after the Western European devaluation (in thousand 1945 Kčs):

Receiving Country	September 1949	October 1949
France and colonies	15.6	12.8
Netherlands	14.3	10.6
Switzerland (did not devalue)	12.1	10.4
East Germany	17.8	17.8

[8] Under the second postwar currency reform, internal values in Kčs have been deflated at the ratio 5:1 while the exchange rate has been raised at the ratio 6.94:1; consequently, the exchange rate for one U.S. dollar has been changed from 50 Kčs to 7.20 Kčs instead of to 10 Kčs, which would correspond to the general deflation (see Chapter 7, Section 1).

dwell at length on the changes in the exchange rate when dealing with the dollar value of exports and imports. Such changes exercised an influence only on the balance sheet of the state monopoly of foreign trade, as will be discussed in Section 6.

By dividing the unit export price index by the unit import price index, the author has obtained (in Table 6.14) an index of the terms of trade. This table shows that, over the entire decade under review, the terms of trade with the East were turning less against Czechoslovakia than in trade with the market economies. This was caused, among other factors, by the extremely low prices charged by Czechoslovakia to the underdeveloped countries (which, in fact, is a hidden economic aid, besides that described in Section 7) and by Czechoslovak underbidding in the Western market.

In 1957, Czechoslovak terms of trade, in relation to the centrally planned economies, worsened as compared with 1956, but they remained unchanged in relation to the market economies. In 1958, there was a noticeable improvement in terms of trade in relation to both areas (in the market economies this was due solely to the fall in the import unit price). Terms of trade slightly surpassed the 1953 levels; they were thus higher for trade with the centrally planned economies than for trade with the market economies. Yet terms of trade with the centrally planned economies still remained substantially below the exceptionally favorable terms of 1954. But the movement of terms of trade from 1948 on can hardly be taken as a reliable measure of the relative profitability of trade without further study of the price levels in trade with both areas.

In a system of comprehensive central planning, with state monopoly of foreign trade, it is possible not only to divorce completely the internal and external price levels but also to vary substantially the export prices charged to buying countries (import prices also vary as to the goods imported from individual centrally planned economies). For instance, in March 1950, the passenger car "Tatraplan" was exported at the following prices, free at the Czechoslovak border (in 1,000 Kčs, 1945 currency): Hungary, 73; Poland, 70; Belgium, 64.8; Canada, 43.3.[9] It is more difficult to give an example of an identical product imported from several countries at very different prices. For most imported goods, quality variations by the supplying countries as well as price must be taken into account. However, there is a schedule of quality of imported goods, according to the estimate made by the central planning authorities—the so-called "internal

___

[9] It may be useful to stress here that the internal wholesale price was 156,000 Kčs, so that a very large export subsidy was applied; foreign trade subsidy will be discussed in Section 6.

transaction price," or state wholesale price. This applies to the price at which the foreign trade monopoly sells imported goods to nationalized industry (or the price at which the foreign trade monopoly buys goods to be exported). For example, the import price, free at the Czechoslovak border, and the corresponding internal transaction price for cotton, per kg in prewar Kčs, in February 1950, were officially reported to be as follows:

	Import Price	Internal Transaction Price
From the USSR	44.50	41.90
From the United States	39.60	42.55
From Egypt	53.00	64.00

If these reported prices really applied, it is obvious that the state monopoly of foreign trade—in this particular case Centrotex, the export-import company for textile raw materials and products—was making a profit on imports of American and Egyptian cotton and sustaining a loss on the import of short-stapled Soviet cotton, as the internal transaction price in the first two cases was higher and in the latter case lower than the import price. Similarly, in January 1950 the Koospol State Company for import of food was purchasing Soviet wheat reportedly at 471 Kčs (1945 currency) per 100 kg and reselling it at 403 Kčs. More recent evidence is available on import prices being higher than internal wholesale prices for specific commodities; e.g., V. Komárek, in an article in *Plánované hospodářství*, No. 11, 1959, stated that the internal wholesale price for Krivoj Rog iron ore (55 per cent iron content) was 83.70 Kčs per metric ton, while the actual import price paid to the USSR can be confidently estimated, at the official exchange rate, at 90–120 Kčs per ton. Such a surplus expenditure on imports seems to be limited to some basic materials. On imports of most other products from both West and East, the state monopoly was making a profit.

Prices mutually charged by the centrally planned economies in 1948 for several kinds of goods were higher than the world market price.[10] A lower index of import unit prices in 1956 in relation to the centrally planned economies does not, therefore, necessarily mean that the prices charged by the East actually fell, at the official exchange rate, below the prices charged by the West.

[10] In January 1950 the price for Czechoslovak imports of Soviet wheat, for example, was $2.56 a bushel (at the official exchange rate), free at the border, when the Chicago price for wheat was only $2.17.

The export prices that Czechoslovakia was getting—from 1948 to 1953 —from the other centrally planned economies were higher for most goods (mainly industrial consumers' goods), substantially the same for other goods (e.g., sugar), and lower for specific commodities (especially strategic goods), than the corresponding prices obtained from the West. It is well known that up to 1953, the people's democracies had to supply strategic materials to the USSR at very low prices. Hungary, for example, exported bauxite to the USSR until 1953 for less than half the price charged to other countries, including Czechoslovakia.[11] Again, a statement was made by the Polish Prime Minister, Jozef Cyrankiewicz, in November 1956, that Poland supplied six million tons of coal to the USSR from 1946 to 1953 at an unduly low price and that the Soviet government would deliver goods to the value of two million rubles in compensation to Poland for the loss sustained. No similar statement has ever been made by the Czechoslovak government; yet some goods—for example, oil pipes—were exported in large quantities to the USSR until 1953 at a price about one-third below the internal transaction price at a time when the export price to the West did not yet imply such a loss regarding the same kind of goods.

On the other hand, when a new export drive to the market economies started in 1954, export prices to the West were reduced more than those charged to the East. This applies especially to prices for capital goods exported to underdeveloped countries and for consumers' goods exported to Western Europe and North America.

From 1954 to 1957, the Czechoslovak government stated several times that trade with the USSR and other people's democracies is carried out at world market prices (plus half the transportation costs). But some export prices in mutual trade within the centrally planned area continued to diverge from world market prices even after 1954, and were also far from uniform in relation to all centrally planned economies.[12]

In 1957, new price relations were fixed in trade within the centrally planned area by the Council for Mutual Economic Aid, admittedly different from the world market price relations.[13]

[11] *Economic Survey of Europe*, 1957, Chap. VI, p. 3, footnote.

[12] For example, in 1955 Czechoslovakia paid $23.7 per ton for crude petroleum from Hungary at the official exchange rate, while East Germany paid $17.8 and Poland paid $18.0 per ton (*Economic Survey of Europe*, 1957, Chap. VI, p. 28).

[13] J. Vaněk, editor of the Czechoslovak economic monthly *Politická ekonomie*, wrote in the January 1958 issue: "Foreign trade turnover of the countries of the Socialist camp amounts to only 12 per cent of world trade, and only 4 per cent of this accounts for trade with the capitalist countries (8 per cent being mutual trade within the Socialist market). Consequently, the influence of the countries of the

As Table 6.14 indicates, the Czechoslovak export unit price in trade with the centrally planned area fell in 1957. It is difficult to say whether this was a first consequence of the price structure in the "Socialist world market." (In any case, it has to be borne in mind that a change in the export unit price can be caused by changing the commodity pattern of trade.) The slight increase in unit price of Czechoslovak exports to the centrally planned area in 1958 did not compensate for the previous decrease in 1957. On the other hand, the unit price for Czechoslovak imports from the centrally planned area went down noticeably in 1958. One suspects that, on the whole, the new price structure, as applied from 1958 in intra-Eastern European trade, reduced the price levels somewhat, although some intra-Eastern European export prices seem to have still remained above (Western) world market prices. Some indications of this can be obtained from a comparison of value data in Table 6.8 and quantity data in Table 6.9. The following price approximations, in 1958, at official exchange rates, can be derived—which are, however, subject to doubts in view of the different classification of goods in the above-mentioned tables, varying quality, etc.:

Export prices per metric ton of refined sugar, free at the Czechoslovak border: to the USSR, 832* Kčs; to Switzerland, 664* Kčs; to the United Kingdom, 430* Kčs.

Import prices per metric ton of hard coal: from the USSR, 111* Kčs ($15.40 at the official exchange rate); from Poland, 122* Kčs ($17.20 at the official exchange rate). In Western Europe, prevailing wholesale prices for hard coal were noticeably lower in 1958.

As may be gathered from the preceding observations, the state monopoly of foreign trade and central planning make it possible to manipulate freely not only the exchange rate but every export price. The price manipulation may be more efficient than exchange rate changes in achieving specific aims in export-import policy, as they are a powerful instrument in discriminating among countries and among categories of goods.

Socialist camp on the formation of value relations in the capitalist world market area is very limited for most goods. Only in exceptional cases can Socialist countries influence price movements (e.g., in the fur, timber, and flax markets). Therefore, if Socialist world market prices are pegged to so-called world market capitalist prices, without further examination of them, it would mean that the Socialist market is being tied to the capitalist market with all its fluctuations due to business cycles and speculation." However, Vaněk adds that "some common points in the price formation in capitalist and Socialist markets" exist; he argues that a "balanced regard" should be given both to the "planned development of the Socialist camp" and to the "profitability of foreign trade."

6. Foreign Trade Net Subsidy

The following questions arise, however: What was the expense of such general price manipulations in Czechoslovak external trade? How was the external and internal balance maintained?

In the *Economic Survey of Europe*, 1957, figures have been published on the foreign trade net subsidy in Hungary and East Germany.[14] By comparing exports and imports at domestic prices and foreign trade prices, surplus expenditure on exports and surplus receipts from imports have been obtained; by subtracting surplus receipts from surplus expenditure, the net foreign trade subsidy was calculated. According to pertinent figures of the Economic Commission for Europe, surplus expenditure on exports in Hungary in 1956 was 222 per cent of the domestic price of goods exported, surplus receipt from imports was 57 per cent of the domestic price of imported goods, and the net subsidy was 80 per cent of external turnover. Foreign trade subsidy in East Germany, according to the *Economic Survey of Europe*, 1957, amounted to only 38 per cent of the turnover in 1956. Thus, at the official exchange rate, the Hungarian foreign trade net subsidy should have amounted to $1,050 million and the East German subsidy to only $720 million, although East German external trade was much larger. The *Economic Survey of Europe* explains this difference by the greater importance of domestically high-priced foods in Hungarian exports and of domestically low-priced raw materials in Hungarian imports. In the author's opinion, two other factors may be involved as well. First, part of such a foreign trade net subsidy may be just a statistical shadow, due to an artificial exchange rate. Such a shadow may have been greater in Hungary than in East Germany. Second, in 1956, East Germany was the only centrally planned economy that still maintained the rationing system,[15] while the other countries in the centrally planned area had already replaced quantitative restrictions on civilian consumption by "rationing by price" through the "turnover tax" (see Chapter 7). If the "domestic price" for Hungarian exports included the high turnover tax and for East German exports excluded it, the resulting, much higher Hungarian subsidy on exports is natural.

In Czechoslovakia a better, though not perfect, method is to estimate the net loss in, or net subsidy on, foreign trade by comparing the internal transaction prices, paid or obtained by the export-import companies on the state wholesale level (which exclude the very high turnover tax on

[14] Chap. VI, p. 28 ff.

[15] The rationing system was abolished and consumers' prices increased in East Germany only in 1958.

goods for final civilian consumption; see Chapter 7, Section 3), with the actual export-import prices. The "internal transaction" or state wholesale prices in Czechoslovakia include a varying rate of profit, as well as of planned losses on certain commodities, due to underpricing (see Chapter 7, Section 3), and they cannot therefore be compared with Western wholesale prices. Their pattern, however, is not so extremely different from the Western patterns as that of Czechoslovak consumers' prices.

In the preceding section, the example of a great gap between a high internal wholesale price and a low export price for a Tatraplan car is given. Such great export subsidies seem to be exceptional, but the internal transaction price and the export price for motorcycles and for sugar were unofficially reported in 1950 as follows (in 1945 currency, see Chapter 7, Section 1):

	Internal Transaction Price	Export Price "Free, Czechoslovak Border" (Average of Prices Charged to All Buyers in the Importing Country) at Official Exchange Rates	
Motorcycle JAWA-250, per unit	16,400	Hungary	14,500
		Finland	10,950
		France	11,400
		Holland	9,600
		Switzerland	8,950
		United Kingdom ..	8,050
		United States	11,500
Sugar refined, per kg[a]	From 9.10	USSR	6.40
	(crystal)	Austria	6.80
	to 9.40	Switzerland	6.15
	(finest cube)	Norway	6.35

[a] Even before the war, Czechoslovakia subsidized its sugar exports.

On the other hand, the internal transaction price in 1950 for most imported goods was unofficially reported to be above the import price. For example, prices for sunflower seeds (the most important raw material of the Czechoslovak vegetable oils and fats industry) were said to compare as follows (in prewar Kčs per metric ton):

	Internal Wholesale Price	Import Price at Official Exchange Rate, Free, Czechoslovak Border
From the USSR	1,040	800
From Bulgaria	1,040	850
From Rumania	1,040	850
From Hungary	1,040	885
From Turkey	1,040	810

Unfortunately, no more recent information on the difference between internal wholesale prices and export-import prices for various commodities is available to the author. However, some semiofficial statements confirm that the limits of minimum export price and maximum import price are not set by the internal wholesale price. For instance, V. Čerňanský stated, in *Predvoj* of June 11, 1959:

> International trade is carried on at so-called world market prices. . . . The criterion is the price charged by other competitors. . . . Our internal price, or our costs of production, cannot be used as a criterion because the specific value from the point of view of one single exporter cannot determine the situation on the world market . . . We would make a great mistake if we judged the utility of exports or imports according to the difference between the internal and the external price of a commodity . . .

The continuing existence of surplus expenditure on exports has also been implicitly acknowledged.[16] Czechoslovak planning authorities know the amount of total difference between export and import prices, on the one side, and the corresponding internal wholesale prices, on the other. For individual commodities, and for individual trading partners, an index of "foreign trade rentability" (based in principle on surplus expenditure on exports and surplus receipts from imports) is being computed. Its construction has been described by Czechoslovak economists,[17] but the results have not been published so far.

Under the circumstances, the author made his own rough approximation of surplus expenditure on exports and surplus receipts from imports, and of the resulting foreign trade net subsidy, as described above.

Such a foreign trade net subsidy amounted to 7–9 billion Kčs in Czechoslovakia in 1957, or 36–46 per cent of the turnover in foreign trade. There are some indications that this estimated ratio of net subsidy to foreign trade is not exaggerated.[18]

[16] See Dr. Nachtigal, "Projecting the Results of Foreign Trade in the Balance Sheet of the National Economy," *Statistický obzor*, No. 5, 1958.

[17] A short summary of J. Navrátil's description of the "index of foreign trade rentability" was published in English in the *Economic Bulletin for Europe*, XI, No. 1, 70 n. The criticism therein of Navrátil's index—that it regards profits retained by the producing company as domestic cost—is of little practical consequence, because the "profits retained by the company" are very limited in Czechoslovakia—approximately 5–8 per cent (see Chapter 7, Section 3).

[18] E.g., the *Economic Bulletin for Europe*, XI, No. 1, 47, quotes from *Nová mysl* that, in 1956, Czechoslovakia's foreign trade turnover amounted to 24 per cent of its national income (under Marxist definition). Starting from the turnover of 18.6 billion Kčs in actual export-import prices, the above percentage ratio would suggest a national income under Marxist definition of only 77 billion Kčs. If, however, the rate of foreign trade subsidy, as estimated by the author for 1957, is also applied to the 1956 foreign trade turnover, to recompute it roughly in terms of internal whole-

Valtr Komárek gave more conclusive evidence on the existence of a sizable foreign trade net subsidy in Czechoslovak trade with the USSR:[19]

Assuming that one ton of iron ore, 55 per cent iron content, which is imported mainly from the USSR, cost 50 rubles, or 90 Kčs at the official exchange rate, and assuming that the index of rentability [profitability] in trade with the USSR is 0.75, which means that production at 1 Kčs at exchange parity will cost 1.35 Kčs, we shall have to export goods at the [internal wholesale] price of 120 Kčs to buy iron ore priced at 50 rubles.

Komárek stressed that his data should serve as a theoretical model only. He went on to say, however, that the Czechoslovak internal state wholesale price for one ton of Krivoj Rog ore is 83.71 Kčs and that the equivalent value of Czechoslovak export goods in buying a ton of Soviet ore is approximately 140 Kčs in terms of internal wholesale prices. On the basis of these data, which he did not qualify as a "theoretical model only," the foreign trade net subsidy rate, in trade with the USSR, appeared to amount to 39 per cent in 1959. In the author's opinion, the foreign trade net subsidy in relation to the USSR is lower than in relation to the market economies, especially the underdeveloped ones. This 1959 estimate was made after a certain worsening of Czechoslovak terms of trade with Eastern Europe. In 1957, the rate of net subsidy in trade with the USSR may have been lower than 39 per cent, and the author's estimate of 36–46 per cent for the over-all rate of foreign trade net subsidy seems to be well within reality.

The "statistical shadow due to an artificial exchange rate" seems to be limited, in Czechoslovakia, mainly to the subsidy within the export surplus in visible trade with the market economies. The greatest part of the estimated net foreign trade subsidy is, in the author's opinion, a real subsidy. If so, the question arises as to why foreign trade is carried out at such a great loss. The main factors that may be involved are as follows:

a) Import and export plans have been computed and integrated into the over-all economic plan in terms of physical quantities. Value relations have been neglected to a great extent (only in recent years have some "indicators of rentability" [profitability] been applied when the "fulfillment of the foreign trade plan" was being considered).

---

sale prices, the above-mentioned percentage ratio would suggest a Marxist national income of 125† billion Kčs, as compared with the author's estimate of Marxist national income (after adjustment for domestic transfer payments; see Chapter 10, Section 3) of 129 billion Kčs.

[19] "Problems of the Pricing System Involved in an Examination of the Efficiency of the National Economy," *Plánované hospodářství*, No. 11, 1959.

b) After the total nationalization of external trade, state export-import agencies were hastily set up in 1949 with inexperienced personnel, which resulted in losses in foreign trade. But it would be unfair to the export-import companies not to say that, after the disruption of most of the old Czechoslovak trade relations with the West between 1949 and 1953, it was difficult to regain some Western markets without underselling, especially in view of the quality of some of the Czechoslovak goods. (The quality of exports has improved only in recent years.)

c) Czechoslovakia has tried to break through the Western export "black list" by paying high prices for imports of Western strategic materials and has tried to break through a certain amount of discrimination against Czechoslovak goods by underbidding.

d) Advertising of Czechoslovak goods and Czechoslovak marketing and servicing organizations in the West are inadequate; foreign trade companies try to make up for this handicap by underbidding in Western markets.

e) A great part of the net foreign trade subsidy, especially in trade with underdeveloped countries, is by deliberate policy. The very low export prices are a kind of hidden economic aid. This concealed aid is seldom considered as such in Western surveys of international economic aid. Nor will the author try to include it in his estimates of the economic aid granted by Czechoslovakia, as described in the next section. Yet it is very important to know that, besides the "open" economic aid, Czechoslovakia is subsidizing some foreign economies, through deliberately accepting a net loss in foreign trade, to the extent of several hundred million dollars a year.

7. *Foreign Aid*

Czechoslovakia's contributions to multilateral economic aid have been negligible in recent years; from 1954 to 1956 it contributed only $400,000[20] for international technical assistance and international relief organizations and nothing to the international lending organization.

On the contrary, in the field of bilateral foreign aid, both economic and military, Czechoslovakia plays an important role. The aid is given mostly in the form of long-term credits (except for grants to Hungary in 1956–57 and to Korea in 1953–54). Officially, these credits are not denoted as foreign aid by the Czech government. But the low interest rate (mostly 2 per cent—or a mere half of the rate of interest applied to U.S. foreign aid credits), the long period of repayment (up to 15 years), and

---

[20] Of this, $200,000 went to UNEXPTA, $100,000 to other technical agencies, and $100,000 to the U.N. Children's Fund.

other unusually favorable conditions for the debtor countries make it clear that these credits fall in the category of foreign aid.

The known economic foreign aid granted by Czechoslovakia in the years 1956–57 and 1958–59 is contained in Table 6.15; it makes no claim to completeness or accuracy. It is to be stressed that the data refer to the commitments and not to the amounts actually spent on economic aid.

It is not known to what extent the Czechoslovak commitments have already been carried out; some loans—e.g., to Yugoslavia—seem to have remained partly unutilized. Nor is it to be expected that the Czechoslovak economic aid will continue from year to year like the American aid. With these qualifications in mind, it is very interesting to note that, in the two-year period 1956–57, the known foreign economic aid granted per capita amounted in Czechoslovakia to approximately $47, in the United States to $20, and in the USSR to approximately $14. After a noticeable decrease in 1958, the flow of new "foreign aid" credits granted by Czechoslovakia seems to have been resumed in 1959.

There are no reliable data available on military aid granted by Czechoslovakia. Some unconfirmed reports by Western journalists suggest that military aid may not be lower than economic aid.[21]

8. Summary

A specific foreign trade policy, consistent either with the general theory of employment or with the theory of comparative costs, cannot be traced in Czechoslovakia in the decade under study. In fact, the main task of the state monopoly of foreign trade seems to have been as follows: in relation to other centrally planned economies, to export and import fixed quantities of raw materials and capital goods according to the output plans; in relation to the underdeveloped countries in Asia and Africa, to export fixed quantities of machinery and to take certain amounts of agricultural products; in relation to the developed market economies in the West, to import planned quantities of raw materials and capital goods that are needed to fulfill output plans. Quantity has been the primary consideration and value secondary. Only in exports to the West has the primary task been to obtain enough foreign currency to pay for imports and to

---

[21] For example, reporter Leacacose of the American *Plain Dealer* reported, after having visited Prague in the autumn of 1957, that Egypt owed $240 million and Syria $150 million to Czechoslovakia for arms deliveries. There is no guarantee that this report is not grossly exaggerated. On the other hand, it is known that Czechoslovakia is supplying arms on credit at a very low rate of interest or at very low prices to countries of the centrally planned areas, to Afghanistan, Indonesia, and other countries in Asia and Africa.

TABLE 6.15—LONG-TERM CREDITS GRANTED BY CZECHOSLOVAKIA

(Dollar equivalents, in million U.S. dollars)

Receiving Country	Year	Amount	Purpose, or Kind of Supplies on Credit	Repayment
			1956–57 PERIOD	
Communist countries:				
Albania	1956	...	"Aid"	...
Hungary	1956	12		—
	1956, Mar.	25	Raw materials, other goods	Due 1960–67
Poland	1957, Mar.	27.5	Machinery	...
	1957, May	25ᵃ	Development of Polish sulfur output	Due 1961–67
	1957, Oct.	62.5ᵃ	Extension of Polish coal mines	...
Outer Mongolia	1957, Jan.	2.5	Shoe factory	...
Total known		154.5		
Yugoslavia	1956, Feb.	50ᵇ	Economic development, use until 1960	Due in 10 years
	1956, Feb.	25ᵇ	Purchase of consumers' goods, use until 1960	Due in 10 years
Total known		75		
Non-Communist countries:				
Afghanistan	1956–57	8	Cement factory, use for 5 years after completion	...
Egypt	1957	56	Economic development	Due in 12 years
Indonesia	1956, May	...	Equipment, use for 5 years	...
Syria	1957, Mar.	168	Factory equipment, use for 3 years	...
India	1957, Jan.	61	Postponed payment for steel foundry, use immediately	Due in 3 years
Total known		293		
Estimate to others (Indonesia, Burma, China, etc.)		80–100†		
Grand total		610†		

TABLE 6.15—*Concluded*

Receiving Country	Year	Amount	Purpose, or Kind of Supplies on Credit	Repayment
			1958–59 PERIOD	
Albania	1959?	25[e]	To promote Fe and Ni ore mining	...
Bulgaria	1959	...	Machinery and equipment to promote Cu mining, MEDET[d]	
East Germany	1959	27.5[e]	Machinery for K industry	In K fertilizers
Rumania	1959	...	Two power plants at 300 mw each[f]	In electric power
India‡	1959?	50[g]	...	"Eight years' credit at an advantageous rate of interest for India"
Ghana	1959	...	Investment goods[h]	"Long-term credit"
Grand total		150–400		

This list has been drafted on the basis of official or semiofficial statements in Czechoslovakia and/or the receiving countries. It is necessarily incomplete. A 2 per cent rate of interest can be assumed, with the exception of Egypt, which in the 1956–57 period paid 2.5 per cent.

[a] Confirmed by *Výstavba Slovenska*, September 24, 1959: 100 million and 250 million rubles, respectively.
[b] Probably not being fully used according to schedule, but the Vesnik Jugoslovenske Investicione Banke in January 1959 confirmed the $50 million credit.
[c] *Pravda*, June 13, 1959 (100 million rubles).
[d] *Rudé právo*, November 15, 1959.
[e] *Rudé právo*, September 15, 1959 (110 million rubles).
[f] *Rudé právo*, October 3, 1959.
[g] *Rudé právo*, November 25, 1959 (350 million Kčs).
[h] *Rudé právo*, July 10, 1959.

make other payments. To achieve its goal, the state monopoly has resorted to reducing prices of exports and to increasing volume of exports.

In a market economy, running external trade on these lines would have resulted in serious disturbances in internal balance. In a centrally planned economy, however, there is no such direct interaction between external and internal balance. In Czechoslovakia, the lack of value considerations in external trade has been compensated by manipulating domestic real income, as mentioned in Section 5. But the foreign trade net subsidy, in the region of one billion dollars a year, as described in Section 6, is of course a matter for concern, especially in view of other sources of inflationary pressure. Recently, there have been discussions in Czechoslovakia on the optimum returns in foreign trade.[22] Yet, with the rather arbitrary internal price structure and in view of the elimination of the market function, it may be as difficult to find the limits of a profitable basis in external trade as it is to assess the marginal productivity of capital investments.

The stress on volume and the lack of value considerations are reflected in the statistics: the dollar value of exports rose substantially more slowly than the volume of exports, as described in Sections 2 and 4. But even the volume of trade rose more slowly than industrial production over the decade under study, while in Western Europe external trade showed a greater rate of growth than output in mining and manufacturing. The export unit price fell (except in 1951 and 1952, the years of the Korean war) and the terms of trade turned against Czechoslovakia, owing mainly to the sharply reduced prices in exports to the West, as shown in Section 5. This unfavorable development resulted not only from deliberate dumping but also from the previous disruption of established commercial relations during the first period of the state monopoly of foreign trade, in 1949–53, and from a lack of ability of a centrally planned economy to respond quickly to the changing demand and supply in world markets. Over the entire period 1948–58, the general terms of trade turned noticeably against Czechoslovakia.

On the other hand, Czechoslovakia's central planning system attained some specific goals which a market economy would hardly be able to achieve, e.g., the far-reaching change of pattern of exports and imports, as described in Section 3, and the stepping up of the export of machinery to a per capita level twice as high as in the West. A surprisingly large amount of foreign aid granted by Czechoslovakia (as described in Section 7) is also noteworthy.

[22] See J. Navrátil et al., "Zahraniční obchod a výroba," a study on the "profitability" of foreign trade.

Chapter 7

MONEY AND PRICES

1. The Currency Reform of June 1953

There is no monetary policy in the Western sense to be discovered in Czechoslovakia; under central planning, the internal balance is supposed to be maintained by fixing consumers' prices and incomes rather than by a systematic effort to avoid inflationary or deflationary pressure. An excess of liquid assets which may result from a rigid system of wages and consumers' prices—under which demand and supply are not always equated by pricing on the domestic market—may become very detrimental to sound development. Such a situation did arise, in fact, during the first industrialization drive prior to 1953, and in June of that year a second postwar currency reform was carried out. A few comments on the postwar currency reforms in Czechoslovakia are necessary for an understanding of subsequent economic developments.

In the autumn of 1945, the government of the National Front took steps to cure the wartime money inflation by blocking all cash and money deposits in special accounts, by introducing a general levy on property and a much higher and much more progressive levy on increase of property during the war, and by setting up the "Fund for National Reconstruction." Through selling confiscated German property—obtained as reparations for losses suffered under the occupation—the Fund was supposed to acquire enough money in new currency to cover what remained on blocked accounts after deducting levies from property and property increase.

Prewar money in circulation amounted to about 8 million prewar koruny. Immediately after the 1945 currency reforms, price ceilings set by the Price Control Office were increased threefold in order to bring the official prices—which remained almost at the prewar level in view of wartime control—and the black-market prices, supply and demand, closer together. In view of the higher ceiling, the official estimate of sound money in circulation was also three times higher than prewar—24 billion postwar Kčs. But free exchange of old currency for new brought circulation to 28.2 billion Kčs by the end of 1945. This was done for the benefit of the Allied occupation armies, of political parties, and of nationalized industries (at that time only large-scale industries, the mining industry, and banks were nationalized). Later, this increased, to 46.6 and 61.7 billion Kčs by the end of 1946 and 1947, respectively. After the introduction of comprehensive central planning, based on almost complete nationalization of industry and trade under the new Communist-controlled government, circulation reached 75.6 billion Kčs by the end of 1948. Since 1949, publication of data on money circulation has been discontinued.

Meanwhile, price and money inflation persisted, especially during the stepped-up industrialization drive of 1951–53, with enormous money premiums for fulfilling and overfulfilling the output plans in heavy industry and with a rapidly increased rate of investments. A political decision to "dissolve" the purchasing power of the money holdings of the "bourgeois classes" also may have been involved, although, by 1953, money inflation was greater than price inflation, and the excess liquidity seemed to be concentrated in the hands of miners and workers in heavy industry.

In any case, at the end of May 1953, the government considered a new currency reform—the second in eight years—to be useful.

Under the law of May 30, 1953, a series of far-reaching economic measures dealing with currency, prices, and wages was decreed. The main points were:

a) General deflation of prices, wages, and claims. All these money values (including taxes, tariffs, etc.) were lowered as of June 1, 1953, at a ratio of five old koruny to one new koruna.

b) Severe reduction of personal cash holdings, deposits, and claims. Only 300 koruny per person were exchanged at the above-mentioned general deflation ratio of 5:1. All other cash in private hands was exchanged at the ratio of 50:1, which meant a 90 per cent confiscation. Deposit money was exchanged at varying ratios, according to the amount in the possession of each person; the average confiscation of deposit money can be estimated to have been 75 per cent. (Holdings of the state, nationalized industries, unified agricultural cooperatives, and other collective bodies were exchanged at the general deflation ratio, i.e., with no confiscation.)

c) All blocked accounts from the 1945 currency reform (amounting, according to the latest available data of June, 1947, to 70 billion Kčs or $1.4 billion) were invalidated and the Fund for National Reconstruction was dissolved without publication of final accounting for the confiscated German property. The entire internal public debt (dating from the time before the Communist-controlled Government took over and amounting to approximately 93 billion Kčs or $1.9 billion) was repudiated. It is interesting to note in this connection that—contrary to the practice in the USSR, Hungary and other East European countries—no State loans have been launched by the Czechoslovak Government ever since.

d) New official exchange rates of the Kčs were fixed, and the new currency unit defined as 0.123426 gram of pure gold. The exchange rate for the ruble was fixed at 1.80 Kčs, and for other currencies accordingly; for the U.S. dollar it was fixed at 7.20 Kčs, as compared with the old exchange rate of 50 Kčs for one U.S. dollar. This means that, while the internal revaluation ratio was 1:5, the external revaluation of the Kčs was 1:6.94. The impact on Czechoslovak exports was countered by lowering export prices in terms of Kčs at the corresponding ratio to maintain export prices unchanged in terms of foreign currency (see Chapter 6, Section 5).

e) The high-priced state free market and the low-priced rationed market for food and consumers' goods were merged into a new uniform market. When the general deflation ratio is taken into account, with the ratio of purchases on the rationed and the free market at approximately 2:1,[1] the uniform market prices certainly meant an increase in the cost of living. Following is a comparison of prices in Kčs in May–June 1953 (on the old free and old rationed markets in terms of new currency units, actual prices in terms of old currency were, of course, five times higher):

	May 1953 Old Rationed Market	May 1953 Old Free Market	June 1953 New Uniform Market
Butter (kg)	20	96	44
Beef (kg)	12	50	25
Sugar (kg)	3.04	28	14

The range of increase in the cost of living is indicated by the amount of food that various categories of the population had been able to buy on monthly rations:

	Normal Worker	Worker in Heavy Industry	Miner
Bread (pounds)	10.5	15.5	20.75
Meat (pounds)	3	5	10.75
Butter (pounds)	.33	.33	.33
Sugar (pounds)	2.5	2.5	3.5

In addition to the above-mentioned rations, which probably fully covered the average food consumption of workers in heavy industry, and

---

[1] The ratio of total purchases on ration and on the free market will be discussed in more detail in connection with the cost-of-living index in the next section.

may have exceeded that of miners, there were supplementary rations for the fulfillment of the working norm, which included two pounds of bread, one pound of meat, two pounds of margarine, and one pound of sugar a month.

Cheaper textiles "on points" (sold against points on the rationing card) were withdrawn.

The government maintained at first that the second currency reform meant a decrease in the cost of living. This argument, however, was later implicitly abandoned when the official figures on the decline of personal consumption in 1953 were published. This decline occurred in spite of the increase in wages and salaries, decreed simultaneously with the currency reform, as described below.

f) Wages and salaries were increased, in terms of new currency units, as follows: for miners, up to 0.70 Kčs an hour; for other workers in industry, between 0.34 and 0.60 Kčs an hour; for salaried workers with monthly pay of less than 1,000 Kčs, by 60 Kčs a month; for salaried workers with monthly pay between 1,000 and 1,200 Kčs, by 40 Kčs; there was no increase for salaried workers with monthly pay exceeding 1,200 Kčs (or 6,000 Kčs in terms of old currency). Thus, in the most favorable cases, wages were increased approximately 15 per cent, and salaries approximately 6 per cent. The average increase in money wages and salaries was far from sufficient to counterbalance the increase in the cost of living (see Section 4), so that real earnings went down (see Chapter 9, Section 2).

There is no doubt that large state financial reserves were built up through the second currency reform, in view of the increase in average consumers' prices (coupled with an increase in the turnover tax; see Chapter 7, Section 1). It should be mentioned, in this connection, that an increased turnover tax draws off possible excess liquidity.

After the 1953 currency reform, a period of economic "thaw" followed in 1954–57, with a slower rise in the rate of investments in production and with a better balanced output between capital and consumer goods. With the new production drive of 1958–59, more attention has been given by the central planning authorities to the dangers of inflation; the new pricing policy is described in Section 3. But, first, the external value of the present Czechoslovak currency is discussed.

2. External Value of the Czechoslovak Koruna

In the field of visible trade, a uniform—and artificial—exchange rate of the Kčs is applied; its artificiality and inelasticity are corrected, at least in trade with the market economies, by manipulating export-import prices through the state trade monopoly (see Chapter 6, Section 4). An official acknowledgment of the artificiality of the exchange rate is the state shop TUZEX where Czechoslovak citizens can use remittances from abroad, gifts in hard currency, to buy various goods; foreign money is exchanged at the official rate of the Kčs (7.18 Kčs for a dollar, buying rate), but the TUZEX prices in Kčs are approximately one-third of the normal domestic market prices.[2]

In the field of tourist traffic, however, multiple exchange rates are applied. They come nearer to the actual relationship in purchasing power than the official exchange rate.

The exchange rates (buying rates) and the author's rough estimate of the internal consumer's purchasing power of the Kč in 1958 compare as follows:[3] Exchange rates: official, 7.18 Kčs per dollar; "tourist," 14.32 Kčs; special (for a limited amount of Čedok hotel bonds and at certain periods of time only), 21.50 Kčs. Purchasing power (money spent according to the Czechoslovak and American patterns of consumption, respectively): Czechoslovak weighting, 17† Kčs; American weighting, 23† Kčs.

The ratio of official exchange rate to purchasing power of the Kčs, however, varies widely according to the kinds of goods. At the present Czechoslovak consumers' price structure, the purchasing power of the Kčs, as compared with American and roughly also West European prices, is very much below the official exchange rate for buying shoes, food, and textiles; it is considerably below the exchange rate for buying durables; and it roughly corresponds to the official exchange rate for buying services (this is due, among other factors, to the very low housing rent and inexpensive cultural services in Czechoslovakia, whereas some other services are relatively more expensive than in the West, at the official exchange rate; medical services are free in Czechoslovakia).

While the Kčs is officially overvalued in relation to most Western currencies, it is undervalued in relation to the ruble. Whereas the official rate is 180 Kčs for 100 rubles, the actual purchasing power lies between 110 and 130 Kčs for 100 rubles. This has been acknowledged by fixing the ruble tourist rate below the official rate.

[2] On the black market in Czechoslovakia, TUZEX bonds in 1958 were sold at a price five times higher than the official exchange rate. But this also reflects scarcity value and higher quality of certain goods available in TUZEX, as well as a speculation margin and a risk premium, since receivers of TUZEX bonds are forbidden to sell them to any but Czechoslovak citizens.

[3] Weights used are from *Internationaler Vergleich der Preise für die Lebeshaltung* (West German Statistical Office, Wiesbaden, 1957).

3. System of Prices

A detailed study of pricing problems in a highly developed centrally planned economy would be most useful. The question whether it is possible to arrive at a satisfactorily working pricing system at a high stage of economic development without using any functions of the market (and, as we shall see, without applying the labor theory of value when fixing the price) is closely connected with the question whether central planning of the present Czechoslovak (and Soviet) type is able to achieve, in the long run, superior economic efficiency. But these considerations would lead us too far afield.

There are two main categories of price:

The state wholesale price, at which the state and state-controlled bodies buy goods and services from other state enterprises, cooperatives, and individuals, and at which they sell goods and services only to other state or state-controlled organizations (irrespective of the quantities bought or sold).

The retail price, at which goods and services are sold to buyers other than the state or state-controlled bodies (again irrespective of the quantities sold).

According to a series of lectures on "Planning the National Economy" by the Economic Faculty in Prague,[4] the wholesale price applies when, after the transaction, the products remain or the services are consumed within Socialist ownership; and the retail price applies when the products or services go to private or individual ownership or consumption. Thus, prices for energy and fuel, materials, semifinished products, investment goods, consumption goods, and services purchased by the state administration as well as by enterprises in industry, construction, transportation, and trade (all these sectors are completely nationalized), by state farms, and by unified agricultural cooperatives of the third and fourth types, come under the first category. (There are also special state wholesale prices for armaments.) So do the "internal transaction prices" at which the export-import state monopolies buy home-produced goods for export and sell imported goods to the state wholesale trade organizations and state industrial enterprises, etc. The state procurement and state purchase price for agricultural produce is a somewhat special category of wholesale price; this is described in Chapter 4. On the other hand, prices paid by con-

[4] Vysoká škola ekonomická, *Sborník statí o plánování národního hospodářství* (Prague, 1954).

sumers for all consumers' goods and services and prices paid for production goods by the remaining small number of individual farmers and by a negligible handful of self-employed workers come under the retail price category.[5]

Both categories of prices are fixed by the State Planning Office; prices respond only by decision of the planners either to changing demand or supply or to changing cost or to inflationary or deflationary pressure. They are uniform for the whole country, and do not reflect varying transportation costs or other variations in cost among individual enterprises.

a) The *wholesale price* contains "cost of production," turnover tax, if applied (all capital goods seem to be entirely exempt since 1958), and the profit or loss of the enterprise. "Cost of production," in turn, includes "cost of raw materials and of semifinished or finished products, services from other enterprises for purposes of production, other materials, fuel, total wages, contributions paid by the enterprise for national insurance, depreciation of basic funds and of tools, etc., and miscellaneous."[6]

The capital discount rate is not included in the accounting of costs. ("Depreciation of basic funds" refers only to wear-and-tear of fixed capital assets.) Costs refer only to "present and past expenditure of labor." However, through underpricing of basic materials and of capital assets (with resulting undervaluation of the depreciation rate of capital assets), the costs as officially accounted do not always fully cover total wage costs at all stages of production.

The rate of tax, if applicable to some commodities at the wholesale price level, is added to the above wage costs, and the margin between the fixed wholesale price of the final product (from the point of view of the producing enterprise) and the sum of cost and turnover tax is described as "profit" or "loss." The ratio of profit to total costs at fixed prices is officially described as rentability (in Czech, *rentabilita*; the literal translation is profitability, or rate of profit, but the specific meaning is different).

---

[5] Prices charged by a private individual to another private individual are of limited importance. The amount of agricultural produce remaining for free sale after the state delivery quotas are fulfilled is rather small. Under the Czechoslovak law, it is a criminal offense for any person to sell services, such as painting a house, to another person for payment. These services are the monopoly of "communal industry." It is a criminal offense to sell privately secondhand articles, such as carpets. These can be sold only to "Bazar," the state shop for secondhand articles. It is also an offense for a doctor to have private patients, etc.

[6] According to *Sborník statí*, Chap. 11, p. 49. It should be noted that changes in import prices do not enter into the accounting of costs, nor do changes in export prices enter into the accounting of profits. All changes in external prices are absorbed in the budgets of foreign trade monopolies (see Chapter 6, Sections 5 and 6).

Rentabilita refers only to "accumulation in form of enterprise profits" (decentralized profit of the State monopoly), whereas the greatest part of the "socialistic accumulation" (state profit) is centralized in the turnover tax: see Chapter 8, Section 1, and Chapter 10, Sections 1 and 3.

It should be stressed that, in calculating the rentability of a whole sector of the national economy, not only the wholesale but also the retail turnover tax is assumed to be collected within the sector of production. For instance, the rentability in industry developed as follows (in percentage of total sales):[7]

		1953	1955	1956	1957
a.	Turnover tax[a]	26.3	24.4	21.9	20.6
b.	Profit	8.0	6.2	5.5	7.4
c.	Total "production cost"	65.7	69.4	72.6	72.0
d.	Total sales	100	100	100	100
	Rentability (ratio b:c)	12.2	8.9	7.5	10.3

[a] Total sum of "wholesale" and "retail" tax on all industrial goods.

There is an increasing tendency to keep the "accumulation" (sum of turnover tax and profits) very low at the basic stages of production, and there is a theory that the rate of turnover tax, concentrated in the final products, could serve as an indicator of relative scarcity (see below, in description of "retail prices").

Unfortunately, no information is available on the actual development of state wholesale prices or their level. The computation of the old wholesale price index was discontinued in 1951 (publication of the results was discontinued in 1949), and the new index of wholesale prices, which was tentatively computed (but not published) in 1957, has proved unsatisfactory.[8] The planning authorities examine the development of the state wholesale price level only on the basis of a derived index, obtained by comparing reports of enterprises on annual sales at current prices and at prices valid on July 1, 1954. Yet even this derived index has been published only for the most recent period. However, we can roughly assess trends in wholesale prices.

Only in 1949, the first year after the introduction of the centrally

[7] From *SRRC*, 1958, p. 118.

[8] A member of the State Statistical Office, A. Červený, stated in an article in *Statistický obzor*, No. 8, 1959: "Until 1951, an index of wholesale prices was calculated, based on 69 price series (mostly for raw materials and agricultural produce). This single way of statistically reporting the wholesale price level was not considered adequate, and its computation was discontinued in 1952. A new index of wholesale prices, based on selected price series, was reintroduced in 1957, but it did not succeed in correctly reflecting changes in the wholesale price level . . ."

planned economy, did the Price Control Office fix wholesale prices on the basis of submitted calculations of cost, plus a justifiable rate of profit. Until 1950, therefore, wholesale prices increased in line with increasing labor and other costs, and state price subsidies were limited to some kinds of food. But in 1950 the Price Control Office was abolished, and state wholesale prices were rigidly fixed for long periods by the State Planning Office, as described above. From the beginning of this new pricing system, investment goods seem to have been somewhat underpriced. In spite of the absence of a wholesale price index, there is some evidence that the level of state wholesale prices remained virtually unchanged in the 1951–57 period; labor costs, on the other hand, increased rapidly, especially in connection with the industrialization drive of 1951–53. Table 7.1 shows how a derived index of price investments compares with the index of earnings of workmen in capital goods industries, and with the index of wages and salaries in construction.

The lag of state wholesale prices behind wage costs was not fully compensated by increased productivity per worker, or by decrease of non-labor costs. In 1956, it was more or less officially acknowledged that in

TABLE 7.1—COMPARISON OF DERIVED INDEX OF INVESTMENT PRICES WITH INDICES OF WAGES AND SALARIES

	Derived Index of Investment Prices[a]		Index of Wages in Investment Goods Industries[b]	Index of Wages and Salaries in Construction[c]
1948	100	100	100	100
1949	135		106	110
1950	141		119	126
1951	145	140†	129	131
1952	145		145	150
1953	145		157	148
1954	145		169	157
1955	...	140†	171	161
1956	...		177	167
1957	...	141†	176	169
1958 (Jan. 1)	...	126†	181†[d]	...

[a] The first column is according to the *Economic Survey of Europe*, 1955. The second column is the author's estimate, obtained by comparing official retrospective data on total gross investments at 1948, 1956, 1957, and January 1, 1959, prices.

[b] From *SRRC*, 1958, p. 131. No index is available on total wage costs (the sum of wages *and* salaries, plus contributions paid by the enterprise). See also Chapter 9, Section 1.

[c] Index calculated by the author on the basis of data on average wages and salaries, *SRRC*, 1958, p. 174. See also Chapter 9, Section 1.

[d] Calculated by the author on the basis of the report on the *Results of the Fulfillment of the State Plan of Development*, giving average increase in the whole industry, under the assumption that the 1958 increase in wages was equally divided between investment and consumers' goods industries.

some branches the state wholesale price fell below cost. For example, an article by Jiří Typolt[9] described how the cost of production topped the state wholesale price in metallurgy. He stressed the resulting undervaluation of cost in the metal-using industry (engineering), giving the following example of fictitious and actual costs of production of a railway car:

	Based on Fixed State Wholesale Prices (Kčs)	Based on Actual Costs of Foundry Products (Kčs)
Foundry products	15,000	18,700
Other materials	5,600	5,600
Finishing costs	6,400	6,400
Total cost	27,000	30,700

Typolt implied that the "state wholesale price below cost" was also being applied in other branches of industry, and he described the curious way in which the low price for foundry products had a distorting effect on the costs of production within the metallurgical branch itself:

> In metallurgy, as well as in other branches of the national economy, prices involving a loss—a loss not due to uneconomical output but to external causes—cannot create the proper conditions to interest managers in rational output. An enterprise is better off using semifinished products bought from outside rather than its own, since the former cost less . . . The great gap between the price of materials bought and of one's own costs to produce them—as much as 30–40 per cent—not only makes up for the higher consumption of fuel needed to reheat the outside products, but also enables the enterprises to achieve a fictitious lowering of costs of production, although in reality the national economy has suffered a loss.

On March 14, 1956, the Czechoslovak government issued a directive that state wholesale prices should be determined, *in principle*, by an enterprise's own cost of production.[10] It was stated, however, that wholesale prices could be changed only once a year and that the first general revision of wholesale prices would be carried out only in 1958. The directive added that, as an exception to general principle, "individual wholesale prices may be fixed in such a way as to be in line with the economic relationships stipulated by the plan."

[9] "K úpravě státních velkoobchodních cen v hutním průmyslu," *Plánované hospodářství*, No. 10, 1956.

[10] I.e., labor cost and depreciation only, with no rate of interest on "basic funds" (capital assets) used.

Typolt indicated in his article that the planned increase in steel prices for 1958 was in the range of one-half, as compared with 1955–56 prices. He gave as an example construction steel (smooth steel for reinforced concrete, 18–24 mm), for which the wholesale price valid in 1955 was 640 Kčs per metric ton and that planned for 1958 was 970 Kčs, an increase of 51 per cent.

Other economists also pointed out the ill effects of wholesale price below cost, and stressed the necessity of doing away with large-scale price subsidies in heavy industry.[11]

In 1957, the level of state wholesale prices remained largely unchanged, as the derived index of investment prices indicates, but the planners tried to reduce somewhat the discrepancy between higher costs and lower wholesale prices by reducing wage costs. They stepped up their efforts to achieve a much faster rise in productivity of labor as compared with the rise in wages. In fact, the rise of wages in the investment goods industries was checked completely in that year, whereas productivity continued to rise (see Table 2.11).

Nevertheless, the announcement by Minister of Finance Ďuriš in his 1958 budget speech that the level of state wholesale prices would not be raised but *reduced* (see Chapter 8, Section 1) came as a surprise. On closer examination, the reductions appear to have been concentrated in branches where presumably there had been no large-scale subsidy; in metallurgy and in fuel, where the price-below-cost problem had been most serious, there has even been a slight increase in wholesale prices.[12]

Unfortunately, no systematic evidence on the change in wholesale prices is available, and it would be rather futile to attempt, in the absence of published data on wholesale prices, to derive a price index, with subdivisions for "machinery" and for "construction," from the investment statistics of 1957 and 1959 prices, because of the change of statistical coverage.[13] Nevertheless, it is reasonable to assume that the planners, in spite of the reduced general wholesale price level, tried to keep the net price subsidy down.

Where the turnover tax was formerly applied, although the price was below cost and the producing enterprise had to be subsidized, it was now

[11] See F. Zeman, *Predvoj*, September 12, 1957.

[12] As suggested by Červený's information on the movement of wholesale prices by industrial branches; further below.

[13] Statistics of 1957 prices include the cost of assembly work under "building construction investments," whereas those for 1959 prices include this cost in "machinery and equipment," and so forth. See Chapter 8, Section 2.

abolished and the fixed "loss" of the enterprise was reduced, and possibly done away with accordingly. For example, the 26 per cent tax on coal was abolished, with no change in the wholesale price of coal,[14] so that the receipts of the coal industry increased by 26 per cent. The main difference was that the state budget was deflated: in receipts, through lower turnover tax, and in expenditure, through lower price subsidy; this is discussed in the next chapter, on state budget and investments.

In spite of the efforts of the planners to bring about a somewhat more rational wholesale price structure, as described above, there is no doubt that the 1958 wholesale price reform did not entirely close the gap between higher cost and lower price and that underpricing continues to exist in important sectors of heavy industry.

Information on the change in wholesale prices between 1954 and 1958 was given by A. Červený of the State Statistical Office; it is based on derived index numbers from the output reports (Červený pointed out that price movements have not been statistically reported):[15]

STATE WHOLESALE PRICES IN 1958
June 1954 = 100

Industry, over-all average 98.7
Production goods 98.3
Consumers' goods 99.3

Branches:
Electric power 100.0
Fuel 122.3
Ferrous metallurgy, including iron ore............. 112.0
Nonferrous metallurgy 93.0
Chemical and rubber industries 89.3
Building materials 95.4
Wood-working industry 103.8
Wood pulp and paper 113.8
Glass, china, ceramics 94.6
Textiles 91.3
Ready-to-wear clothing 89.4
Leather goods, shoes, furs 96.2
Graphic arts industry 90.2
Food processing 109.1
Other branches of industry....................... 101.1

Unfortunately, no information is available on wholesale price changes between 1954 and 1956; yet it can be assumed that they were rather small. In ferrous metallurgy we can assume that the 12 per cent rise in the average

[14] According to K. Rozsypal, deputy chairman, State Planning Office, "Summary of the Discussion on Wholesale Prices," *Plánované hospodářství*, No. 2, 1959.
[15] *Statistický obzor*, No. 8, 1959.

wholesale price, as indicated by the above index, actually occurred between 1956 and 1958; Typolt's information (see footnote 9) indicated
that in 1956 the wholesale price for steel involved such a loss for the producing enterprise that an increase of approximately 50 per cent was needed
to bring it to the cost level by 1958. It is fairly safe to assume that the
actual increase in the wholesale price of steel was not very different from
the 12 per cent average price increase for all ferrous metallurgy, and
thus was insufficient to close the gap. The remaining gap seems not to
have been closed from the cost side either. According to an article by
A. Červený,[16] over-all costs of production in industry in the first half of
1958 were only 1.2 per cent lower than in 1956. Even if we allow for a
possible faster reduction of production costs in the "deficit" branches like
metallurgy, it is almost certain that there was still a considerable discrepancy between higher (though somewhat reduced) costs of production and
lower (though somewhat increased) wholesale prices for steel and probably also for other products of heavy industry.

The deputy chairman of the State Planning Office, K. Rozsypal, in his
above-mentioned article left no doubt about the continuing existence of
prices below cost; he agreed that wholesale prices in proportion to "value"
(i.e., labor costs at all stages of production) could make measuring of
efficiency easier, and that the calculation would not be distorted by dissimilar pricing of various materials and goods; but he argued that the
"discrepancy between price and cost of individual commodities" should
be dealt with "through taxation policy" (which obviously means to subsidize state wholesale prices for certain commodities from receipts of turnover tax on consumers' goods). The aim of such a pricing policy, according to Rozsypal, is "to achieve certain specific aims," for example, to
induce enterprises to use (artificially low-priced) machinery of a new
design, domestic materials instead of imported ones, etc.[17] Furthermore,

---

[16] "Index Numbers of Costs of Industrial Output," *Statistický obzor*, No. 12, 1958.

[17] However, some of Rozsypal's arguments seem to be contradictory. Stressing
that state wholesale prices should remain pegged for a period of approximately five
years, he gives an example of a new invention in the motorcycle industry which
would allow production of a more efficient type of motorcycle at reduced cost; he
argues that the price for the old type, which has become obsolete, should not be
changed and that the price for the new type should be fixed higher in proportion
to its better performance, although its cost of production is lower; he accepts the
fact that this would give the factory producing the new type a rate of profit much
above the average rate of profit in the motorcycle industry. Such pricing of newly
introduced products—if applied, for example, to machine tools—would work just
opposite to "inducing enterprises to use machinery of a new design." When claiming that underpricing should induce enterprises to use domestic materials instead of

Rozsypal recommended certain measures to reduce existing state wholesale price subsidies in the long run, for example, by using substitutes for products that involve a deficit wherever possible, by concentrating the output of a deficit product in enterprises where the deficit (and the subsidy necessary to cover the cost) is lowest, etc.

V. Komárek was even more explicit on the continuing state wholesale price subsidies and their distorting effects: "If iron ore is priced too low and the wholesale price of coke allows for no profit (rentability of cokeries is zero and the wholesale price for coke coal involves a loss), it is obvious that . . . metallurgy enjoys an unjustified advantage in our calculations."[18]

But the most recent, and most convincing, evidence of continuing large-scale deficits in industry comes from M. Vojta in his previously quoted article on net value of output.[19] He computed an index of profit per worker (average index of profit in the industry as a whole equals 100) and found that, in 1958, in ferrous metallurgy this index was only 3.5. In view of the generally low level of profits in industry (in 1958, 5.9 per cent of the total value of sales, the so-called "realized price," from *SRRC*, 1959, Table 7.8), profits in this large branch amounted to only 0.2 per cent of the value of sales; this means that if some lines of output in ferrous metallurgy produced at a profit exceeding 0.2 per cent, as they probably did, other lines must have produced at a loss. In the field of nonferrous metallurgy, Vojta's evidence on the necessity of a general subsidy is irrefutable: his "index of profit per worker" has a *negative* value, −74.9 per cent. Vojta further stressed that all enterprises with a net value of output of less than 30,000 Kčs per worker and year (also in other branches of industry) had a "negative index of profit per worker," and that this index was lowest for large enterprises, those with 5,000 and more wage earners.

For some specific groups of goods, the wholesale price subsidy may even have been increased recently; for example, there was a reduction in the wholesale price of agricultural machinery supplied to state farms and unified cooperatives by 30 per cent in June 1959,[20] although the previous price had already been officially stated to be below the cost of production. But this was an exceptional case; the reason for the new deficit price for

---

imported ones, Mr. Rozsypal seems to disregard the fact that internal wholesale prices for some imported commodities are below the actual import prices, as in the case of iron ore (see Chapter 4, Section 6).

[18] *Plánované hospodářství*, November 1959.

[19] *Statistický obzor*, 1960.

[20] According to *Práca*, July 7, 1959.

agricultural machinery was obviously to make up for the loss of advantage to the Socialist sector in agriculture when the double-pricing, discriminating in favor of state farms and agricultural cooperatives, was abolished in 1959 (see Chapter 4, Section 4).

Czechoslovak planning authorities are well aware of the distorting effects of underpricing, but they do not seem to give enough attention to the resulting waste of nonlabor input, especially of capital assets. They tend to gradually eliminate "prices below cost" by "continuously lowering the cost of production," especially through a faster rise of productivity of labor as compared with the rise in real earnings. The cautious policy toward increasing real per capita income in spite of the fast increase in material product in 1958 was probably designed not only to raise the rate of investments but also to correct the ratio of wholesale price to cost.[21] But to close the gap entirely will be a long-term program, which will go beyond the third Five-Year Plan of 1960–65, unless there is a change in the present pricing policy.

The problem of state wholesale prices has been discussed at length in order to establish that, in the 1951–58 period, wholesale prices for important commodities, especially in heavy industry, were much below cost and that underpricing of that kind has continued in Czechoslovakia to a somewhat reduced extent since the 1958 wholesale price reform, although some experts on Eastern European economies claim that large-scale underpricing is contrary to the current Soviet practice. We shall need the subsidy argument when examining Czechoslovak economic growth on the basis of gross national product and expenditure.

b) Retail prices are widely divorced from costs as well as from wholesale prices. They "depend on the tasks that the retail prices help us to fulfill";[22] those tasks are to achieve a fixed rate of accumulation through

[21] Marxist national income (net product in the "productive sphere," see Chapter 10, Section 1) increased in 1958 by 8 per cent. Fixed investments increased by 9 per cent, and if we allow for a possible faster increase in stocks, the increase in total investments—fixed and nonfixed—may have been around 10 per cent. Assuming an approximate 1:1 ratio between total personal income and "surplus value," we can estimate that the increase in personal income, corresponding to an 8 per cent increase in Marxist national income and to a 10 per cent increase in accumulation, would be around 6 per cent (all percentages based on constant prices). But real earnings in the "Socialist sector" increased by only 2 per cent, and real incomes in agriculture by not much more than 2 per cent. Obviously, the actual increase in accumulation was faster than the 10 per cent increase in expenditure on fixed and nonfixed investments; part of the difference was probably used to build up state reserves to improve the wholesale price structure and to check money inflation.

[22] Vysoká škola ekonomická, *Sborník statí o plánování národního hospodářství* (Prague, 1954), Part II, p. 62.

turnover tax and to use the varying incidence of turnover tax on various consumers' goods to adapt demand to the planned scope and pattern of output, exports, and imports and of the existing stocks of goods.

Public opinion does not differentiate between turnover tax and other constituents of the retail price. A reduction in turnover tax on consumers' goods is officially described simply as "reduction in retail prices." To the author's knowledge, the rates of turnover tax are not being currently published. As a rough estimate, the *average* rate of turnover tax on food and food products in 1958 was around 95 per cent and on industrial goods other than processed food it was approximately 100 per cent. In 1959, the turnover tax on industrial goods was reduced slightly more than that on food (see the cost-of-living index, Table 7.2). These averages, however, are very theoretical because, in reality, the rate of turnover tax varies widely according to the kinds of goods.

Since the 1953 currency reform, the rate of turnover tax and consumers' prices have been reduced by six stages so far. At every stage, the turnover tax on selected kinds of goods, and on selected assortments within the same kinds, was reduced by a varying percentage. The resulting change in consumers' prices will be discussed in the next section, on the cost-of-living index. The changes in consumers' prices were not linked with a corresponding change in state wholesale prices. In most recent times, there has been an increased tendency to keep wholesale prices low, to concentrate the full amount of turnover tax in consumers' prices, and to make the latter even more independent of the former. Deputy Chairman Rozsypal of the State Planning Office stated:[23]

> Low prices at basic stages of production make it possible to judge the degree of satisfaction of the needs of the population according to the rate of turnover tax applied on various consumers' goods. The more the accumulation is concentrated in the basic stages of production preceding the final product, the more difficult it is to assess the rate of accumulation in relation to the final product concerned [accumulation in the form of turnover tax]. A high rate of accumulation in the basic stages of production would prevent lowering consumers' prices, because turnover tax could not be allowed for in the final product: it would be impossible to reduce the retail price even if the output of the product in question could be increased, because such a reduction would necessitate a simultaneous reduction in the wholesale price.

[23] "Summary of the Discussion on Wholesale Prices," *Plánované hospodářství*, No. 2, 1959.

Mr. Rozsypal apparently starts from the assumption that wholesale prices must remain pegged for a long period and that a fixed over-all rate of accumulation through turnover tax must be achieved.

A discussion on the margin between state procurement and state purchase price for agricultural produce and the consumers' price for food, by a member of the teaching staff of the Economic Faculty in Prague, M. Křížek, also helps to clarify the present function of the retail price in Czechoslovakia:[24]

> In our country, every enterprise is supplied with raw materials, machinery, etc., at prices below their real value [presumably labor value]. This is so in agriculture too. Agriculture also obtains various means of production, has the use of machinery, has fertilizers and fodder delivered, etc., at low prices. This enables our farmers to produce at relatively low costs. [Křížek obviously refers to farmers on state farms and in unified cooperatives, and not to individual farmers (see Chapter 4, Section 4).] But it is only a fiction that costs of production are low. To produce, for instance, a hundredweight of wheat, a much greater amount of labor [than reflected by cost at official wholesale prices] must be expended. Thus, if we buy a kilogram of bread, its price includes not only the farmer's labor but that of the miner and of the workers in the metal-working industry, in engineering, in the chemical industry, and so on. . . .

Having explained that the great difference between prices paid to the farmers and the consumers' prices for food is due mainly to the turnover tax, Křížek continued:

> Why should we apply a turnover tax instead of supplying the means of production at their real [labor] value? In principle, the second solution would be possible, but it would not change consumers' prices. The present method, however, is more advantageous. It makes possible an elastic price policy, elastic in the sense that we can adjust prices more quickly to changing conditions of production; the second reason is that, by means of the turnover tax, the state secures immediate and continuous revenue which is indispensable for a continuous acceleration of the process of production in the national economy.

Only the last two arguments hold, in the author's opinion. The high and varying rate of turnover tax does serve to adjust consumers' prices to

[24] This was a commentary, broadcast by Radio Prague on January 12, 1959. The author apologizes for possible inaccuracies in taking down Mr. Křížek's talk.

changed conditions of production, or rather, to adapt demand for various goods to planned supply by pricing; and the turnover tax is, in fact, the main source of state revenue and state accumulation (see Chapter 8, Section 1). The first argument, that consumers' prices would not change if the turnover tax were reduced, is valid only on the assumption that the full amount of this tax is used to subsidize the price of the means of production. But this is far from reality. Only one-third of the revenue from the turnover tax was used in 1957 to keep prices of basic commodities, machinery, etc., low.[25] Most of the receipts from the turnover tax are being used for fixed investments, which Křížek implies by stating that the tax is indispensable for continuous acceleration of the process of production, for nonfixed investments including undesired increase in stocks of goods, for subsidizing state farms, etc., and for foreign trade net subsidy. A reduction in the turnover tax expended on other purposes than a genuine price subsidy could be accompanied by a reduction in consumers' prices.

In contrast to the situation on wholesale prices, a fair amount of statistical information is available on retail prices (including turnover tax). List prices for a number of products are published regularly (some price series are shown in Table 7.3), and so is the year-to-year index of retail prices (see *SRRC*, 1959, Tables 15.11 and 15.12). This index, however, is computed in such a way that it reflects not only price movements but substitution effects.[26]

J. Mach of the State Statistical Office calculated the percentages of price change by six retail price reductions since the 1953 currency reform in the following way:[27]

Year	Date of Price Reduction	Total Retail Sales (*Billion Kčs*)	"Savings" of the Population on Purchases (*Billion Kčs per year*)	"Price Reduction" (*Per cent*)
1953	October 1, 1953	67.1	4.5	6.7
1954	April 1, 1954	74.6	5.6	7.5
1955	April 1, 1955	80.1	1.3	1.6
1956	April 1, 1956	84.8	2.1	2.5
1957	December 3, 1956	89.2	1.4	1.6
1958	March 8, 1959	90.5	2.3	2.5

[25] See Chapter 8, Section 1.

[26] The index is based on 118 group price series, covering total value of sales. It is constructed on the Paasche formula $I = \Sigma p_1 q_1 / \Sigma p_0 q_1$, where p_0 is the price of the previous year, p_1 is the price of the current year, and q_1 is the quantity sold in the current year, where $\Sigma p_0 q_1 = \Sigma (p_1 q_1 / p_1)/p_0$.

[27] "Price Reductions and Family Cost of Living," *Statistický obzor*, No. 5, 1959.

In contrast to the "retail price index," Mach forecasts the "savings" of the population—except for 1959—on the basis of the change in list prices, assuming that elasticity of demand is zero, so that the change in consumers' prices does not influence the scope and pattern of purchases. His "price reduction" is a percentage obtained by simply comparing the forecast "savings" to total sales.

Furthermore, a cost-of-living index is being published, as described in the next section.

4. Cost-of-Living Index

Publication of the prewar index of the cost of living for "workers' families" and for "employees' families" was discontinued in 1949. For the years 1953 up to the present, numerical results have been published of the new cost-of-living index, based on $1937 = 100$, and of the same index based on June $1953 = 100$ (i.e., the month following the second postwar currency reform).[28] The index is calculated for "workers' and employees' families" and for "farmers' families." Its construction has been disclosed only in general terms.[29] Nevertheless, two shortcomings of the new index can be detected. First, some of the 1937 consumers' prices, as listed in *SRRC*, 1958, refer to high-quality products, whereas the prices in the same series for 1953–58 are those for medium or lower quality.[30] Second, the index is obviously based on list prices, disregarding the fact that lower-priced goods often disappeared from the state retail shops (there are no private shops left) in the 1956–58 period.[31] Both these short-comings create a downward bias. But even if these shortcomings are accepted, the index could not be used for the purpose of studying real wages over the decade 1948–58, since no official data on the cost of living have been published for the years 1948–53. Yet this period was the time

[28] The index is based on the Laspeyres formula $I = \Sigma p_1 q_0 / \Sigma p_0 q_0$, thus probably overrating the price changes.

[29] The index for workers' and employees' families is based on 1955 consumption according to the "family budgets." It contains 133 food and drink items, 178 manufactures, and 61 services.

[30] For example, the 1937 price of a pair of men's leather shoes is quoted as 79 Kč, when prices ranged from 59 to 99 Kč. The 1957 price in the same series, according to the Statistical Yearbook, is 179 Kčs, though at that time prices for a pair of men's shoes with leather soles ranged from approximately 150 to 400 Kčs.

[31] A letter from a worker, published by *Rudé právo* on December 13, 1958, says: "After the currency reform, a good men's shirt cost 39 Kčs. Today, there is no shirt available under 50 Kčs. The cheaper kind of silone [Czech nylon] stockings at approximately 23 Kčs a pair are not to be got either; only the more expensive ones at 42 Kčs a pair are in the shops."

TABLE 7.2—ESTIMATE OF THE COST-OF-LIVING INDEX OF
WAGE AND SALARY EARNERS IN CZECHOSLOVAKIA

	Weight	1948 Year	1952 Year	1953 June	1954 Apr.	1955 Apr.	1956 Dec.	1957 Dec.	1958 Dec.	1959 March
BY STAGES OF POSTWAR CONSUMERS' PRICE REDUCTIONS										
1937 = 100[a]										
General	100	104	155	180	162	157	152	153	156	150
Food, drink	42	100	176	213	201	200	191	192	193	179
Clothing, footwear	14	184	256	341	281	259	251	257	273	268
Other manufactures	10	137	251	234	177	177	177	177	177	152
Rent, fuel, light	14	47	50	44	44	44	44	45	46	46
Other expenditures	20	85	80	80	79	78	78	78	78	78
1948 = 100[a]										
General	100	100	150	174	156	151	147	148	150	144
Food, drink	42	100	176	213	201	200	191	192	193	179
Clothing, footwear	14	100	139	185	153	141	136	140	148	145
Other manufactures	10	100	183	170	129	129	129	129	129	112
Rent, fuel, light	14	100	106	94	94	94	94	96	98	98
Other expenditures	20	100	94	94	93	92	92	92	92	92
June 1953 = 100										
General	100			100	89	87	84	85	86	83
Food, drink	42			100	94	93	89	90	91	85
Clothing, footwear	14			100	82	76	73	75	80	78
Other manufactures	10			100	76	76	76	76	76	67
Rent, fuel, light	14			100	100	100	100	102	104	104
Other expenditures	20			100	99	98	98	98	98	98

	1948	1952	1953	1954	1955	1956	1957	1958
YEARLY AVERAGES (CALENDAR YEARS)								
General index 1948 = 100	100[a]	150[a]	164	160	152	147[b]	148	150
1953 = 100			100	97	93	90	90	91

The estimate of the cost of living is based on 23 price series, to be found in Table 7.3, together with detailed weights. The group "other expenditures," however, is based only on a very rough estimate obtained by linking the "other expenditures of a worker's family" in the prewar official index, up to 1948, with the author's estimate, up to 1952, and with the "services" group in the present official index, from 1953 to 1959.

[a] Index numbers for the postwar years prior to the second currency reform of June 1953 are calculated on the basis of prices in terms of 1953 currency units. In terms of the first postwar currency, they would be five times higher (thus, in 1948, in terms of the then-valid currency, the cost of living amounted to 520 per cent of the 1937 basis). (See Chapter 7, Sections 1 and 3.)

[b] Including both price reductions of 1956 (April and December).

of greatest industrial expansion, with accompanying inflation and rapidly rising cost of living. Only the entire decade 1948–58 can be considered as a reasonable cross-section of economic development both under the rigid expansion policy and under the economic "thaw," which seem to alternate in the centrally planned economies.

Therefore, the author was compelled to attempt his own estimate of the cost of living covering the entire period 1948–58, at least for workers' and employees' families (which now represent in Czechoslovakia over two-thirds of the total population). Three main difficulties were encountered in computing it:

a) In 1948, a fairly important black market existed, with much higher prices than those established by the official low-priced rationing. In 1949, an official state "free market" was introduced, parallel to the rationed market, with many prices as high as, or even higher than, those on the black market. It is very difficult to guess what portion of civilian consumption was covered by rationed low-priced goods and what portion by high-priced black-market, and later free-market, goods. The ratio varied according to categories of workers; for instance, workers in heavy industry, and especially miners, enjoyed very large supplementary rations.[32] Additional rations were also granted to children. An accurate weighting of the rationed and black-market or free-market purchases is almost impossible. As an estimate, the population purchased, on the average, one-third of the total consumption on the black market in 1948 and on the free market in 1952.[33]

b) The pattern of consumption in a system of state monopoly of retail trade, with prices often fixed irrationally and with varying availability of goods, is subject to sudden changes. Averages of the prewar consumption pattern, the pattern in 1948, and the 1957 pattern have been used as weights in the estimate, but this of course is not a satisfactory answer to the problem of weighting.[34]

c) The 1945 currency reform—though it introduced a new symbol for the currency unit, Kčs, and though it was followed immediately by a

[32] Frant. Skoupil (*Tvorba*, August 6, 1951) estimated the value of additional ration cards for a heavy-industry worker at 10,157 Kčs a year (one-sixth of his money earnings) and for a miner at 19,526 Kčs a year (one-fourth of his earnings), as compared with the rations of an ordinary worker in industry. These amounts have probably been calculated as a difference between the rationed price and the free-market price of the volume of additional rations.

[33] A ratio of 2:1 between official and black-market prices was estimated by many members of the Economic Council and of the State Planning Office in 1948. On June 27, 1951, the then Deputy Secretary General of the Communist Party, Josef Frank, announcing a sharp increase in free-market prices, stated that "purchases of meat in the free market have reached one-third of the total meat purchases." Since the meat ration was reduced at the same time, it is likely that, in spite of the higher free-market prices, the share of free-market purchases did not go down. Meat is, of course, not representative of the breakdown of total purchases into "rationed" and "free," but there are other indications that the over-all ratio of purchases on the rationed market to those on the free market remained roughly 2:1.

[34] Technically the Laspeyres formula was used, with 1948 weighting. The ficti-

rise in official prices to a level three times higher than prewar—maintained, formally, a unit continuity of the prewar legal tender (Kč) and of the war tender (K in Bohemia and Moravia and Ks in Slovakia). There was no general change in nominal wages or other nominal claims. The price indices, naturally, went up accordingly. (The index of the cost of living, on a 1939 = 100 basis, went up to 325 in 1947.) On the other hand, the second currency reform, of May 1953, though maintaining the Kčs name of the monetary unit, introduced a new currency unit, equal, in theory, to five old units. (There was a general deflation of all wages, salaries, pensions, and other money claims by 5:1, as described in Section 1.) This coefficient was also one of the factors in fixing new uniform state retail prices, which replaced the old rationed and free-market prices. Czechoslovak official statistics published after June 1953 quote retrospectively all value figures in terms of 1953 currency units, that is, data for 1945–53 are deflated by 5:1. Thus the 1948 prices in Table 7.3 have also been given in terms of 1953 currency units. The original prices, in terms of 1945 currency units, were five times higher.

The difficulties described in *a*) and *b*) necessarily make the estimate of the cost of living during the double-pricing period very doubtful. Since any claim to accuracy would be very illusory, the consumption picture has been simplified and the number of price series on which the estimate is based has been kept down to 23: food (11 items), manufactured goods (9 items), rent, electricity, and coal.

In spite of this very rudimentary construction, the estimate shows a certain correlation with the official index during 1953–58, the period of continuing consumer price reductions and increasing supplies of consumer goods in a uniform market. Converted on the June 1953 base, this index compares with the official index as follows:

	1953 June	1954 April	1955 April	1956 Dec.	1957 Dec.	1958 Dec.
Author's estimate	100	89	87	84	85	86
Official postwar index	100	87.4	86.1	82.2	82.5	83.0

---

tious 1948 consumption pattern, based on official rationed purchases only and disregarding the black market, was roughly corrected by giving some regard to the average change in consumption of goods covered by the index between 1937 and 1957 (in these years, the pattern of consumption was not distorted by the double market). The 1948 = 100 index was then calculated back to 1937 and arithmetically rebased on that year. In view of the uncertainties of weighting, it would be futile to use the ideal Fisher formula.

The 1937–48 movement of the cost of living, as reflected by the author's estimate, seems to be also supported by a semiofficial index, computed at the beginning of 1949 by V. Aulický, a member of the Government Price Control Office. Aulický's index is based on the prewar "market basket" with rationed market prices for the food obtainable on ration and free-market prices for the prewar food consumption exceeding the rations. This is not quite realistic, because the market basket priced in this way cost over 100,000 Kčs (1945 currency) at the beginning of 1949; only 2 per cent of the workers had such a high income. (Even in prewar times, the prewar market basket used as weighting for the official index was not realistic; in 1937, the cost was 16,872 Kč [prewar currency], and only one-tenth of the workers had an income of that amount or more.) Obviously, an average worker's family could not afford to buy so large a part of their food on the high-priced free market as suggested by Aulický's index. On the other hand, his index priced all manufactures at official rationed prices, whereas a certain amount was purchased on the black market, and later on the free market, at much higher prices. The upward bias resulting from overweighting the free-market purchase of food may have been compensated by the downward bias of disregarding the purchase of manufactures on the black market, so that the index may reflect fairly well the actual change in the cost of living.

Aulický used "free market" prices for food purchased above the ration price, whereas the author had to use black-market prices for 1948 (the free market was introduced only in 1949). But black-market prices of 1948 were on the whole only slightly lower than free-market prices of 1949 (the latter started to increase rapidly only in connection with the intensified industrialization drive after the revision of the first Five-Year Plan in 1951); from this angle, there is no severe limitation of comparability of the two indices.

The official index, Aulický's index, and the author's estimate (rebased to 1937 = 100) compare as follows:

Official prewar index (prewar consumption pattern, rationed market prices only), 1948 .... 321.6

Aulický's index (prewar consumption pattern, combined rationed and free-market prices for food, rationed prices for manufactures), beginning 1949 595

Author's estimate (average of simplified 1937, 1948, and 1957 consumption patterns, combined rationed and black-market prices for all goods), 1948 .... 518[a]

[a] Figure from Table 7.2 converted from 1953 currency units into old currency units.

TABLE 7.3—CONSUMERS' PRICES IN CZECHOSLOVAKIA

(Prewar data in Kč, postwar data in Kčs [1953 currency])

Kind, Quantity	Weight	1937	1948 Rationed	1948 Black Market	1952 Rationed	1952 Free Market	June 1953 (after 2d currency reform)	April 1954	April 1955	Dec. 1956	Dec. 1957	Dec. 1958	March 1959
Rye bread (kg)	4	2.10	1.00	1.50	1.60	3.10	2.80	2.60	2.60	2.60	2.60	2.60	2.60
Wheat flour, coarse (kg)	4	2.90	1.40	3.00	3.60	7.60	6.00	4.90	4.90	4.40	4.40	4.40	4.40
Butter, med. quality (kg)	5	16.50	16.00	35.00	16.00	90.00	44.00	42.00	42.00	42.00	42.00	42.00	38.00
Lard, medium quality (kg)	4	14.85	15.00	30.00	15.00	90.00	36.00	36.00	36.00	32.00	32.00	32.00	28.00
Milk, av. price (liter)[a]	4	1.45	0.90	2.00	0.95	1.60	2.00	2.00	2.00	2.10	2.10	2.10	2.10
Eggs, av. price (each)[a]	3	0.60	0.60	1.50	0.75	1.80	1.40	1.30	1.30	1.25	1.20	1.20	1.20
Sugar (kg)	5	6.35	3.20	12.00	3.20	28.00	14.00	11.00	11.00	11.00	11.00	11.00	9.60
Beef, hind quarter, boneless (kg)	5	17.00	8.50	20.00	9.60	40.00	25.00	25.00	25.00	24.00	24.00	24.00	24.00
Pork, joint (kg)	5	13.30	10.00	25.00	10.00	52.00	29.40	29.40	29.40	28.00	28.00	29.00	29.00
Coffee (kg)	1	36.00	23.00	100.00	—	500.00	300.00	240.00	240.00	210.00	210.00	210.00	210.00
Beer, 10% (liter)	2	2.60	1.60	—	3.60	—	3.60	3.00	2.40	2.40	2.40	2.40	2.40
Man's suit, mixed wool	3	200.00	260.00	600.00	540.00	1280.00	740	505	505	486	490	500	486
Woolen fabric (m)	2	80.00	100.00	400.00	112.00	590.00	510	436	436	400	400	420	420
Man's cotton shirt, medium	3	28.00	35.00	90.00	44.00	130.00	64.00	46.50	46.50	46.50	48.00	53.00	45.00
Lady's dress, artificial silk	3	130.00	150.00	400.00	260.00	620.00	330	271	140	140	150	160	140
Leather shoes, med. (pr)	3	59.00	59.00	150.00	112.00	200.00	167.00	167	167	167	180	190	190
Washing soap, average of 3 cheapest kinds (kg)	3	5.30	6.00	15.00*	10.00*	25.00*	17.00	13.00	13.00	10.00	10.00	10.00	8.80
Furniture, bedroom, med.	2	2100	3000	4000	—	4100	4000	4000	4000	3650	3650	3650	3650
Motorcycle, Jawa 250	2	4990	3600*	8000*	—	16300*	12600	8800	8800	8800	8800	8800	8800
Sewing machine	2	1250	1200*	3000*	—	3300*	2300	1450	1450	1450	1450	1450	1450
Rent (1 room and kitchen)	8	90	50	50	50	—	50.00	50.00	50.00	50.00	52.00	54.00	55.00
Electricity, mo. rate (kwh)	3	2.70	0.90	—	—	0.80	0.80	0.80	0.80	0.80	0.80	0.80	0.80
Hard coal (100 kg)	3	29.10	16.00	28.00	19.20	35.20	16.00	16.00	16.00	16.00	16.00	16.00	16.00

Prices for 1937, from prewar price statistics (Cenové zprávy Státního úřadu statistického, Prague), are not available for most manufactures; prices for manufactures are taken from postwar statistical and other publications. Black-market prices are estimated by the author. Other postwar prices up to 1953 from various official statistics and statements. Author's estimates (*) are subject to a large margin of error. Prices for 1953–59 are according to official price statistics, except for manufactures in the 1956–58 period, which have been estimated by the author according to unofficial reports, taking into account the nonavailability of low-priced goods on the uniform market. Prices for 1937 are in Kč; for 1948 and 1952 in Kčs units of 1953 ("new currency"; original prices deflated 5:1); for 1953–59 in Kčs (new 1953 currency). Weights are those used in the author's estimate of the cost-of-living index (Table 7.2).

After the first draft of this book was completed, another estimate of the cost-of-living index, by J. Mach, was published by the Czechoslovak State Statistical Office.[35] It is linked with the calculation of the "necessary working time" to buy the most important items of consumption and is based on 32 series; in addition to the 23 price series used by the author, it also covers rolls, rice, sausage, ham, margarine, potatoes, apples, wine, rum, cigarettes, gas, bricks, and cement, but omits important manufactures, especially textiles, which are covered in the author's index: woolen fabrics, artificial silk, furniture, motorcycles, and sewing machines.

This index involves the following factors of downward bias—most of which have been mentioned by Mach himself:

a) The weights given to rent, electricity, and gas are based on actual purchases, while the rest of the "market basket" is fictitiously limited to the items covered by the index. Thus, rent, electricity, and gas are greatly overweighted, being just the low-priced items (rent has hardly increased at all since prewar years).

b) On the other hand, high-priced manufactures are not covered by the index.

c) Some prices used for the base year 1937 are valid for Prague only, such as those for potatoes, fruit, and especially rent; these are compared with the postwar averages for the whole country. Under the prewar market economy, prices in Prague were considerably higher than in the rest of the country: the average 1937 rent for a worker's flat, as estimated in the author's computation, was 90 Kč a month, whereas Mach's estimate for Prague is 250 Kč.

d) He compares prewar prices for high-quality goods and services with postwar prices for medium-quality goods. This probably applies to rent, and it certainly does to shoes. The prewar price of 79 Kč for a pair of men's shoes is for above-average quality, but the postwar price of 176 Kčs is for only medium quality.

e) For the 1953–59 period, Mach uses list prices, although lower-priced assortments often were not available on the market.

The downward bias in *c*), *d*), and *e*) has already been discussed in connection with the official cost-of-living index.

After having studied Mach's index carefully, the author still feels

[35] "Comparing the Development of Wages and Prices on Czechoslovakia's Territory, 1914–1959," *Statistický obzor*, No. 8, 1959.

justified in using his own estimate of the cost of living for further computations. The results of the two indices compare as follows (cost of living, 1937 = 100):

	1914	1937	June 1953	April 1959
Mach's index	14	100	152	119
Author's index (arithmetically rebased to 1937)	...	100	180	150

In any case, the author is compelled to use his own estimate for the 1948–53 period, for which the results of Mach's index are not available.

More detailed results of the estimate of cost-of-living trends can be found in Table 7.2. As compared with the prewar period, the cost of living increased most in clothing and footwear, followed by increases in food and other manufactured goods, whereas there was a decrease in rent, fuel, light, and other expenditures.

The weights and price series used can be found in Table 7.3.

A comparison by countries of the cost-of-living indices is included in Table 9.6, together with a rough comparison of real wages in industry. Although comparability among countries is subject to great limitations, it is obvious that the cost of living in Czechoslovakia moved rather independently from the general trends in the market economies. It went up until 1953, and after a sudden jump during the currency reform of that year, it fell substantially until 1958. Over the whole period 1948–58, the cost of living probably rose faster than in West Germany, Great Britain, or the United States, but slower than in France or Austria.

Chapter 8

STATE BUDGET AND INVESTMENTS

1. State Budget

The purpose of this section is not to discuss public finance in a centrally planned economy but to give basic information which may be necessary in order to elucidate the preceding chapter on prices, to understand the meaning of Czechoslovak statistics on investments in the next section of this chapter, and to discuss some of the problems that will emerge in connection with the attempt to estimate Czechoslovak national income and gross national product in Chapter 10.

As is to be expected, the proportion of gross national product going through the state budget is much larger in Czechoslovakia than in the market economies. State receipts and state expenditures reach a level equal to almost two-thirds of gross national product (provided the estimate of the latter, in Chapter 10, is not too far from reality). In West Germany and in the United States[1] less than one-fifth, and in the United Kingdom less than one-fourth, of the gross national product has been reallocated through the state budget in recent years.

Yet the really important difference lies in the different economic function of the state budget in Czechoslovakia rather than in its scope. In market economies state budgets serve, from the economic point of view, as important tools to redistribute income. This is not so in Czechoslovakia. Tables 8.1 and 8.2 show the Czechoslovak budget in recent years by main categories of receipts and expenditures. Direct taxation comes under the official heading of "receipts from the population." This amounts to only 11–12 per cent of the budgetary state revenue. The main component of the "receipts from the population" is the "wage tax," which, in 1958, provided 92 per cent of actually collected personal taxes.[2] The rates of the wage tax, and of some other personal taxes, are much less progressive than

---

[1] Referring to the federal budget.

[2] Personal taxes collected in 1958 were as follows (from *SRRC*, 1959, Table 21.6), in million Kčs: wage tax, 9,340; agricultural tax (paid by individual farmers), 131; tax on incomes from literary and artistic activities, 15; tax on other personal incomes, 176; tax on entrepreneurship (paid in addition to "tax on other incomes" by all nonagricultural self-employed workers), 43; "house tax" on private house ownership, 405.

TABLE 8.1—CZECHOSLOVAK STATE BUDGET:
PLANNED EXPENDITURES AND RECEIPTS

(In billion Kčs, at current prices)

	1954	1955	1956	1957	1958	1958 "Comparable Basis" with 1957[a]
Receipts:						
"From the Socialist sector".	...	73.1	77.2	85.1	80.4	93
Turnover tax	46.5	44.9	...	44.5	49.8	46.7
Paid-off profits	16.6	...	...	17.3	13.4	20
"From the population"	...	10.3	10.7	10.7	11.3	11
Other receipts	...	2.8	2.3	2.5	3.0	...
Total receipts	87.8	86.2	90.3	98.2	94.7	104
Expenditures:						
"To promote the national economy"	48.5	43.9	48.1	53.2	45.3	60
Education, culture, social welfare	27.4	28.3	28.8	31.9	36.9[b]	32[c]
Defense and security	7.8	10.4	9.6	9.3	8.9	9
Administration	3.9[d]	3.5	3.4	3.5	3.4	3
Total expenditures	87.6	86.0	89.9	97.9	94.4	104
Budget surplus	0.2	0.2	0.4	0.3	0.2	...

Data are from *SRRC*, 1958, Table 21.1, completed by data from budget speeches as reported in *Rudé právo*. Figures are not quite comparable from year to year, owing to changes in budget structure. They do not sum up accurately into totals because of rounding [by the author].

 [a] Figures estimated on the basis of statements by Minister of Finance Ďuriš on the new state wholesale prices, as reported in *Rudé právo*, April 16, 1958.

 [b] Including housing, previously under "promotion of the national economy."

 [c] Excluding housing.

 [d] Including service on state debt of 0.2 billion Kčs.

in the West. On the expenditure side there is, in fact, a considerable category of expenditure on "education, culture, and social welfare" (approximately one-third of total budgetary expenditures), which has a bearing on the pattern of the sum of individual and collective incomes of the population; but the main item within this category is the benefits paid to the population through national health and social welfare insurance. As we shall see in the course of further examination, national insurance in Czechoslovakia is financed autonomously: contributions cover cost, and no *net* subsidy from state budget can be traced.[3]

The main economic function of the state budget in Czechoslovakia

 [3] National insurance itself, of course, contributes somewhat toward more equality in incomes. Family allowances and, to a lesser extent, old-age benefits are designed under the most recent regulation, of March 1959, so as to assist some groups of people in the lowest income brackets (see Chapter 9, Section 2).

TABLE 8.2—CZECHOSLOVAK STATE BUDGET:
OPERATIONS—ACTUAL STATE RECEIPTS AND EXPENDITURES

(In billion Kčs, at current prices)

	1956	1957
Receipts:		
"From the Socialist sector"	...	87.8
Turn-over tax	45.4	44.5
Paid-off profits	13.7	17.3
"From the population"	...	10.8
Other receipts	...	...
Total receipts	97.3	101.8
Expenditures:		
"To promote the national economy"	55.2	55.3
State fixed investments	20.6[a]	18.4[b]
General overhauls	6.7[c]	7.3[c]
Technical research and development	...	2.6
Increase in stocks	...	1.9
Total investments financed from state budget	30†	30†
Education, culture, social welfare	28.2	33.0
Defense and security forces	9.1	8.7
Administration	3.4	3.3
Total expenditure	95.9	100.9
Actual surplus	1.3	0.9

Data are from speeches by the Minister of Finance, as reported in *Rudé právo*, unless stated otherwise. Figures are not quite comparable in price pattern from year to year, owing to the increasing transfer of public receipts and expenditures from the state budget to the budget of the "national committees," etc. Figures on "investments" are lower than figures on "public investments" in Table 8.4, since the latter are financed also by local administration (national committees) and in part by the state enterprises themselves.

[a] Excluding general overhauls (see Chapter 8, Section 2), but possibly including a small amount of nonfixed investments.

[b] Excluding general overhauls.

[c] Rough estimate by the author, at 1956–57 investment prices, based on data at 1959 prices in Table 8.5 and the derived investment price index (Chapter 7, Section 3).

(and, in fact, in all centrally planned economies) is to secure "Socialist accumulation," that is, capital formation under Socialist systems in the Soviet area. There are two sources of such a centralized accumulation: the state's share in the profits of nationalized enterprises of all kinds (until 1957, approximately one-fifth of total state revenue) and the turnover tax (until 1957, half of state revenue; a shift between those two items in 1958 will be discussed further below). The turnover tax and its role in price fixing was discussed in Chapter 7, Section 3. The turnover tax, though collected within the sectors of production, is concentrated in retail prices, whereas wholesale prices are practically exempt from it. Therefore, a reduction in the wholesale price, with unchanged fixed retail price, means a higher rate of turnover tax. At the same time a lower wholesale price level reduces both sides of the state budget. A statement by Minister of Finance Ďuriš in his 1958 budget speech confirms the analysis in Chapter 7:[4]

> Through a new adjustment of state wholesale prices as of January 1, 1958—an adjustment undertaken to give more weight to the function of profits and efficiency—total receipts and total expenditures of the state budget were reduced by over three billion Kčs. Through lower state wholesale prices,[5] the profits of state enterprises went down and the receipts from turnover tax went up. The price reduction also lowered the total cost of investments and other budgetary expenditures. All this, however, had no bearing on the material scope of the budget. Lower state wholesale prices led, above all, to lower expenditures of state enterprises. This is the reason why, in the new budget, the share of expenditures for the national economy fell to 47.9 per cent of total budgetary expenditures. (In 1957 the corresponding percentage was 54.3 per cent.[6]

Ďuriš further stated that on a *comparable* basis, budgetary revenue and expenditure are *increasing* by 10 per cent. In absolute current figures, however, revenue *went down* from 98.8 billion Kčs in 1957 to 94.7 billion Kčs in the 1958 budget. Budgetary expenditure went down from 98.2 billion Kčs to 94.5 billion Kčs.

A comparison of Ďuriš's 1958 budget figures in terms of billion Kčs at current 1958 wholesale prices and in terms of percentage increase based on comparable prices suggests that the wholesale price level may have decreased by approximately 12 per cent. In Chapter 7 (Section 3) it was seen that the reduction in wholesale prices seems to have been concentrated in the building sector, whereas prices for machinery and equipment, which had been considerably below cost, may have been slightly raised. Therefore, the reduction in the wholesale price level did not necessarily mean an increase in the subsidy of wholesale prices. This subsidy may, on the

---

[4] *Rudé právo*, April 16, 1958.

[5] Ďuriš refers, in fact, to the price level. Some wholesale prices have been increased (for steel etc., see Chapter 7, Section 3).

[6] An important factor in the smaller share of "expenditures in the national economy" in the total 1958 budget was the shift of housing from this category to that of "social welfare expenditures"; see Tables 8.1 and 8.2.

contrary, have been reduced to a "net deficit"; but the reduction in the wholesale price level also meant lower profits for enterprises. The resulting loss of state revenue from the state's share in profits, however, was compensated by increased revenue from turnover tax (which covered the increased margin between the lower wholesale price level and the unchanged retail price level). In the 1958 state budget the share of turnover tax in total revenue thus went up to more than half, while the state's share in profits went down to one-eighth of the total revenue (see Table 8.1).

All this did not entail any great change in the rate of accumulation. Both the state's share in profits and the full amount of turnover tax are included in the so-called "accumulation plan." In the estimate of Marxist national income in Table 10.6, the assumption is made that there is no difference between turnover tax and profits of the state.[7] In the official budget figures, turnover tax is subsumed under "receipts from the Socialist sector," although in the last instance almost the full amount of it is collected from the population in retail prices. (It is interesting to note that, for instance, total contributions to national insurance are also subsumed under "receipts from the Socialist sector," although only half is paid by the nationalized enterprises, whereas the other half is deducted from earnings.)

In recomputing national income under the Western definition, however, some corrections have to be made in the sum of profits and turnover tax in order to arrive at the genuine net accumulation (capital formation). The expenditure side of the state budget provides a clue for such a rough correction.

Official Czechoslovak figures on budget expenditure give only very broad and heterogeneous categories; the largest item is "expenditure for the national economy." Until 1957, its share in the total budgetary expenditure at state-fixed prices amounted to over half, whereas expenditures on culture and social welfare, including the autonomously financed national insurance benefits, amounted to one-third, expenditures on defense and security to less than one-tenth, and expenditures on administration to one-thirtieth of the total budgetary outlay (see Tables 8.1 and 8.2). The author endeavored to subdivide "expenditures for the national economy" into two basic groups: one comprising investments (fixed and nonfixed, including increase in unsalable stocks) and the other which can be described as subsidies. Of the latter, however, only part can be considered price subsidies. The other part is so-called endowments (*dotace*)

---

[7] "Economically speaking, there is no difference between turnover tax and profits" (*Politicá ekonomie*, June 1954).

to individual enterprises or for unprofitable forms of production (e.g., state farms).[8]

This subdivision of "expenditures for the national economy" can be found in Table 8.2. Some of the subdivided figures are overlapping. Yet, it is possible to estimate roughly the following breakdown of "expenditures in the national economy" in 1957, at current state-fixed prices (in billion Kčs):

Fixed investments financed by the state budget	18.4[a]
Improvement of technology and technical research	2.6[a]
Increase in stock	1.9[a]
Other investments, including "general overhauls" (see Section 2 of this chapter)	6.7†
Total state-financed investments, fixed and nonfixed, approximately	29*
Foreign trade net subsidy (see Chapter 6, Section 6)	8†
Domestic wholesale price subsidies, endowments to individual companies and state farms, and financing of other deficits	18†
Total	55.3[a]

[a] Official figures, given by Minister of Finance Ďuriš (*Rudé právo*, December 12, 1958).

(The above figures on investments are lower than the data on "investments by state organs" in Table 8.5, as they do not include fixed investments financed through the budgets of national committees or by individual enterprises themselves.)

The above approximation of subsidies from the state budget is subject to a large margin of error, but it will be very useful in connection with the estimate of Czechoslovak national income and gross national product under the Western definition.

The pattern of the Czechoslovak state budget is absolutely incomparable to Western state budgets because of the very different price structure. On the other hand, a comparison with the scope and pattern of state revenue and expenditure in other centrally planned economies is of some validity. This can be found, for 1958, in Table 8.3. It is noteworthy that in the other most developed centrally planned economy, East Germany,

---

[8] Such direct subsidies to state farms have been officially confirmed; see F. Kord, "Changes in the Planning and Financing of State Farms" (*Plánované hospodářství*, No. 2, 1959). Subsidies to individual enterprises in industry also exist, but some of them are clearly connected with a wholesale price fixed below the average cost, or just at the average cost, with a loss to all enterprises below average efficiency. M. Kocman (*Ekonomický časopis*, No. 3, 1959) stated that, although the price for steel, which had been fixed below cost and thus generally brought a planned loss to steel factories, has been "abolished in principle since 1958," the new price for steel still does not cover the cost of output in the great steel combine SONP in the traditional steel industry center of Kladno.

TABLE 8.3—STATE BUDGETS FOR 1958 IN SOME EUROPEAN
CENTRALLY PLANNED ECONOMIES

	Czecho-slovakia	East Germany	Hungary	Poland	USSR
Receipts (in billion dollars at official exchange rates)	13.3	9.5	4.3	40.0	160.8
Per cent of total receipts:					
Turnover tax	52.6	...	...	...	46.9
Paid-off profits of state enterprises	14.2	...	...	...	20.3
Total accumulation[a]	66.8	50.4	74.9	72.5	67.2
Direct taxation	11.9	10.5	11.2	11.3	9.7
Receipts from national insurance	18.6	15.2	2.8	12.2	5.1
Other receipts	2.7	21.9	11.1	4.0	20.0
Expenditures (in billion dollars)..	13.2	9.5	4.3	39.5	156.9
Per cent of total expenditures:					
"National economy"	47.9	55.3	51.7	56.1	41.0
Education, culture, social welfare	39.1	35.7	29.2	24.0	33.9
Defense, security	9.4	2.5⎫	⎱12.7	7.8⎱	15.3
Administration	3.6	6.5⎭		3.0⎰	1.9
Other expenditures	—	—	6.4	9.1	7.9

Data are from "State Budgets in the Countries of CMEA" (Council for Mutual Economic Aid), *Statistický obzor*, No. 12, 1958. The scope of the budget depends on the varying importance of the "state sector" in the national economy, and comparability among countries is limited. For example, the East German budget is relatively small, because of the smaller share of the state sector and the larger share of the private sector in the East German economy. The percentage distribution is not quite comparable either, because of the differences in pattern of prices and in the structure of state budgets.

[a] Total accumulation equals turnover tax plus paid-off profits of state enterprises; calculated by the author.

the share of accumulation is substantially lower, and the scope of the state budget substantially smaller, in spite of its greater population. This is due to the fact that nationalization is far from being so complete in East Germany as it is in Czechoslovakia. Table 8.3 also shows that the revenue from national insurance is relatively higher in Czechoslovakia than in other Eastern European countries. In fact, on the basis of percentages in Table 8.3, this revenue amounted to 17–18 billion Kčs in 1958, whereas the sum of national health cost and of social insurance benefits amounted to only 16–17 billion Kčs.[9] This confirms the previously mentioned assumption that Czechoslovak national insurance is not subsidized from the state budget.

[9] The sum of social insurance benefits in 1958 amounted to 9.7 billion Kčs. The total cost of national health in 1958 amounted to 6.6 billion Kčs. In addition to these costs, specific medical care, including preventive care, may also have been financed through national health insurance.

2. Gross Fixed Investments

It would require a special study to try to examine the investment policy of Czechoslovak planning authorities. Under the existing artificial pricing, they encounter considerable difficulties in finding a workable criterion for the ratio of marginal output to investments in order to allocate investments more rationally to various branches of the national economy and to individual enterprises. So far political decisions seem to have been more important than economic considerations. The over-all rate of investments in the national economy, in particular, seems to be a political issue.[10]

As in most of the other chapters of this book, the comments will be compressed into a descriptive framework, telling what happened in the field of investments rather than why it happened. Yet, even a purely factual study involves certain problems.

Official Czechoslovak statistics on "investments" refer, in principle, to domestic gross fixed investments. They do not cover stocks of materials, finished or semifinished products, or foreign investments. Investments data are defined as "expenditure on acquiring new basic funds (fixed capital assets, see Section 3), or on enlarging, reconstructing, or maintaining the existing basic funds," as well as "expenditure that does not lead to a higher value of basic funds but is directly connected with their development." Basic funds, the life of which is shorter than one year or the price of which is less than 600 Kčs per independent unit, are excluded from Czechoslovak investments statistics. Also excluded are all goods purchased by individuals—not only consumers' durables such as automobiles (although all motor vehicles purchased by the state administration or nationalized enterprises are included), but tools purchased by individual farmers as well. On the other hand, investments data cover cost of geological prospecting and even such unusual items as the pay of directors of factories under construction until they have started to produce.

The coverage of official "investment" statistics also varies slightly from one statistical yearbook to the other. For instance, in the *SRRC*, 1959, the cost of drilling for oil was added to the previous coverage of "construction" investments; previously separate data on "investments in assembly work" were included under the heading "investments in machinery and equipment." And the relatively unimportant "other investments" have been cut from the investment statistics altogether. All this,

---

[10] Planning and financing of investments in Eastern Europe has been described in the *Economic Survey of Europe*, 1959, Chapters 7 and 8.

however, is of limited practical importance. The real difference, in comparison with Western statistics on gross fixed investments, is that Czechoslovak data on investments do not include so-called general overhauls (*generální opravy*). These are defined as "removing the wear and tear or the damage done to basic funds, so that they are rehabilitated, without improvement of their technical properties . . . General overhauls of machinery imply replacement of a considerable number of spare parts. . . . General overhauls of buildings imply replacement of substantial parts of buildings."[11] The exclusion of "general overhauls" from Czechoslovak investment statistics is rather contradictory to the previously mentioned definition of the latter, which explicitly covers "reconstruction and rehabilitation of existing basic funds." Nevertheless, there is no doubt that Czechoslovak data on "investments" do not include the value of "general overhauls" (capital repairs),[12] for which separate statistics are to be found in official Statistical Yearbooks.

But another limitation of comparability arises from the unusually great delay in putting new capacities into use in Czechoslovakia. In this respect the comparison of official data on expenditures on investments with the figures on actual increase in basic funds (stock of capital assets) provides a useful indication, as discussed below. Another difficulty, which arises from artificial pricing, cannot be corrected satisfactorily: the degree of underpricing varies for different types of investment groups and distorts the structure of investments by branches of the national economy as well as by "construction" and "machinery and equipment" investments, and by state capital and nonstate investments.

It should also be pointed out that no systematic information on net

[11] *SRRC*, 1959, p. 105. Definition of "investments" can be found *ibid.*, p. 103.

[12] According to the *Results of the Fulfillment of the State Plan*, 1959, Chapter III, "investments and general overhauls" amounted to 45.4 million Kčs, "that is, 15.6 per cent more than in 1958." In 1958, "investments" at January 1, 1959, prices, amounted to 31.9 billion Kčs (*SRRC*, 1959, Table 6.1), and "general overhauls" to 7.2 billion Kčs (*ibid.*, Table 6.30). A comparison of the *sum* of Tables 6.1 *and* 6.30 with the amount of "investments and general overhauls" in 1959 suggests an increase of 12 per cent (the difference from the official 15.6 per cent increase may be due to a different statistical coverage and/or the lack of reference in the plan fulfillment report to the price levels at which the increase has been measured). On the other hand, a comparison of 1958 data on "investments" only with the 1959 value of "investments and general overhauls" would suggest, at 1959 constant prices, an increase of 42 per cent, which is out of the question. It should be pointed out that the ECE and other U.N. statistics on gross fixed investments in Czechoslovakia refer to Czechoslovak "investment" figures only, and do not add the "general overhauls" data.

investments is available in Czechoslovak statistics, and statistical information on depreciation is incomplete.[13]

For all these reasons the examination of investments in Czechoslovakia is not easy.

To see investment trends in proper perspective, we must say a few words about the scope and distribution of fixed investments in the years immediately preceding the introduction of comprehensive central planning. Estimates of 1948 investments, as quoted below, have been computed with the usual Western breakdown by gross and net investments.

The first postwar estimate put the total amount of gross fixed investments in 1948 at 35 billion Kčs at current prices, and net investments at 19 billion Kčs. Net investments, according to this estimate, amounted to only 6 per cent of national income under Western definition at market prices. Later it was argued that the over-all depreciation rate that was applied (5 per cent of national income) was too low. (In these old statistics, "general overhauls" are, of course, not excluded from "investments" data.) The depreciation quota was revalued and the following picture obtained (1948 investments at current prices, 1945 currency units, in billion Kčs):

	Gross Investments	Depreciation	Net Investments
Industry and handicrafts	13.1	12.0	1.1
Agriculture and forestry	2.3	3.1	−0.8
Transportation	7.1	3.5	3.6
Construction	0.1	0.3	−0.2
Housing	8.5	(0.8)	(6.7)
Public administration	6.7	3.0	3.7
Trade, banking, etc.	0	0.5	−0.5
Total fixed investments	37.8	24.2	13.6

The above tabulation indicates that the gross investment rate in 1948 was unduly low and that net disinvestment occurred in some branches of the national economy. Therefore, a certain increase in gross investments in later years was justified.

The increase in gross fixed investments under central planning, as reflected by data in Tables 8.4 and 8.5, was spectacular. In terms of comparable 1959 prices, yearly expenditure on gross fixed investments was stepped up threefold between 1948 and 1958. The expenditure on gross fixed investments thus increased faster than the gross value of production in the national economy, so that the marginal gross output–gross

[13] Net investments could be estimated with the aid of Dogmar's formula (see the *Economic Survey of Europe*, 1955, p. 200).

TABLE 8.4—GROSS FIXED INVESTMENTS, EXCLUDING GENERAL
OVERHAULS, BY CATEGORIES OF INVESTMENTS

(*At comparable 1959 prices, in million Kčs*)

Year	Total	Investments			
		In Pro-ductive Basic Funds	In Non-productive Basic Funds	In Build-ing and Con-struction	In Ma-chinery[a]
1948	9,819	6,244	2,674	6,230	2,688
1949	11,823	8,573	3,250	7,601	4,222
1950	14,207	10,440	3,767	8,884	5,323
1951	17,113	12,687	4,426	10,602	6,511
1952	20,088	14,841	5,253	12,977	7,111
1953	20,595	14,484	6,111	13,850	6,745
1954	20,012	13,967	6,045	13,512	6,500
1955	21,883	14,874	7,009	14,565	7,318
1956	26,670	17,429	9,241	17,941	8,729
1957	29,325	19,571	9,754	19,446	9,879
1958	31,983	23,523	8,460	19,849	8,460

Data are from *SRRC*, 1959, Tables 6.1 and 6.2. They refer to expenditures on investments, whether completed or not.

[a] Including cost of assembly work, equipment, and tools.

TABLE 8.5—GROSS FIXED INVESTMENTS, EXCLUDING GENERAL
OVERHAULS, BY INVESTORS

(*At comparable 1959 prices, in million Kčs*)

Year	State, State Organs, and State-owned Enterprises[a]	Cooperatives and Other Collective Bodies[b]	Unified Agricultural Cooperatives	Private Persons and Organ-izations[c]	Housing within Private Investments
1948	7,590	127	—	1,200	821
1949	10,648	86	—	1,089	813
1950	12,920	339	214	948	780
1951	15,250	995	860	868	793
1952	17,867	1,352	1,259	869	832
1953	17,906	1,777	1,679	912	891
1954	17,467	1,500	1,283	1,045	1,019
1955	18,419	1,983	1,554	1,481	1,448
1956	20,830	2,742	2,176	3,098	3,021
1957	23,136	3,005	2,479	3,184	3,102
1958	26,668	3,695	3,263	1,620	1,552

Data are from *SRRC*, 1959, Tables 6.1 and 6.2. They refer to expenditures on investments, whether completed or not.

[a] Including investments by "national committees" (local governments), "Action Z" (labor brigades working to improve public places), and all fixed investments abroad such as construction of embassies, etc.

[b] Including investments by organizations of the National Front, led by the Communist Party.

[c] Including investments by agricultural cooperatives of the first and second types—nonexistent in recent years. (See Chapter 4, Section 4.)

fixed investment ratio deteriorated by some 20 per cent in these ten years.

Table 8.4 subdivides fixed investments (excluding general overhauls) into "building and construction" and "machinery, including assembly work and equipment." Investments in machinery and equipment, most of which are labor-saving, amounted to less than one-third of the total gross investment outlay, whereas investments in "buildings" took two-thirds. Even if we allow for the probably more serious underpricing of machinery and equipment, their share in total gross investments is surprisingly low, especially in view of the labor shortage in Czechoslovakia. Even in the sector of industry alone, the share of investments in machinery and equipment remained far below half the total fixed investments, as can be seen from the following data:[14] Machinery and equipment investments, in per cent of total gross fixed investments in Czechoslovak industry—1948, 39.5; 1949, 43.4; 1950, 45.2; 1951, 45.8; 1952, 41.8; 1953, 41.0; 1954, 35.3; 1955, 44.0; 1956, 39.5.

In the developed Western market economies, the share of machinery and equipment in total industrial fixed investments usually is around two-thirds.

Table 8.4 also subdivides fixed investments (excluding general overhauls) into "productive" and "nonproductive" (see Chapter 10 on the division of Czechoslovakia's economy into "productive" and "nonproductive" spheres). The latter include especially investments in services for the population, covering civilian housing, passenger transportation, health institutions, etc. An increase in the share of "nonproductive" investments therefore indicates that, at a given investment rate, greater attention is being given to improving the standard of living and that the industrialization drive is being eased.[15]

A comparison by countries of the pattern of gross fixed investments by branches of the national economy has been attempted in Table 8.6. Data are also given on investments in national currencies and the percentage share of state investments in total investments. It must be borne in mind that all Czechoslovak investment data are distorted by a different price structure and a different statistical coverage, with particular emphasis on the fact that the cost of "general overhauls" is omitted from the

[14] *Plánované hospodářství*, No. 1, 1959.

[15] In the *Economic Bulletin for Europe*, Vol. 11, No. 1, Table 1, the annual overall increase in investments in Czechoslovakia appears to be higher for 1956 than for other years. This could be misunderstood as an indication of a stepped-up production drive, whereas, in reality, 1956 was a year of economic "thaw"; the increase in fixed investments was due solely to increased investments in the "nonproductive" sphere, while investments in the "productive" sphere decreased, as compared with previous years.

TABLE 8.6—PERCENTAGE DISTRIBUTION OF GROSS FIXED INVESTMENTS BY
ECONOMIC BRANCHES. SHARE OF STATE INVESTMENTS
IN TOTAL INVESTMENTS

(*At current prices; in Czechoslovakia at 1957 constant prices*)

		Percentage Distribution						
Year	Total Gross Fixed Investments[a]	Agriculture	Industry[b] Incl. Constr., Public Utilities	Transportation	Dwellings	Public Administration	Other	Share of State in Total Investments (*Per cent*)
CZECHOSLOVAKIA								
	Million Kčs							
1949 13,321		7	51	14	15	13		91
1953 32,109		11	44	15	14	17		88
1956 29,792		15	39	9	22	15		79
1957 32,792		14	40	10	21	15		73
1958[b] 33,210		...	...	...	16	...		78
FRANCE								
	Billion fr							
1952 2,377		10	37	15	19	11	8	11
1956 3,161		9	32	12	28	12	7	11
WEST GERMANY								
	Billion DM							
1952 .... 25.5		9	40	13	24	7	7	11
1956 .... 44.1		9	37	15	25	7	7	13
UNITED KINGDOM								
	Million £							
1952 2,077		5	43	10	25	8	9	54
1956 3,084		3	44	11	22	7	13	43
YUGOSLAVIA								
	Billion din							
1952 287		5	69	18	5	2	1	95
1956 466		11	44	21	11	8	5	93
POLAND								
	Billion zl							
1956 .... 51.7		41	19	9	30			...

Data for Czechoslovakia are from, or calculated on the basis of, the official National Statistical Year-books. Data on Czechoslovakia exclude "general overhauls," since corresponding figures are available only at 1959 prices (see Table 8.6). If general overhauls were included, the percentage share of industry and construction in total gross fixed investments would be higher than in this table, especially from 1953 on (for example, in 1957 it would amount to approximately 41–42 per cent, as compared with 40 per cent in this table). Data for other countries are from the *Economic Survey of Europe,* 1957, Table V.

Comparison between countries should be made with great reservation. In particular, the state share in total investments in Czechoslovakia is not comparable with the corresponding figures for other countries, in view of the lower prices of capital goods for state investments.

[a] Excluding general overhauls in Czechoslovakia.
[b] At current 1958 prices. Not comparable with previous years (investment prices have been reduced by approximately one-sixth).

TABLE 8.7—GROSS FIXED INVESTMENTS IN CZECHOSLOVAKIA, INCLUDING GENERAL OVERHAULS
BY BRANCHES OF NATIONAL ECONOMY

(In million Kčs at comparable 1959 prices)

	Industry	Construction	Agriculture* and Forestry	Transporta-tion, Com-munications	State Supply of Materials	Trade and Catering	State Procure-ment of Agric. Products	Other Produc-tive Branches	Science and Research	Communal Services	Housing	Health, So-cial Welfare	Educ., Cul-ture, Physi-cal Culture	Public Ad-ministration	Total
1948															
"Investments"	4,375	84	375	1,351	11	32	13	2	22	136	1,660	302	346	208	8,918
General overhauls	347	30	29	204	—	23	—	—	6	11	40	14	32	14	750
Total investments	4,722	114	404	1,555	11	55	13	2	28	147	1,700	316	378	222	9,668
1953															
"Investments"	8,311	435	2,372	3,058	62	159	78	9	133	212	2,943	374	401	2,048	20,595
General overhauls	1,269	136	90	778	9	46	8	4	23	47	161	58	120	44	2,793
Total investments	9,580	571	2,462	3,836	71	205	86	13	156	259	3,104	432	521	2,092	23,388
1954															
"Investments"	8,251	370	2,338	2,467	97	311	120	13	152	198	3,699	313	678	1,005	20,012
General overhauls	1,952	220	134	1,089	17	58	16	8	40	70	270	83	171	50	4,178
Total investments	10,203	590	2,472	3,556	114	369	136	21	192	268	3,969	396	849	1,055	24,190
1955															
"Investments"	8,192	460	3,187	2,343	75	474	135	8	175	302	4,392	335	870	935	21,883
General overhauls	2,106	204	205	1,573	23	81	33	17	35	73	290	103	219	72	5,034
Total investments	10,298	664	3,392	3,916	98	555	168	25	210	375	4,682	438	1,089	1,007	26,917
1956															
"Investments"	9,581	505	4,043	2,488	142	513	135	22	303	498	6,059	401	1,013	967	26,670
General overhauls	2,613	244	273	1,646	30	104	42	10	45	111	302	131	254	212	6,017
Total investments	12,194	749	4,316	4,134	172	617	177	32	348	609	6,361	532	1,267	1,179	32,687

TABLE 8.7—Concluded

	Industry	Construction	Agriculture and Forestry^a	Transportation, Communications	State Supply of Materials	Trade and Catering	State Procurement of Agric. Products	Other Productive Branches	Science and Research	Communal Services	Housing	Health, Social Welfare	Educ., Cul., ture, Physical Culture	Public Administration	Total
1957															
"Investments"	10,514	862	4,300	2,994	184	574	110	33	280	586	6,333	437	1,198	920	29,325
General overhauls ...	2,972	262	332	1,496	34	163	35	17	64	100	369	169	255	264	6,532
Total investments....	13,486	1,124	4,632	4,490	218	737	145	50	344	686	6,702	606	1,453	1,184	35,857
1958															
"Investments"	13,085	960	5,216	3,260	168	676	91	67	259	680	5,068	432	1,160	861	31,983
General overhauls ...	3,559	272	350	1,551	35	173	36	20	55	114	391	173	244	198	7,171
Total investments....	16,644	1,232	5,566	4,811	203	849	127	87	314	794	5,459	605	1,404	1,059	39,154

Data on "investments" and "general overhauls" are from *SRRC*, 1959, Tables 6.4 and 6.30. Total investments are total gross fixed investments, roughly comparable with the Western definition, under the assumption that "general overhauls" outside the state plan of investment are negligible. These figures were calculated by the author.

The division into branches of the national economy is according to the official Czechoslovak classification, listing first all the "productive" and then the "non-productive" branches. (See Chapter 10, Section 1.) Therefore, industrial research comes under "investments in industry" and not under "research," and investments in administrative buildings of state-owned industry come under "investments in industry" and not under "investments in state administration," and so on. All data refer to expenditure on investments, including expenditure on unfinished or abandoned investments.

^a Excluding tools purchased by individual (independent) farmers. The value of tools purchased by individual farmers—which is excluded from official Czechoslovak investment statistics—was of some importance in 1948; in later years, it was negligible, with the possible exception of the 1954–55 period (during the relaxed collectivization drive, see Chapter 4, Section 4).

179

value data on investments. In spite of these limitations of comparability, it is safe to state that the portion of gross fixed investments reserved for industry is much higher in Czechoslovakia than in the listed market economies and that the portion reserved for housing, transportation, and trade is much lower. The percentage share of state investments in total investments is naturally much higher in Czechoslovakia. Its decrease (from 85 per cent in 1948 to 73 per cent in 1957, rising again to 78 per cent in 1958) is due not only to an increase in nonstate investments in Czechoslovakia but also to a certain shift from state investments to investments financed autonomously by nationalized enterprises and other collective bodies; and to a relative shift of state expenditure from "investments" as covered by Czechoslovak statistics under this heading and applied in Tables 8.5 and 8.6 to "general overhauls" (see Table 8.7).

TABLE 8.8—STATE-PLANNED FIXED INVESTMENTS[a] BY
BRANCHES OF NATIONAL ECONOMY

(In million Kčs at comparable 1959 prices)

	1948	1953	1954	1955	1956	1957	1958
Industry	4,302	8,269	8,229	8,126	9,495	10,428	12,963
Construction	83	433	366	444	486	843	950
Agriculture, forestry ...	123	684	1,043	1,619	1,828	1,796	1,937
Transportation, etc.	1,346	3,054	2,456	2,334	2,466	2,958	3,224
Supply of materials	11	62	97	75	142	181	168
Trade, public catering ..	22	131	200	222	232	282	481
Procurement of agricultural products	13	78	120	135	135	110	88
Other "productive" investment	2	9	13	8	22	33	67
Science and research....	22	133	152	175	303	280	259
Communal services	136	212	198	301	497	586	680
Housing	839	2,048	2,676	2,939	3,016	3,195	3,513
Health, social welfare..	248	369	307	319	363	414	414
Education, etc.	240	381	622	831	970	1,164	1,111
Public administration ..	203	2,043	988	891	875	866	813
Total	7,590	17,906	17,467	18,419	20,830	23,136	26,668

Data are from *SRRC*, 1959, Table 6.5.
[a] Contents of investments by state authorities in "investments" in Table 8.7, i.e. excluding general overhauls.

So far we have been discussing *expenditure* on gross fixed investments. The increase in the stock of capital assets has lagged much behind the increase in investment expenditure (excluding expenditure on general overhauls). Large amounts of money have been spent on projects which for many years remained unfinished (for example, the construction of a large steel combine, HUKO, in eastern Slovakia) or have been totally abandoned (Table 8.8). The President of the State Planning Office, O. Šimůnek, described the 1958 situation as follows:[16]

> We can see that the plan of putting new productive capacity into use remains much further from fulfillment than the investment plan itself. Under the plan for this year we counted on construction cycles being accelerated and efficiency of investments improved; yet the amount of unfinished investment work was not reduced; indeed, it increased by 5 per cent as compared with last year. This means that we are building more, but the effect is less. . . .
>
> We cannot be blind to the fact that the present disposition of new construction is unsatisfactory from the economic point of view, as can be seen from the high investment costs as well as from the uneconomical working of new productive capacities. It often happens that the output in new productive capacities is more costly than in the old production units.

The necessary information could not be found in Czechoslovak statistics for measuring the ratio of marginal net investment to net output and thus for examining the unsatisfactory working of new productive capacities, as mentioned by Šimůnek. But some indication of the gap between the expenditure on gross fixed investments and the increase in fixed capital assets may be of interest. A clue comes from the statistics on basic funds, as defined in the next section. Absolute data on the yearly amount of new basic funds are available, however, for the state sector only, and the comparison must be limited accordingly (i.e., to approximately three-fourths of the total gross fixed investments).[17] A comparison of the yearly expenditures on gross fixed investments (excluding general overhauls) and of new capital assets put to use, in terms of constant prices, can be found in Table 8.9. New basic funds should not be confused with net investments, as they cover all capital assets being put into use, whether to enlarge, improve, or just replace the existing fixed capital stock.

A smaller part of the discrepancy between the higher expenditure of gross fixed investments (excluding general overhauls) and the lower value of new basic funds is due to the Czechoslovak definition of investments, which, as mentioned above, also includes such items as geologists' pay in

[16] *Rudé právo*, November 27, 1958.

[17] After this manuscript had been completed, data on the yearly increase in basic funds were made available for the entire national economy (including the nonstate sector) in *SRRC*, 1959, Table 6.13.

TABLE 8.9—INVESTMENTS WITHIN THE STATE INVESTMENT PLAN
COMPARISON OF EXPENDITURES ON GROSS FIXED INVESTMENTS
AND OF COMPLETED BASIC FUNDS (ASSETS)
BRANCHES OF NATIONAL ECONOMY

(In million Kčs, at comparable 1957 prices)

Year	Total		Productive Sphere		Nonproductive Sphere	
	Invest-ments	Basic Funds Completed	Invest-ments	Basic Funds Completed	Invest-ments	Basic Funds Completed
1948	8,635	6,717	6,693	5,148	1,942	1,569
1949	12,052	8,139	9,354	6,041	2,698	2,098
1950	14,649	11,404	11,371	8,563	3,278	2,841
1951	17,360	14,077	13,362	10,795	3,998	3,282
1952	20,355	16,107	15,464	11,836	4,891	4,271
1953	20,242	16,351	14,468	11,478	5,774	4,873
1954	19,667	19,289	14,326	14,657	5,341	4,632
1955	20,624	21,802	14,670	15,311	5,954	6,491
1956	23,387	21,162	16,802	14,878	6,585	6,284
1957	25,925	24,978	18,866	18,652	7,059	6,326

Data are from *SRRC*, 1958, Tables 6.3 and 6.6. "Investments" contain a small amount of nonfixed investments.

connection with prospecting for new mineral deposits, etc. But the greatest part of the gap denotes the increase in the share of long-term investments, longer building periods, and investment projects abandoned after a certain expenditure on them. In 1957, this gap was somewhat narrower than at the beginning of central planning in Czechoslovakia. This is only natural in view of the fact that long-term investments had only started in the first postwar years. In view of the easing of long-term investments in heavy industry in 1955–56, one would have expected that the amount of new basic funds (capital assets put to use) would be at least equal to the expenditure on gross fixed investments in 1956–57. If the volume of new basic funds still remained below the investment expenditures, the gap may be interpreted as indicating a further slowing down of the construction cycle and wasted capital outlay.

Finally, Table 8.10 gives a comparison of state investments in the last four years, at 1957 and January 1959 prices. On the basis of these data the derived investment price index for 1958 was obtained in Chapter 7, Section 3.

3. Basic Funds

The term "basic funds" as used in Czechoslovakia and other Eastern European countries denotes fixed capital stock. (In the 1957 Statistical Yearbook "basic funds" also included land and forests, but in *SRRC*,

TABLE 8.10—INVESTMENTS WITHIN THE STATE INVESTMENT PLAN
COMPARISON OF EXPENDITURES ON GROSS FIXED INVESTMENTS
AT 1957 AND JANUARY 1959 PRICES

(In million Kčs)

Year	Total		Machinery and Equipment		Building Including Housing		Housing Only	
	1957	1959	1957	1959	1957	1959	1957	1959
1955	20,624	17,822	6,768	7,011	13,791	10,811	3,145	2,939
1956	23,387	20,065	8,027	8,267	15,268	11,798	3,227	3,016
1957	25,925	22,171	9,209	9,394	16,620	12,777	3,426	3,195
1958	...	25,780	...	11,542	...	14,238	...	3,513

Data at 1957 prices are from *SRRC*, 1958, Table 6.3. The sum of the subdivisions "machinery and equipment" and "building" does not tally with official data on total investments; the difference (of only 0.2 per cent) is due to the inclusion of "other investments" in the data on total investments. This rather negligible, undefined category of investments has been excluded from investment statistics that have been published—also retrospectively—since 1958. Therefore, according to data at 1959 prices, the sum of "machinery and equipment" and "building" tallies with "total investments." Data on "basic funds completed" and on investments at 1959 prices have been published in *SRRC*, 1959, not only for investments within the state investment plan, as above, but also for the whole national economy, since the manuscript of this book was completed. Special details on Czechoslovak investments can be obtained from this source, Tables 6–13 ff.

1958, the coverage was limited to fixed capital assets and a rather negligible item of domestic animals.) Statistics on basic funds, in terms of 1955 constant prices, refer, however, to the purchase price—that is, to replacement costs—with no allowance for depreciation. Only actual retirements of assets are subtracted.

So far, only index numbers and percentage distribution of the existing basic funds have been published. These are shown in Table 8.11, in breakdown by branches of the national economy within the "productive" as well as the "nonproductive" spheres. Basic funds in the form of machinery and equipment also are specified in this table. The index numbers show that fixed capital assets increased most in construction and industry, but only very little in agriculture and transportation. The share of the latter two branches of the national economy in total fixed capital stock went down considerably between 1948 and 1957.

Data on basic funds may become very important for assessing the relative economic efficiency of gross fixed investments among various branches of the national economy as well as among individual enterprises; the important element is the planned rate of accumulation, which is inherent in the centrally planned economies. To achieve the planned accumulation, every unit of basic funds must yield, in theory, an average rate of accumulation. Comparing such a theoretical average yield of basic funds with the actual basic funds–accumulation ratio in individual enter-

TABLE 8.11—BASIC FUNDS (CAPITAL ASSETS) IN CZECHOSLOVAKIA

(Data based on purchase price, in terms of constant 1955 prices; figures for end of year)

	Index 1948 = 100				Percentage Share				
	1953	1956	1957	1958	1948	1953	1956	1957	1958
Industry	124.9	148.5	158.1	168.0	24.3	26.6	28.0	28.5	28.9
Building and construction	134.4	150.9	168.6	188.8	0.8	0.9	0.9	1.0	1.0
Agriculture and forestry	111.4	128.5	136.5	147.7	8.5	8.4	8.6	8.7	9.0
Freight transport, communications servicing production	108.1	117.2	119.9	123.4	9.7	9.2	8.8	8.6	8.5
Other "material production"	110.2	127.1	135.1	144.9	2.2	2.1	2.2	2.2	2.3
Subtotal: "Productive sphere"	118.2	137.1	145.0	153.9	45.5	47.2	48.5	49.0	49.7
Science and research	126.0	178.0	204.0	224.6	0.3	0.3	0.4	0.4	0.5
"Communal" services	107.1	114.5	118.8	122.8	3.1	2.9	2.7	2.7	2.7
Housing	109.1	121.2	126.3	130.4	26.0	24.9	24.5	24.4	24.1
Passenger transportation, communications servicing population	107.1	113.1	115.4	118.1	15.1	14.2	13.3	12.9	12.6
Health, social welfare	118.5	129.4	133.3	138.5	1.8	1.9	1.8	1.8	1.8
Education, culture	112.0	125.1	130.8	135.6	4.5	4.4	4.4	4.4	4.4
Administration	129.4	150.0	156.8	162.9	3.7	4.2	4.4	4.4	4.3
Subtotal: "Nonproductive sphere"	110.5	121.5	125.9	130.0	54.5	52.8	51.5	51.0	50.3
Total basic funds	114.0	128.6	134.6	140.8	100.0	100.0	100.0	100.0	100.0
Machinery and equipment	134.1	167.2	181.4	197.7	12.8	15.1	16.7	17.3	18.0
In industry	137.9	171.0	183.6	198.0	7.3	8.8	9.7	9.9	10.2

Total value of basic funds in 1956 (in billion Kčs, at 1955 prices):

Productive sphere (of which industry was 182†) .... 315†
Nonproductive sphere (of which housing was 159†) .... 335†
Total basic funds .... 650†

Data are from *SRRC*, 1958, Table 1.10; *SRRC*, 1959, Tables 1.14 and 1.15. Basic funds include domestic animals. No allowance has been made for depreciation; only actual retrieving of capital assets has been deducted. Valuation is based on replacement costs at 1955 prices.

prises and branches, one can assess relative efficiency, at least in theory. This may help the planning authorities to allocate marginal assets to various enterprises in a better proportion to their relative efficiency to the accumulation per unit of basic funds. They could even transfer existing assets for one branch or one enterprise, where the actual yield of output per unit of basic funds is lower than the average, to another branch or enterprise, where it is above the average. In this way the net national product would increase, while all other factors, including the over-all rate of accumulation, would remain unchanged. Using Western economic terms, the planners could in this way maximize the profits on capital.

In practice, however, this scheme of assessing the relative efficiency of investments is not workable, because of shortcomings in the statistics of basic funds and because of distortions by artificial pricing. If, however, the basic funds were valued year by year at their actual value in terms of labor costs, and if state wholesale prices were calculated in proportion to labor costs, a rational factor could be brought into central planning of investments, even without applying a rate of interest on capital.[18]

Furthermore, this would enable the planners to bring wage costs and capital costs to a common denominator (adding the average yield per unit of basic funds required to fulfill the planned accumulation to the present calculation of the cost of production; see Chapter 7, Section 3). Thus, the relative economic efficiency of individual enterprises and of individual branches of the national economy could be ascertained in terms of the ratio of the wage and capital costs to value of production (comparing the input of labor and basic funds with the output of goods).

In Table 8.11 the actual value of basic funds in Czechoslovakia is estimated under the current statistical definition. Such an approximation is necessary for estimating the over-all depreciation in connection with the estimates of gross national product in Chapter 10. Furthermore, such an approximation may also serve for estimating the scope of the actual retirements of capital assets (scrapping old machinery, pulling down old buildings, etc.). According to a very rough estimate, total basic funds, valued at 1955 replacement costs, amounted to approximately 550 billion Kčs in 1948, 650 billion Kčs in 1956, and 670 billion Kčs in 1957. Thus, over the years 1948–57 the total value of basic funds (existing capital stock) increased by 120 billion Kčs. On the other hand, the "basic funds put to use" (completed capital assets) over the same period amounted to

---

[18] A similar argument on "accounting relative capital intensity" was very well presented by the Economic Commission for Europe in connection with problems of export efficiency in Eastern Europe, in *Economic Bulletin for Europe*, Vol. 11, No. 1, p. 71 ff.

approximately 180–90 billion Kčs at 1957 prices.[19] There was probably no great difference in investment price between 1955 and 1957; thus comparison of the actual increase in basic funds (existing capital stock) with the amount of basic funds put to use suggests that the total amount involved in scrapping machinery, pulling down old buildings, etc., in the nine years 1948–57 amounted to approximately 60–70 billion Kčs (average of 1955 and 1957 prices). If these estimates are not too far from reality, they indicate that the yearly rate of retrieving old assets was only around 1 per cent, much below the average depreciation rate of 5 per cent, as assumed by the author. This in turn suggests that the average age of capital assets must have increased considerably in Czechoslovakia. In fact, according to official and semiofficial statements, in some branches of industry the average age of machinery is around 50 years, and the average age of buildings may be even more than 50 years. It is obvious that the major part of investments in Czechoslovakia, in the years under study, has been used for enlarging rather than for modernizing fixed capital assets.

Table 8.12 contains data on what could be called "national wealth," excluding minerals in the earth (that is, data on "basic funds" under the

TABLE 8.12—DISTRIBUTION OF NATIONAL WEALTH[a]

(In per cent; 1956, at 1955 purchase price)

	National Share in Total Wealth	Breakdown by Ownership	
		Socialist	Private
Total	100	82.7	17.3
Industry	27.2	99.7	0.3
Agriculture	8.7	58.3	41.7
Forestry	4.7	100.0	0
Building	1.0	94.6	5.4
Transportation	20.6	100.0	0
Communications	0.8	100.0	0
Trade and public catering......	1.3	97.9	2.1
State procurement and supplies	0.6	100.0	0
Communal services	3.0	98.2	1.8
Housing stock	24.0	43.7	56.3
Social welfare, health, education, culture	6.2	100.0	0
Public organizations	0.2	100.0	0
Administration	1.7	100.0	0

Data are from *Czechoslovak Statistical Abstract, 1958.* Valuation is at 1955 replacement costs.
[a] Basic funds (capital assets), land, and forests, but excluding deposits of minerals.

[19] Basic funds acquired under the state investment plans amounted to 160 billion Kčs in 1948–57 (see Table 8.6), and state investment accounted for approximately 80 per cent of total investments.

old broader definition, including fixed capital assets and domestic animals as well as land and forests, at 1955 costs of replacements), by economic branches and by Socialist and private ownership. The table shows that, in 1956, 82 per cent of this national wealth was in collective ownership and less than 17 per cent in private ownership of individuals. Within the Socialist ownership, the state's share was 95 per cent and the cooperatives' share only 5 per cent. With collectivization of agriculture nearing completion, in 1959 probably nine-tenths of the national wealth and almost 100 per cent of the means of production were in Socialist ownership; if socialism can be defined simply as collective ownership of the means of production, Czechoslovakia has become a fully Socialist country.

Chapter 9

INCOME OF THE POPULATION AND
STANDARD OF LIVING

1. Earnings in the Socialist Sector and Per Capita Income

Under the heading "Average wages in the Socialist sector of the national economy," Czechoslovak statistics provide data referring to the average per capita monthly earnings of wage and salary earners, including overtime pay and all kinds of premiums, before deduction of direct taxes (wage taxes), of contributions to national insurance, and of compulsory contributions to unified trade unions ROH. These data exclude the pay of apprentices.

In 1957, data on "average wages" covered 4,532 thousand wage and salary earners out of 6,100 thousand persons "working in the national economy" (see Chapter 1, Section 2), or 74 per cent of the population "working in the national economy." The remaining 26 per cent were members of unified agricultural cooperatives, individual farmers, apprentices, and a handful of self-employed workers, of no economic importance.

Data on "wages in the Socialist sector" cover income of employees of state farms and unified cooperatives; but their number is rather small (8 per cent in 1957), so that the "average wages" are fairly representative for the average per capita income of the nonagricultural population, if we disregard the groups generally excluded from Czechoslovak statistics (the armed forces, police, prisoners, etc.). Today in Czechoslovakia there is no personal income of importance outside agriculture other than from employment; the entrepreneur is practically nonexistent. Income from property is limited to interest from relatively small money deposits in the state banks and other unearned personal income is limited to Health and Social Welfare benefits (see Section 2) and to winnings from state football pools and lotteries; rent from the remaining private houses has to be deposited in blocked accounts, and can be used only for repair of the house.

Average monthly earnings before taxes, etc., in the "Socialist sector," as described above, are to be found, by economic branches, in Table 9.1.[1]

---

[1] Data on gross earnings for the years 1948–56 are from *SRRC*, 1957. In *SRRC*, 1958, they have been retrospectively reduced; on page 88 the following reason is given: "Under the Act on National Health Insurance, No. 54, 1956, which became effective January 1, 1957, workers with monthly pay will no longer receive their

Practical value of these data is limited. They represent averages of earnings of all salary and wage earners within the branch, from directors of the largest enterprise to charwomen. But at least for two economic branches —industry and construction—official data on gross earnings are available, subdivided for most years into main employment groups: manual workers, technical staff, office workers, and auxiliary personnel. These subdivisions have also been included in Table 9.1. In 1948, average monthly earnings of manual workers in industry were 17 per cent lower than the weighted average of the pay of the technical staff and the office employees; in 1957, they were 1 per cent higher than the average pay of the technical and office staff. In a similar way, manual workers' earnings in construction over the period under study surpassed office workers' pay, and came much nearer to the technical staff pay.

Over the entire decade 1948–58, average nominal earnings of manual workers in industry before taxes and contributions rose 85 per cent, whereas the corresponding increase in earnings, in the over-all average within the Socialist sector (excluding members of unified agricultural cooperatives), was only 56 per cent.

In agriculture per capita income was lower than in nonagricultural branches for many years. The gap between per capita personal income in agriculture and earnings in industry may even have increased in the 1948–51 period, although no data are available to the author for these years. Between 1951 and 1956, per capita income in agriculture increased fairly rapidly, as illustrated by average net income in Table 4.8. (These data, from an article by Josef Nikl in *Nová mysl*, No. 7, 1958, however, include income of farmers from nonagricultural activities, which brings the figures, especially for individual farmers, above the true income from agriculture.) Nevertheless, in 1956, per capita personal income in agriculture remained below the average per capita earnings of the nonagricultural population and considerably below the earnings of manual workers in industry, as

---

basic salary when they are unable to work because of sickness, accident, or motherhood [previous stipulations granted six weeks' pay]; from the start of disability, they will now receive national health insurance benefits, which do not come from wage funds. In order to make the data comparable, it has been necessary to adjust data on average wages up to 1957 by reduction coefficients obtained by the sampling method."

Such an adjustment of the figures on earnings for the 1948–56 period does not seem justified. The data should reflect actual wage costs. A discontinuation of pay for sickness, etc., by the employer actually reduces wage costs (or slows down their increase). On the other hand, higher benefits paid by national health insurance are reflected, in due course, in the relating data on social security, as well as in the figures on net per capita income of the population.

TABLE 9.1—MONTHLY EARNINGS IN CZECHOSLOVAKIA
BY ECONOMIC BRANCHES[a]

(*In Kčs—new currency units of 1953*)

	1948	1953	1954	1955	1956	1957	1958
Average earnings in the Socialist sector	819	1,095	1,169	1,197	1,243	1,251	1,277
Industry	759	1,182	1,263	1,280	1,315	1,314	1,357
Manual workers	715	1,138	1,235	1,252	1,285	1,237	1,325[b]
Technical staff	975*	1,522	1,591	1,637	1,694	1,641	1,756
Office workers		1,046	1,093	1,109	1,133	1,136	1,172
Auxiliary workers	...	932	967	975	995	1,010	...
Construction	829	1,256	1,335	1,364	1,421	1,430	1,455
Technical staff	1,391	1,551	1,633	1,668	1,766	1,744	1,732[c]
Office workers	1,039	1,120	1,155	1,159	1,196	1,163	1,164[c]
Agriculture	...	790	843	913	1,013	1,049	1,054
Forestry	...	920	992	1,078	1,067	1,085	1,136
Freight transportation	...	1,207	1,285	1,335	1,368	1,384	1,382[c]
Personnel transportation	...	1,207	1,274	1,322	1,354	1,375	1,344[c]
Trade and public catering.....	...	848	985	1,000	1,051	1,041	1,034
Communal services	...	920	970	1,019	1,011	1,032	984[c]
Housing services	...	740	811	723	800	815	...
Health and social welfare	...	1,009	1,011	1,033	1,029	1,089	1,126
Science and research	...	1,339	1,443	1,499	1,550	1,526	1,552[c]
Education	...	985	1,029	1,057	1,125	1,150	1,168
Administration and justice	...	1,118	1,160	1,233	1,242	1,265	...

Data for the period through 1956 are from *SRRC*, 1957, Tables 5.4, 7.12, and 8.4. Data on gross earnings in industry and construction are not weighted averages of earnings of workers, technical staffs, office workers, and auxiliary workers; they are slightly higher, probably because they also include the higher pay of the central management staff. Data for 1957 are from *SRRC*, 1958, Tables 5.5, 7.13, and 8.7. They reflect discontinuation of pay from the "wage fund" during sickness. Data for 1958 are from *Statistické zprávy, Results of the Fulfillment of the State Plan*, 1958, and from *SRRC*, 1959, Tables 5.6, 7.16, and 8.10.

[a] These are average earnings of all wage and salary earners within the branch, excluding apprentices, before deduction of taxes and before contributions to National Insurance and to trade unions, unless otherwise stated. Data cover Socialist (nationalized) sector only.

[b] Average earnings, reflecting the organizational change in industry, are not comparable with previous years. Comparable earnings in 1957 amounted to 1,298 Kčs.

[c] Some of the series on average earnings in *SRRC*, 1959, have been retrospectively changed, so these 1958 data are probably not fully comparable with those of previous years.

shown by the following approximations (in Kčs per month, before taxes and contributions):[2]

[2] Estimates of income in agriculture are based on Josef Nikl's data plus 25 per cent taxation, contributions, etc., for individual farmers, and 20 per cent for members of cooperatives (the difference in estimated taxation is smaller than the difference in the rate of agricultural tax, since the above incomes also contain income not subject to agricultural tax). These estimates of income in agriculture are higher than estimates of income per economically active person, based on Bezouška's data, in Table 9.8. This difference is described in the footnote to Table 4.9.

	1951	1953	1956
Average earnings in the Socialist sector, excluding co-operatives	1,006	1,095	1,243
Average earnings of manual workers in industry	945	1,138	1,285
Average income of members of unified agricultural co-operatives, including income in kind and income from nonagricultural activities	800†	1,130†	1,200†
Average personal income of individual farmers, including income in kind and income from nonagricultural employment	750†	1,070†	1,170†

The years 1953 and 1956, with the drives toward industrialization and collectivization relaxed, were relatively good years for individual farmers. It is likely that in later years the gap between their income and the higher earnings of the nonagricultural population and of members of unified agricultural cooperatives increased.

Information on the distribution of personal income by income brackets within the various social groups (classes) is very scarce. Data on the distribution of manual workers' wage rates and earnings before taxes, etc., are given according to eight "classes" in the "State Catalogue of Work Norms" in its most important schedule, which in May 1957 was applied to 64 per cent of the wage earners receiving time wages, and to 76 per cent of those receiving piecework wages.

The distribution of hourly wages in industry seems to be more equal, according to Table 9.2, than it was in 1948 or in prewar times. But it cannot be ascertained how premiums—which are a large part of earnings —are distributed among the individual workers. Many complaints have been raised in this respect.

In connection with the new wage system introduced in 1959–60, it was officially stated that the ratio of lowest and highest "wages" (probably earnings before taxes) in the Socialized sector of the national economy would increase from $1:2$ to $1:2\frac{1}{2}$. Unfortunately, no information was given on the stratification upon which the ratio between "lowest" and "highest" wages was based. Yet it appears that a somewhat greater inequality in earnings according to the nature of the work performed is being considered.

No recent figures are available on distribution of income of the entire population by kinds of employment. The following estimates, in Kčs per month, for the period 1956–57 give a very rough idea of the differences in personal gross income; they include total money income, with premiums, etc., before taxation, and income in kind, but exclude "collective wages" (social services, etc.; see Section 2) and the value of special facilities

TABLE 9.2—STRATIFICATION OF WAGES AND EARNINGS IN CZECHOSLOVAK INDUSTRY[a]

	Category of Workers, According to the (pre-1958) "State Catalogue of Work Norms," May 1957								Total or Average
	1	2	3	4	5	6	7	8	
HOURLY WAGES									
Tariff wage, Kčs/hr	1.98	2.18	2.40	2.64	2.92	3.24	3.58	3.98	2.86
Premiums, including compensation for stoppages,[b] Kčs/hr	0.71	1.37	1.73	2.28	2.58	3.08	3.60	3.58	2.49
Average earnings, Kčs/hr	2.69	3.55	4.13	4.92	5.50	6.32	7.18	7.56	5.35
Hours worked, in per cent of total actual working time paid by hourly wages	0.2	3.9	18.6	27.3	20.1	19.2	8.8	1.9	100.0
PIECEWORK WAGES									
Tariff at 100 per cent work norm fulfillment; work norms based:									
On estimates, Kčs/hr	2.16	2.38	2.62	2.88	3.18	3.53	3.90	4.34 }	3.14
On time studies, Kčs/hr	2.34	2.57	2.83	3.12	3.45	3.82	4.22	4.70 }	
Average fulfillment of work norm, in per cent	171	175	183	195	208	203	201	202	194
Other premiums[b] than pay for overfulfillment of work norm, Kčs/hr	0.11	0.24	0.26	0.23	0.17	0.10	0.25	0.14	0.22
Average earnings, Kčs/hr	4.02	4.68	5.36	6.18	7.08	7.57	8.33	9.15	6.31
Hours worked, in per cent of total actual working time paid by piecework wages	0.8	9.6	23.4	26.2	21.5	13.8	4.1	0.6	100.0

Source: "Některé statistické údaje k dopisu ÚV KSČ v souvislosti s přestavbou dělnickyxh mezd" (Some Data in Connection with the Letter of the Central Committee of the Communist Party on Reorganization of Wages), *Special Supplement, Statistický obzor*, No. 12, 1958.

[a] These incomplete data, referring only to the "most frequently applied wage schedule," cover 64 per cent of hourly wage workers and 76 per cent of piecework workers.

[b] Pay for stoppages (idle time on the job; see Chapters 1 and 2) cannot be legitimately added as premiums to hourly earnings. However, this inaccuracy was of limited importance in 1957, since this kind of pay amounted to only 1 per cent of earnings.

(such as allotment of a flat, permission to buy a car at a "normal" price, vacations for selected workers free of charge or at a reduced charge):

Pension of former self-employed worker:

If other family workers have incomes	100[a]
If family is living on old-age benefits[b]	190[a]
Pension of widow of former factory worker or employee[b]......	280
Pension of former factory worker[b]	480
Woman shop assistant...................................	650
Woman worker in textile factory	700
Postman	750
Owner of shoe repair shop	750
Pension of former miner[b]	850
Average office worker	950
Pension of former heavy-industry worker[c]	1,000
Individual farmer (income per working member of family)...	1,050
Average factory worker in light industry	1,100
Foreign language correspondent	1,100
University research assistant	1,400
Member of prosperous unified agricultural cooperative.......	1,500
Young architect	1,700
Truck driver	1,800
Average factory worker in heavy industry	1,800
Coal miner	2,000
Chief engineer in average factory (400 employees)	3,000
Chief surgeon in average hospital (120 beds)	3,000
Uranium ore miner	3,000
Average newspaperman	3,000
Director of average-sized factory (400 employees)	5,000
Editor in chief of the Communist Party *Rudé právo*	9,000

[a] Not granted to persons sentenced on charges of antistate activities and some economic crimes (speculation, etc.).

[b] Pension granted before 1957.

[c] Pension granted after 1957.

The highest incomes accrue to prominent artists and scientists, generals, and members of the Cabinet and of the Politburo of the Party.

Direct taxation (wage tax on wages and salaries, agricultural tax on incomes of cooperatives and individual farmers, disregarding the trade tax on the handful of nonagricultural self-employed workers) is lower and less progressive in Czechoslovakia as compared with the Western market economies (except the high taxation of individual farmers owning more than 15 hectares of land, the so-called kulaks). The wage tax amounted to approximately 10 per cent of average earnings in the 1955–58 period; contributions to national insurance were at approximately the same rate as the wage tax. Thus, the distribution of income after taxes and contributions may not substantially differ from the distribution before taxation (excluding the incomes of kulaks, etc.). As compared with the Western market economies, distribution of income in Czechoslovakia is definitely

more equal in terms of income "before taxes," and probably more equal
even "after taxes." It should be mentioned, however, that certain groups
of old people must live on incomes just at the level of the living wage:
this applies not only to former entrepreneurs who lost their property
through nationalization without compensation, but also to former members
of professions who lost their savings, including life insurance claims,
through two postwar currency reforms, and are receiving only very low
social welfare benefits, with no additional income.

2. *"Collective Incomes" and Cost of Social Services*

Czechoslovak planning authorities claim that the "collective wage"
and "collective consumption" increased much faster than individual earnings and individual personal consumption. In a special economic survey
(*Statistické zprávy*, May 1958) published on the occasion of the Eleventh
Congress of the Communist Party of Czechoslovakia, the following comparison was made:

Index of personal (individual) and collective consumption
1948 = 100

	1953	1955	1956	1957
Personal consumption (paid for from individual incomes)	120.3	148.3	157.4	169
Consumption of institutions providing services to the population	309.5	357.3	367.1	...

This comparison needs some clarification. "Collective consumption"
includes total costs of services provided and the benefits paid to the population by Social Security and National Health Insurance. Under the heading of "health insurance benefits" even such items as family allowances or
costs of vacation for selected good workers are subsumed. Detailed data
on total costs and description of the items included in social security and
national health are to be found in Tables 9.3 and 9.5. In fact, the costs of
national insurance increased faster than individual income. But, as mentioned in Chapter 8, Section 1, they are financed by contributions of the
employees and employers themselves, each party paying about half of the
total contributions. The author could not discover any *net subsidy* to national insurance through the state budget. Thus, as far as national insurance is concerned, only the part of the contributions paid by the employer
(the state) can be considered additional income of the population, or as
"collective consumption by the population." It amounted, in the period
1953–57, to approximately one-tenth of the total wage bill.

Furthermore, the number of recipients of state social security benefits
should be considered. This number increased through incorporating pri-

TABLE 9.3—OLD AGE, DISABILITY, AND OTHER SOCIAL WELFARE BENEFITS
IN CZECHOSLOVAKIA
(Excluding national health benefits)

	1949	1953	1956	1957	1958
NUMBER OF RECIPIENTS (*in thousand persons*)					
Old age, disability (including benefits paid to wage earners' wives)	568.2	757.4	937.6	1,121.8	1,207.7
Widows' and orphans' benefits ...	346.1	388.6	443.4	537.3	555.9
Industrial injuries indemnities ...	131.3	130.5	128.0	—	—
Social welfare and other benefits based on old legislation	244.5	313.2	298.4	403.2	383.8
Special benefits for distinguished persons	—	4.0	2.6	2.5	2.3
Benefits paid to victims of war ...	257.3	221.4	211.7	—	—
Civil servants' benefits not under national insurance	200‡	—	—	—	—
Total	1,624.2	1,815.2	2,021.9	2,062.3	2,147.4
TOTAL AMOUNTS PAID (*in million Kčs*)					
Old age, disability, etc.	1,677	3,483	4,455	5,992	6,701
Widows and orphans	630	1,301	1,589	2,029	2,139
Industrial injuries indemnities...	170	207	253	—	—
Social welfare, etc.	502	698	726	875	821
Special benefits	—	9	8	13	18
Benefits to victims of war........	469	382	355	—	—
Civil servants	1,260	—	—	—	—
Total	4,729	6,080	7,386	8,910	9,681
AVERAGE YEARLY BENEFITS PER RECIPIENT (*in Kčs*)					
Old age, disability, etc.	2,951	4,599	4,741	5,341	5,549
Widows and orphans	1,820	3,348	3,584	3,776	3,848
Industrial injuries indemnities ...	1,294	1,586	1,977	—	—
Social welfare, etc.	2,053	2,229	2,433	2,170	2,139
Special benefits	—	2,222	3,077	5,200	7,826
Victims of war	1,823	1,754	1,677	—	—
Civil servants	6,300	—	—	—	—
Over-all average	2,911	3,379	3,653	4,320	4,508

Data on number of recipients and total benefits paid are from *SRRC*, 1957 and 1958, and *Statistický obzor*, No. 6, 1959. Average yearly benefits per recipient are calculated by the author.

vate insurance into state social security. Average benefits per recipient increased more slowly than total cost, and real per capita benefits were even decreasing at certain periods (see Table 9.4).

In a similar way, national health insurance now covers medical and other health services, part of which used to be provided outside the state

TABLE 9.4—INDEX NUMBERS OF BENEFITS FROM NATIONAL INSURANCE, 1949 = 100
(Excluding health insurance)

	1953	1956	1957	1958
NOMINAL BENEFITS PER RECIPIENT				
Over-all average	115.0	125.5	148.4	154.8
Old age and disability of workers and employees	155.8	160.7	177.6	188.0
Widows' and orphans' benefits	184.0	196.9	207.5	211.4
Social welfare benefits and other benefits under old legislation	115.0	125.5	148.4	154.8
BENEFITS PER RECIPIENT AT CONSTANT COST OF LIVING				
Over-all average	77	94	110	114
Old age, disability	105	120	132	138
Widows and orphans	123	148	154	155
Social welfare benefits, etc.	73	88	78	76

Index numbers were calculated from data in Table 9.3. Figures for constant cost of living were based on the cost-of-living index in Table 7.2, under the assumption that the cost of living in 1949 was 10 per cent above the 1948 level. The index applied here is as follows: 1949 = 100, 1953 = 149, 1956 = 134, 1957 = 135, 1958 = 136. In view of serious changes in the pattern of benefits, the index numbers show approximate trends only, and no year-to-year comparisons should be made. For instance, after the abolition of special pensions with higher benefits for civil servants and their widows, old-age and widows' benefits increased because of inclusions of the former benefits of civil servants. On the other hand, social welfare benefits include most former self-employed workers whose private insurance was blocked, etc.

social services. Everyone in Czechoslovakia is now entitled to free medical care, free hospitalization, etc., so that the number of persons benefiting from national health increased. The cost of national health per inhabitant will be discussed in the next section.

Besides the "collective consumption" through national insurance, other kinds of social services are financed or subsidized by the state, by the unified trade unions ROH, etc. Again, the part of these services financed by contributions of the population to ROH, etc., cannot be considered as collective income in addition to individual income. In any case, in 1958 the total "collective consumption" by the population, or "social wage," hardly exceeded 20 per cent of the total wage and salary bill. Thus it is probably not higher in Czechoslovakia than the social expenditure on labor, in addition to the wage bill, in France or Great Britain.

For comparison with fair accuracy of the actual individual and "collective" net incomes of the population, a special study of taxation and of the manner of financing the social services, etc., would be necessary. In this book, the intercountry comparisons are limited to the development of workers' real earnings in industry before taxes, where the problems of

TABLE 9.5—COST OF HEALTH INSURANCE IN CZECHOSLOVAKIA
(Health insurance benefits, including family allowances)

(*In million Kčs*)

	1948	1953	1954	1955	1956	1957	1958
Sickness benefits and cash payments during hospitalization..	520	1,231	1,422	1,566	1,695	3,005	2,327
Cash payments during sickness of family member	—	—	—	—	—	45	36
Maternity cash benefits	41	136	150	157	165	291	285
Grants for newlyweds	30	69	80	84	98	—	—
Maternity grants and grants for layettes	77	144	148	147	146	140	132
Family allowances	722	2,075	2,798	2,890	2,984	3,218	3,362
Funeral grants	18	59	19	18	18	22	20
Selective recreation, organized by ROH (unified trade unions) and financed through health insurance	—	—	144	125	146	65	85
Treatment in health resorts.....	109	152	239	207	214	332	325
Other health benefits	3	33	31	29	31	9	...
Total	1,570	3,899	5,031	5,223	5,497	7,127	6,572
Average health insurance cost per inhabitant (in *Kčs*)	1,276	3,046	3,870	3,987	4,164	5,318	4,869
Index	100	239	303	312	326	418	382
Index at 1948 constant cost of living	100	159	189	205	222	282	257

Data are taken from *SRRC*, 1958, Table 18.1, and 1959, Table 18.3. The yearly cost of health insurance per inhabitant and index numbers have been calculated by the author. For the index of cost of health insurance at 1948 cost of living, the index of the cost of living from Table 7.2 has been used. Data are not fully comparable from year to year. There are serious interruptions of comparability between 1948 and 1953; all special kinds of health insurance and all private sickness and other health insurance have been incorporated in unified national health insurance. Between 1956 and 1957, salary payments of employees for the first six weeks of sickness have been shifted from the employer (wage fund) to health insurance. (See also remarks to Table 9.1.)

comparability are not so extremely difficult. The development of average per capita incomes and social benefits in Czechoslovakia, as different from the trends in real earnings in industry, will be discussed in the following section.

3. *Real Per Capita Earnings in Industry, Real Per Capita Personal Income, and Real Social Security Benefits Per Recipient*

Table 9.6 provides an index of manual workers' real earnings in Czechoslovak industry (including mining, manufacturing, electricity, and gas) compared to an index of real earnings in manufacturing in the de-

TABLE 9.6—INDEX OF TRENDS IN THE COST OF LIVING AND IN REAL EARNINGS
IN MANUFACTURING, INTERNATIONAL COMPARISON

	1948	1952	1953	1954	1955	1956	1957	1958
COST-OF-LIVING INDEX[a]								
Czechoslovakia	100*	150*	164*	160*	152*	147*	148*	150*
Austria	100	202 ‖	(200)	(206)	(210)	(216)	(224)	(228)
France (Paris) ...	100	144	143	143	144	147	151	171
West Germany	100	109	107	107	109	113	114	118
United Kingdom ..	100 ‖	(126)	(130)	(132)	(138)	(145)	(150)	(155)
United States	100	110	111	111	111	113	117	120
INDEX OF NOMINAL EARNINGS IN MANUFACTURING BEFORE TAXES[b]								
Czechoslovakia[c] ...	100	146	159	173	175	180	181	185
France	100	183	188	200	216 ‖	(233)	(251)	(280)
West Germany	100	167	176	183	196	210 ‖	(223)	(235)
United Kingdom ..	100 ‖	(129)	(136)	(146)	(159)	(170)	(181)	(184)
United States	100	126	132	133	141	148	152	(154)
INDEX OF WORKERS' REAL EARNINGS IN MANUFACTURING[b]								
Czechoslovakia[c] ...	100	97	97	108	115	122	122	123
France	100	127	131	140	150	(158)	(166)	(164)
West Germany	100	153	164	171	180	186	(197)	(199)
United Kingdom ..	100 ‖	(102)	(105)	(111)	(115)	(117)	(120)	(119)
United States	100	114	119	120	127	131	130	(128)

The cost-of-living index for Czechoslovakia is taken from Table 7.2 (not the official index; see Chapter 7, Section 4); for other countries from various issues of the U.N. *Statistical Yearbook*, U.N. *Monthly Bulletin of Statistics*, and *International Labour Review, Statistical Supplement*. Index of nominal earnings is calculated on the basis of data on earnings in manufacturing from U.N. sources. Index of real earnings was obtained by dividing the nominal-earnings index by the cost-of-living index. Figures for 1958 are taken from the *International Labour Review, Statistical Supplement*, 1959.

There are serious limitations of comparability between countries. Serious interruptions of comparability of national index series are marked ‖. Index numbers derived from an incomparable base are set in parentheses. Comparisons between countries should be made only in respect to approximate trends, and should not be used as measurements of year-to-year developments.

[a] Rebased to 1948 = 100, irrespective of limited convertibility in some countries.

[b] Figures for Czechoslovakia are on a monthly basis, for France on an hourly basis, and for West Germany, the United Kingdom, and the United States on a weekly basis.

[c] Figures are for industry, that is, including mining and public utilities.

veloped market economies (index numbers of per capita nominal earnings divided by the cost-of-living index). In spite of severe limitations of comparability, it is safe to state that, from 1948 to 1953, workers' real earnings in Czechoslovak industry decreased, whereas real earnings in manufacturing in the developed market economies increased. From 1953 to 1957, Czechoslovak real earnings rose faster than earnings in the listed market economies, but this rise was not sufficient to catch up, over the whole 1948–58 period, with the increase in real earnings in manufacturing in France or West Germany, or to surpass that in the United States, in spite of the much higher starting level of American earnings. Only in Great Britain the increase in real earnings in manufacturing was slightly slower than the increase in real earnings in Czechoslovak industry (which may be due, among other factors, to the inclusion of fast-rising miners' earnings in the Czechoslovak data).

It was demonstrated in the previous section that manual workers' earnings rose faster than average earnings in the whole Socialist sector in Czechoslovakia. It may be of interest to compare the trends in real workers' earnings and real per capita average incomes of the population.

TABLE 9.7—APPROXIMATION OF AVERAGE NET INCOME IN CZECHOSLOVAKIA IN 1948
(Based on personal income in national accounts)

(*In billion Kčs*)

	Money Income	Income in Kind	Total Personal Income
Wages and salaries	137.8	2.5	140.3
As entrepreneurs: farmers	10.3	18.0	28.3
As entrepreneurs: others	21.0	1.0	22.0
Pensions, old-age benefits, other transfers	28.0	—	28.0
Unblocked pre-1945 accounts	5.9	—	5.9
Income from property (rent, interest, etc.)	5.0	1.0	6.0
Total	208.5	22.5	231.1
Minus direct taxes			11.0
Minus employees' contributions to national insurance			9.7
Personal income after taxes			211.4
In 1953 currency units (5 : 1)			42.28

Source: Unpublished, semiofficial computations.

A rough estimate has been made of average net per capita personal income in Czechoslovakia (including transferred income), after taxes and contributions, for 1948 and 1956 (necessary data for other years are not available). In 1948, the source of statistical information was personal income in national accounts; in 1956, family budgets. The results of such a comparison can be found in Tables 9.7 and 9.8. From Table 9.7, it was calculated that the average per capita net personal income after taxes (1953 currency) was 3,438 Kčs. From Table 9.8, the 1956 personal income, in per cent of 1948, was as follows:

Average per capita personal income (including income in kind), after
taxes and contributions 162
Cost of living (from Table 7.2) 147
Average *real* per capita personal income after taxes and contributions 110

TABLE 9.8—APPROXIMATION OF AVERAGE NET PER CAPITA
INCOME IN CZECHOSLOVAKIA IN 1956
(Based on "net money income of households")[a]

| | Weight in Total Sample (30,948 house- holds) (per cent) | Average Number of Members in Household | | Net Money Income after Taxes | | Net In- come per Capita Including Income in Kind (Kčs) |
		Total	Econom- ically Active	Per Capita (Kčs)	Per Eco- nomically Active Person (Kčs)	
Wage earners	27.7	3.49	1.51	6,006	13,873	6,350*
Salary earners	25.6	3.35	1.52	6,643	14,703	6,650*
Members of agricultural co-operatives	5.7	3.51	1.94	4,756	8,610	6,700*
Independent farmers	13.7	3.54	2.18	3,848	6,256	5,000*
Wage earners with own farming lot	10.2	3.96	1.94	5,057	10,392	7,000*
Pensioners	15.7	1.94	0.27	4,646	...	4,650*
Entrepreneurs (small handicrafts	0.1	2.94	1.36	5,202	11,261	5,200*
Weighted average ...	100	3.26	1.48	5,515	12,140*	5,550*

[a] J. Bezouška, *Statistický obzor*, No. 11, 1958.

In view of the different nature of the statistical data used, these results are subject to many qualifications. Nevertheless, a 10 per cent increase in real per capita personal income over the eight years 1948–56, as estimated on the previous page, seems to be fairly supported by the increase of 4 per cent in average real earnings in the "Socialist sector," excluding agricultural cooperatives, over the same period.[3] A faster increase in per capita personal income may be explained by a faster rise of incomes in agriculture, and especially of "collective" incomes. For example, the cost of social security and national health per inhabitant, which is included in the estimate of per capita personal income, rose faster than earnings in the "Socialist sector." This was due especially to a fairly rapid increase in the cost of national health per inhabitant (by 122 per cent between 1948 and 1956, in terms of constant cost of living), as shown in Table 9.5. On the other hand, it should be pointed out that the real old-age benefits from social security *per recipient* were decreasing until 1956; that is, the purchasing power of the average old-age pension went down. Even after 1956, the average old-age benefit in the lowest category of "social welfare benefits and other benefits based on old legislation" remained below the

[3] The nominal increase in 1956, based on data in Table 9.1, was 152 on the 1948 = 100 basis, to which the author's cost-of-living index of 147 was applied.

1948 level, in terms of constant cost of living. This is demonstrated in Table 9.4.[4]

If the estimate of per capita real personal income has fair validity, it means that in the 1948–56 period manual workers' real earnings in industry rose at least twice as fast as real personal incomes on the average of the whole population (increases of 22 per cent and 10 per cent respectively). It also means that in Czechoslovakia real per capita personal income, including "collective income," was rising in the 1948–56 period by less than 1.5 per cent a year—noticeably more slowly than in the developed market economies, where, in contrast to Czechoslovakia, the per capita personal income rose almost as fast as, and in some countries faster than, average earnings in manufacturing (even after taxes).

The question arises now whether the development of per capita real income over the period under study can be considered representative of long-term trends in the Czechoslovak centrally planned economy.

Limiting the tentative answer to real earnings in the "Socialist sector," which represent incomes of three-quarters of the population, it is obvious that the decrease in real earnings because of inflation in the first period of central planning, up to 1953, was an abnormal one. In the future, even under a new industrialization drive, Czechoslovak planning authorities will certainly try hard to avoid such a drastic inflation as occurred before 1953. On the other hand, the rapid increase of real earnings in the 1953–57 period, brought about by rapid consumers' price reductions as well as by a rapid increase in money earnings, cannot be considered as a normal development either (the increase was almost checked in 1957–58, as shown in Table 9.6). Under the long-term plan up to 1965, the rapidly increasing rate of investments would hardly allow a continuous lowering of turnover tax (and thus reduction of consumers' prices) at a pace comparable to the average consumers' price reductions between 1953 and 1957. Nominal earnings, under the new wage system, will certainly rise much more slowly in future years than they did in the 1953–57 period.[5]

---

[4] Changes in social security and family allowances, and the new rules of March 1959 have been described in *Industry and Labour* (International Labour Office, Geneva), Vol. XII, No. 7, October 1959.

[5] According to a broadcast by Radio Bratislava on September 5, 1958, the "average wage" (nominal per capita earnings in the Socialist sector, excluding agricultural cooperatives) is planned to increase, under the long-term plan, at a yearly rate of only 1.6 per cent. The comparable increase in gross nominal earnings per capita in 1954 amounted to 6.7 per cent, in 1955 to 2.3 per cent, in 1956 to 3.9 per cent, in 1957 to 1.9 per cent, and in 1958 to 2.4 per cent.

Thus, the long-term development of real earnings in Czechoslovakia may not be very different from the 1948–58 average.

4. Some Other Indicators of the Standard of Living

Table 9.9 provides data on per capita consumption of food in Czechoslovakia in prewar times and in recent years. While, on the whole, food consumption has surpassed the prewar level, consumption of some important items, like milk and vegetables, still remains below it. The present national diet seems not to be well balanced, as analyzed by V. Zápotocký in *Statistický obzor*, No. 2, 1959. Table 9.10 contains a comparison by countries of net per capita supplies of meat, fats, and sugar. Consumption of these high-quality foodstuffs in 1957 was slightly lower in Czechoslovakia as compared to the Western average, but higher than in other Eastern European countries (with the exception of consumption of fats, and possibly also of meat, in East Germany).[6]

TABLE 9.9—PER CAPITA CONSUMPTION OF FOOD IN CZECHOSLOVAKIA

	(In kilograms)					
	1936	1948	1953	1956	1957	1958
Meat[a]	32.9	28.4	(40.1)	(48.4)	(51.0) ‖	54
Fats and oils[b]	15.1	9.8	(14.8)	(17.1)	(17.4) ‖	17.5
Milk (*liter*)	164.2	124.9	148.0	141.2	133.7 ‖	118.6
Eggs (*each*)	137	95	185	167	174 ‖	170
Wheat flour	65.2	74.9	89.8	92.6	82.9 ‖	81.3
Bread (rye)	84.7	74.7	88.4	75.7	72.8 ‖	74.5
Sugar, refined	23.8	22.7	(28.3)	(34.2)	(33.5) ‖	34.9
Potatoes	118.9	95.2	127.2	126.7	131.7 ‖	107.3
Fruit, all kinds	46.0	52.2	65.7	48.4	34.1 ‖	61.5

Data for 1936–57 are from an article by V. Zápotocký in *Statistický obzor*, No. 2, 1959. Figures in parentheses possibly include, besides human consumption domestically, food processing for exports. Data for 1958 are from *SRRC*, 1959, Table 15.1. They seem not to be fully comparable with Zápotocký's data for previous years.

    [a] Beef, veal, pork, mutton, lamb, horse, poultry and game, including products, in terms of carcass weight, including offal.
    [b] Fat content.

Table 9.11 contains approximations of the necessary working time of a worker in industry to earn the retail price of various foodstuffs and cigarettes. In spite of many inaccuracies involved, this table shows that the necessary working time is longer in Czechoslovakia than in the de-

    [6] A detailed comparison of per capita consumption of other kinds of food and of a number of manufactures in Eastern Europe can be found in the *Economic Survey of Europe*, 1958.

TABLE 9.10—PER CAPITA CONSUMPTION OF MEAT, FATS, AND SUGAR,
COMPARISON BETWEEN COUNTRIES

(In kilograms)

Country	Year	Meat, All Kinds (carcass weight)	Fats and Oils (fat content)	Sugar, Refined
Czechoslovakia	1957	51	17	33
Austria	1957/58	49	18	34
France	1957/58	70	17	26
West Germany	1957/58	53	25	28
United Kingdom	1957/58	71	23	49
United States	1957/58	92	20	41
East Germany	1957	45[a]	26	27
Hungary	1957	42	22	25
Poland	1957	47[b]	...	26
Yugoslavia	1957/58	20	9	8

Data for the centrally planned economies are from *Statistický obzor*, No. 2, 1959. Data for the market economies and Yugoslavia are from the U.N. *Statistical Yearbook*, 1958. There is limited comparability between these sources.

[a] Net weight, excluding bones and offal.
[b] Including animal fat.

veloped Western market economies, except for cigarettes and potatoes. But the working time is shorter for those goods listed than in Hungary, Poland, or the Soviet Union[7] (and also shorter than for a worker in the less developed market economies in Southern Europe, which are not listed in this book).

Table 9.12 gives figures on cars per 1,000 inhabitants. It shows that the density of motor vehicles in Czechoslovakia, though much higher than in other Eastern European countries, lags much behind the Western market economies, in spite of some development of Czechoslovak motoring in recent years.

Table 9.13 gives data, in international comparison, on radio and television sets. In this respect, Czechoslovakia has reached a high level, comparable to Western European countries (which, however, in 1958 remained below the British and American levels for television sets).

Table 9.13 also provides data on yearly film attendance. In 1957, it was higher in Czechoslovakia than in other centrally planned economies

---

[7] Except for eggs; a number of comparable data on necessary working time to buy various commodities in the USSR are not, however, available to the author.

TABLE 9.11—WORKING TIME PER KILOGRAM NECESSARY TO EARN THE PRICE OF BASIC FOODSTUFFS, ELECTRICITY, AND CIGARETTES IN 1957

Time per Worker in Manufacturing (Western Countries) or Industry (Eastern Europe)

(Time in hours and minutes)

Commodity	Czecho-slovakia[a]	Austria[b]	West Germany	United Kingdom[c]	United States[d]	Poland	Hungary	USSR
Butter (kg)	5h21m	1h45m	3h15m	1h40m	48m	9h50m	9h20m	7h00m
Eggs (each)	08[e]	08	07	05	02	04	...	07
Milk (standard liter)	15[f]	13	12	14	07	21	25	29
Beef sirloin (kg)	3 23	4 18	2 19	2 11	1h02m	...	...	...
Pork cutlet (kg)	3 23	3 18	2 38	2 07	57	...	...	...
Wheat flour (kg)	27	26	21	17	07	54	40	...
Rice (kg)	51	34	28	24	11	...	1 30	...
Potatoes (kg)	06	06	05	08	03	...	...	...
Sugar (kg)	1 21	37	33	17	08	1 42	1 33	2 10
Coffee (kg)	29 49	8 24	9 08	4 05	1 03	33 —	57 —	...
Tea (kg)	25 —	12 —	15 —	41 —	...	32 —	32 —	17 —
Electricity (kwh)	06½[g]	03	06	02½	02	04	05[h]	...
Cigarettes (pack of 20)	25	26	45	52	08	...	...	...
AVERAGE HOURLY WAGE	7.10 Kčs	10 Sch.	2.20 DM	57 d.	$2.07	7 Zl.	7 Ft.	4 rub.

Sources: For Czechoslovakia, *Rudé právo*, March 14, 1959; for Western countries, *ILO Statistical Yearbook*, 1958; for Poland, Hungary, and the USSR, figures are based on newspaper reports only and are subject to a great margin of error.

The data refer to approximate standard quality and to consumers' prices and wages before taxes; for Czechoslovakia, Hungary, Poland, and the USSR the data include premiums, overtime, etc. Comparison between countries is subject to very severe limitations, in view of the varying quality, the varying taxation of wages, etc. In no case should the comparison be regarded as representative for the comparative workers' standard of living, since important consumption items, for which international comparison is especially difficult, are missing. For example, rent, in terms of the necessary working time, is much lower in Czechoslovakia than in the West (but living space is rationed), and cultural services and health services are free. In contrast to the West, however, prices of manufactures are much higher.

[a] Based on prices in March 1959, after the latest price reduction. [b] Based on prices in 46 large towns, except for electricity, which is for New York only.
[c] Based on prices in the seven largest cities. [d] Based on prices in Vienna.
[e] At the summer price, April–September. At the winter price, the figure would be 13 minutes.
[f] At the summer price, April–September. At the winter price, the figure would be 17 minutes.
[g] For the first 15 kilowatt hours; there is a surcharge for excess consumption. [h] For the first 25 kilowatt hours; there is a surcharge for excess consumption.

TABLE 9.12—NUMBER OF PASSENGER CARS IN USE PER 1,000 INHABITANTS
(Excluding military and police vehicles)

	1948	1956	Month	1957	Month	1958
Czechoslovakia	8	11[a]	Dec.	13[a]	Dec.	15[a]
Privately owned	7*	...		...	Dec.	12
Austria	5	27	Oct.	33	Oct.	41
France	37[b]	79[b]	Jan.	88	Jan.	100
West Germany	6	43	July	48	July	58
United Kingdom	40	76	Sept.	83		...
United States	227	323	Dec.	326		...
East Germany	...	...		6[c]		...
Poland	...	...		2[c]		...
Hungary	...	...		2[c]		...
USSR	...	...		2[c]		...
Yugoslavia	0.5	1	Dec.	1		...

Figures for Czechoslovakia were obtained by taking the total number of cars in use in 1948, 105,000, adding production and imports and subtracting exports and scrapped cars, for the years 1956, 1957, and 1958:

	In 1,000 Units		
	1948–56	1957	1958
Production	136.8	34.6	43.4
Plus imports	14†	10.5	9.5
Minus exports.	−96.6	−15.9	−25.0
Minus scrapped cars	−10†	− 1.2†	− 1.9†
Increase of cars in use	44*	28*	26*
Number of cars in use at end of period	149*	177*	203*

(Cars in use at end of period probably include a certain number of cars not actually in use, as well as military and police cars; thus not comparable with other countries.)

Figures for Czechoslovakia, privately owned cars in 1958, are based on a total of 162,900, as given in *Hospodářské noviny*, No. 46, 1959 (November 13). Figures for other countries: for 1948 and 1956, from *American Automobile*; for 1957 and 1958, from *Statistisches Jahrbuch für die Bundesrepublik Deutschland*, 1958, 1959.

[a] Including a certain number of cars not actually in use, as well as military and police vehicles.

[b] Excluding all government cars.

[c] Without indication of the month of census; the comparable figure for Czechoslovakia, as given in *Statistisches Jahrbuch*, is 9; in the author's opinion, this may be a slight underrating.

except East Germany and the USSR, but lower than in all the listed market economies, except France (it is a well-known fact that the Latins are less inclined to watch television or to go to the films than the Anglo-Saxon, Germanic, or Slav nations).

Finally, Table 9.14 contains figures on the number of books published (titles), and on newspaper circulation. The number of books published is relatively higher than in the larger Western countries; but this is a usual phenomenon in a small country, where, in spite of fewer inhabitants, the

TABLE 9.13—RADIO AND TELEVISION SETS AND ATTENDANCE AT FILMS, COMPARISON BY COUNTRIES

(End 1958–beginning 1959)

| Country | Sets in Use (or Licenses Granted), thousands | | | | No. of Persons per Radio Set | No. of Persons per TV Set | Yearly Film Attendance per Person, 1957 |
| | Radio | | | Television | | | |
	Wireless	Wired	Total				
Czechoslovakia	3,055	262	3,317	328	4	41	13.9
Austria	1,956	14	1,970	60	4	117	15.8
France	11,484	—	11,484	1,000	4	45	9.7
West Germany	16,050	159	16,209	2,000	3	26	15.4[a]
Great Britain	15,584	1,048	16,632	9,300	3	6	17.8
United States	161,000	—	161,000	52,000	1	3	14.0
Yugoslavia	1,380	175	1,555	7	13	2,630	6.0
East Germany	5,500	...	5,500	274	3	63	17.2
Hungary	1,800	...	1,800	12	6	82	11.5
Poland	3,600	...	3,600	100	8	288	8.2
USSR	10,700	...	10,700	2,600	19	80	15.1

Data on radio and television sets: for Czechoslovakia, from *SRRC*, 1959, Tables 11.26 and 11.27 (for end of 1958); for other countries, from *U.S. Information Agency*, March 2 and 13, 1959. (Some of these data are obviously estimates; number of persons per set calculated by the author.) Data on film attendance are from U.N. *Statistical Yearbook*, 1958, Table 183.

[a] 1956.

TABLE 9.14—BOOK PUBLICATION AND NEWSPAPER CIRCULATION
IN 1957, COMPARISON BY COUNTRIES

	Books		Newspapers		
Country	Total Number	Number per 100,000 Persons	Total Number	Circulation (*Thousands*)	Circulation, Copies per Thousand Persons
Czechoslovakia	7,187	53.8	17	2,200	166
Austria	4,102	58.7	34	1,306	187
France	11,917	27.1	137[a]	10,692[a]	246[a]
West Germany	15,710	31.1	481	14,700	273
United Kingdom	20,719	40.3	114[b]	29,100[b]	573[b]
United States	13,142	7.3	1,824	56,596	337
Yugoslavia	5,768	31.8	18	858	48
East Germany	...	...	37[b]	2,131[b]	116[b]
Hungary	3,456	35.2	25	1,200	121
Poland	6,444	22.9	40	4,161	150
USSR	59,530[c]	29.7[c]	385	21,475[d]	407[d]

Data are from U.N. *Statistical Yearbook*, 1958, pp. 626 ff., 634 ff. (Figures per 100,000 persons were calculated by the author.)

[a] 1955.

[b] 1954.

[c] Of these, 21,238 were placed on the market (or 10.6 per 100,000 persons); the rest were books and pamphlets distributed free of charge.

[d] Excluding 5.6 million copies of specialized dailies and 6.8 million copies of dailies put out by individual factories and collective farms.

variety of publications is approximately the same as in much larger countries. (This is one of the reasons that the number of published books per 100,000 persons is highest in small countries like Switzerland and Austria.) Total number of published books in Czechoslovakia, however, until 1957 remained below the prewar figure: 1937, 10,994; 1955, 4,399; 1956, 4,842; 1957, 7,181.

Circulation of newspapers is much lower in Czechoslovakia than in Western countries, but higher than in other Eastern European countries. It is noteworthy that the circulation of dailies per inhabitant per year decreased from 193 in 1950 (approximately the prewar level) to 166 in 1956.

Table 9.15 provides data on foreign tourists in 1957. It shows that international tourist travel was extremely limited in Czechoslovakia, as compared with Western countries. (The number of total journeys abroad, including official travel, was four times higher than tourist travel.) In

TABLE 9.15—FOREIGN TOURIST TRAVEL IN 1957

Country	Foreign Tourist Arrivals		Travel of Nationals Abroad (Each country visited counted as one trip)	
	Visitors (*Thousands*)	No. of Visitors per Thousand Persons of Country Visited	Trips (*Thousands*)	Trips Abroad per Thousand Persons of Home Country
Czechoslovakia	82	6	73[a]	5[a]
Austria	3,040	434	2,700[†]	386[†]
France	4,310	98	6,300[†]	144[†]
West Germany	3,090[†,b]	61[†]	8,700[†]	170[†]
United Kingdom	1,180	23	5,400[†]	147[†]
United States (excl. travel to and from Canada and Mexico)	950	6	4,500[†]	26[†]
Yugoslavia	1,970	107	150[†]	8[†]
Poland	80	3	90[†]	3.2[†]
USSR	550[c]	3[c]	75[†]	0.4[†]

Data for Czechoslovakia are from *SRRC*, 1959, Table 14.8; for other countries, from U.N. *Statistical Yearbook*, 1958, Table 143 (based, in turn, on information compiled by the British Travel and Holiday Association). These data are subject to many qualifications, as indicated in the source, and their international comparability is very limited. In principle, they cover stays by foreign nationals of 24 hours or more, excluding transit. (An exception is the West German statistics in terms of nights spent by foreign tourists: the author estimated the number of arrivals in Germany by assuming, arbitrarily, that the average stay of foreign tourists was three days.)

Only data on arrivals of foreign tourists are complete, and taken directly from the source. Data on national traveling abroad as tourists have been obtained by summing up data on arrivals of the nationals of the country concerned, in the countries of arrival. Since the list of the countries of arrival in the U.N. *Statistical Yearbook* is incomplete, data on nationals traveling abroad as tourists are incomplete too. (Most important tourist countries of arrival have been covered, however, and the author also made a correction for travel of German, Polish, and Soviet tourists to Czechoslovakia— omitted in the U.N. *Statistical Yearbook*.)

It is hoped that data in this table reflect trends in foreign tourist travel fairly well but they cannot be regarded as a reliable measure of comparative foreign tourist travel. Furthermore, the intensity of tourist travel from any country cannot be regarded as indicative of the standard of living without considering many other factors. (For instance, it is only natural that the number of Austrians traveling abroad as tourists is very high, since Austria is a small land-locked country, within easy reach of the seaside in Italy and Yugoslavia, and with neighboring Germany speaking a similar language.)

[a] Actual number of tourist trips abroad, irrespective of the number of countries visited (usually only one foreign country was visited by Czechoslovak tourists). Actual number of tourists going abroad can be ascertained in Czechoslovakia, in contrast to Western countries, because tourist travel abroad is organized only through the official travel agency, Čedok. Number of border crossings, including official and business trips, transit, and transportation personnel, was, of course, much higher: 1,171,000 persons entering and 1,162,000 leaving Czechoslovakia were counted (including both foreign and Czechoslovak nationals; *SRRC*, 1959, p. 361).

[b] Rough estimate on the basis of 9,246,000 nights spent by foreign tourists in West Germany.

[c] Including delegations and business trips. Actual tourist travel was probably less than half of this.

absolute figures, international tourist travel developed as follows (in thousand persons):[8]

[8] Data for 1955 and 1956 are from *Hlas Domova*, VII, 14; for 1957 and 1958 from *SRRC*, 1959, Table 14.8.

	1955	1956	1957	1958
Foreign tourists visiting Czechoslovakia.....	8	32	82	80
From East Germany	...	...	34	24
From Hungary	...	...	6	11
From Poland	...	...	3	10
From USSR	...	...	9	8
From Austria	...	...	8	8
From U.S.	...	...	1	4
Czechoslovak tourists going abroad	4	53	73	89
To Bulgaria	...	...	10	11
To East Germany	...	...	29	26
To Hungary	...	...	6	15
To Poland	...	...	7	8
To Rumania	...	...	7	9
To USSR	...	...	10	11
To Belgium (world exposition)	...	...	—	4

In spite of recovery in the most recent years, international tourist travel remains only a small fraction of prewar travel. Facilities for both international and internal tourist travel decreased rapidly after introduction of the centrally planned system and after nationalization of all hotels. The total number of beds in hotels and boarding houses fell from 145.4 thousand at the end of 1949 to 69.7 thousand at the end of 1957.

Finally, the number of inhabitants per physician is given, in international comparison, in Table 9.16. From this angle, medical care in Czecho-

TABLE 9.16—NUMBER OF PHYSICIANS AND SURGEONS IN 1957,
EXCLUDING DENTISTS

	Physicians and Surgeons (*Thousands*)	No. of Persons per Physician or Surgeon
Czechoslovakia	19.3	868
Austria	11.5	599
France	45.6	958
West Germany	68.3	732
United States	207.9[a]	817[a]
Yugoslavia	10.3	1,735
Hungary	13.6	713
Poland	20.2	1,376
USSR.	329.0	1,644

Data from U.N. *Statistical Yearbook*, 1958, pp. 596 ff.
[a] 1955.

slovakia is on the Western level (higher than in France) and much better than in above-listed Eastern European countries, except Hungary.

5. Summary

Over the period 1948–58, manual workers' real gross earnings in industry increased by approximately one-fourth, that is, slightly faster than the not quite comparable workers' real earnings in manufacturing in Britain, but noticeably slower than in France or West Germany. Taxation and the amount of social services provided probably did not change these trends very much, except for the United States.

But workers' earnings in Czechoslovakia developed more favorably than average per capita income of the population. These rose, in terms of average yearly compound rates, in the period 1948–56, by just slightly over 1 per cent a year—much more slowly than in the developed Western market economies. Some indicators, such as net per capita food supplies, the necessary working time to buy basic food, etc., seem to corroborate the fact that the standard of living in Czechoslovakia, while remaining above that in less developed centrally planned countries, in most respects has not been catching up with Western standards.

Any more systematic and accurate comparison of the standard of living would have to take into account the factors of quality and availability. Under central planning, changes in quality are not reflected by consumers' prices. Even after the abolition of rationing, some goods are not available on the market. (There has been a shortage for many years of quality razor blades, electric bulbs, spices, citrus fruit, etc., and there have been local shortages of meat, vegetables, and even fresh bread; the latter kind of non-availability may be in connection with a rather reduced network of retail shops.) Since internal trade is not analyzed in this book, it may be useful to give here at least the number of retail shops per 10,000 inhabitants:

Czechoslovakia, 1956	61	East Germany (still with shops	
France, 1954	164	two-thirds private), 1956	115
West Germany, 1950	120	Hungary, 1956	36
Great Britain, 1950	112	Poland, 1956	50
		USSR, 1956	24

Rationing still applies, in Czechoslovakia, to "living space" (flats are allotted by authorities), to cars at "normal price," to hard-coal supplies for households, etc.

On the evidence given in this book, personal consumption in Czechoslovakia developed much more slowly than production. Such a conclusion may be drawn also on the basis of national income and expenditure aggregates, as discussed in the next chapter.

Chapter 10

NATIONAL INCOME, GROSS PRODUCT,
AND EXPENDITURE AGGREGATES

1. Conceptual Framework of National Income and
Social Product in Centrally Planned Economies

Two basic national aggregates have been used so far in centrally planned economies: national income and gross social product. Both are basically different from national income and gross national product under the definition generally accepted in the West.[1]

National income and social product, as presently defined in Eastern Europe, refer only to the sphere of material production or the "productive" sphere. This does not mean that they exclude all services. They include services connected with the production and distribution of material products, such as trade (wholesale, retail, and foreign), transportation of goods, legal services, etc. In the Czechoslovak framework, the branches of material production are industry (mining, manufacturing, electricity, and gas); construction; agriculture; forestry; transportation (in principle, freight transport only); communications and servicing production; state supplies of materials and state procurement of agricultural produce; trade and public catering.

Explicitly excluded from the official Czechoslovak computations of national income are the following branches of the "nonmaterial" or "nonproductive" sphere: passenger transportation; communications (the part servicing the population); science and research (but probably not industrial research); communal services (such as barbers, cleaners, etc.);

---

[1] In some centrally planned economies—for example, Poland—the concept of "gross national income" or "net product" has been introduced. It is, in fact, gross national product limited to the sphere of material production (merely a difference in terminology). In *Dochód Narodowy Polski,* 1956, the "net product" is defined as follows: "Value of material goods which, as the ultimate result of material production, is at the disposal of the community; on the other hand, national income corresponds to the *newly produced* value of material production. The difference between net product and national income is the value of fixed investments consumed (amortization) by which net product exceeds national income." In Czechoslovak statistics such an aggregate is not used.

housing, health, and social welfare; education, cultural services, physical culture; administration (civil service) and justice; banking and insurance (though banking and insurance directly connected with production and distribution of goods are probably included in the branches of material production); community organizations (such as united trade unions, the Association of Youth, etc.). Defense, of course, is also excluded from national income as well as from statistics on the working population, total wage fund, etc.

The above-described aggregate will be referred to in this chapter as "national income by Marxist definition," or shortly as "Marxist national income."

No distinction is made between national income at factor cost and at market prices. (We shall see in the course of our further analysis that such a distinction depends on whether the turnover tax is considered to be state profit or indirect taxation.)

The difference in magnitude between the Eastern European national income and the Western national income, under current definitions, boils down to the exclusion, in the former, of a part of services.

There is a much greater difference between gross social product (or, simply, social product) in Eastern Europe and gross national product in the West. While the latter embraces only the final product before subtraction of provisions for fixed capital consumed in the course of production (that is, it is equal to net product plus depreciation), the former includes the multiple counting of the value of material products at all stages of production. All the final and intermediate products and raw materials enter into gross social product as many times as they are transferred from one enterprise to another within the "sphere of material production."[2] Social product is equal to the sum of the gross value of material production. (This includes "material services"; "immaterial services" are excluded from gross social product in a way similar to the exclusion of these services from Marxist national income in the present Eastern European concept.) In view of the repeated rotation of the products and services included in gross social product, its numerical value must far exceed the numerical value of gross national product by Western

---

[2] In Czechoslovakia and some other centrally planned economies including the USSR, however, this "enterprise method" seems to be applied only in industry and agriculture, whereas in freight transport, trade, and other less important branches of "material production" the "branch method" is applied, so that the repeated rotations of products *within* these branches are eliminated from computations of social product.

definition; there is, of course, also a very great difference between Marxist national income and gross social product.[3]

Any reader familiar with the Marxist scheme of economic reproduction will notice that national income, as described above, is equal to the sum of variable capital and surplus value, and social product is equal to the sum of constant capital, variable capital, and surplus value.

In *SRRC*, 1959, p. 17, the following definitions can be found, which, however, are not very satisfactory and which do not indicate the actual method of computing the relating aggregates:

National income is the remainder of social product produced, after allowing for consumption of the means of production within a year. Social product is formed by the total amount of material goods—means of production and consumption goods—produced in the community within a year. National income, which represents the amount of expended labor, contains, in its original material form, all consumption goods produced and that part of means of production that is allocated for expanding output.

Another aggregate, for which the index is also found in *SRRC*, 1958 and 1959—personal consumption—is also different from the corresponding Western idea. It includes not only consumption of consumers' goods, including material services, by households, but also "maintenance of individual housing." In Western accounts, at least a part of such "maintenance" of housing is usually subsumed under gross fixed investments. On the other hand, personal consumption by Marxist definition excludes "nonproductive" services. It can be argued that, as long as "nonproductive" services are excluded, the inclusion of maintenance of housing is not without justification. In Western accounts, such maintenance is *de facto*

---

[3] Under the Polish computations for 1956, gross social product—carefully described only as "gross production" (*produkcija globalna*)—amounted to 589 billion zlotys at current prices, while national income (by Marxist definition) amounted to only 259 billion. A similar great difference can be noted between the value of the East German gross social product (*Brutto Sozialprodukt*) and the Marxist national income (*Volkseinkommen*). In 1958, they amounted, at current prices, to 114.9 and 65.1 billion DM respectively (according to an article by J. Kazimour in *Statistický obzor*, No. 11, 1959). By Western definition, the difference between gross national product and national income boils down to consumption of capital, and thus never exceeds one-tenth. The basic difference between Western gross national product and Marxist gross social product has been officially acknowledged in Czechoslovakia; when comparisons with Western per capita GNP were made, the Czechoslovak aggregate, used for this purpose, was Marxist national income, with qualifications, and not Marxist social product (*Postavení ČSR ve světovém hospodářství*, p. 172).

also included in personal consumption by means of the cost of rent. But other qualifications of the data on personal consumption in Czechoslovakia are necessary. Their statistical coverage is as follows:[4] purchases by the population in retail trade, purchases by the population in the farmers' market, consumption in kind by persons working in agriculture, other consumption (water, gas, electricity, maintenance of individual housing, etc.). This means that Czechoslovak data on personal consumption also include purchases of tools, fertilizers, and other means of production by individual farmers (see Chapters 2 and 7).[5] There is no economic justification for including these production goods in personal consumption.

It should be mentioned that the method of computing Marxist national aggregates varies in detail from country to country within the central planning area.

In 1958, a special commission of the Council of Mutual Economic Aid in Moscow (with membership of all *European* centrally planned countries: Albania, Bulgaria, Czechoslovakia, the German Democratic Republic, Hungary, Rumania, Poland, and the USSR) embarked on a study of a new uniform methodology of national income calculations. So far, the author does not know of any published report with new Eastern European definitions of national income aggregates.[6]

Before studying the recent trends in national aggregates, it may be useful to explain in some detail the computations of Czechoslovak national income in 1948 by a group of economists at the Economic Council of the Czechoslovak government. They are the more interesting as they provide

[4] From a study by M. Misař, *K otázkám rozvoje a plánování osobní spotřeby v ČSR*, p. 19. Misař also describes two other categories of consumption in Czechoslovakia: "institutional consumption" (national health scheme, education, communal services such as restaurants, laundries, barbers), and "consumption by state administration, defense, etc." In contrast to personal consumption, these last two categories come under a common heading of "community" or "social" or "collective" consumption (*spotřeba společenská*).

[5] Purchases for resale by the few remaining self-employed craftsmen and owners of private shops are also included in "personal" consumption. But these purchases, and the resulting duplications, have been negligible in recent years. On the other hand, consumption in kind by this rapidly disappearing category of nonagricultural self-employed workers is not included in personal consumption.

[6] After this manuscript had been completed, an important study of national accounting methodology in Eastern Europe (including Czechoslovakia) was published in the *Economic Bulletin for Europe* (Vol. 11, No. 3, November 1959). But even in this recent study, the new method of computing Marxist national income, as proposed by the CMEA, has been described only in general terms, with limited information on the proposed manner of computing national income and gross social product. Nor does this study contain any new statistical material on Czechoslovak national income and gross social product.

data on national income in Czechoslovakia computed by both Marxist and Western definitions.

2. Czechoslovak National Income and Expenditure in 1948, Computed by Western and Marxist Methods

Table 10.1 shows the difference between national income at factor cost, by Western definition, and national income computed according to Marxist definition.[7] It can be seen that a certain part of services, by Marxist definition, enters into national income originating in industry and other branches of "material production," so that the final numerical difference between the two aggregates by Western and Marxist definition is smaller than one would expect.

TABLE 10.1—CZECHOSLOVAK NATIONAL INCOME BY ECONOMIC ORIGIN IN 1948, COMPARISON OF MARXIST AND WESTERN COMPUTATIONS

(In billion Kčs, in terms of first postwar currency units, at current prices)

Origin	Marxist Definition	Western Definition
Agriculture and forestry	40.0	37.4
Industry and handicraft	123.4	89.0
Building	13.0	11.0
Transportation	11.4	16.6
Trade	12.0	13.6
Public catering	3.2	3.5
Administration		24.7
Services		12.0
Rent		5.3
National income in "productive sphere"	203.0	
National income at factor cost		213.1

Source: Unpublished semiofficial computations.

Table 10.2 shows national income and expenditure at market prices, by Western definition, and Table 10.3 shows the changing structure of national income (wages and salaries, profits, rent, and other income from property) between 1937 and 1948. The rapid increase in the proportion of wages and salaries in national income and the rapid fall of income from entrepreneurship and property over this period are noteworthy.

All data in Tables 10.1–10.2 are in terms of first postwar currency units. They can be converted into 1953 currency units—the legal tender

[7] In the Soviet conception, based at that time on prewar Soviet literature on national income, by D. I. Tchernomodik, M. B. Kolganov, *et al.*

TABLE 10.2—CZECHOSLOVAK NATIONAL INCOME IN 1948 BY WESTERN
DEFINITION; BY TYPE, ORIGIN, AND EXPENDITURE

(In billion Kčs, in terms of first postwar currency units, at current prices)

A. TYPE		C. EXPENDITURES	
Wages, salaries	146.0	Personal consumption	189.0
Profits, interest	61.1	State and public consumption..	48.1
Rent	6.0	Net investments (domestic) ...	20.1
		External balance	− 2.2
National income at factor cost..	213.1		
		National expenditure at market prices	255.0
B. ORIGIN			
"Socialist" sector	123.3	Minus indirect taxes plus subsidies	−41.9
"Capitalist" sector[a]	52.2		
"Personal" sector[b]	31.6		
Rent	6.0	Expenditure of national income at factor cost	213.1
National income at factor cost..	213.1		

Source: Unpublished semiofficial computations. (Independent from Table 10.1, hence minor discrepancy in Rent.)
   [a] Nonnationalized enterprises employing labor.
   [b] Self-employed workers, not employing labor except family members.

of today—at the approximate ratio of five to one.[8] Such a conversion suggests Marxist national income in 1948 (at present-day currency units, but at 1948 prices) of 40.6 billion Kčs. The 1948 computations of Marxist national income seem to have covered a smaller amount of services than later retrospective official computations. This is obvious from the fact that the percentage share of national income originating in trade, which can be calculated on the basis of Table 10.1, is lower than the

TABLE 10.3—DISTRIBUTION OF NATIONAL INCOME, COMPARED
WITH PREWAR TIMES

(In per cent of national income at factor cost, at current prices)

Type	1937	1946	1947	1948
Wages and salaries	59.0	67.9	68.2	68.5
Profits	32.2	28.6	28.5	28.4
Rent..............................	8.8	3.5	3.3	3.1

Source: Unpublished semiofficial computations.

   [8] This ratio does not apply to foreign trade or to cash holdings and savings of the population (see Chapter 7, Section 1). It should be stressed that the conversion into new currency units is made independently of price movements. Converted data are "at current prices," and price indices must be applied to obtain figures "at constant prices."

corresponding percentage for 1948 according to *SRRC*, 1959 (see Table 10.4). When comparing the approximations of Marxist national income in 1953, 1956, and 1957 with the year 1948, the author estimated the 1948 national income at 42 billion Kčs (in order to include a comparable amount of services in the 1948 Marxist national income, as well as to make a slight correction of the 5 : 1 ratio of currency units).

3. Czechoslovak National Income by Marxist Definition, 1948–58 Period

In contrast to Bulgaria, East Germany, Hungary, and Poland, Czechoslovakia has not yet published any recent absolute figures on national income (by Marxist definition). Only index numbers of the growth of national income (over-all growth and by branches of material production), percentage distribution of national income by economic origin, and index numbers of personal consumption have been published so far. These are to be found in Table 10.4.

All index series are based on aggregates at constant prices of April 1, 1955 (that is, prices after revaluation of "basic funds"; see Chapter 8, Section 3). No index numbers based on aggregates at current prices have been published until now, so that it is not possible to arrive at absolute figures, starting from the known data for 1948; nor is it possible to derive a price index of Marxist national income. Data on percentage structure of national income by branches of material production, however, have been published in terms of both constant and current prices. The share of industry, over the 1950–53 period, increased faster in terms of current prices than of constant prices. This indicates that prices in industry were increasing substantially faster, on the average, than those of the total "sphere of material production." This is in line with the remarks on the industrialization drive during the 1951–June 1953 period (see Chapter 2 and Chapter 7, Section 1). From 1955 to 1956, the share of industry in Marxist national income increased, in terms of constant prices, from 64 to 66 per cent, but in terms of current prices it remained unchanged at 62 per cent. This indicates that prices in industry decreased faster, on the average, than those in "material production" as a whole. Wholesale prices probably remained unchanged from 1955 to 1956 (see Chapter 7, Section 3). On the other hand, retail prices for industrial products (consumers' goods) decreased, according to the official index, by 3 per cent.[9]

[9] The official cost-of-living index, in the subsection on industrial products, amounted to 139.9 in 1955 and 136.0 in 1956 (1937 = 100) (from *SRRC*, 1959, Table 15.13; see also Table 7.2).

TABLE 10.4—CZECHOSLOVAKIA'S NATIONAL INCOME BY MARXIST DEFINITION

Official index numbers and percentages

	1948	1949	1950	1951	1952	1953	1954	1955	1956	1957	1958
					A. AT CONSTANT PRICES OF APRIL 1955						
Index 1948 = 100											
National income	100	110	121	133	146	155	161	178	189	203	219
Originating in:											
Industry	100	105	111	129	142	148	154	170	185	200	218
Agriculture and forestry	100	120	132	121	115	127	112	123	119	119	122
Construction	100	109	122	138	192	214	220	252	298	319	330
Other branches of "material production"	100	132	190	193	221	237	297	324	294	326	357
Personal consumption	100	103	120	122	124	120	137	148	158	172	174
Percentage share of personal consumption in national income[a]	74	69	73	67	62	57	62	61	61	62	59
Structure of National Income, in per cent; total national income = 100											
Industry	67	64	61	65	65	64	64	64	66	66	67
Agriculture	17	19	19	16	14	14	12	12	11	11	10
Forestry	1	1	1	1	1	1	1	1	0	0	0
Construction	8	8	8	8	10	10	10	10	12	12	11
Freight transport and communications servicing material production	1	2	2	3	3	3	3	3	3	3	3
State supply of materials and procurement of agricultural produce	1	1	1	1	2	2	2	2	2	2	2
Trade and public catering	5	5	7	5	5	5	7	7	5	5	6
Remaining branches of material production	0	0	1	1	1	1	1	1	1	1	1

TABLE 10.4—*Concluded*

B. AT CURRENT PRICES

Structure of National Income, in per cent; total national income = 100

	1948	1949	1950	1951	1952	1953	1954	1955	1956	1957	1958
Industry	58	63	61	66	69	67	64	62	62	62	62
Agriculture	20	17	16	13	11	13	12	15	16	15	13
Forestry	2	2	1	1	1	1	1	1	0	0	1
Construction	7	8	9	9	9	9	10	10	12	12	11
Freight transport and communications servicing material production	4	3	3	3	3	3	3	3	3	3	3
State supply of materials and procurement of agricultural produce	1	1	1	1	1	1	2	2	2	2	2
Trade and public catering	8	6	8	6	5	5	7	6	4	5	7
Remaining branches of material production	0	0	1	1	1	1	1	1	1	1	1

Sources: *SRRC*, 1959, Tables 1.4, 1.5, 1.7, 1.9. Index numbers and percentages refer to unpublished official computations of Marxist aggregates. Adjustment made in official aggregates for transfer payments through turnover tax is open to doubt, especially in breakdown by branches of material production. Because of this and because of the great variation in the (net) rate of turnover tax, data on the structure of Marxist national income are of very limited practical value. The percentage share of Marxist personal consumption in Marxist national income in the first part of the table also should be interpreted with utmost caution because of possible divergencies of coverage of the two aggregates. Index numbers of Marxist national aggregates are not comparable with Western data.

[a] From the *Economic Survey of Europe*, 1958, extrapolated by the author (for 1958) on the basis of the official national income and personal consumption index numbers.

Considering that industry's share in total Marxist national income was two-thirds; that the share of other branches forming the Marxist national income moved parallel in terms of constant and current prices, except in agriculture; that the share of agriculture in Marxist national income was less than one-sixth; and that output of consumers' goods made up only approximately one-half of total industrial production,[10] the relatively small reduction in retail prices for industrial products seems to have been fully reflected by the change of the structure of Marxist national income at current prices. We know from Chapter 7 that—assuming unchanged wholesale prices—the change in retail prices is determined by changing turnover tax. Therefore, the above-mentioned remarks might be interpreted as an indication that almost the full amount of turnover tax, if not all of it, is included in Marxist national income. But the change in the share of industry in Marxist national income at current prices over one year was too small, and possibly also due, in Table 10.4, to rounding of percentages, so that no definite answer is possible to the question of what amount of turnover tax is included in official figures on national income and what amount is excluded as transfers (see below). This question can be answered only after more detailed information on the method of computation or detailed absolute figures on Marxist national income have been published.

The unchanged share of industry in Marxist national income at current prices between 1957 and 1958, in contrast to the increased share in terms of constant prices, is due, in the first place, to the reduction of wholesale prices in that year (see Chapter 7, Section 3, as well as Chapter 8, Section 1).

The share of agriculture decreased, over the period 1948–54, faster in terms of current prices than of constant prices, thus denoting the lag in the price of agricultural products behind prices in other branches of "material production" (weighted average of wholesale and retail prices). From 1955 to 1956, the share increased, in terms of current prices, from 15 to 16 per cent, but in terms of constant prices it decreased from 12 to 11 per cent. This contrast may be partly due to the increase in state prices paid for quota and above-quota deliveries of agricultural produce (see Table 4.8).

However, percentage figures on the origin of Marxist national income have little real meaning. Even if adequate adjustment has been made for subsidies (and this is almost impossible by branches of material sphere,

---

[10] In terms of gross value, consumers' goods amounted to 43.7 per cent and means of production to 56.3 per cent of industrial output in 1956 (*SRRC*, 1959, Table 7.10).

in view of the very complicated artificial pricing),[11] the official data still include a widely varying rate of "net" turnover tax.

The index of personal consumption in Table 10.4 commands greater interest. It shows that personal consumption decreased absolutely in 1953 (which is in accordance with the remarks on currency reform in that year in Chapter 7, Section 1). The percentage share of personal consumption in Marxist national income in the same table is, of course, not comparable with Western national accounts, in view of the different definitions and the very different price structure in Czechoslovakia. Nevertheless, it is noteworthy that the share of personal consumption in Czechoslovakia's Marxist national income decreased unmistakably during the first industrialization drive up to 1953, and again in 1958.

In addition to relative data on national income, as given in Table 10.4, other economically interesting, though rather unusual, index numbers on the "influence of factors of growth of national income" have been published recently.[12] They are defined as the "growth in national income which would have been achieved if the factor concerned had alone determined national income." Therefore, an index of factor influence over 100 denotes that the contribution of the factor concerned toward formation of Marxist national income increased, as compared with the base year 1948; an index below 100 means that the contribution decreased (or the negative contribution became even more negative). This information is shown in Table 10.5.

The indices of influence of productivity of "living," or currently expended, labor (defined as social product per worker, that is, gross value of output per worker in the "productive sphere") and of the share of national income in social product are independent of other factor indices.

---

[11] Price subsidy on production goods can be ascertained fairly well only in the producing branch; it is difficult to break down such a subsidy by branches, using the subsidized means of production. For example, it is difficult to find out to what extent industry, agriculture, construction, freight transport, foreign trade, etc., profit from the directly subsidized wholesale price of coal, coke, steel, oil, or from directly or indirectly subsidized steel and oil products, etc. But even in the producing branches certain difficulties are involved in the statistical reporting of subsidies (for instance, steel factories achieve a fictitious lowering of cost and a fictitious profit by mutually selling and buying subsidized semiproducts, as described by Typolt in Chapter 7, Section 3).

[12] SRRC, 1959, Table 1.11; furthermore, Table 1.12 gives data on the "percentage share of factors in the increase of national income" for 1957 and 1958 by three principal branches of the "productive sphere": industry, agriculture, and construction. But here again the practical value of these figures is extremely limited by the very unequal distribution of subsidies, for which an adequate adjustment is hardly possible, and by the very unequal rate of turnover tax.

TABLE 10.5—INFLUENCE OF FACTORS OF GROWTH OF NATIONAL INCOME (MARXIST DEFINITION)

Based on constant prices, of April 1, 1955

1948 = 100

	1949	1950	1951	1952	1953	1954	1955	1956	1957	1958
Index of national income	110	121	133	146	155	161	178	189	203	219
Index numbers of factor influence:										
Number of workers in the "productive sphere" (excluding foreign trade)	100	100	100	99	101	103	105	106	107	107
Social productivity of labor (excluding foreign trade) :	111	122	135	148	154	156	170	181	194	206
Productivity of "living labor"	110	126	139	151	158	160	174	187	201	213
Change in ratio of national income to social product	100	97	98	98	98	97	98	97	96	97
Influence of foreign trade	100	99	98	99	100	100	100	98	98	99

Source: *SRRC*, 1959, Table 1.11. Definitions of factors can be found in the text of Chapter 10, Section 3.

National income, in the above table, is determined only by the following three factors: number of workers in the "productive sphere," excluding foreign trade; social productivity of labor (defined as national income, or net value of production per worker in the "productive sphere"); and influence of foreign trade.[13] The inclusion of the last-named factor suggests that Marxist national income in Czechoslovakia, though defined as national income produced, probably has been adjusted for foreign trade net subsidy ("net gain or loss in foreign trade").[14]

As Table 10.5 shows, the main factor of growth in Marxist national income since 1948 has been the increasing social productivity of labor. The factor "number of workers in the productive sphere" has increased only since 1953. The index of the "influence of foreign trade" in no year since 1948 exceeded 100, and in the years 1950–52 and 1956–58 it fell below 100. This means that the contribution of foreign trade toward the formation of Marxist national income produced in 1949 and in 1953–55 remained the same, and in all other years was lower, as compared with the base year 1948. There is no doubt that in 1948 this "contribution" was negative (a sizable foreign trade net subsidy existed), and that the "net loss in foreign trade" in 1950–52 and again in 1956–58 exceeded the corresponding loss in 1948.[15] The index of the "influence of foreign trade" is based on differentials between internal prices and export-import prices. One factor in these differentials is the terms of trade. Thus some correlation is only natural between the index of the influence of foreign trade on Marxist national income and the index of terms of trade as computed by the author in Table 6.14. (For instance, the increasing index of influence of foreign trade in 1953 and in 1958 coincided with improving terms of trade.)

It is noteworthy that the index of "social" productivity of labor in-

[13] The index of national income, divided by index numbers of two of the mentioned factors, equals the index of the remaining third factor in any year (very slight discrepancies are easily explainable by rounding of percentages); and the mathematical product of the index numbers of the three factors, of course, equals the index number of national income.

[14] In this, Czechoslovak national income by Marxist definition probably differs from the Polish national income produced. It also differs from Poland's definition of national income distributed, because it still contains the surplus or deficit of foreign trade (at foreign trade prices).

[15] On the basis of the author's approximation of the current value of Marxist national income, as described below, and of the index numbers of Marxist national income and of factor influence in 1955–56, the *increase* of foreign trade net subsidy in 1956 over 1955, at 1955 constant internal prices, can be estimated at roughly 3 billion Kčs. This is consistent with the author's estimate of 7–9 billion Kčs for total foreign trade net subsidy in 1957.

creased, in most years, more slowly than that of "productivity of living labor." This means that net output per worker in the "productive" sphere increased more slowly than gross output, and a part of the increase in productivity of "living" labor was expended on rising material costs of output. A deterioration in the ratio of the net value to gross value of output is also reflected by the falling index of the share of national income in social product.

In the absence of available official data on the actual value of Marxist national income, the author had to make his own rough computations. Accuracy of method or findings is not claimed; yet the approximations are probably not far from reality. In any case, these estimates are the only possible starting point for at least a rough comparison of trends in Czechoslovak national income and expenditures with Western national aggregates —until either the official Czechoslovak absolute figures on national income or detailed Western recomputations have been published.[16]

The manner in which the relating estimates have been made can be seen in Table 10.6. Total wage costs (the total wage fund plus contributions to national insurance paid by the enterprise; in agriculture, total net income before taxation), plus profits of enterprises, plus full amount of turnover tax, plus statistical adjustments for the movement of stocks, etc., have been summed up for all branches of the "productive" sphere (sphere of material production), and this sum is regarded as Marxist national income *before adjustment for transfer payments through turnover tax.* This aggregate, plus the sum of material costs and amortization, so far as can be ascertained from the official Czechoslovak data, is what is described as social product.

The question as to which services are of "material character" and should be included in Marxist national income and which are "immaterial" and should be excluded has been much discussed both in the East and in the West. Fortunately, for practical purposes of approximation, the dividing line has been set by the Czechoslovak Statistical Office: data on wage funds have been officially divided into "productive" and "nonproductive" spheres (*SRRC*, 1958, Table 5.5). The estimate of turnover tax and profits by branches of the material sphere involved some problems, but at least for the largest branch—industry—profits and turnover tax also could be ascertained.

---

[16] In fact, a detailed computation of national accounts for Czechoslovakia is being undertaken for the four years 1948, 1949, 1955, and 1956 by a team of economists under a special Eastern European National Income Project at Columbia University: Thad P. Alton and associates, *National Income and Product of Czechoslovakia in 1948–1949 and 1955–1956.*

Another point open to discussion is whether Marxist national income must be computed on the production side. There are some indications that in Czechoslovakia and in other Eastern European countries the "income approach" is also being used.[17] This is definitely the case in Poland;[18] but, in order to balance the aggregates computed from production and income, a distinction is made between "national income produced" and "national income distributed," the difference being foreign trade surplus or deficit (at foreign trade prices) and "net gain or loss in foreign trade" (differentials between foreign trade and internal wholesale prices). In Czechoslovakia, adjustment for "net loss or gain in foreign trade" seems to have been made in the aggregate defined as national income produced (aggregate "national income distributed" is not used in *SRRC*, 1957–59).

But besides the problem of differentials between foreign trade and internal prices, there is another, even more important adjustment to be made in the estimated aggregate in Table 10.6.

We know from Chapter 7, Section 3, that the wholesale prices of certain commodities do not cover the wage costs and that some branches as a whole, as well as some individual companies, must be subsidized from the state budget (mostly from turnover tax revenue). Yet, in the estimate of Marxist national income in Table 10.6, the full amount of wage costs and the full amount of revenue from turnover tax are included. Obviously there is some duplication; the transfer payments from turnover tax to wage costs have to be subtracted from the estimate of Marxist national income.[19]

In Chapter 8, Section 1, the scope of subsidies of all kinds in 1957 was roughly estimated as a residual of "expenditures for the national economy" from the state budget, after having subtracted state capital outlay on fixed investments, research, increase in stocks, and other ascertainable fixed and

---

[17] Czechoslovak economists J. Kolár and O. Turek, in an article in the East German review *Wirtschaftswissenschaft* (No. 8, 1957), confirmed that in Czechoslovakia both the product and the income approaches were followed recently in computing Marxist national income.

[18] "The computation of national income (net production) has been carried out simultaneously by the production method—that is, subtracting the value of material costs (value of the means of production and of material services consumed in the process of output) from the value of gross production—and by the primary income method (that is, by computing the elements of the primary division of national income)." *Dochód Narodowy Polski 1956.*

[19] A rather primitive but perhaps also convincing argument for subtracting part of the turnover tax can be presented as follows: in the estimate of Marxist national income, the total accumulation (turnover tax and profits) has been included, but some enterprises produce at a loss. The sum of losses must be subtracted from the sum of profits in the broader sense (from "accumulation") to arrive at net profit (net accumulation).

TABLE 10.6—Czechoslovakia's National Income and Gross Social Product by Marxist Definition
Approximations at current prices charged to the final user, in billion Kčs, before adjustment for transfers

Branch of Material Sphere	Year	1 Consumption of Raw Material, Semiproducts, Fuel and Energy[a]	2 Depreciation	3 Total Wage Costs (personal income in agriculture)	Gross accumulation (4+5)		6 Increase in Stocks, Statistical Corrections	7 National Income "before Adjustment"[b] (3+4+5+6)	8 Gross Social Product[c] (1+2+3+4 +5+6)
					4 Turnover Tax	5 Profits			
Industry	1953	65.4	3.7	28.0	38.8	11.8	3‡	82	151*
	1956	75.5	9.0	33.9	35.7	9.0	10‡	89	173*
	1957	82.1	9.2	35.2	36.2	13.0	10‡	94	186*
Agriculture	1953	8‡		15‡				20‡	28‡
	1956	9‡		18‡				23‡	32‡
	1957	10‡		18‡				23‡	33‡
Forestry	1953	0.9*	0.1*	1.2		0.1‡		1.3	2*
	1956	1.0*	0.2*	1.4		0‡		1.4	2.5*
	1957	1.0*	0.3*	1.4		0‡		1.4	2.5*
Construction	1953	9.5‡	0.2‡	7.1		5‡		12*	22*
	1956	11.4‡	0.4‡	8.5		8‡		17*	30*
	1957	11.9‡	0.5‡	8.8		9‡		18*	31*
Freight transport, communications, servicing production	1953	2.1*	0.5*	2.7		1.2*		4*	7*
	1956	2.9*	1.9*	3.5		1.2*		5*	9*
	1957	3.2*	2.0*	3.8		1.3*		5*	10*
Trade, public catering..	1953	4‡	0.1‡	3.8		3‡		6‡	10‡
	1956	5‡	0.1‡	4.9		3‡		7‡	12‡
	1957	5.5‡	0.2‡	5.5		3‡		8‡	14‡

TABLE 10.6—Concluded

Sphere Branch of Material	Year	Consumption of Raw Material, Semiproducts, Fuel and Energy^a	Depreciation	Total Wage Costs (personal income in agriculture)	Gross accumulation (4+5)		Increase in Stocks, Statistical Corrections	National Income "before Adjustment"^b (3+4+5+6)	Gross Social Product^c (1+2+3+4 +5+6)
					Turnover Tax	Profits			
Other branches of material production	1953	1‡	0.1‡	1.1		1‡		2‡	3‡
	1956	1‡	0.1‡	1.2		2‡		3‡	4‡
	1957	1‡	0.1‡	1.2		2‡		3‡	4‡
Total	1953	95*		59*		67*		126*	224*
	1956	118*		71*		74*		145*	263*
	1957	124*		74*		78*		152*	276*

Marxist national income and gross social product have been characterized in Section 1. The way of computing the approximations of these aggregates has been described in Section 3.

Sources (all tables quoted below are from *SRRC*, 1958): *All data on wage costs:* calculated from Table 5.5 (number of wage and salary earners in the "branches of material production," multiplied by corresponding average monthly earnings), plus 10 per cent estimated contribution to national insurance paid by the employer. These data exclude pay of apprentices and earnings of a negligible number of nonagricultural self-employed workers. Correction for this has been made in column 6 (statistical corrections). *Industry:* estimates of columns 1–5 based on percentage shares of wage costs in total costs (Table 7.3) and percentage structure of "realized value" of industrial output (Table 7.7; "realized value" includes, besides costs of production, turnover tax and profit). *Agriculture:* rough estimates are based on article on money income by J. Bezouška, *Statistický obzor*, No. 11, 1958, and on statistics in agriculture by V. Hladík, *Statistický obzor*, No. 10, 1959, on Table 9.34 (persons working permanently in agriculture), and on various approximations by the author (especially on incomes in kind). It should be stressed that the main factor in increase of income originating in agriculture was the increase in state purchase prices for agricultural produce in the 1953–57 period (in contrast to the generally decreasing price level; see Tables 4.7 and 10.4). In terms of constant prices, income originating in agriculture probably decreased in the 1953–57 period (whereas total Marxist national income increased, in terms of constant prices, even faster than in terms of current prices). Data on gross value of production in agriculture at constant prices given by Bartiněk in *Plánované hospodářství*, No. 7/8, 1959. *Forestry:* Table 10.19 (structure of costs), and various approximations. *Construction:* Tables 8.18, 8.20b, and various approximations. *Freight transport and communications:* Table 11.9 and various approximations. *Trade and public catering:* Tables 13.18, 13.19, 13.20, 13.21, and various approximations, including a guess concerning income of employees in foreign trade monopolies. Foreign trade net subsidy has been disregarded at this stage of computations of Czechoslovak national income (see Sections 3 and 4).

The usual marking of the probable margin of error does not apply in this table. All data are to be regarded as estimates only. The asterisk denotes a likely margin of error of 5–10 per cent, the dagger denotes a margin of error probably exceeding 10 per cent; figures with the double dagger are mere guesses.

^a Official Czechoslovak data on structure of cost of production in industry, which have been used for estimating consumption of raw material, exclude "material wasted." (*SRRC*, 1959, Table 7.27.)

^b Before adjustment for transfer payments through turnover tax (see Chapter 10, Section 3).   ^c Excluding waste of material in industry (see footnote *a*).

227

nonfixed investments. Of the residual of 28 billion Kčs, 8 billion were estimated to be foreign trade "net" subsidy (see Chapter 6, Section 6) and 18 billion were estimated to be "domestic wholesale price subsidies, endowments to individual enterprises including state farms, and financing of other deficits of enterprises." It is possible that the last item contains a certain amount for allotments to increase working capital of firms in addition to the budgetary item "increase in stocks." Therefore, the "transfer payments," to be deducted from the 1957 aggregate in Table 10.6, have been estimated at only 16 billion Kčs. A similar procedure was used for the years 1953 and 1956 to obtain "Marxist national income free of transfer payments through turnover tax"[20] (although, in these two years, the results are subject to an even greater margin of error, in view of the even less complete information on the breakdown of "expenditures of the national economy" in the state budget).

After further subtracting foreign trade net subsidy from the last-named aggregate, one should arrive, at least in theory, at a magnitude not very different from the unpublished national income by official computation.[21] The pertinent approximations can be found in Table 10.7.

[20] The term "transfer payments" is used rather than "subsidies" so as to avoid the problem of the extent to which the transfers involved in the computations in Table 10.6 are comparable with net subsidy. More light on the subsidy problem in 1948–49 and 1955–56 may be shed in the study by Dr. Alton (see footnote 16), although it is extremely difficult to trace subsidies unless and until more information becomes available on the phases of distribution and redistribution of national income in Czechoslovakia. It is to be regretted that Dr. Alton's study does not cover the years 1953 and 1954, the period that separates the economic and political turmoil of 1948–49, with its inflationary policies, and the industrialization drive of 1951–52, from the policy of economic *détente* following the second postwar currency reform in June 1953. In no case will it be possible to use the findings on the scope of subsidies in Czechoslovakia in 1948–49 and in 1955–56 for an appraisal of Czechoslovakia's economic growth since 1958, because of the substantial revision of the wholesale price structure (see Chapter 7, Section 3).

[21] But there are some differences. For instance, the official calculation of the price correction factor for foreign trade—as described recently in the *Economic Bulletin for Europe* (Vol. 11, No. 3, pp. 57–58)—is different from the "net foreign trade subsidy" as characterized in Chapter 6, Section 6. The officially computed "net loss in foreign trade" is likely to be lower than the author's estimate of "net subsidy." In fact, it is not justifiable to subtract the entire "foreign trade net subsidy" as estimated in Chapter 6, from national income: not only because a small part of it may be just a statistical shadow, due to the artificial exchange rate of the Czechoslovak currency, but because a substantial part of it originates in deliberately low prices charged by Czechoslovakia to underdeveloped countries both inside and outside the centrally planned area. Such a "hidden economic aid" could be legitimately deducted only as a difference between "national income produced" and "national income domestically distributed." (In the approximation of gross national product

In the absence of a published official index on national income at current prices, the only possible check is in terms of constant prices. This also has been calculated in Table 10.7. The index, based on the author's approximation of Marxist national income in Czechoslovakia, comes reasonably close to the official index of national income. This is, of course, no definite proof that these approximations do not differ considerably from the unpublished official absolute figures on national income in Czechoslovakia. A fairly constant component may be added, or missing, in the author's approximations, as compared with the official computations. It is to be hoped that the Czechoslovak planners, by publishing official data on national income and its constituents in Czechoslovakia, will help to discover mistakes in the approximations in Tables 10.6 and 10.7.

TABLE 10.7—CZECHOSLOVAK NATIONAL INCOME BY MARXIST DEFINITION
Approximations adjusted for transfers and foreign trade net subsidy

	1948[a]	1953	1956	1957
	BILLION KČS			
Marxist national income before adjustment for transfer payments through turnover tax	...	126†	145†	152†
Transfer payments	...	− 18†	− 16†	− 16†
Foreign trade net subsidy	...	− 6*	− 8*	− 8*
Marxist national income, excluding transfer payments and after deduction of foreign trade net subsidy, at current prices	42*	102†	121†	128†
	INDICES			
Index 1953 = 100 (based on approximation at current prices)	41	100	118	125
Price index used[b]	62	100	94	94
Index 1953 = 100 (based on constant prices)	66	100	125	133
Official index of national income at April 1955 prices (rebased to 1953 = 100) ..	64.5	100	122	131

[a] In new currency units.
[b] These figures are a weighted average of the cost-of-living index (from Table 7.2, weight 2) and of the derived index of investment prices (from Chapter 7, Section 3, weight 1). This, of course, is a methodological weakness, which, however, seems not to have seriously distorted the results obtained.

by Western definition in the next section of this chapter, no portion of "foreign trade net subsidy" has been subtracted from GNP, and it has been considered only within the expenditure on GNP.) The portion of turnover tax to be excluded from Marxist national income as transfer payments (domestic subsidies) also may differ in the author's approximation as compared with the official computation.

4. Approximations of Czechoslovak National Income, and Gross National Product and Expenditure, Analogous to Western Definition

In order to arrive at national income roughly comparable with Western aggregates, the author started with "Marxist national income before adjustment for transfer payments," making the following adjustments:

Only "transfer payments through turnover tax" (domestic subsidies) were deducted to obtain what can be described as Marxist national income free of transfers, in the domestic economy, but including the foreign trade net subsidy.[22]

The second adjustment necessary is the inclusion of immaterial services (which are not covered by the Marxist definition of national income). The wage fund within the "immaterial sphere" can be estimated with sufficient accuracy from data on monthly earnings in SRRC, 1958 (Table 5.5). Remuneration of apprentices, which is excluded from official data on earnings, and contributions to national insurance were added to obtain total wage costs in the "immaterial sphere." Under the (methodologically incorrect, but probably not too unrealistic) assumption that, in the immaterial sphere, accumulation is equal to subsidies,[23] total wage costs represent total income.

A certain group of gainfully active persons and their incomes seem to be generally excluded from Czechoslovak statistics on "working population," "wage fund," etc. (the armed forces, security forces, etc.; see Chapter 1, Section 2). In the Western market economies, the pay of armed forces and security forces is contained in national income data. Therefore, a very rough guess has been made of the income of armed and security forces in Czechoslovakia.[24]

[22] It can be argued that foreign trade net subsidy is also a transfer payment through the state budget, but its special character is obvious. The author thinks it useful to include foreign trade net subsidy in national income and gross national product of Czechoslovakia and to treat it as an item of external balance within the expenditure on gross national product. The correct procedure would be to split this subsidy into "unwanted foreign trade net subsidy," to be deducted from national income and GNP, and the "hidden economic aid," to be treated within the expenditure on GNP. This, however, is not possible because statistical information is lacking.

[23] A certain correction which it may be necessary to make in the "immaterial sphere" may have been, in fact, already included in the estimates of transfer payments in the "material sphere."

[24] It could be argued that these incomes are also just transfer payments; they are financed from the state budget, and the greatest part of state revenue has already been included (income tax within wage fund, turnover tax within accumulation).

TABLE 10.8—APPROXIMATION OF CZECHOSLOVAK NATIONAL INCOME AND
GROSS NATIONAL PRODUCT
Analogous to Western definition at market prices

	1948	1953	1956	1957
BILLION KČS, AT CURRENT PRICES				
Marxist national income before adjustment for transfer payments through turnover tax (domestic subsidies)	...	126	145	152
Minus transfers (domestic subsidies)	...	− 18*	− 16*	− 16*
Income originating in the "nonproductive sphere"	...	12*	15*	16*
Income of groups not included in Czechoslovak statistics (armed forces, police, etc.)	...	5*	4*	4*
National income—analogous to Western definition, at current market prices	52ᵃ	125	148	154
Replacements of fixed capital consumed in the "productive" and "nonproductive" spheres..	6ᵃ	10*	16*	17*
Gross national product—analogous to Western definition, at current market prices........	58ᵃ	135	164	171
INDEX NUMBERS, 1953 = 100				
Gross national product at current prices........	43	100	122	127
Price index used	62	100	94	94
Gross national product at constant prices.......	69	100	130	135
Population	96.2	100	103.1	104.2
Per capita gross national product at constant prices	72	100	126	129

The usual marking of the margin of error does not apply in this table. All data are to be regarded as subject to a possible margin of error up to 10 per cent, and data marked with an asterisk are subject to a margin of error possibly exceeding 10 per cent. The method of computing the approximations of GNP has been described in Section 4.

ᵃ Official data, converted into new (1953) currency units 5 : 1. These data have been computed by members of the National Income Commission at the Economic Council of the Czechoslovak government. The method of computation used was that of Dr. Miloš Stádník, as described in *Národní důchod a jeho rozdělení se zvláštním zřetelem k Československu*. Data on national income of Czechoslovakia for previous years can also be found in Stádník's book, and his computations of national income for 1947 and 1948 can be found in U.N. *Statistical Yearbook*, 1949.

The total obtained in this way can be found in Table 10.8. It can be described as analogous to the Western definition of national income at market prices. If we consider turnover tax—excluding domestic subsidies —to be just state profit, this agglomerate, of course, would be "at factor cost." But in the author's opinion, it represents "a valuation approximating marginal utility to the buyer" rather than "marginal cost to the producer" and therefore comes nearer to the Western concept of national income "at market prices."[25]

[25] Contrast national income "at factor cost" and "at market prices," as described in the U.N. *National Accounts Statistics*, Part A-2. In any case, with the present Czechoslovak institutional background, with the state being the only producer in all branches of the "productive sphere" except agriculture, a distinction between "market prices" and "factor cost" is highly artificial.

Having estimated national income analogous to Western definition, the author cannot resist the temptation to compare between countries the absolute level of per capita national incomes converted into common currency—however inaccurate such comparison will be. It seems to be legitimate to adjust further the approximation from Table 10.8 to make it more comparable with the Western aggregates "at factor cost." Assuming rather arbitrarily that one-half of turnover tax is genuine tax to be subtracted from national income at factor cost, and adding estimated domestic subsidies and one-half of the foreign trade subsidy (assuming that the other half is "hidden economic aid"), the "national income at factor cost" of 147 billion Kčs in 1957 has been arrived at. This has been converted into dollars at the tourist exchange rate of 14.32 Kčs for one U.S. dollar (which approximates the weighted average of lower purchasing power parity of the Kčs for consumers' goods [see p. 143] and higher parity for investment goods). The per capita national income obtained in this way was of the order of $760 for 1957, that is, less than 40 per cent of the corresponding U.S. figure of $2,120. The relating figures for Western Europe were: Austria $560, West Germany $740, France $860, and the U.K. $940, if national aggregates (from the U.N. *Statistical Yearbook*, 1959, Table 166) are converted at official dollar exchange rates; but these rates considerably understate the relative purchasing power of the Western European currencies (see *OEEC, General Statistics*, 4, 1960, p. vii). In proportion to actual domestic purchasing power, the Western European per capita national income would be about one-third higher. In spite of the difficult conversion problem and of the limits in international comparability of national account data, it can be confidently stated that, in 1957, per capita national income—at roughly comparable purchasing power—was higher in Czechoslovakia than in Austria and probably not much lower than in West Germany.

The next step is to estimate very roughly the Czechoslovak gross national product at market prices, and expenditure on it, by Western definition. On the basis of available statistics, it is difficult to cut out all material costs (energy, fuel, raw materials, intermediate products, depreciation) from the gross social product (or "gross value of production") in the whole national economy (agriculture presents special difficulty in this respect). In order to obtain the approximate magnitude of gross national product, we simply added an *estimated* depreciation[26] to national income

[26] Based on replacements of fixed capital, as reflected by official (only relative and incomplete) data on amortization. This involved serious underrating of the depreciation rate until revaluation of basic funds in 1955. The official amortization

at market prices, as described above. The result can be found in Table 10.8. This table does not contain the breakdown of the approximation of Czechoslovak gross national product by economic origin, because the proportion of agriculture is subject to a particularly great margin of error. Yet it is interesting to note that the share of industry in gross national product in Czechoslovakia in 1956 at current prices amounted to approximately 45 per cent, and after adjustment for the unequal distribution of the rate of turnover tax it amounted to approximately 42 per cent. Corresponding figures were 42 per cent in West Germany, 42 per cent in the United Kingdom, and 34 per cent in the United States.

Finally, in Table 10.9 Czechoslovak expenditure on gross national product in the Western sense was estimated for the year 1956. Personal expenditure was roughly estimated as follows (in billion Kčs at current prices):[27]

Personal consumption by Marxist definition...................... 87†
Minus purchases of production goods "by the population," especially by individual farmers, depreciation of private housing, and statistical duplications .... − 7†
Plus personal consumption of immaterial services................. 10†

Personal consumption by Western definition.................... 90†

---

was so low that basic funds (fixed capital assets) would have to be scrapped before being amortized in the accounts. After the revaluation of basic funds in 1955, which was carried out independently of wholesale prices for investments (wholesale prices hardly changed between 1953 and 1957), the official depreciation rate almost doubled. In industry, for instance, amortization, as officially applied, amounted to 4.5 per cent of cost of production in 1953, and to 8.2 per cent in 1956.

Official relative data on amortization in industry (*SRRC*, 1959, Table 7.27), compared with the author's estimate of the value of basic funds (Table 8.11), suggest an amortization rate of approximately 5 per cent in most years since 1955. Such a depreciation rate seems to be fully justifiable, and the author cannot subscribe to the opinion of some economists in the West that the increased official amortization contains a camouflaged rate of interest on capital.

[27] If the author's index of the cost of living and the official index of personal consumption at constant 1955 prices are applied to 1948 personal consumption (Table 10.2) (converted into new currency units), a figure of 88 billion Kčs at current prices is obtained for 1956. The same figure is obtained when applying the percentage ratio of personal consumption to national income (Table 10.4) to the author's estimate of Marxist national income before adjustment for transfer payments (Table 10.6). Application of the same percentage ratio to Marxist national income after adjustment for domestic subsidies, as estimated by the author, gives a figure of 79–80 billion Kčs. (Application of the percentage ratio to Marxist national income after adjustment for both domestic subsidies and foreign trade net subsidy would be futile; the foreign trade net subsidy is estimated in a different way from what seems to be the official computation of "net loss in foreign trade," or "influence of foreign trade on national income"; in any case, it is contained in the

NATIONAL INCOME, GROSS PRODUCT, AND EXPENDITURE

Until official absolute figures on personal consumption have been published in Czechoslovakia, or recomputed in detail in the West (such a recomputation would exceed the framework of this study), there is no choice but to accept the margin of error involved in the above approximation of personal consumption. It is to be hoped that this margin of error is not too great.

The remaining gross national product was spent in Czechoslovakia on state and other collective consumption (estimated roughly by the author), on gross fixed investments (official data), on increasing stocks (estimated by the author), on surplus of exports over imports (official data at foreign trade prices), on foreign trade net subsidy (estimated by the author; see Chapter 6, Section 6), and on a limited external flow of income. The relating figures can be found in Table 10.8. Data at fixed official prices charged to final users (i.e., retail prices for personal consumption and part of collective consumption, state wholesale prices for all other expenditure on national product) are distorted by artificial prices: retail prices include a very high and widely varying rate of turnover tax, and part of the wholesale prices are below cost and have to be subsidized.[28]

---

estimate of GNP in this section, and will be treated as a separate item of expenditure on GNP.) Needless to say, all three above estimates are methodologically incorrect: in the first case—disregarding the problem of the price index to be applied—Marxist personal consumption is applied to non-Marxist personal consumption in the base year. In the last two cases, the ratio of personal consumption to Marxist national income at *constant* 1955 prices is applied to the author's approximation of Marxist national income at *current* 1956 prices.

Another way of estimating personal consumption is to start from the percentage of contents of retail sales in personal consumption: according to *SRRC*, 1959 (Table 1.13), the pattern of Marxist personal consumption in 1956 was as follows: purchases by the population in retail trade, 87.3 per cent; purchases on the farmers' market, 1.4 per cent; consumption in kind, 8.1 per cent; other personal consumption, 3.2 per cent. Total retail sales, in 1956 at current prices, amounted to 83.5 billion Kčs (defined as "sales to final consumer for personal consumption," including sales in public catering). A comparison of this figure with the 87.3 per cent figure of retail sales in personal consumption would suggest a personal consumption in 1956 of 95 billion Kčs, but this estimate certainly exceeds Marxist personal consumption as well as personal consumption by Western definition. On the one hand, retail sales statistics cover at least a part of immaterial services; on the other hand, they also cover sales of production means to independent farmers and other self-employed workers, sales to institutions ("collective consumers") for their own consumption, prices charged for repair of objects of consumption, etc.

[28] The undervaluation of gross investments, and of "accumulation" at official prices, has been acknowledged by Czechoslovak economists. For example, Valter Komárek (in *Plánované hospodářství*, No. 11, 1959) stated: "Existing prices do not enable us to assess economic relations correctly [that is, to analyze national income]: in the present balance sheets of the national economy, the portion of accumu-

TABLE 10.9—APPROXIMATION OF CZECHOSLOVAK EXPENDITURE ON
GROSS NATIONAL PRODUCT IN 1956

(*In billion Kčs at current official prices and at conventional prices*)

	At Official State-fixed Prices	Minus Turnover Tax	Plus Domestic Subsidies	"At Factor Cost"[a]	Percentage Share "at Factor Cost"	At Conventional Prices
Personal consumption (adjusted as analogous to Western definition).	90	−41*	2*,[b]	51	37.9	62
State and collective consumption	26*	− 4*	4*	26*	19.3*	32*
Gross fixed investments (including "general overhauls")	35	—	9	44	32.6	53½
Increase in stocks	3*	—	½*	3½*	2.6*	4½*
Export surplus	2	—	½[c]	2½	1.8	3
Foreign trade net subsidy	8*	—	—	8*	5.8*	9½*
External flow of income[d]						
Gross national product..	164	−45	16	135	100.0	164
Plus net accumulation through turnover tax........				29		
GNP "at market prices"				164		
Minus foreign trade net subsidy				− 8*		
"Disposable" GNP				156		

The usual marking of the margin of error does not apply in this table. All data are to be regarded as subject to a possible margin of error up to 10 per cent (except the official data on gross fixed investments including general overhauls, and net exports), and data marked with an asterisk are subject to a margin of error possibly exceeding 10 per cent. The method of computing the expenditure on GNP at state-fixed and conventional prices has been described in Section 4.

[a] Factor cost under official accounting of "cost," i.e., with no rate of interest on capital.

[b] Domestic subsidies on personal consumption concentrated on rent.

[c] Domestic subsidy on export surplus as difference between cost and domestic wholesale price of export goods (not to be confused with foreign trade net subsidy, resulting from the difference between export-import prices and domestic wholesale prices).

[d] Although there was a certain inward and outward flow of income, the net external flow was probably not more than half a billion Kčs. No statistical information on external flow of income in Czechoslovakia in 1956 is available.

To eliminate these most serious distortions, the main constituents of national expenditure have been estimated in Table 10.8 "at factor cost," deducting estimated amount of turnover tax and adding an estimate of domestic subsidies. This "factor cost" in the Czechoslovak institutional background covers only labor cost (including incomes of individual farmers), depreciation, and the rather low "accumulation in the form of enterprise profits." It does not contain any rate of interest on capital. The

lation appears to be lower than it actually is." Before the 1958 wholesale price reform, the undervaluation of accumulation may have been even more serious (see Chapter 7, Section 3) than in 1959.

percentage structure of national expenditure "at factor cost" was calculated, and the accumulation in the form of turnover tax excluding subsidies was then spread over the constituents in proportion to their share "at factor cost." In this way, "national expenditure at conventional prices" was obtained. Its sum is equal to gross national product ("at market prices"), and its pattern is based on "factor cost" plus an equal rate of net accumulation through turnover tax. All this procedure can be gathered from data in Table 10.8.

The structure of national expenditure at conventional prices appears to be very different from the structure at state-fixed prices: the share of personal consumption falls much below one-half, that of gross fixed investments rises to one-third of gross national product.

Finally, Table 10.10 gives a comparison by countries. Per capita

TABLE 10.10—GROSS NATIONAL PRODUCT AND EXPENDITURE,
INTERNATIONAL COMPARISON

	Czecho-slovakia	Austria	France	West Germany	United Kingdom	United States
INDEX OF PER CAPITA GNP AT CONSTANT MARKET PRICES, 1953 = 100						
1938	58[a,b]	...	79	...	...	58
1948	72[b]	66	93[c]	80[c]	88	86
1953	100	100	100	100	100	100
1956	126	129	114	123	108	103
1957	129	136	121	128	110	103
EXPENDITURE ON GNP IN 1956[d]						
Personal (private) consumption	37.9	63.7	68.0	58.5	65.0	63.2
Government (public) consumption	19.3[e]	13.0	15.0	13.8	17.4	17.5[f]
Gross domestic fixed investments	32.6	22.1	17.7	22.9	15.0	17.4[f]
Increase in stocks	2.6	1.0	1.4	1.3	1.2	1.0
Export surplus	1.8	0.2	1.6	3.8	0.5	0.3
Net foreign trade subsidy..	5.8	—	—	—	—	—
Factor income from abroad	p.m.	—	−0.5	−0.3	0.9	0.5
Gross national product	100	100	100	100	100	100

Data for Czechoslovakia are approximations from Tables 10.8 and 10.9. Data for other countries are from U.N. *Statistical Yearbook*, 1958, Tables 161 ff. (Percentages were calculated by the author.) Comparison between countries is subject to severe limitations; the data should be regarded only as indications of trends.

  [a] 1937.

  [b] The increase in per capita GNP, 1937–48, was caused by the decrease in population (see Chapter 1, Section 1).

  [c] 1950.

  [d] Percentage shares are based on current prices (in Czechoslovakia, on conventional prices; see Section 4).

  [e] Including "collective consumption."

  [f] Some items overlap.

gross national product, as estimated by the author, seems to have increased in Czechoslovakia, from the beginning of the central planning period until 1957, in a fairly similar way to that of those market economies with a similar starting level of economic development—France, Germany, and Austria.[29] Czechoslovakia's rate of economic growth in terms of gross national product may have been even somewhat faster than the average in Western Europe. But the really striking difference is the different pattern of expenditure in gross national product. In spite of all the uncertainties involved in the estimates in Table 10.9, and in spite of the severe limitations of international comparability in Table 10.10, it is safe to state that personal consumption in Czechoslovakia had a much smaller share and gross fixed investments had a much larger share in gross national expenditure than they had in the developed market economies. The importance of foreign trade net subsidy in Czechoslovak national expenditure is also noteworthy.

[29] Data in Table 10.10 suggest that the increase was somewhat faster than in France (since 1950), the same as in West Germany (since 1950), and somewhat slower than in Austria. It should be borne in mind that the relatively faster increase of per capita GNP in West Germany and Austria, as compared with other developed market economies, was due, among other things, to retarded postwar reconstruction in those countries.

CONCLUSION

If the approximations of national accounts in Chapter 10 have fair validity—and the quantitative analysis by branches of the Czechoslovak economy in Chapters 2 to 6 seems to support this—the over-all increase in per capita production of goods and services over the period 1948–57 in Czechoslovakia was approximately the same as in the Western Euro-pean market economies that had a comparably advanced economic level: Austria, West Germany, and France. (Czechoslovak growth of production, measured in the above-described way, appears to have been somewhat faster than the growth in the United Kingdom or the United States; how-ever, the higher level of production in these two countries in the base year of our comparisons is to be taken into account.)

Yet, to achieve a comparable, or slightly higher, growth of per capita output, a much greater input of both labor and fixed capital assets was needed in Czechoslovakia during the period under study.

The percentage of economically active population in the total popula-tion is the same, or slightly higher, as compared with Western market economies (especially because of a noticeably higher percentage of work-ing women in Czechoslovakia, as described in Chapter 1). Practically the entire nonagricultural economically active population consists of wage and salary earners. Contrary to the Western market economies, there is officially no unemployment, and in reality only very small unemployment, in Czechoslovakia; even frictional unemployment hardly occurs, in view of the direction of labor. Working hours seem to be longer in Czecho-slovakia: in 1958, for example, hours worked per week in manufacturing compared as follows: Czechoslovakia (author's estimate, including mining and electricity), 48.4;[1] West Germany, 45.7; the United Kingdom, 45.4; Austria and France, 45.0; the United States, 39.3.[2] A certain amount of time worked in Czechoslovakia was wasted by stoppages caused by break-

[1] The legal normal working time was 46 hours (less in mining and in other hazardous work); according to *Statistické zprávy*, No. 11, 1959, overtime worked in 1958 in industry amounted, on the average, to 6.8 per cent of normal working time.

[2] In some Western market economies, shorter hours worked in 1958 were partly due to a reduced employment level (1958 was a year of recession in some Western countries). But even at a normal employment level, as in 1957, the hours worked in Czechoslovakia were longer than in the West (see Table 2.9). On the other hand, allowance should be made for a relatively greater number of persons in the United States who have two jobs.

down of power supply or machinery or by shortage of materials; the working time wasted in this way, however, has been cut down in recent years. On the other hand, with the exception of a strike wave following the 1953 currency reform, there have been only local strikes in Czechoslovakia; no strikes are being organized by trade unions. In the West, a great amount of working time fell off through large-scale strikes, most of them officially organized by trade unions. There is no doubt that in the years under study, 1948–58, more labor per unit of output was expended in Czechoslovakia as compared with the developed Western market economies.

The relative expenditure of fixed capital assets (basic funds) was even greater. In 1956, well over one-fourth and possibly one-third of Czechoslovak gross national product was spent on gross fixed investments, whereas in West Germany and Austria the proportion was only one-fifth, in France and the United States one-sixth, and in the United Kingdom one-seventh. As compared with the developed market economies, a much greater part of total fixed investments in Czechoslovakia was earmarked for expanding output, and a much smaller part for improving housing and services to the population. Furthermore, even within investments in the "productive" sphere, the share of investments reducing the use of labor (such as outlay on modernizing machinery) was relatively small in Czechoslovakia; stress was put on "widening" rather than on "deepening" investments.

These higher labor-output and capital-output ratios suggest that the economic efficiency of the central planning system in Czechoslovakia, in its first ten years of existence, remained behind that of the market economies at a comparable, rather advanced stage of development; the relatively much greater input of resources cannot be explained by a more rapid structural change alone (industrialization of previously agricultural Slovakia, general shift toward heavy industry), although this factor should not be overlooked.

A similar comparison of economic efficiency between Czechoslovakia and the other, less-developed centrally planned economies is not possible in this book for lack of statistical data on other Eastern European countries. Yet the fragmentary information in Chapters 1 to 8 suggests that their economic efficiency was by no means higher than that of Czechoslovakia. A faster increase in gross value of industrial production in some of these countries was partly due to a low starting level and to a larger input of resources in industry, including credits from abroad.

A relatively faster increase in input of material resources into production in Czechoslovakia as compared with the developed market economies was naturally accompanied by a relatively slower increase in personal consumption. In the Western market economies, personal consumption at present takes almost two-thirds of gross national product; in Czechoslovakia, less than half. There is also evidence available on the slower development of average per capita personal income in Czechoslovakia.[3] Over the entire period 1948–58, real earnings in industry did not rise faster than in the listed Western market economies, except possibly in Great Britain; yet workers' earnings in industry, including mining, were rising in Czechoslovakia much faster than real incomes of other groups of the population. There was no such contrast between workers' earnings and real incomes of other groups of the population in Western market economies. The increase in average per capita real income in Czechoslovakia lagged considerably behind the trends in Western Europe and in the United States.

On the other hand, the development of personal income in Czechoslovakia brought somewhat more equality in distribution of income (if we disregard the extremely low old-age benefits for former self-employed workers who lost all their savings through two postwar currency reforms). In very recent times, Czechoslovak authorities have found that the leveling off in pay of labor went too far, and the increase in earnings seems now to be concentrated on skilled labor, while wages in some unskilled categories are kept stationary or are reduced.

Czechoslovak planners claim that the lag in personal real income behind the Western developments has been compensated by a faster increase in so-called collective consumption. The share of state and collective consumption in the author's estimate of expenditure on gross national product in Czechoslovakia seems to be only slightly higher than in the developed market economies, but it is difficult to say how much of it is genuine collective consumption by the population and how much is state or other public consumption. In fact, collective consumption in the form of real costs of national health increased considerably in Czechoslovakia. Yet national health seems to be financed autonomously through contributions, half of which are paid by the wage and salary earners themselves. On the other hand, real old-age benefits remained fairly stationary (the purchasing power of the nominal value of average old-age benefits decreased up to 1957, and even in very recent years the purchasing power of some categories of pensions has remained below the 1948 level). A

---

[3] Savings from personal incomes have been negligible in Czechoslovakia in recent years. (Contrary to the situation in some other centrally planned economies, no internal state loans have been launched.) Personal savings amount at present to less than 2 per cent of personal income, so that there is no great difference between personal income and personal expenditure.

noticeable increase in collectively financed cultural and educational costs can be traced. But on the whole, the ratio of collective consumption of the population to personal consumption is probably not very different in Czechoslovakia from the corresponding ratios in France or in some of the other Western European countries. Collective consumption of the population in Czechoslovakia, in addition to personal (individual) consumption, is probably not greater than one-fifth to one-fourth of the latter.

The standard of living seems to have risen more slowly, and at present to be lower, in Czechoslovakia as compared with the Western European market economies; but it is noticeably higher than in other centrally planned economies, with the possible exception of East Germany, as illustrated by some indicators in Chapter 9. The lag behind the Western European standard of living seems to be more serious than one would expect on the sole evidence of the higher fixed investment rate in Czechoslovakia. The explanation lies partly in the external flow of goods and services. Over the entire period under study, Czechoslovakia had a sizable net export surplus, and it also granted considerable foreign credit. Even more important than this open economic aid is the net foreign trade subsidy, a great part of which also can be regarded as a deliberate aid to the less developed centrally planned economies as well as to underdeveloped countries in Asia and Africa.

In this respect Czechoslovakia differs very much from most of the other centrally planned economies, which, with the exception of the USSR and East Germany, were receiving net foreign credits. The Czechoslovak contribution toward the industrialization of less developed countries is also illustrated by the almost 50 per cent proportion of machinery and equipment in its total exports. (In East Germany, exports of machinery in the period under study were even more considerable, but per capita foreign aid, granted either openly in the form of credits or concealed in foreign trade net subsidy, seems to have been lower.)

Various branches of the Czechoslovak economy developed in accordance with the above-described use of gross national product: the increase in output was concentrated in heavy industry and building (except for housing) while light industry, housing, and services were relatively neglected. The very low share of services in national income and product is sometimes explained by the absence in Czechoslovakia of such services as a stock exchange, excessive advertising, etc. In fact, in 1957 the cost of advertising in Czechoslovakia, including make-up of goods, amounted to only 9 per cent of the total costs of retail trade and to only 0.1 per cent of the total costs of wholesale trade. But services of undoubted positive utility to a large element of the population, such as passenger transportation, barbers, dry cleaners, etc., are also in short supply. Inadequate distribution services (retail trade) added local shortages of some consumers' goods to temporary general shortages of other kinds of goods (electric bulbs, razor blades) originating in inadequate production.

The unsatisfactory development of Czechoslovak agriculture during the years under study, with output remaining below the prewar level, is of a special nature. In the first period, up to 1953, it was mainly due to an insufficient input of resources; in the second period, the increased input was used to promote collectivization rather than to rationally expand agricultural output.

The foregoing critical remarks may appear to amount to a general condemnation of central planning in a developed country like Czechoslovakia. Such is not the intention. Centrally planned economy has been applied in Czechoslovakia only for a relatively short time. The author's judgment of the market economy in the early days of capitalism would have been even more negative. It took the market economy more than a century to discover the course of business cycles and to try to counteract economic depressions and unemployment (yet the problem of unemployment in the market economies still exists). Furthermore, comparisons in this book refer only to the developed market economies; yet two-thirds of the world's population live in underdeveloped countries where the market economy works less satisfactorily than in countries with a high capital intensity and a traditional parliamentary system.

It is possible that in the years ahead, by improving the central planning system, some of the waste of toil and material resources will be reduced in Czechoslovakia. (Chapter 8 discusses in broad outlines the possibility of distributing fixed investments in a more rational way.) But any far-reaching improvement in economic efficiency through a more rational system of pricing seems to be a long-term program.

A fast increase in industrial output is planned in Czechoslovakia under the third Five-Year Plan, up to 1965. Yet, as described in Chapter 2, Section 2, Czechoslovak industrial growth outstripped industrial growth in comparable market economies only during the first part of the period under study, up to 1953, while in the years 1953–57 increase in industrial output remained slightly behind that in France, West Germany, and Austria. The period prior to 1953 was marked by strains and stresses and inflation. When a new production drive started in 1958–59, after relaxation of industrialization and a fairly rapid increase in the standard of living in the years 1953–57, the Czechoslovak planners tried to avoid some of the economic drawbacks that existed before the 1953 currency reform.

They now pay more attention to the dangers of inflation. But the anti-inflationary device used is keeping the increase in real wages considerably below the increase in productivity of labor (see Chapter 7, Section 3). This will again decelerate the growth in real income of the population, as is known from the 1953–57 period. However, catching up with the Western European standard of living does not seem to be a short-term goal. But there are economic liabilities from past developments other than the lag in the standard of living that will have to be honored in the near future. Fixed investments, however vast in scope, have been used, in the years under study, for expanding the capacity of production rather than for maintaining and modernizing existing capital assets. A large part of "basic funds" is overdue for being demolished or scrapped, and a large portion of future gross fixed investments will be needed just for replacements.

It is very difficult to predict future developments in the Czechoslovak centrally planned economy without studying in more detail the planning technique and the probable future economic policy. This has not been the aim of the present book. Yet, it is fairly safe to state that *simultaneous long-term* increases *in both* production and personal consumption, which would noticeably surpass the rates of increase in comparably developed Western European market economies, as known since the end of the second World War, do not seem to be within sight.[4]

On the other hand, some specific achievements of Czechoslovakia's present economic system cannot be discarded as unlikely. The great discriminatory power inherent in central planning makes it easier than in a market economy to concentrate resources on great economic, technological, and scientific projects; to make quick changes in the economic pattern in connection with technological progress or with a sudden change in the pattern of armaments; to participate in a sweeping program of international economic integration; and so on.

The ultimate success or failure of central planning, as described in Czechoslovakia in this book, will depend on the human factor. This book is strictly limited to a description of economic developments in a rather narrow materialistic sense.

[4] According to the new targets for 1965, which were published after this book had been set in type, Czechoslovak output, especially in industry, is planned to grow faster, whereas personal consumption is planned to increase at approximately the same rate, as compared with the long-term postwar trends in France, West Germany, and Austria (see Appendix).

Appendix

RESULTS OF THE 1959 PLAN; PLAN FOR 1960
AND TARGETS FOR 1965 UNDER THE
THIRD FIVE-YEAR PLAN

In September 1959, the Central Committee of the Communist Party of Czechoslovakia issued directives for the Third Five-Year Plan, cover-ing the years 1961–65,[1] on the basis of a report by the chairman of the State Planning Office, O. Šimůnek.[2] Many of these targets surpass those outlined by the first secretary of the Communist Party and President of the Republic, A. Novotný, at the Eleventh Congress of the Party in June 1958 and described as long-term plans in Chapter 2, Section 7, and Chap-ter 4, Section 5, of this book. In *Plánované hospodářství*, No. 11, 1959, the following comparison was given (all index numbers 1957 = 100, based on gross value):

	Targets for 1965	
	Under Di-rectives of June 1958	Under Di-rectives of September 1959
Index of industrial production............	190–95	201
Index of agricultural production..........	140	140
Index of volume of construction...........	170–80	179.8
Index of output in engineering............	230	260
Index of output in chemical industry.......	250	300
Hard coal, million tons	35–36	35.5
Coke, million tons	10.7	11.6
Crude steel, million tons	9.2–9.7	10.5
Electricity, billion kwh	38	37.7
Plastics, thousand tons	90–95	105.6
Cement, million tons	7	8.6

Stepping-up of targets for 1965 was motivated by the fast growth of the national economy in 1958–59.[3] In fact, as far as industry is concerned, the increases in gross value of output in these years were the highest since the currency reform in 1953; comparable costs of production were low-ered; and contrary to the first industrialization drive of 1951–53, there

---

[1] The first Five-Year Plan covered 1949–53, the second 1956–60.

[2] His speech of September 23 was published in *Rudé právo* of September 29, 1959.

[3] This also was the motivation for increased 1960 targets under the revised second Five-Year Plan, by decision of the Czechoslovak government of July 24, 1959.

was practically no increase in wages in industry in 1958, and in 1959 it was considerably below the increase in output per man-year,[4] which worked as an anti-inflationary device. The plan of output was being fulfilled more equally over the subbranches of industrial production, and so was the investment plan.[5] On the other hand, the targets for agricultural production in 1965 were not lowered, although the plan in agriculture was not fulfilled in the years 1958–59. (In the latter year, the gross value of agricultural production actually fell below that of 1958.)

A number of self-explanatory data on the development of Czechoslovakia's economy in 1959, together with the planned figures for 1960 and the targets for 1965 under the latest directives for the third Five-Year Plan, can be found in the tables at the end of this Appendix, with the following breakdown: basic national account data, industry, construction, agriculture, transportation, foreign trade, and the standard of living.

These tables also contain index numbers of the planned growth under the revised second Five-Year Plan, 1956–60, under the third Five-Year Plan, 1961–65, and over the whole period since the beginning of comprehensive central planning in 1948, up to 1965. When comparing the percentage increases under the second and third Five-Year Plans, it should be borne in mind not only that the third Five-Year Plan starts from a substantially higher level, but also that the second Five-Year Plan covers two years of economic *détente*, from 1956–57, as well as three years of a very pronounced, resumed industrialization drive, from 1958 to 1960. In fact, the acceleration of the yearly flow of gross fixed investments and of the rate of growth in some basic subbranches of heavy industry seems to have been concentrated in the first three years of the long-term plan 1958–60 rather than in the remaining five years, 1961–65.

The main characteristics of the third Five-Year Plan, 1961–65, are as follows:

[4] Increase in wages (earnings) in industry in 1959 has not been given in the *Results of the Fulfillment of the State Plan*, 1959. But it can be assumed, in view of the new system of wages which was introduced, that, in contrast to past developments, the 1959 increase in wages in industry did not outstrip, and probably remained below, the average increase in wages in the whole Socialist sector. Real wages in the Socialist sector increased by 5 per cent (and nominal wages even less; see Table A.7), as compared with the increase in "productivity of labor" (gross value of output per man-year) in industry, by 8 per cent (see Table A.1).

[5] A certain decentralization of planning, as described in Chapter 2, Section 6, seems to have borne fruit. It also should be mentioned that the plan of gross value of output was overfulfilled by 1.8 per cent in industry as a whole, and the "comparable cost of output" was reduced more than planned, so that, in terms of net value, the production plan—if such an unpublished net output plan exists—also must have been overfulfilled.

A. Production drive, with new stress on selected subbranches of heavy industry. From 1961 to 1965, Marxist national income ("net value" of output of commodities and "material" services) is planned to increase by 43 per cent; gross value of industrial production by 50 per cent[6] (of which output of means of production is planned to increase by 60 per cent); and output in engineering by 72 per cent and in chemical industry by 86 per cent, in terms of gross value of output. The share of output of the means of production in total gross value of output in industry is planned to increase from 60 per cent in 1955 to 64 per cent in 1960 and to 68 per cent in 1965; the share of engineering alone is planned to exceed 30 per cent of total gross value of industrial output by 1965.

The pattern of industrial production is planned to change as follows (in per cent of total gross value of output in industry):[7]

	1957	Planned 1965
Fuel industry (solid fuel)	7	5
Power	3	4
Metallurgy	11	12
Engineering	24	31
Chemical industry	8	10
Building materials	3	4
Consumers' manufactures	15	11
Food industry	17	12

Within the engineering branch, the planned growth of output of some specific products exceeds considerably the average planned increase of gross value of engineering (by 72 per cent under the third Five-Year Plan) (index of gross value of output 1960 = 100):[8]

Power machinery and equipment	186
Machinery and equipment for chemical and rubber industries	340
Electric and diesel locomotives	275
Machinery and equipment for production of building materials	304

In consequence, some other lines of output within engineering must be planned to increase by less than 72 per cent, and some may even be planned to decrease. The resulting change of pattern of machinery production is certainly connected with the new division of production of machinery over the whole area of member countries of the Council for Mutual Economic Aid.[9]

[6] The increase in terms of *net* value under Marxist definition is planned to be even faster (see *C. Efforts to improve economic efficiency*).

[7] From *Plánované hospodářství*, No. 11, 1959.

[8] *Ibid.*

[9] According to *Plánované hospodářství* (No. 11, 1959), "In engineering, far-reaching changes in pattern have to be carried out; these have been made necessary by increased needs of heavy machinery products for our own investments as well as

Other main branches of the "material sphere of production" are planned to grow more slowly than industry; for instance, the gross value of output in agriculture is planned to increase, under the third Five-Year Plan, by 21 per cent[10] and in freight transport by 31 per cent. Only construction is planned to grow, parallel with industry, by 50 per cent in terms of gross value.

Gross social product (see Chapter 10, Section 1) is thus planned to change in pattern as follows (in per cent of total gross social product):[11]

	1955	Plan 1960	Target 1965
Industry	65.2	67.7	70.5
Agriculture (presumably including forestry)	14.3	11.8	10.3
Construction	8.9	10.8	10.7
Other branches of the "material sphere," including trade (see Chapter 10, Section 1)	11.6	9.7	8.5

B. Stepped-up rate of investments. Gross fixed investments, excluding general overhauls, are planned to increase faster, in terms of constant prices, than gross value of output under the third Five-Year Plan (and even more so under the 1960 Plan); see Table A.1. The increasing ratio of gross fixed investments to gross output suggests a further decrease in the marginal yield of investments.[12]

An increasing portion of the stepped-up investments is planned to be allocated to industry:

---

by commitments of our engineering in the Socialist camp, to cover some of the needs of the Soviet Union and other countries of the Socialist camp in the field of the means of production. . . . Cooperation and division of programs of output among the countries of the Socialist camp will influence the structure of our engineering industry. In the course of preparations for the third Five-Year Plan, further negotiations concerning the division of labor among the member countries of the Council of Mutual Economic Aid will take place. At the same time some earlier agreements will be carried out. For instance, Czechoslovakia will produce electric locomotives, water turbines, rubber and shoe machines, etc. The People's Republic of Poland will supply Czechoslovakia with construction machines, the People's Republic of Hungary with combines, the German Democratic Republic with printing and paper-making machines, etc."

[10] A faster yearly increase is planned for 1960; see Table A.3.

[11] From *Plánované hospodářství*, No. 11, 1959.

[12] Any estimate of the actual deterioration of the ratio of gross investments to gross output would necessitate, among other things, reduction of the comparison of increase in gross fixed investments to the "material sphere" as covered by Marxist gross social product.

	(In per cent of total gross fixed investments, excluding general overhauls)		(In billion Kčs at 1959 prices)
	1959–60	1961–65	1961–65
Industry	40.2	45.4	120*
Construction	2.6	2.3	6*
Agriculture (presumably including forestry)	15.9	15.2	40*
Transport and communications	9.8	10.8	28*
Education and culture	3.9	4.1	11*
National health	1.5	1.9	5*
Housing and communal services	25.1	20.3	40†
Other investments			62*
Total	100	100	312

Percentages are from *Plánované hospodářství*, No. 11, 1959; prices are author's estimate on the basis of percentages and total amount of investments, as announced by O. Šimůnek.

The 120 billion Kčs planned to be invested in industry represents an increase of 80 per cent, in terms of constant 1959 prices, over the corresponding investments for 1956–60, as compared with the planned increase in gross value of output of only 50 per cent. Thus, if we limit our comparison to the sector of industry alone, we can suspect a further deterioration of the ratio of gross fixed investments to gross output by approximately 16 per cent over the years 1961–65. Such a deterioration is not unexpected in view of the "widening" rather than "deepening" investments and of the rather neglected maintenance and renewals in the past, since 1948, and in view of the further change of the pattern of production as planned in 1961–65.

C. Efforts to improve economic efficiency. Great efforts are being made to improve economic efficiency, however, even as to the use of fixed investments. In the absence of the rate of interest on capital, enterprises are being induced by other means to use their fixed capital more fully. At a special meeting of economic experts, reported in the Czechoslovak daily press on November 17, 1959, the chairman of the State Planning Office, O. Šimůnek, insisted that a second shift of work be introduced in industrial concerns, and he declared that enterprises that failed to do so would not be allotted new investments to widen their capacity.[13]

Under the third Five-Year Plan, more stress will be placed on modernizing and labor-saving than hitherto. This is necessary in view of the fact that 94 per cent of the planned increase of Marxist national income is to be achieved by increase in output per worker (increased "productivity of

[13] Šimůnek also stated that, at present, 1,100,000 workers in industry are in the first shift and only 300,000 are in the second shift.

labor") and only 6 per cent by the increased number of economically active persons.[14]

The new system of wages (see Chapter 9), with more stress on piecework wages and premiums, is also devised to increase productivity.

New, modern technology is to be introduced, and it is interesting to note in this connection that the Czechoslovak planners seem to realize some of the shortcomings of their previous economic policy. For instance, in Chapter 8, Sections 2 and 3, the small share of machinery in total investments has been pointed out. According to Šimůnek,[15] the share of expenditures on machinery in total fixed capital outlay is to increase from 29.1 per cent under the second Five-Year Plan to 33.1 per cent under the third Five-Year Plan. In consumption of energy, Chapter 2 points out the relatively great share of solid fuel and the small share of liquid fuel and electricity in Czechoslovakia. The pattern of energy sources is now planned to change as follows (in per cent of total domestic consumption of energy):[16]

	Actual 1955	Plan 1960	Target 1965
Solid fuel	93	89	83
Liquid fuel	4	7	13
Electricity	3	2	3

In Chapter 5, the low electrification of Czechoslovak railways was mentioned. Under the third Five-Year Plan, electric traction is planned to reach more than half of the total railway traffic, as follows (in percentage share):[16]

	Actual 1955	Plan 1960	Target 1965
Steam traction	97	72	26
Electric traction	3	25	51
Diesel engine traction	...	3	23

In these respects, Czechoslovak planners seem to have reached their correct conclusions, in the absence of domestic market indicators, by study-

[14] The total labor force ("working population") is planned to increase in 1961–65 by 420,000 persons. This is more than the prospective increase in the population of productive age. In view of the already existing full employment, the "labor force plan" can be fulfilled only by increased employment of partially disabled persons, of old persons, and of housewives.

[15] In a speech on September 23, 1959.

[16] From *Plánované hospodářství*, No. 11, 1959. (Atomic energy seems not to be planned for economic use in any important quantity.)

ing the trends in developed Western market economies rather than by applying their own specific guide for comparison of investment alternatives.[17] However, for the future they are trying to construct a guide to the relatively most productive investments, in the absence of interest rates and price indicators. They are also giving more attention to a complex study of the optimum allocation of all national resources. V. Komárek informs us[18] that a special commission for the study of the "economic efficiency of investments" has been set up. He postulates "a complex approach" to the problem of allocation of investments and points out that not all import-reducing investments are justifiable.

Great efforts are also being made to reduce material waste and costs of production in general. In industry, comparable costs of production are planned to be lowered at a yearly rate of 2.6 per cent.[19] Official cost accounting in Czechoslovakia, as we know from Chapter 7, does not cover any rate of interest on fixed capital (basic funds). Wage costs, on a comparable basis, are being lowered because output per man-year is increasing faster than workers' earnings.

The chairman of the State Planning Office, O. Šimůnek, stated that the share of industry in Marxist national income would increase faster than its share in gross social product.[20] This, too, suggests an improving ratio of net to gross output, but here again the increasing use of fixed investments per unit of output is left out of the picture, and only depreciation of "basic funds" is included.[21]

D. Development of foreign trade. No official data on the planned increase of foreign trade are known to the author. V. Komárek stated that "foreign trade turnover rose by 16 per cent in 1959 and will continue to

---

[17] In Western market economies, in the author's opinion, price—under the present imperfect competition—does not reflect satisfactorily costs of production, or utility (and a perfect competition, besides being impossible under the present institutional pattern, would run against the requirements to increase social security and social justice, and would hardly achieve any better economic performance). Nevertheless, the author feels that, on the whole, the existing price structure in developed market economies involves less economic irrationalities than the existing artificial pricing in Czechoslovakia.

[18] In an article, "Efficiency of Investments Connected with Foreign Trade," in *Plánované hospodářství*, No. 4, 1960.

[19] From O. Šimůnek's speech of September 23, 1959.

[20] *Ibid.*

[21] It should be noted that in Czechoslovakia fixed capital stock (basic funds) was revalued in 1955, whereas in the Soviet Union such a revaluation is only being carried out now. Depreciation, as officially applied in Czechoslovakia, seems not to be so underrated as in most other centrally planned economies.

rise rapidly."[22] According to unofficial data published in the *Economic Bulletin for Europe* (XI, No. 1, 1959), foreign trade turnover (presumably at 1958 foreign trade prices) is planned to increase, between 1958 and 1965, by 58 per cent. Thus, the development of the volume of external trade would be more or less in line with the growth of "net value" of output, as approximately reflected by Marxist national income at constant prices, whereas in most years of the 1948–58 period the growth of foreign trade was lagging behind the growth in output.[23]

The planned increase seems to be due, above all, to increasing Czechoslovak contributions toward industrialization of underdeveloped countries and of the Soviet Union. It was officially stated that the share of machinery and industrial equipment in total exports (presumably at constant foreign trade prices) is to go up from 43.3 per cent in 1958 to 55.3 per cent in 1965 (see Table A.6). If the information on planned increase of external turnover is correct, and if both exports and imports are planned to develop in a fairly parallel way, this would mean that the volume of Czechoslovak exports of machinery and industrial equipment would double over these seven years.

E. Efforts to maintain a moderate, steady increase in consumption and to check inflation. Personal consumption by Marxist definition is planned to increase over the five years 1961–65 by 31 per cent, retail trade turnover by 30 per cent, and real *per capita* earnings in the Socialist sector (closely correlated with real per capita personal income) by an estimated 20 per cent (see Table A.7).[24] These increases are well below the

[22] From *Plánované hospodářství*, No. 4, 1960. Komárek also stated that exports (presumably at domestic wholesale prices) amount to 12 per cent of gross value of production in Czechoslovakia (presumably in 1959).

[23] In breakdown by economic areas, the turnover would increase, according to information from the *Economic Bulletin for Europe*, as follows: in trade with the USSR by 100 per cent; in trade with other member countries of the Council for Mutual Economic Aid (i.e., other centrally planned economies in Europe) by 56 per cent; in trade with centrally planned economies in Asia and with Yugoslavia, it would *decrease* by 25 per cent; and in trade with market economies, including underdeveloped countries in Asia and Africa, it would increase by 39 per cent.

[24] A slower increase in real *per capita* personal income, as compared with the increase in personal consumption and in retail trade turnover, is caused not only by expected increase in population; but it can be easily explained by the unusually broad definition of personal consumption in Czechoslovakia and by duplications in the statistical coverage of retail trade (see Chapter 10). It is noteworthy that nominal incomes are planned to increase more slowly than real earnings in view of the planned further reduction in retail prices. In no case can the faster increase in "personal consumption," as compared with the increase in real earnings, be interpreted as expected drawing on cash savings.

planned increases in output and in productivity of labor (see *A. Production drive*).[25] Keeping the increase in personal incomes below the increase in output and in productivity of labor as an anti-inflationary device is discussed in Chapter 7.

On the other hand, it is noteworthy that—in contrast to the first industrialization drive of 1950–53—with decreasing output of consumer goods, inflation, and decreasing real incomes, the planners now take care to maintain a steady though moderate increase in consumption by the population, especially of consumers' manufactures. This serves not only to raise the standard of living but also to withdraw excess liquidities from circulation via high turnover tax on durables and, curiously enough, to promote a propensity to save.[26]

Summary

If the third Czechoslovak Five-Year Plan is fairly fulfilled, the average yearly rate of growth in the "material sphere of production" would be around 8 per cent, of which the rate of growth in industry would be around 10 per cent (in terms of "net value" by Marxist definition and by official pricing; the yearly growth of the official index of gross value of production is planned to be slightly less, 9.4 per cent). Real *per capita* personal income is planned to increase by slightly less than 4 per cent per year, and personal consumption by Marxist definition by slightly over 5 per cent. Assuming that the change in output in the "immaterial sphere" would not distort the above-mentioned production trends, and assuming that the general production and consumption long-term postwar trends in developed market economies will continue without much change, Czechoslovakia

[25] According to *Odborář*, 1959, the increase in wages in 1959 was coupled with the increase in productivity of labor (gross value of output per man-year) as follows:

Index of Productivity	Index of Wages
105	99.0
106	100.4
107	101.2
108	102.0

According to this information, enterprises with an increase in productivity of labor below 7 per cent do not obtain any money from the state bank to increase wages, and those with an increase in productivity below 5 per cent are bound to cut wages.

[26] Consumers' credit is extremely limited in Czechoslovakia. Most durables must be fully paid on delivery, and automobiles must be prepaid by two-thirds of the price several months before delivery. The propensity to save has been falling rapidly in Czechoslovakia, following two postwar currency reforms.

would surpass the rate of production growth in market economies at a comparable level[27] and would maintain, at the same time, a more or less comparable rate of consumption growth. Thus, Czechoslovak planners would be able to claim to have achieved a superior economic performance. Their success would be the more remarkable as Czechoslovakia is likely to continue to use a considerable portion of her resources for granting net foreign aid (see Chapter 6).

But even if we disregard the difficult problem of finding an adequate comparable yardstick to measure the economic growth in centrally planned economies and in market economies, several other questions remain open:

1) The fulfillment of the third Five-Year Plan, at least in some sections, is subject to doubt. When in 1958 the yearly growth in industrial output surpassed the average growth as planned under the Five-Year Plan up to 1965, personal consumption was practically stationary. In 1959, industrial output increased at a rate comparable to that under the Five-Year Plan, as did personal consumption. But both 1958 and 1959 showed the effects of the economic *détente* of 1954–57, when material and psychological reserves were built up. Therefore, these two years cannot provide proof of attainability of the 1965 targets: the Czechoslovak planners may find it increasingly difficult to maintain, over a long period, both a very high rate of growth of industrial output with the very high investments it requires at the present juncture, and a fairly high rate of consumption growth. In agriculture, the postwar developments up to the present do not at all warrant the high 1965 targets.

2) With ever higher starting levels, it will be increasingly difficult to maintain yearly rates of growth, even if, in theory, the "saturation point" does not exist under central planning in the same sense as it exists in a market economy, and Czechoslovak planners will not be faced with all the problems of distributing the national income as experienced by the most developed market economies.

3) So far, the Czechoslovak planners could use the trends in more developed market economies as a certain guide in allocating investments and other national resources. When Czechoslovakia becomes a fully de-

---

[27] In specific fields of heavy industry, Czechoslovakia may be catching up with, or even surpassing, the per capita output in the most developed market economies. Chairman Šimůnek of the State Planning Office stated in his speech on September 23, 1959: "By 1965 we shall produce approximately 739 kg of steel per inhabitant, which is substantially above the per capita steel output in the United States in recent years." (Per capita output of crude steel in the U.S. including Alaska and Hawaii amounted to 443 kg in 1958 and 477 kg in 1959.)

veloped economy, it will need its own reliable guide for further development. The problem of how to choose the most efficient alternative allocation of resources is far from solved under the present artificial pricing.

4) Consumption of goods and services alone is not a satisfactory
measure of the standard of living. The latter involves such factors as free
availability of goods and services, at least a relatively free choice of employment (and, of course, availability of employment), and a number of
psychological factors, which have not been discussed in this book at all.

In any case, the answer to the question of which of the two systems, a
"developed market economy in a parliamentary democracy" or a "developed centrally planned economy in a people's democracy," is superior
would exceed by far this descriptive economic study. Which of the two
systems can provide a larger portion of the population with a happy life
free from want, and limit mental and material suffering to the absolute
minimum? This depends not only on the economic system but also on
the methods and policies applied at any particular time in any particular
country.

After studying the third Czechoslovak Five-Year Plan, the author had
nothing to add to what was basically stated already in the Conclusion of
this book: that the potential economic achievements of central planning
in Czechoslovakia should not be underestimated and that its ultimate
success, or failure, will depend greatly on the human factor.

APPENDIX TABLES

The following tables give basic data for 1959, plans for 1960, and
targets for 1965 in the long-term perspective, since 1948.

Unless indicated otherwise, all data for 1948, 1955, 1958, planned
figures for 1960, and targets for 1965, as well as of the indices of increase
for 1955–60, 1960–65, and 1948–65, are from *Čísla 3. čs. pětiletky* (Figures on the Third Czechoslovak Five-Year Plan), a special supplement to
Statistický obzor, No. 11, 1959. All data for 1959, unless indicated otherwise, are from *Zpráva o rozvoji národního hospodářství ČSR za rok 1959*,
(Report on the Development of the Economy of the Czechoslovak Republic
in 1959), a special supplement to *Statistický obzor*, No. 2, 1960. The index
numbers of increase, based on 1955 = 100, 1960 = 100, and 1948 = 100
respectively, cover in part actual, in part planned, figures.

TABLE A.1—BASIC NATIONAL ACCOUNT DATA

					Plan		Index of Increase		
	1948	1955	1958	1959	1960	Target 1965	1955-60	1960-65	1948-65
Index of national income under Marxist definition, at 1955 constant prices..........	100	178	219	230	244	349	137	143	349
Index of gross fixed investments, excluding general overhauls, at 1959 constant prices[a]	100	245	359	426	464	689	189	149	689
Ratio of gross fixed investments to Marxist national income, based on official prices†,[b]	16	21	26	29	30	31	—	—	—
Index of personal consumption under Marxist definition, at 1955 constant prices.....	100	149	174	183	197	257	133	131	257
Ratio of personal consumption to Marxist national income*,[c]	74	61	59	59	59	55	—	—	—
Index of total labor force in the Socialist sector of the national economy[d]	100	170	182	185	186	203	110	109	203

TABLE A.1—*Concluded*

[a] No data on planned "general overhauls" for 1960 and 1965 have been published; the above index is therefore based on gross fixed investments excluding general overhauls and is thus somewhat distorted (probably involving a downward bias).

Absolute figures up to 1959 are as follows (at 1959 prices, in billion Kčs):

	1948	1958	1959
"Gross fixed investments"	8.9	32.0	37.9
"General overhauls" (see Chapter 8, Section 2)	0.7	7.2	7.5
Total fixed investments	9.6	39.2	45.4

[b] This percentage share is absolutely not comparable with expenditure on "gross fixed investments" in Western national accounts, (1) because "gross fixed investments" official data do not include "general overhauls" (see note *a*); (2) because the ratio is based on official prices of investments which are heavily subsidized (see Chapter 7, Section 2, and Chapter 10, Section 4); and (3) because Marxist national income is not comparable with national income and gross national product under Western definition (see Chapter 10). It should be noted that the share of gross fixed investments at current "conventional" prices in gross national expenditure in 1956 (roughly comparable to Western definitions) amounted to one-third (see Table 10.9). The above approximation of the ratio of gross fixed investments (excluding general overhauls) to Marxist national income at official prices should be regarded only as an indication of trend; it is based, in turn, on the following approximations (in billion Kčs, 1953 currency):

	1948	1955	1958	1959	Plan 1960	Target 1965
Marxist national income at 1955 prices	63.6	113.9	138.3	146.3	155.2	221.9
"Marxist gross fixed investments" (excluding Marxist "general overhauls") at 1955 prices	9.9	24.3	35.5	42.2	45.9	68.2

[c] At official 1955 constant prices. It should be noted that "personal consumption" includes a very high rate of turnover tax. At current "conventional" prices, the share of personal consumption in gross national expenditure in 1956 amounted to approximately 38 per cent.

[d] Excluding total labor force in unified agricultural cooperatives. The above index covers practically the total nonagricultural working population, plus a relatively small number of employees in state farms. (In other words, it covers total "working population," see Chapter 1, Section 2, except members of unified agricultural cooperatives, individual farmers, a negligible handful of other self-employed workers, and apprentices.)

TABLE A.2—INDUSTRY

	1948	1955	1958	1959	Plan 1960	Target 1965	Index of Increase		
							1955–60	1960–65	1948–65
Index of gross value of output	100	224	300	332	357	535	159	150	535
Means of production	100	249	340	384	420	672	168	160	672
Consumers' goods	100	198	261	282	288	374	145	130	374
Index of labor force	100	128	140	143	146	156	114	107	156
Index of gross value of output per man-year ("productivity of labor")	100	176	215	232	247	346	140	140	346
Index of gross value of output in engineering	100	341	497	...	652	1,122	191	172	1,122
Index of gross value of output in chemical industry	100	282	405	453*	489	909	173	186	909
Electricity, billion kwh	7.5	15.0	19.6	21.9	24.2	37.7	161	156	501
Hard coal (gross output), million metric tons[a]	18.6	23.2	27.2	28.6*	29.6	35.5	128	120	191
Brown coal, million tons	22.6	36.7	54.3 }	53.0*	55.4 }	73.2	143	132	324
Lignite, million tons	1.0	2.0	2.5 }	...	3.1 }	4.2	152	135	414
Coke, million tons	4.3	7.0	7.4	...	8.4	11.6	120	138	272
Pig iron, million tons	1.6	3.0	3.8	4.2	4.7	7.7	159	161	465
Crude steel, million tons	2.6	4.5	5.5	6.1	6.8	10.5	152	154	401
Rolled steel, million tons	1.8	3.0	3.8	...	4.7	7.3	156	157	412
Nitrogenous fertilizers, thousand tons N	29	60	108	133	145	293	239	202	995
Phosphoric fertilizers, thousand tons P_2O_5	54	98	117	135	146	285	150	194	525
Staple fiber, thousand tons	...	49	55	...	64	106	130	166	...
Plastics, thousand tons	...	24	48	...	56	184	240	326	...
Steam turbines, MW	122	911	863	942	1,185	1,990	130	168	1,631
Steel rolling machines, thousand tons	1	16	21	23	34	59	214	174	7,400
Ball bearings and other bearings, million units	2	14	27	...	36	65	159	179	4,180
Main-line locomotives, units	171	125	152	...	286	790	229	276	462
Tractors, thousand units	9	13	25	29	34	43	268	128	474

258

TABLE A.2—*Concluded*

	1948	1955	1958	1959	Plan 1960	Target 1965	Index of Increase 1955-60	Index of Increase 1960-65	Index of Increase 1948-65
Trucks, thousands	7[b]	12	14	15	15	20	121	133	274
Private cars, thousands	18	13	43	51	56	110	447	196	612
Household refrigerators, thousands	8	31	80	104	120	265	399	221	3,500
Television sets, thousands	—	17	134	197	247	400	1,432	162	3,200
Cement, million tons	1.7	2.9	4.1	4.7	4.9	8.6	171	174	519
Wool fabrics, billion meters	42	39	43	45	45	52	115	116	125
Shoes, million pairs[c]	64	63	80	87*	90	101	143	112	157
Meat, carcass weight, thousand tons	163[d]	345	415	413	442	583	128	132	...
Dairy butter, thousand tons	23[e]	43	58	55	61	80	142	130	...
Sugar, refined, thousand tons ...	518	659	856	...[f]	974	1,203	148	123	233

[a] I.e., including consumption of pits, waste, etc. Net output, in million metric tons, was as follows: 1955, 22.1; 1958, 25.8; 1959, 26.5.
[b] Excluding chassis without mounted body; in later years these are included.
[c] All kinds, leather, rubber, and other materials. Output of leather shoes only developed as follows, in million pairs: 1948, 28; 1955, 23; 1958, 34; 1959, 39.
[d] A considerable amount of meat production by individual farmers was not statistically reported; therefore it is not comparable with later years.
[e] The share of dairy butter in total butter production was lower than in later years.
[f] It was officially stated that the 1959 output remained below that of 1958.

TABLE A.3—CONSTRUCTION

	1948	1955	1958	1959	Plan 1960	Target 1965	Index of Increase 1955-60	Index of Increase 1960-65	Index of Increase 1948-65
Volume of construction[a]	100	249	334	384*	422	635	170	150	635
New housing units put into use, thousands...	21.6[b]	50.7	53.4	67.0*	76.2	109.4	151	144	505

[a] Undefined index 1948 = 100, based probably on budget expenditure at constant budget prices.
[b] Average floor space 53.2 square meters, as compared with 39.3 square meters in 1955 and 38.3 square meters in 1958.

TABLE A.4—AGRICULTURE

	1948	1955	1958	1959	Plan 1960	Target 1965	Index of Increase 1955-60	1960-65	1948-65
Index of gross value of agri. production	100	127	133	131*	148	180	117	121	180
Crops	100	118	117	111*	133	162	113	122	162
Livestock production	100	143	158	162*	174	211	122	121	211
Agricultural land, million hectares	7.6	7.3	7.4	...	7.4	7.2	101	98	95
Arable land, million hectares	5.3	5.1	5.1	...	5.2	5.2	101	101	98
Hectare yields, 100 kg/ha:									
Wheat	16.4	20.4	18.3	22.8	22.0	27.0	108	123	165
Rye	15.5	18.9	19.0	20.2	20.5	25.0	108	122	161
Barley	15.4	20.1	17.9	21.9	21.8	26.5	108	122	172
Sugar beets	236	285	299	200*	295	325	103	110	138
Potatoes	110	127	109	105*	153	180	120	118	164
Livestock, million head, at end of year:									
Cattle	3.7	4.1	4.2	4.3	4.4	4.8	106	110	131
Pigs	3.2	5.3	5.3	5.7	5.5	5.5	104	100	170
Sheep	0.5	1.0	0.8	0.7	0.7	0.6	70	86	131

TABLE A.5—TRANSPORTATION

	1948	1955	1958	1959	Plan 1960	Target 1965	Index of Increase 1955-60	1960-65	1948-65
Public freight transportation, million tons:									
Rail	75	140	174	181	198	259	141	131	348
Road	25	75	107	115	126	220	166	175	884
Inland water	0.9	2.8	3.2	3.1	3.6	5.7	127	158	614
Public passenger trans., million passengers:									
Rail	460	583	596	558	607	620	104	102	135
Road	293	758	694	1,050	1,084	1,330	143	123	454
Inland water	2.4	2.3	2.3	2.3	2.6	3.6	114	140	152
Air	0.1	0.2	0.4	0.6	0.6	1.5	276	248	1,500

TABLE A.6—FOREIGN TRADE
(In billion Kčs and percentage)

	1948	1955	1958	1959	Plan 1960	Target 1965	Index of Increase 1955-60	Index of Increase 1960-65	Index of Increase 1948-65
Exports[a]	5.4[b]	8.5	10.9	12.9	...	...	...	...	...
Imports[c]	4.9[b]	7.6	9.8	11.5	...	...	...	...	...
Turnover	10.3[b]	16.1	20.7	24.4	...	32.7[d]	...	...	317[a]
With centrally planned economies, including Yugoslavia:									
Exports[a]	2.0[b]	5.8	7.7	9.0	...	...	...	...	...
Imports[c]	1.9[b]	5.4	6.9	8.3	...	...	...	...	...
Turnover	3.9[b]	11.2	14.6	17.3	...	24.3[d]	...	...	623[a]
With market economies:									
Exports[a]	3.4[b]	2.7	3.2	3.9	...	...	...	...	...
Imports[c]	3.0[e]	2.2	2.9	3.2	...	...	...	...	...
Turnover	6.4[e]	4.9	6.1	7.1	...	8.4[d]	...	...	131[a]
Percentage share of machinery and industrial equipment in total exports[f]	20.3	43.5	43.3	...	48.7[g]	55.3	—	—	—
Percentage share of raw materials in total imports[f]	56.5	53.6	54.7	...	52.7[g]	51.5	—	—	—

[a] At current foreign trade prices, free at the Czechoslovak border (analogous to f.o.b. exports).
[b] Original data in 1945 currency units converted into 1953 currency units at the ratio 6.94:1 (see Chapter 6, Section 5), so that the dollar exchange rate of 7.20 Kčs per dollar applies for the whole series.
[c] At current foreign trade prices, free at the border of the supplying country (analogous to f.o.b. imports).
[d] Based on information, in dollars, in the *Economic Bulletin for Europe*, XI, No. 1.
[e] Excluding UNRRA supplies; see also note a.
[f] Presumably based on current value at foreign trade prices.
[g] Plan 1961.

TABLE A.7—STANDARD OF LIVING

	1948	1955	1958	1959	Plan 1960	Target 1965	Index of Increase 1955-60	Index of Increase 1960-65	Index of Increase 1948-65
Average per capita monthly earnings in the "Socialist sector" of the national economy, in Kčs[a]	819	1,197	1,277	1,305	1,339[b]	1,524[b]	112	114	187
Index of the above data	100	146	156	160	163[b]	187[b]	112	114	187
Approximation of the cost-of-living index[c]	100*	152*	150*	146*,[d]	143*,[e]	...	94*	...	...
Approximation of the index of real per capita earnings in the "Socialist sector" of the national economy[f]	100*	96*	104*	109*	114*	136†,[g]	119*	120†	136†
Index of retail trade at constant prices	100	151	182	195	212	276	140	130	276
Index of benefits from national insurance per recipient at constant cost of living[h]	100[i]	94[j]	114	118†,[k]	120†,[l]	...	127†	...	...
Index of health insurance expenditure per person at constant cost of living[m]	100	205	257	...	...	...	...	...	...
Number of beds in hospitals and maternity homes, thousands	71	92	100	...	105	115	114	110	162
Number of places in kindergartens, thousands	6	35	38	...	43	58	124	135	936
Number of households:									
Per passenger automobile	344†,[n]	...	28.7[o]	...	...	9.4[p]	—	—	—
Per television set	—	...	18.5[o]	...	...	1.9[p]	—	—	—
Per refrigerator	...	...	18.2[o]	...	...	3.0[p]	—	—	—
Increase in private deposits, billion Kčs per year	3.8†,[q]	1.1[r]	2.8[r]	2.7	...	...	...	...	...

[a] Data up to 1958 from Table 9.4.
[b] Based on a statement by the chairman of the State Planning Office, O. Šimůnek, that the "average wage" in the Socialist sector of the national economy would increase in 1960 by 2.6 per cent, and over the third Five-Year Plan by 13.8 per cent (Plánované hospodářství, No. 3, 1960).
[c] From Table 7.2.

TABLE A.7—Concluded

[a] Three months at 150, nine months at 144 (after the retail price reductions of March 1959; see Table 7.2).

[e] Estimate based on the statement that, through the retail price reductions of April 1960 (reported in *Rudé právo*, April 23), the population "will save 1.8 billion Kčs," on the assumption that retail sales would be around 100 billion Kčs and that there would be no further reduction in retail prices in 1960 and with due regard to the reduction, from 0.80 Kčs to 0.70 Kčs per kwh, of the price of electricity for lighting and to the abolishment of surplus charges for excess consumption of electricity in households.

It should be stressed that for the first time, in connection with the official announcement of retail price reductions, it was stated that "good care will be taken that the reduced articles remain available on the market in unchanged quality for at least two years." Thus, for the first time since 1953, it can be assumed that the announced price reductions will be fully reflected in the lowering of the cost of living and will not refer only to list prices. (The substitution effect, however, remains to be ascertained.)

[f] Not to be confused with the index of workers' real earnings in industry, Table 9.6. A comparison of the two index series confirms that workers' real earnings in industry were increasing faster than real per capita incomes in the whole Socialist sector.

[g] Based on the official statement at the meeting of the Central Committee of the Communist Party on September 23, 1959, that the real income per person in terms of "material consumption, consumption of services paid for by the population, of services provided for the population in education, health insurance, etc." would increase by 20 per cent under the third Five-Year Plan, 1960–65; on the assumption that real average incomes in agriculture (unified agricultural cooperatives and individual farmers) would develop parallel with real average incomes in the Socialist sector, including employees of state farms. Even if this assumption were not correct, the distorting effect would not be great, since total personal income in agriculture, excluding state farms, amounts at present to less than one-fifth of total personal income in Czechoslovakia. Furthermore, total real personal income in unified agricultural cooperatives outweighs total real personal income of individual farmers, and the former cannot be expected to develop too differently from total real income in the Socialist sector. A further assumption is that individual and collective real incomes of the population will also develop in a parallel way.

[h] From Table 9.4.

[i] Index 1949 = 100.

[j] 1956.

[k] Rough estimate, based on the announced slight increase in nominal benefits of individually selected pensioners. The increase in benefits at constant cost of living was brought about also by the fall in the cost of living.

[l] Rough estimate, based on the announcement that individually selected benefits would be increased by amounts totaling 120 million Kčs, which is less than 0.1 per cent of the sum of social security benefits. The increase in average benefits at constant cost of living was brought about by the fall in the cost of living in 1960.

[m] From Table 9.5.

[n] Estimate based on the number of cars, from Table 9.12, and on the estimated number of 3,600,000 households in 1948.

[o] 1957; from *Plánované hospodářství*, No. 11, 1959.

[p] From *Plánované hospodářství*, No. 11, 1959.

[q] 1947; based on reliable estimates in old (1945) currency units as follows: increase in deposits on savings books, 11 billion Kčs; in primary deposits on personal current accounts, 8 billion Kčs; converted into new (1953) currency units at 5 : 1. It should be stressed that personal current accounts, with payment by personal check, are not at all common on the continent of Europe as they are in the United Kingdom or in the United States.

[r] From *SRRC*, 1959, Table 21.8, deposits on savings books of all kinds, including premium books. There were hardly any deposits on personal current accounts. This excludes savings through advance payments for passenger automobiles, which in 1958 amounted to approximately 0.1 billion Kčs. (In Czechoslovakia, an advance of 20,000 Kčs, or approximately two-thirds of the consumers' price of the most current Škoda car, must be paid approximately one year before delivery to a private person.)

BIBLIOGRAPHY OF WORKS CITED

BOOKS AND ANNUALS

Alton, Thad P., and associates. *National Income and Product of Czechoslovakia in 1948–1949 and 1955–1956.* Columbia University Press, New York (to be published).

Čáp, V., J. Kazimour, M. Skoupý, J. Smrčina, and J. Votýpka. *Národohospodářská evidence v nové soustavě řízení* (Economic Accounting under the New System of Direction). Orbis, Prague, 1959.

Conseil de l'Europe: Données Statistiques (Council of Europe, Statistical Data). Section de la Documentation, Conseil de l'Europe, Strasbourg, 1959.

Czechoslovak Economic Papers. Czechoslovak Academy of Sciences, Prague, 1959.

Czechoslovak Statistical Abstract, 1958. Orbis, Prague, 1959.

Demografická příručka (Demographic Handbook). State Statistical Office, Prague, 1959.

Dochód Narodowy Polski 1956 (National Income of Poland, 1956). Central Statistical Office, Warsaw, 1958.

Dubský, S. *The Economic Development of Czechoslovakia.* Orbis, Prague, 1958.

Economic Survey of Europe, 1954, 1957, 1958. Economic Commission for Europe, Geneva, 1955, 1958, 1959.

European Housing Trends and Policies, 1956, 1958. Economic Commission for Europe, Geneva, 1957, 1959.

FAO Statistical Yearbook (Production), 1954–58. Food and Agricultural Organization of the United Nations, Rome, 1955, 1956, 1957, 1958, 1959.

ILO Statistical Yearbook, 1957, 1958. International Labour Office, Geneva, 1958, 1959.

Internationaler Vergleich der Preise für die Lebenshaltung (International Comparison of Cost-of-Living Prices). [West] German Statistical Office, Wiesbaden, 1957.

Kubík, J. *Úkoly perspektivních plánů hospodářského rozvoje ČSR* (The Tasks of the Prospective Plans of Economic Development of the Czechoslovak Republic). Orbis, Prague, 1959.

Magyar Statistikai Zsebkönyv 1958 (Hungarian Statistical Yearbook, 1958). State Statistical Office, Budapest, 1959.

Margolin, N. S. *Voprosy balansa dieniezhnykh dokhodov i rozkhodov naseleniya* (Problems of the Balance of Money Incomes and Expenditure of the Population). Moscow, 1939.

Misař, M. *K otázkám rozvoje a plánování osobní spotřeby v ČSR* (Problems of Developing and Planning Personal Consumption in the Czechoslovak Republic). Státní nakladatelství politické literatury (State Publishing House for Political Literature), Prague, 1957.

Narodnoe Khoziaistvo SSSR v 1958 godu (National Economy of the USSR in 1958). Moscow, 1959.

Navrátil, J. *Zahraniční obchod a výroba* (Foreign Trade and Production). Státní nakladatelství politické literatury (State Publishing House for Political Literature), Prague, 1958.

Nykryn, J., K. Štěpán, K. Heřman, and J. Kalinová. *Obchodní operace v čs zahraničním obchodu* (Trade Operations in Czechoslovak Foreign Trade). Orbis, Prague, 1959.

Postavení ČSR ve světovém hospodářství (Position of the Czechoslovak Republic in the World Economy), by a collective of authors. Státní nakladatelství politické literatury (State Publishing House for Political Literature), Prague, n.d. (probably 1958).

Results of the Fulfillment of the State Plan of Development of the National Economy of the Czechoslovak Republic. State Planning Office, Prague. Annually, 1955 to 1959.

Rocznik Statystyczny 1958 (Statistical Yearbook, 1958). Central Statistical Office, Warsaw.

Stádník, M. *Národní důchod a jeho rozdělení se zvláštním zřetelem k Československu* (National Income and Its Distribution, with Special Reference to Czechoslovakia). Knihovna Sborníku věd právních a státních, Prague, 1946.

Statistical Digest of the Czechoslovak Republic. State Statistical Office, Prague, January 1948. (See second item below.)

Statistical Pocket Book of Jugoslavia. Federal Statistical Office, Belgrade, 1959.

Statistická příručka ČSR 1948 (Statistical Digest of the Czechoslovak Republic, 1948). State Statistical Office, Prague, January 1948. (See second item above.)

Statistická ročenka Republiky Československé, 1957, 1958, 1959 (Statistical Yearbook of the Czechoslovak Republic).[1] State Statistical Office, Prague, 1957, 1958, 1959. Referred to as *SRRC* in the text.

Statistisches Jahrbuch der DDR 1958 (Statistical Yearbook of the German Democratic Republic). [East] German Statistical Office, Berlin.

Statistisches Jahrbuch für die Bundesrepublik Deutschland, 1955, 1958, 1959 (Statistical Yearbook of the German Federal Republic). [West] German Statistical Office, Wiesbaden.

United Nations. *Demographic Yearbook*, 1954–58. Statistical Office of the U.N., New York, 1955–59.

[1] No postwar statistical yearbooks were published in Czechoslovakia until 1957.

United Nations. *National Accounts Statistics,* 1956, 1957, 1958. Statistical Office of the U.N., New York, 1957–59.

United Nations. *National and Per Capita Incomes in Seventy Countries,* 1949. Statistical Office of the U.N., New York, 1950.

United Nations. *Per Capita National Product in Fifty-five Countries,* 1952–1954. Statistical Office of the U.N., New York, 1957.

United Nations. *Statistical Yearbook,* 1949–58.[2] Statistical Office of the U.N., New York, 1950–59.

Vysoká škola ekonomická (Economic Faculty). *Sborník statí o plánování národního hospodářství* (Anthology of Essays on Planning the National Economy). Pedagogické nakladatelství, Prague, 1954.

Zauberman, A. *Industrial Development in Czechoslovakia, East Germany and Poland.* Chatham House Memoranda, distributed for the Royal Institute of International Affairs by Oxford University Press, London, 1958. (A revised edition is to be published.)

PERIODICALS AND NEWSPAPERS[3]

Monthlies, Quarterlies, and Triannuals

Cenové zprávy státního úřadu statistického (Price Reports of the State Statistical Office). State Statistical Office, Prague, 1948.

Czechoslovak Economic Bulletin. Czechoslovak Chamber of Commerce, Prague.

Demografie (Demography). State Statistical Office, Prague.

Direction of International Trade, U.N. Statistical Papers, Series T. Joint publication by the Statistical Office of the United Nations, the International Monetary Fund, and the International Bank for Reconstruction and Development, New York.

Economic Bulletin for Europe. Economic Commission for Europe, Geneva.

Ekonomický časopis (Economic Journal). Slovak Academy of Sciences, Bratislava.

Finance a úvěr (Finance and Credit). Czechoslovak Ministry of Finance and the State Bank of Czechoslovakia, Prague.

International Labour Review, Statistical Supplement. International Labour Office, Geneva.

Internationale Monatszahlen (International Monthly Data). West German Federal Statistical Office, Wiesbaden.

Měsíční přehled zahraničního obchodu (Monthly Summary of Foreign Trade). State Statistical Office, Prague, 1948.

[2] Some data also from U.N. *Statistical Yearbook,* 1959, which was published when this book was in proof.

[3] Through 1959, unless dated, in which case year refers to latest issues available to the author.

Monthly Bulletin of Agricultural Economics and Statistics. Food and Agricultural Organization of the United Nations, Rome.
Monthly Bulletin of Statistics. Statistical Office of the United Nations, New York.
Nová mysl (New Thought). Central Committee of the Communist Party of Czechoslovakia, Prague.
OEEC Statistical Bulletin—General Statistics. Organization for European Economic Cooperation, Paris.
Odborář (Trade-Unionist). Central Council of Trade Unions, Prague.
Plánované hospodářství (Planned Economy). State Planning Office, Prague.
Politická ekonomie (Political Economy). Czech Academy of Sciences, Prague.
Statistické zprávy (Statistical Reports). State Statistical Office, Prague.
Statistický obzor (Statistical Review). State Statistical Office, Prague.
Statistikai Szemle (Statistical Review). State Statistical Office, Budapest.
United States Information Agency. Washington.
Vestnik Jugoslovenske investicione banke (Reports of the Yugoslav Investments Bank). Belgrade.
Vierteljahreshefte zur Statistik der DDR (Quarterly Statistics of the German Democratic Republic). East German Statistical Office, Berlin.
Za socialistické zemědělství (Toward a Socialist Agriculture). Czechoslovak Academy of Agricultural Science, Prague.
Zahraniční obchod (Foreign Trade). Ministry of Foreign Trade, Prague.
Život Strany (Life of the Party). Central Committee of the Communist Party of Czechoslovakia, Prague.

Bimonthlies and Weeklies

Hlas Domova (Voice of the Home Country). Prague.
Hospodářské noviny (Economic News). Central Committee of the Communist Party of Czechoslovakia, Prague.
Prague News Letter. Czechoslovak Chamber of Commerce, Prague.
Predvoj (Avant-garde). Central Committee of the Slovak Communist Party, Bratislava.
Tvorba (Creation). Communist Party of Czechoslovakia, Prague.
Výstavba Slovenska (Building Up Slovakia). Bratislava.

Newspapers

Lidová demokracie. Czech People's Party, Prague.
Mladá fronta. Unified Youth Organization, Prague.
Práca. Slovak Revolutionary Trade Unions, Bratislava.
Práce. Czech Revolutionary Trade Unions, Prague.
Pravda. Communist Party of Slovakia, Bratislava.
Rudé právo. Communist Party of Czechoslovakia, Prague.

SUBJECT INDEX

(The abbreviation *i.c.* stands for international comparison)

Abortions, 10

Accidents, motor vehicle, 12–13

Accumulation, 146, 169, 183; centralized, 167; "net," 169–70, 235

Afghanistan, aid to, 135n, 136

Agricultural production: collective and private, gross value, by sectors, 82; *i.c.*, 68–69; indexes, 66–67, 260. *See also* Crops, Livestock, Yields

Agriculture: basic funds, 65–66; collectivization, 79, 81–87; development factors, 73–79; importance in economy, 64; investments, 65; manpower, 64–65, 85; mechanization, 78–79; plans to 1965, 87–89, 246; sown area, 74. *See also* Economically active population, Gross social product, Income, Land, Prices

Aid, *see* Foreign aid

Air transportation, 95, 260; *i.c.*, 95

Albania: aid to, 136–37; trade with, 101, 110–11

Alcohol, 51

Aluminum: export, 109; import, 108, 119; output, 48

Amortization, *see* Depreciation

Antimony ore, 48

Apprentices, 18n

Argentina, 102

Australia, 102

Austria, 4; trade statistics compared, 105; trade with, 101, 110–11

Automobiles: export, 109, 112; export and internal prices, 126; households per car, 262; import, 108, 118; output, 49, 259; per capita, *i.c.*, 52; in use, per 1,000 inhabitants, *i.c.*, 203, 205

Baggers, 112

Balance of payments (1948), 103. *See also* External trade

Barley, 70, 116. *See also* Yields

Basic funds (fixed capital assets), 172; by branches of national economy, 184; completed in state investment plan, 182; investments in productive and nonproductive funds, 175, 181, 183; productive capacity, 181; rate of retirements, 186

"Bazar," 145n

Bearings, output, 49, 258

Beer: consumers' price, 162; export, 109; output, 51

Belgium and Luxembourg: trade statistics compared, 105; trade with, 101, 110–11

Bicycles, 49, 113

Birth rate, 7, 7n, 9; *i.c.*, 11

Births, 10

Books published, *i.c.*, 205, 207

Brazil, 102

Bread (rye): consumers' price, 162; consumption, 202

Budget, 165–71; defense, 166–67

Building, *see* Construction

Building materials, 49

Bulgaria, 31; aid to, 137; trade with, 101, 110–11

Burma, 136

Butter: consumers' price, 162; import, 108, 117; output, 259

Cameras, 49

Canada, 102

Capital assets, *see* Basic funds

Cement, output, 50, 259; *i.c.*, 52

Centrally planned economy: distinct from market economy, 1, 2, 243; future prospects, 242–43, 253–55. *See also* External trade

Ceramics, 113

Cheese, 51

Chemicals: chemical industry, 38, 258; *i.c.*, 39; output, 50

China mainland: aid to, 136; trade with, 101, 108

Cinema, *see* Film attendance

Class Structure, 20

Coal: consumers' price, 162; export, 109, 113; import, 108, 115; import price, 129; output, 48, 258 (*i.c.*, 42, 52)

Cocoa beans, 108, 118

Coffee: consumers' price, 162; import, 108, 118

Coke: export, 109, 113; output, 50, 258

Collectivization, agricultural, 79, 81–87

Construction: importance, 58; index of volume, 59, 259; investments, 58–59, 180, 183; manpower, 58; pattern by branches and types, 60

Consumers' goods, shortages, 210

Consumption: collective, 194, 196, 235–36; pattern, 162–63; through black, free, and uniform markets, 159, 161. *See also* Gross national expenditure, Personal consumption

Copper: import, 119–20; output, 48

Cost: of advertising, 241; of production, 145

Cost of living: author's estimate, 158–60; *i.c.*, 198; impact of 1953 currency reform, 141–42; index, 157–64; plan to 1965, 262

Cotton, import, 108, 116; prices, 127

Cotton fabrics: consumers' price, 162; export, 109, 114, 119; output, 51

Cotton yarn: *i.c.*, 52; output, 51

Council for Mutual Economic Aid (CMEA), 171n; Commission on National Income, 214; specialization of machinery output, 247, 248n

Credits granted by Czechoslovakia, *see* Foreign aid

Crops, *i.c.*, 69–71

Currency: exchange rates, 125n, 141–43; postwar reforms, 139–42. *See also* Money

Death rate, 7n; *i.c.*, 11–13

Debt, public, *see* Public debt

Decentralization of industry, 53–54, 246n

Defense budget, 166–67

Deflation, *see* Currency

Deposits, private, increase in, 262, 263n

Depreciation, 174, 186; rate in industry, 232–33n

Diesel engines: export, 109, 119, 123; output, 49

Diphtheria, 13

Divorce rates, *i.c.*, 11

Dysentery, 13

Earnings: average, index, Socialist sector, 262; by branches of national economy, 188–90; compared with average incomes in agriculture, 191; real, index, in industry, *i.c.*, 198; real, index, Socialist sector, 246n, 262; real, per workman in industry, 44

East Germany, 1, 4, 31; aid to, 137; foreign trade net subsidy, 130; national income under Marxist definition and gross social product, 213n; state budget, 171; trade statistics compared, 105; trade with, 101, 110–11

Economic aid, 103–4, 134–37

Economic efficiency, 239, 249–51

Economically active population, 16–19; class structure, 20; distribution by branches of economy, 23–25; *i.c.*, 16. *See also* Working population

Eggs: consumers' price, 162; import, 117; output, 88; per capita consumption, 202

Egypt, aid to, 103, 135n, 136

Electricity: consumption, *i.c.*, 27–28; output, 48, 258; output per capita, *i.c.*, 52

Endowments (*dotace*), 169–70

Energy: per capita consumption, *i.c.*, 27–28; sources, 250

Engineering, 32, 38–39, 258

Excess liquidity, *see* Inflation

Exchange rate, Kčs, 125n, 141–43

Exports: main commodities, 109, 112–15; ratio to national income, 96n; unit value, *i.c.*, 124–26. *See also various commodities*

External trade: commodity pattern, 106–22; dependence on, 96; dollar value, *i.c.*, 96–98; index, influence on Marxist income, 222–23, 225; net subsidy, 130–34; net subsidy in gross national expenditure, 234–35; policy, 135, 138; price policy, 124–29; rentability, 132–33, 138; terms of trade, 124, 126; value by main economic areas, 98–100, 102–3, 261; value by principal trading countries, 101–4. *See also* Prices

Factories, exported, 112

Fats and oils (edible), 51, 202; *i.c.*, 203

Ferroalloys, 119

Fertilizers: in agriculture, *i.c.*, 80; import, 108; output, 50, 258

Film attendance, *i.c.*, 203, 205–6

Finland: trade statistics compared, 105; trade with, 101

Fish, 117

Five-Year Plan: second revised, 245n, 246; third, 245–64

Fodder, 69–71, 74–78, 84, 260; import, 117

Food: consumption, 202; *i.c.*, 203; production, 66–69, 260; prices, 83–85, 162

Foreign aid: economic, 103–4, 134–37; military, 104n, 135

Foreign travel, *see* Tourist travel

Foreign trade, *see* External trade

Forging machines: export, *i.c.*, 123; output, 49

France, 4; trade statistics compared, 105; trade with, 101

Fruit: import, 108, 118; per capita consumption, 202

Fuel, *see* Energy, *individual sources*

Fund for National Reconstruction, 139–40

Gas, output, 48

General overhauls (capital repairs), 173, 178–79; budgetary expenditure on, 167

German population, expulsion of, 6

Ghana, aid to, 137

Glass: export, 113; output, 50
Gold, 48
Gonorrhea, 14
Grain, 69–70; export, 110; import, 111. *See also* Yields
Gross national expenditure, 216, 233–34; at factor cost and at conventional prices, 235; pattern of, *i.c.*, 236–37
Gross national product (Western definition), 231; index per capita, *i.c.*, 236–37. *See also* National income
Gross social product (Marxist definition), 212–13, 224, 226–27, 248
Groundnuts, 117

Harvest, 69, 71n
Hides, import, 108, 116
Highways, 94, 260
Homicide, 12–13
Hops: export, 115; yields, 78n
Hospitals and maternity homes, 262
Housing, 176; floor space, 60; persons per room, *i.c.*, 62; per 1,000 inhabitants, *i.c.*, 61; units completed, 60–63, 259
Hungarian population, transfer of, 6
Hungary, 4; foreign trade net subsidy, 130; state budget, 171; trade statistics compared, 105–6; trade with, 101, 110–11

Illnesses, infectious, 12–14
Imports: main commodities, 108, 115–18; ratio to national income, 96n; unit value, 100. *See also* External trade, *various commodities*
Income, of agricultural population, 85–86. *See also* Earnings, National income, Personal income
Index numbers (reliability), 5
India, aid to, 136–37
Indonesia, aid to, 135n, 136
Industrial production: cost, 44, 251; gross value, 39, 44; index, 29–37 (*i.c.*, 36–37), 258; net in gross value, 39; "net" value, 34; output per man-year, 258; output of commodities (*i.c.*, 41, 43), 47–51, 258–59
Industry: basic funds, 57; decentralization, 53–54, 246n; employment, *i.c.*, 40; growth factors, 44–47; hours worked per week, *i.c.*, 42, 238; importance in national economy, 24–27; investments, 26; manpower, 26, 258; manual workers by branches, 39, 44, 57; method of securing manual labor, 21–22; plans to 1965, 55–56, 258–59; rejects, 34; reorganization, 53–54; statistical coverage, 26. *See also* Gross social product, National income

Infant mortality, *i.c.*, 11, 15
Inflation, 38, 57, 139–40, 201; efforts to check, 252–53
Insurance: health, 195, 200, 262; national, in state budget, 166, 171. *See also* Social security
Inventories: increase in, 170, 226, 235; in GNP, *i.c.*, 236
Investments, gross fixed, 166–67, 256–57; in agriculture, 65; assessing efficiency of, 184–85; in basic funds, 181–82; by branches of national economy, 178, 249 (*i.c.*, 177); by categories, 175–76; in construction, 58–59, 180, 183; in gross national expenditure, 235 (*i.c.*, 236); in industry, 26; by investors, 175; 1957 and 1959 prices compared, 183; ratio to Marxist income, 256; state, 180; statistical coverage, 172–73; in transportation, 91–93
Investments, net fixed, 173–74
Investments, nonfixed, *see* Inventories
Iron, *see* Pig iron
Iron ore: import, 108, 115; import price, 127, 133; output, 48
Italy, 38; trade with, 101

Jute, import, 108, 116

Kindergartens, 262
Koruna, *see* Currency
Kulaks, 193

Labor, in Marxist terminology, 221–24
Land: agricultural, 73, 260; arable, 74, 260; by sectors, 82; unused, 73n
Lard, consumers' price, 162
Lead: import, 119; output, 48
Life expectancy, 14–15
Linen fabrics: export, 114; output, 51
Livestock: *i.c.*, 71–72; by sectors, 84
Locomotives, 258
Losses, planned, 145, 148–53
Lumber: export, 110, 114; output, 50

Machinery: export, 109–12 (*i.c.*, 121–23); imports and exports, 107; output, 49, 258
Maize, import, 108, 117
Malt: export, 115; output, 51
Manganese ore: import, 119; output, 48
Manufacturing, *see* Industry
Market economy, distinct from centrally planned economy, 1, 2. *See also* External trade
Marriage rate, *i.c.*, 11
Meat: consumers' price, 162; import, 108, 117; output, 51, 88, 259; per capita consumption, *i.c.*, 203

Metal-cutting lathes: export, *i.c.*, 123; output, 49

Milk: consumers' price, 162; output, 88; per capita consumption, 202

Mining, output, 48. *See also* Industry

Money in circulation, 139–40. *See also* Currency

Mongolia: aid to, 136; trade with, 101

Motor fuel, 50

Motorcycles: consumers' price, 162; export, 113; export price, 125n, 131; output, 49

Motor vehicles, *see* Automobiles, Motorcycles, Tractors, Trucks

Motors, electric, 112

National expenditure, *see* Gross national expenditure

National income (Marxist definition): approximation for 1959 and 1965 target, 257n; author's approximations, 224–29; comparisons for 1948, 56–57, 215, 217; concepts, 211–13; official index numbers and percentages, 217–21, 247, 253, 256; turnover tax in, 220–21, 226–28

National income (Western definition): after 1948, 231; to 1948, 215–16; per capita, *i.c.*, 232; turnover tax in, 232

National product, *see* Gross national product, National income (Marxist definition), National income (Western definition)

National wealth, by economic branches and by state and private ownership, 186–87. *See also* Basic funds

Netherlands: trade statistics compared, 105–6; trade with, 102

Newspaper circulation, *i.c.*, 207–8

North Korea: aid to, 134; trade with, 101

North Vietnam, trade with, 101

Oats, 70. *See also* Yields

Oil, crude: import, 108, 115; output, 48, 50

Oil, vegetable, *see* Fats and oils

Old-age benefits, *see* Social security

Paper: export, 109, 114; output, 50

Peanuts, *see* Groundnuts

Personal consumption: author's estimates, 233–36; coverage, 213–14; official index numbers and percentages, 142, 218, 221, 256; share in GNP, *i.c.*, 236

Personal income: net per capita, 199–201; planned to 1965, 252–53; by type of employment, 193–94. *See also* Earnings, Income of agricultural population

Physicians and surgeons, *i.c.*, 209–10

Pig iron: import, 119; output, 48; output per capita, *i.c.*, 52

Pigs, 72, 84

Planned losses, 145, 148–53

Plastics, 258

Poland, 4, 31; aid to, 136; gross national income, 211n; national income and gross social product, 213n; state budget, 171; trade with, 101, 110–11

Population, 6–7; by age groups, 8–9; density, *i.c.*, 7; natural increase, *i.c.*, 11; in productive age, *i.c.*, 9; projections to 1970, 8. *See also* Economically active population, Working population

Potatoes, 71, 202. *See also* Yields

Power, *see* Electricity

Price Control Office, 147

Prices, retail, 144–45, 152–57, 262–63n; conventional, 235–36; on rationed, free, and uniform markets, 1953, 141. *See also* Cost of living

Prices, state wholesale, 144–53, 162; below-cost, 145, 148–53; derived index by branches of industry, 150; derived index of investment prices, 147; export/import and internal, 125–29, 131–33; of fertilizers, 83; procurement and above-quota, for agricultural produce, 83–85

Productive and nonproductive spheres (Marxist definition), 211

Profitability, *see* Rentability

Profits: in industry, 146; paid off to the state, 166–67, 169. *See also* Accumulation

Prostoje (work stoppages), 22

Public debt, repudiation of, 141

Public utilities, *see* Industry

Radio, *see* Wireless sets

Railways: steam, electric, and Diesel, 250; total length, 92; transportation, 92–93, 260 (*i.c.*, 93)

Refrigerators: households per refrigerator, 262; output, 49, 259

Refugees, 6

Rent, 160–63, 204n; in 1948 national income, 215–16

Rentability (rate of profit), 145–46. *See also* External trade

Repairs, capital, *see* General overhauls

Replacement of fixed capital, 231, 232n

Resource allocation, 54–55, 251

Retail trade, 234n, 252, 262; shops per inhabitant, *i.c.*, 210

Rice, import, 118

Roads, *see* Highways

Rubber, import, 108, 116

Rumania: aid to, 137; trade with, 101, 110–11

Rye, 69. *See also* Yields

Savings: deposits, 262; private, 240n. *See also* Accumulation

Scarlet fever, 13

Services: in national income, 230; in short supply, 241–42

Sheep, 72, 84

Shipping, 94

Shoes: consumers' price, 162; export, 109, 114–15, 119; output, 51, 259; output per capita, *i.c.*, 52

Shortages, consumers' goods, 210

Silk fabrics: export, 109, 114; output, 51

Silver, 48

Social security: index of benefits per recipient, 196, 202; recipients and benefits, 195. *See also* Insurance

Social welfare, budgetary expenditure on, 166, 195

Soya beans, 117

Standard of living, 202–9, 241, 262. *See also* Consumption, Earnings, Personal consumption, Personal income

Staple fiber, output, 258

State budget, 165–71; compared with other centrally planned economies, 171

State consumption, 235–36

State farms, *see* Agriculture

State Planning Office, price fixing, 145, 167

Statistics, reliability of, 4, 5; of foreign trade, 104–5

Steel, crude: output, 48, 258; per capita, *i.c.*, 52, 254n; per capita consumption, *i.c.*, 29

Steel, rolled, and pipes: export, 109, 113, 119; output, 48, 258

Stillbirths, 10

Stocks, *see* Inventories

Subsidies, 169–70; in external trade, 130–34, 234–35; transfer payments in Marxist national income, 225, 228–29; in wholesale prices below cost, 145, 148–53

Sugar: consumers' price, 162; export, 115; export price, 129, 131; output, 51, 259; per capita consumption, 202 (*i.c.*, 203)

Sugar beets, 70. *See also* Yields

Suicide, 12–13

Sulfur, 108, 116

Sulfuric acid: import, 108, 116; output, 50; per capita output, *i.c.*, 52

Sunflower seeds: import, 117; import price and internal transaction price, 131

Switzerland: trade statistics compared, 105–6; trade with, 102

Syphilis, 12–14

Syria, aid to, 135n, 136. *See also* United Arab Republic

Taxation, 165, 193; of individual farmers in contrast to cooperatives, 85–86; of kulaks, 193. *See also* Turnover tax

Tea, 118

Television sets: households per set, 262; output, 49, 259; in use per inhabitant, *i.c.*, 203, 206

Textile industry, 39; *i.c.*, 38

Textiles, *see individual fabrics*

Tobacco: import, 108, 118; yields, 78n

Tourist travel, foreign, 209; *i.c.*, 207–8

Tractors: export, 109, 112; output, 49, 258; in use, *i.c.*, 79

Trade, *see* External trade, Retail trade

Transfer payments, in national income, 225, 228–29

Transportation, 24, 91–95, 250, 260; earnings, 190

Trucks: export, 109, 112; output, 49, 259

Tuberculosis, 12–13

Turkey: trade statistics compared, 105; trade with, 102

Turnover tax, 130, 156; in national income, 220–21, 225–28, 232; as percentage of sales in industry, 146; receipts from, 166–69; within retail prices, 154–55; within wholesale prices, 149–51. *See also* Accumulation

TUZEX, 143

Underdeveloped countries: aid to, 135–37; trade with, 98–99, 103

Underpricing, 145, 148–53. *See also* Exports, Imports, Subsidies

Unemployment, 21–23

Unified agricultural cooperatives, 81, 83–87

United Arab Republic: trade statistics compared, 105–6, 108; trade with, 104

United Kingdom, 2, 4; trade statistics compared, 105–6; trade with, 102, 110–11

United States, 1, 4; trade statistics compared, 105; trade with, 102

Uranium ore: export, 102; output, 48

USSR, 1, 4, 30; state budget, 171; trade statistics compared, 105; trade with, 101, 119

Vegetables, import, 108, 118

Venereal diseases, 12–14

Wage and salary earners, 16–17, 158; average age, 15n; in economically active population, 19–20. *See also* Industry, Working population

Wages and salaries, 142, 204; lagging behind, productivity in industry, 253n; stratification of wages in industry, 191–92. *See also* Earnings

Washing machines, 49

Waterways, inland, 94

West Germany, 4; trade statistics compared, 105; trade with, 101, 110–11

Wheat, 69; import, 108, 116; import price, 127. *See also* Yields

Whooping cough, 13

Wine: import, 111; output, 51

Wireless sets: output, 49; in use, *i.c.*, 203, 206

Women, 7; in agriculture, 65; employment of, 9, 15–17, 250

Wood pulp: import, 116; output, 50

Wool, import, 108, 116

Wool fabrics: export, 109, 114; output, 51, 259

Wool yarn: output, 51; per capita, *i.c.*, 52

Working population, 15–17, 250, 256

Working time: in industry, 42, 238; necessary to buy food and cigarettes, *i.c.*, 203–4

Yields per hectare, 74–78, 260; *i.c.*, 75–77; by socialist and private sector, 84

Yugoslavia, 2, 4; aid to, 135–36; trade statistics compared, 105; trade with, 101, 120

Zinc, 119

NAME INDEX

Alton, T. P., and associates, 224n, 228n

Aulický, V., 161

Barák, R., 20n

Bartůněk, J., 227n

Bašata, J., 85n

Bezouška, J., 190n, 200, 227n

Čáp, V., 119n

Černaňský, V., 132

Černík, O., 62

Červený, A., 146n, 150–51

Dubský, O., 119n

Ďuriš, J., 149, 166n, 168, 170n

Frank, J., 159n

Havlíček, J., 100n

Hladík, V., 227n

Houštka, V., 66–67

Kazimour, J., 213n

Khrushchev, N. S., 2n, 55, 78n

Kocman, M., 170n

Kocour, O., 103

Kolár, J., 225n

Komárek, V., 127, 133, 152, 251, 252n

Kord, F., 170n

Kučera, M., 8n, 18n

Lenin, N. I., 2

Lukácz, O., 31n

Macek, J., 73n

Mach, J., 156, 161, 163–64

Marx, K., 2

Mencl, K., 86n

Misař, M., 214n

Nachtigal, V., 82n, 132n

Navrátil, J., 132n, 138

Nesvadba, J., 88

Nikl, J., 83n, 84–85, 189, 190n

Nikodém, B., 86n

Novotný, A., 55–56, 245

Román, Z., 31n

Rozsypal, K., 150n, 151–52, 154–55

Šimůnek, O., 181, 245, 249, 251, 254n, 262n

Široký, V., 53

Skoupil, F., 159n

Stádník, M., 231n

Stalin, J. V., 2

Srb, V., 10n, 18n

Štefan, J., 123

Turek, O., 225n

Typolt, J., 148–49, 151, 221n

Vaněk, J., 128–29n

Vašíček, K., 56, 88–89

Vojta, M., 31n, 33n, 39n, 152

Zápotocký, V., 202

Zauberman, A., 31n, 32–33

Zelinka, J., 31n

Zeman, F., 53n